T0374817

THE I TATTI
RENAISSANCE LIBRARY

James Hankins, General Editor

FRACASTORO

LATIN POETRY

ITRL 57

GIROLAMO FRACASTORO
◆ ◆ ◆
LATIN POETRY

TRANSLATED BY

JAMES GARDNER

THE I TATTI RENAISSANCE LIBRARY
HARVARD UNIVERSITY PRESS
CAMBRIDGE, MASSACHUSETTS
LONDON, ENGLAND
2013

Series design by Dean Bornstein

Library of Congress Cataloging-in-Publication Data

Fracastoro, Girolamo, 1478–1553.
Latin poetry / Girolamo Fracastoro ; translated by James Gardner.
pages. cm. — (The I Tatti Renaissance library ; 57)
Includes bibliographical references and index.
ISBN 978-0-674-07271-8 (alk. paper)
1. Latin poetry, Medieval and modern.   I. Gardner, James (Translator)
II. Title.   III. Series: I Tatti Renaissance library ; 57.
PA8520.F7A2 2013
871'.04 — dc23   2012037854

Contents

ॐ৩৫

· CONTENTS ·

Introduction

☙❧❧

Few writers have embodied the ideal of the Renaissance Man more successfully than Girolamo Fracastoro (1476/78–1553). One of the most eminent physicians of his age, indeed, a founder of modern epidemiology, Fracastoro wrote prose works on astronomy and mathematics, philosophy, psychology, and the silting up of the lagoon of Venice. And yet, in an age that abounded in poets who could write Latin verse with style and imagination, few were as widely or as justly admired as he was in that domain.[1]

These twin gifts for science and poetry were united in Fracastoro's best-known work, the three books of the *Syphilis*, in whose title he coined the word by which that disease is known today. In addition to being, perhaps, the best known example of neo-Latin verse, Fracastoro's *Syphilis* has the rare distinction, for a Renaissance Latin poem, of having remained in print, whether in the original or in translation, for much of the past five centuries. But although the *Syphilis* is well known, even famous, within the context of neo-Latin verse, it represents only a third of Fracastoro's poetic output, much of which, until now, has never been translated into English or, indeed, into any other language.

It is difficult, if not impossible, to divorce Fracastoro's poetry from the region of Italy in which he passed most of his life. Born and raised in Verona (where he had a house in the parish of Sant'Eufemia), Fracastoro lived near the Lago di Garda for much of his seventy-five years, a fact eloquently expressed in the poems included in this volume. Latin poetry had always been animated by a potent sense of place and by the conspicuous affection of its poets for the region from which they came: one thinks of Catullus's attachment to Verona and Sirmione, Ovid's to Sulmo,

Propertius's to Perusia and Martial's to Bilbilis. The Sabine farm where Horace spent much of his later years is likewise a fixture of his poetry. It is in this spirit, as well, that Fracastoro writes with such evident affection for the small town of Incaffi, where he had a house on the slopes of Monte Moscal midway between Verona and the Lago di Garda (which he always calls by its ancient name of Benacus). His poetry is rich in references to such local rivers as the Sarca and the Adige (he even named one of his beloved hounds after the latter), as well as to such nearby towns as Malcesine, Bardolino and Salò. He revels in the myths and legends of the region and is well acquainted with its variegated history.[2]

At the same time, Fracastoro's poetry — especially the occasional verse contained in his *Carmina* — is a window onto the intellectual and political life of this part of Italy in the first half of the sixteenth century. He constantly mentions local worthies in and around Verona or farther afield in the Veneto. Among these are Gian Matteo Giberti, the famous reforming bishop of Verona, whose private physician he became; such men of science as Giovanni Battista Ramusio and the brothers Giovanni Battista and Marcantonio Della Torre; the poets Andrea Navagero and Pietro Bembo, both from Venice; and Cesare Fregoso, a soldier of fortune who lived in Verona.

A second circle of acquaintance, resulting from Fracastoro's time as head physician at the Council of Trent, includes Pope Paul III, his grandson Alessandro Farnese, and Pope Julius III. Beyond Rome and Verona, Fracastoro knew Ludovico Ariosto, who sought his opinion of the *Orlando Furioso*, as well as the novelist Matteo Bandello and the satirist Pietro Aretino, not to mention Copernicus and Titian, who may have painted his portrait.[3] There is even a rumor — emblazoned on a plaque that now adorns his house in Incaffi — that Charles V, the Holy Roman Emperor, once visited him there.

*   *   *

The sixth of seven children, Fracastoro was born between 1476 and 1478 to Paolo Filippo Fracastoro, the scion of an old Veronese noble family, and to Camilla Mascarelli, of Vicenza, who died when he was scarcely three years old. According to one legend, she was holding the young Girolamo in her arms when she was struck by lightning and perished, although he was unharmed.[4]

Fracastoro studied medicine in Padua, where he received his diploma *in artibus* in 1502. While there he may have made the acquaintance of his fellow student Copernicus, and he certainly heard lectures by the radical philosopher Pietro Pomponazzi, an important influence on Fracastoro's own scientific studies. In 1505 Fracastoro was admitted to the college of medical doctors in Verona, and from autumn to winter in 1508 and 1509 he took part in the academy founded by Bartolomeo d'Alviano, the condottiere and duke of Pordenone in the Veneto. At this academy, which was largely devoted to composing Latin verse, he befriended the poets Pietro Bembo, Giovanni Cotta, Guilio Camillo Delminio, and Andrea Navagero. Fracastoro was part of d'Alviano's entourage when he led the Venetian forces against the League of Cambrai. But with the condottiere's decisive defeat at the battle of Agnadello in 1509, Fracastoro returned to Verona. There he and Elena Clavi (his wife since at least 1501) had a daughter, Isabella, and four sons, of whom only one, Paolo Filippo, outlived him. Though most of his later life was divided between Verona and his house in Incaffi, Fracastoro was chosen in 1545 as the official physician to the Council of Trent. He died at Incaffi nine years later, on August 6, 1553, of a sudden onset of apoplexy, leaving unfinished his dialogue *De anima* and his biblical epic on the life of the patriarch Joseph.

The great majority of Fracastoro's extant writings are in Latin prose and verse, with a scattering of poetry in Italian and some correspondence (much of it unpublished) in Latin and Italian. His most important prose works can be divided into three categories, astronomical, medical, and philosophical. As regards the first, his preeminent composition is the *Homocentrica*, published in 1538. In it, he took issue with the ancient Greek astronomer Ptolemy, who postulated that some of the stars and planets revolved around the earth in eccentric spheres. Fracastoro sides with Aristotle and Averroes in arguing for an entirely harmonious and centered structure to the universe, in which the stars and planets move round the earth in uniform, hence homocentric, spheres.

Of more lasting importance, however, is Fracastoro's medical text, *De contagione et contagiosis morbis* (1546), the first medical work to argue systematically that the seeds of a disease, which he called its *fomes*, or tinder, could be carried through the air. This opinion differed from later germ theory, however, in that it supposed that these seeds emerged through spontaneous generation from such materials as cotton and wool, without being bio-organisms.

A greater literary interest attaches to Fracastoro's three dialogues. The first of these, *Naugerius* (ca. 1540), was named after his friend, the poet Andrea Navagero. This work on the aesthetic theory of poetry contains "beyond its pedagogical purposes, present in but not essential to the poetic message, [a] notion of poetry and of the *furor poeticus* as a Platonic journey consisting in the progressive sublimation of specific sensual beauties to the purely abstract idea of beauty in itself."[5] Fracastoro's two other dialogues are the *Turrius*, a consideration of how the mind learns and functions, and his *Fracastorius*, a discussion of the soul's immortality. He died, however, before completing the dialogue that bears his own name.

As regards the poems included in the present volume, Fracastoro seems, if we accept the chronology offered by Francesco Pellegrini,[6] to have composed them sporadically throughout his career, even spasmodically, given that they came in spates, followed by lengthy intervals of silence. We do not possess any poetry (or prose) that he wrote prior to the *Syphilis*: this poem was perhaps started as early as 1510, when he would have been in his mid-thirties, but it was not published until 1530. Several other poems included in the *Carmina* can likewise be dated, on circumstantial grounds, to the second decade of the sixteenth century. From the 1520s, however, we possess nothing until the fairly productive period between 1532 and 1536. Afterward, for the next nine years leading up to 1545, according to Pellegrini, "Fracastoro's Muse would be rather silent." But then, in the final decade of his life, he suddenly rediscovered his poetic voice. Because he appears, then, to have composed his earliest works in what — for the time — would have been middle age, it is difficult to discern any clear formal evolution in his verse: given its general smoothness throughout, one has little sense of Fracastoro's passage from a period of apprenticeship to one of mastery.

His earliest published work, the *Syphilis*, is a poem of 1346 lines of dactylic hexameter. Initially it was divided into two books, but that number was increased to three in the first printed edition.[7] In a surprisingly lively and engaging manner — given its unappealing subject — the poem relates the circumstances of the disease's spread after it first appeared in Europe around 1500. Broadly modeled on the four books of Vergil's *Georgics*, the *Syphilis* is a didactic poem that offers the reader scientific and medical lore, enlivened by poetic interludes of Fracastoro's own invention that are (or appear to be) derived from Greco-Roman mythology. A major difference between Fracastoro and Vergil, however, is that whereas Vergil had little or no direct experience of animal husbandry, beekeeping or any of the other topics discussed in the *Georgics*, Fracastoro knew more about syphilis than any doctor of his generation, since he had studied it virtually from its initial appearance and had been among the very first to inquire into the nature of contagious diseases in general.

One of the great and unsolved mysteries of medicine is the origin of this disease whose name Fracastoro coined, perhaps through a corruption of *erysipelas*, a term found in medical Greek that describes a related dermatological ailment with similar symptoms. Whereas many scholars have contended that it was introduced into Europe by the crews of Columbus's ships as they returned from the New World, Fracastoro disputes that account in the first book of his poem, on the grounds that the disease could not possibly appear so promptly in so many places. In his later prose work, *De contagione* (1546), however, he appears less sure of this assertion.

The first book of the *Syphilis*, which includes a dedication to Pietro Bembo, the eminent Venetian poet, historian, and cardinal, examines the causes of the disease and elucidates Fracastoro's belief that its contagion could be airborne. But because Fracastoro discounted physical contact, he failed fully to appreciate the venereal origin of the disease.[8] The latter part of the first book contains a description of the disease's symptoms and effects that, in its graphic nosological precision, is without parallel in earlier poetry.

Much of the first half of the second book is given over to a recital of remedies for the disease, among them the forms of energetic exercise that one must undertake to be rid of the affliction. As a reward for the reader's patience in slogging through this often difficult scientific terrain, Fracastoro concludes his discussion of the curative powers of mercury, or quicksilver, with the charming tale of Ilceus, a gardener in the temple of the gods. In a mistaken tribute to the river goddess Callirhoe, Ilceus hangs in her temple the head of a stag he has killed that was sacred to Diana. Angered by this sacrilege, Diana afflicts Ilceus with a disease very much like syphilis. In a scene reminiscent of the story of Orpheus and Eurydice in *Georgics* 4.4, he must descend into the underworld to find a cure in its murky rivers of molten quicksilver.

The third book begins with a discussion of the other well-known cure for syphilis that was prevalent in the sixteenth century, a decoction made from boiling the wood of the guaiacum tree, which grows abundantly in the West Indies. After a lengthy description of the wood's preparation, Fracastoro relates how its curative powers were discovered. In so doing, he writes what appears to be the earliest poetic account of Columbus's voyages. In one especially evocative passage, the Spaniards, having arrived in the New World, shoot and kill some of the region's brightly colored birds. One of these birds, endowed with the gift of human speech, prophesies the great afflictions that the disease will wreak upon them in punishment for the Spaniards' violence. A local chieftain then tells Columbus of the cure for the disease and explains how it first appeared among his people: once the young shepherd Syphilus insulted the Sun God by saying that the king of the land was a greater deity than he. In revenge the god afflicted him and other inhabitants with the disease, before he relented to the point of providing them with a cure.

Traditionally, the next work to appear in collections of Fracastoro's poetry is a biblical epic on the life of the patriarch Joseph, a labor of Fracastoro's old age that he undertook at the prompting of the eminent cardinal Alessandro Farnese. Fracastoro never lived to complete it, though he composed roughly 1200 lines of finished hexameters in two books. A third book was added, six years after his death, by the Udinese doctor and classical scholar Francesco Luisini.[9] Also comprising some 1200 lines of hexameter, this addition extends the narrative down to the story of Moses and the Exodus.

Fracastoro's *Joseph* follows the general narrative arc of the relevant chapters in the book of Genesis, but it adds little of interest or feeling to the story. Of all the poetic works by Fracastoro, this has usually been the least admired.[10] The only instance of its being translated out of the Latin, apparently, was a rather free version in rhymed couplets by the Jacobean poet Joshua Sylvester: the title of his poem, *The Maiden's Blush*, underscores its focus upon the episode of Joseph and Potiphar's wife. Fracastoro's Latin is a tame reapplication of Vergilian idiom to an Old Testament subject, with little of the startling originality and intense color that often delight the reader in the *Syphilis*. Extrapolating from the portions that Fracastoro completed, *Joseph* was probably intended to be a brief epic or epyllion rather than a full-bore epic in the mold of the *Christiad* by the contemporary Cremonese poet Girolamo Vida. But like that work, *Joseph* follows in what by that time was a fairly established genre of biblical narratives in Vergilian verse, such as Jacopo Sannazaro's *De partu virginis* (published in 1526), as well as sundry poems by Baptista Mantuanus (1447–1516).

The third and final portion of Fracastoro's poetic output is his *Carmina*, a varied collection of compositions written over the last forty years of his life, from his poem on the death of Marcantonio della Torre, datable to around 1512, to a number of poems composed in old age. The first twenty poems of the *Carmina* that appear in the present edition were already included in Fracastoro's *Opera Omnia*, edited by Paolo Ramusio in 1555, two years after his death, and the collection was gradually enlarged by various editors in the course of the sixteenth century.[11] In the standard 1739 edition, published in Padua by Cominus, the editor, Giovanni Antonio Volpi, added a number of other poems to the thirty-one by then included in the *Carminum liber*. He first added twelve poems that had appeared as poetic interludes in various of his prose works (C. 32–43). After these poems Volpi included six more poems that had been discovered by different scholars in various manuscripts (C. 44–49). Also included were seven other unfinished poems contained in an autograph manuscript now preserved in Verona (C. 50–55); these included two tributes to the bishop of Verona, Gian Matteo Giberti, as well as two attempts at a translation of the *Theriaca*, a poem in Greek by the ancient physician Andromachus, an earlier version of the opening of the *Syphilis*, and two short poems of moral instruction. These unfinished poems, especially the first two—with their multiple reworkings of the same passage—offer a welcome opportunity to observe the creative process by which Fracastoro composed his poetry, an opportunity that is exceedingly rare for any poet prior to the seventeenth century. Finally, this I Tatti edition contains as well two other poems attributed to Fracastoro (C. 56–57) that were discovered by Dr. Ornella Rossi in the course of preparing the Latin edition used in this volume.

Though all of the completed poems in the *Carmina* are polished performances, they often present the poet in a charming state of relaxation, especially when he writes of the rustic pleasures of his house in Incaffi, as he does in C. 8. At other times he can exhibit a high-minded and philosophical elevation of tone, as in the poem he addresses to Marcantonio Flaminio and Galeazzo Fiorimonte (C. 7), or the eloquence of panegyric in C. 6, composed for Cesare Fregoso and addressed to Marguerite of Navarre. Other poems, like the two translations of Andromachus (C. 52–53) are informed by a love of scientific lore that recalls some of the denser passages of the *Syphilis*.

Most of Fracastoro's poems, like the *Syphilis* and *Joseph*, are composed in dactylic hexameter, although sixteen are in elegiac distichs. One of his poems, the ode to Bacchus, is in alcaic hendecasyllables and glyconics, while the newly attributed C. 56, his most Catullan poem, is in the hendecasyllables often favored by his ancient Veronese compatriot. And yet, despite his evident affection for Catullus, and despite allusions to that poet's work, Fracastoro is far more influenced by Vergil: his *Georgics* served as a model for the didactic verse included in the *Syphilis*, his *Aeneid* influenced the narrative style of the poem on *Joseph*, and his *Eclogues* were the templates for the diction and occasionally for the substance of several poems in the *Carmina*. Fracastoro's language and meter nevertheless reveal some of the roughness typical of Medieval Latin, to which a doctor's education was inevitably exposed.[12]

As we have seen, Fracastoro had two potent claims to fame, as a scientist and as a poet. It was his misfortune, however, that neither proved sufficient to attract the listless attention of posterity. Beyond the narrow circle of their professions, only the rarest men of science, Aristotle and Archimedes, Galileo and Newton, Pasteur and Einstein, have achieved a renown that endures beyond the grave. And some of the most eloquent voices of early modern Europe have fallen silent because their language was Latin rather than one of the vernaculars. For both of these reasons, the name of Girolamo Fracastoro, famous in his day and for centuries afterward, is known in our day chiefly to scholars rather than to the broader public.

Shortly after his death, however, the citizens of Verona commissioned a life-sized marble likeness of him by Danese Cattaneo, and today, nearly five centuries later, it can still be seen near the statue of Dante in the Piazza dei Signori. All too few visitors to Verona ever learn the identity of the man in whose honor it was raised. But perhaps the present volume, the first complete translation of Fracastoro's poetry into any language, will restore to him some small measure of the renown that he once enjoyed among educated men and women throughout early modern Europe.

My thanks go to James Hankins, the general editor of the I Tatti Renaissance Library, for his encouragement at every stage of this project, as well as to his assistant, Ariane Schwartz, who proved invaluable in procuring essential secondary sources, to Justin Stover for his learned assistance with the annotations, and especially to Ornella Rossi, for her tireless labors on this volume. I owe an immense debt of gratitude as well to Franco and Arianna Baral-

dini for their generosity in showing me their lovely home in In-
caffi, the very house in which Fracastoro wrote much of the poetry
that appears in this volume. They have lovingly restored it, and the
spirit of the poet seems still to dwell therein. *Numen inest!* Finally,
I'd like to thank Tiziano Delibori of Villa Cordevigo for arranging
our meeting in the first place.

I am delighted to dedicate this book to my good friend Orlando
Garcia and to every member of his family.

NOTES

1. As late as 1806 the Scottish poet and linguist John Black could say,
"Fracastoro and our Buchanan are generally supposed to dispute the
sceptre of modern poetical latinity. I have before me a collection of eulo-
gies of each of these poets, transcribed in the course of my reading, and
it is difficult to say on which they are most lavish" (*The Falls of Clyde*,
1806, 91). On Fracastoro's life, see Peruzzi 1997, and the anonymous *Vita*
included in all editions of Fracastoro's *Opera Omnia* since 1555; the latter
was translated into Italian in Pellegrini 1952. (Fuller bibliographical infor-
mation on secondary works cited by author and date may be found under
Secondary Literature in the Bibliography; editions of Fracastoro are cited
by date, and can be found in the section listing Latin Editions of Fracas-
toro's Poetical Works in the Bibliography.)

2. See in particular Pighi 1966, which discusses Fracastoro's appreciation
for the Lago di Garda and its environs.

3. Emil Schaeffer, "Ein Bildnis des Hieronymo Fracastoro von Tizian,"
Jahrbuch der Koniglich Preussischen Kunstsammlungen 31 (1910): 130–38; Georg
Gronau, "The 'Fracastoro' Portrait in the Mond Collection," *Burlington
Magazine* 48, no. 276 (March 1926): 144–149. The portrait, mentioned in
Vasari's life of Titian, is now at the National Gallery in London.

4. See the anonymous life published in Pelligrini 1952 in Italian transla-
tion. According to F. O. Mencke, the life was probably written by Paolo
Ramusio, the son of Giovanni Battista Ramusio (or Rannusio), while
others believe (less plausibly) that the editor was Fracastoro's friend, the

poet Adamo Francesco Fumano. See Fracastoro 1739, 1:xxii, note; the Latin text of the life is found on pp. xxii–xxxi, with Volpi's notes.

5. Peruzzi 1997.

6. Pellegrini 1954.

7. An earlier version of the opening, first published in Fracastoro 1739, has been included below as *Carmina* 55. For the history of the composition of the *Syphilis*, see the Note on the Text, below.

8. Although he does issue a health warning regarding the effects of excessive venery; see *Syphilis* 2.113–15.

9. The text with its preface to Cardinal Alessandro Farnese is given in Fracastoro 1739, 2:77–104. The first edition appeared in Venice in 1569, published by Georgius de Caballis.

10. See Kempkens 1972.

11. For the evolution of this collection, see the Note on the Text, below.

12. For some examples of these features, see Fracastoro 2011.

SYPHILIS
SIVE DE MORBO GALLICO
AD PETRUM BEMBUM

SYPHILIS
OR THE FRENCH DISEASE
TO PIETRO BEMBO

: LIBER I :

Qui casus rerum varii, quae semina morbum
insuetum nec longa ulli per saecula visum
attulerint, nostra qui tempestate per omnem
Europam partimque Asiae Libyaeque per urbes
5   saeviit, in Latium vero per tristia bella
Gallorum irrupit, nomenque a gente recepit;
nec non et quae cura, et opis quid comperit usus,
magnaque in angustis hominum sollertia rebus,
et monstrata deum auxilia, et data munera caeli,
10 hinc canere et longe secretas quaerere causas
aëra per liquidum et vasti per sidera Olympi
incipiam, dulci quando novitatis amore
correptum placidi naturae suavibus horti
floribus invitant et amantes mira Camenae.
15   Bembe, decus clarum Ausoniae, si forte vacare
consultis Leo te a magnis paulisper et alta
rerum mole sinit, totum qua sustinet orbem,
et iuvat ad dulces paulum secedere Musas,
ne nostros contemne orsus medicumque laborem,
20 quidquid id est. Deus haec quondam dignatus Apollo est
et parvis quoque rebus inest sua saepe voluptas.
Scilicet hac tenui rerum sub imagine multum
naturae fatique subest, et grandis origo.
Tu mihi, quae rerum causas, quae sidera noscis,
25 et caeli effectus varios atque aëris oras,
Uranie (sic dum puro spatiaris Olympo,
metirisque vagi lucentes aetheris ignes,
concentu tibi divino cita sidera plaudant),
ipsa ades et mecum placidas, dea, lude per umbras,
30 dum tenues aurae, dum myrtea silva canenti
aspirat, resonatque cavis Benacus ab antris.

: BOOK I :

Now I will sing of the varied accidents of nature and the seeds
that have brought forth a strange affliction: unseen by anyone for
many centuries, it has raged in our time throughout Europe, parts
of Asia and the cities of Libya. It burst upon Italy in the wake of   5
the sad wars of the French and from that nation it took its name.
I will sing as well of the cure of the disease, of the benefits re-
vealed by experience and by man's great resourcefulness in trying
circumstances, and of the help that the gods have granted, to-
gether with the generosity of heaven. Through the clear air and   10
the stars of the vast firmament I will seek the deeply hidden causes
of the disease. Struck by dear love of new things, I take up this
task at the prompting of the peaceful gardens of Nature, with
their sweet blooms, and of the Muses who rejoice in marvels.

   Bembo, resplendent honor of Italy, if perchance Pope Leo   15
should grant you a moment's respite from weighty councils and
from those lofty affairs that sustain the world, and if you take any
pleasure in sparing a few moments for the dear Muses, look not
with contempt upon my labors as a poet and a physician, such as   20
they are. For the god Apollo once found worth in such matters,
and often there is pleasure even in lowly things: beneath this ap-
pearance of a humble subject lies an abundance of nature and fate,
and a grand origin.

   And you be present for me too, Urania, for you know the
causes of nature and the ways of the stars, the varied influences of   25
heaven and the regions of the sky. So may the swift stars applaud
you in divine concert as you pass through pure Olympian air and
traverse the glowing fires of the shifting sky. Wander with me then
through pleasant shades, while soft breezes and myrtle groves in-   30
spire my song, and Benacus echoes from his hollow caves.

Dic, dea, quae causae nobis post saecula tanta
insolitam peperere luem? Num tempore ab illo
vecta mari occiduo nostrum pervenit in orbem,
35   ex quo lecta manus, solvens de litore Hibero,
ausa fretum tentare vagique incognita ponti est
aequora, et orbe alio positas perquirere terras?
Illic namque ferunt aeterna labe per omnes
id morbi regnare urbes, passimque vagari
40   perpetuo caeli vitio, atque ignoscere paucis.
Commercine igitur causa accessisse putandum est
delatam contagem ad nos, quae parva sub ipsis
principiis, mox et vires et pabula sensim
suscipiens, sese in terras diffuderit omnes?
45   Ut saepe in stipulas cecidit cum forte favilla
de face, neglectam pastor quam liquit in arvo,
illa quidem tenuis primum similisque moranti
incedit: mox, ut paulatim increvit eundo,
tollitur, et victrix messem populatur et agros
50   vicinumque nemus, flammasque sub aethera iactat.
Dat sonitum longe crepitans Iovis avia silva,
et caelum late circum campique relucent.
At vero, si rite fidem observata merentur,
non ita censendum, nec certe credere par est
55   esse peregrinam nobis transque aequora vectam
contagem, quoniam in primis ostendere multos
possumus, attactu qui nullius hanc tamen ipsam
sponte sua sensere luem primique tulere.
Praeterea et tantum terrarum tempore parvo
60   contages non una simul potuisset obire.
Aspice per Latii populos, quique herbida Sagrae
pascua et Ausonios saltus et Iapygis orae
arva colunt; specta, Tiberis qua labitur, et qua
Eridanus, centum fluviis comitatus in aequor,

Say, Goddess, what causes, after so many centuries, brought
forth among us this strange affliction. Did it reach our hemisphere,
carried from the Western sea, after a select group of men set sail   35
from Spain, braving the open waves and the unknown waters of
changeful Ocean, as they searched for lands that lay in another
world? For it is said that in those parts this pestilence reigns in
every city with unending affliction, that it wanders abroad because
of a perpetual flaw in the climate, sparing few people. Should we   40
then believe that it was commerce that brought the disease to us,
that, small at first, it gradually gained force and sustenance, spread-
ing itself to every land? As when a spark happens to fall upon   45
some dried twigs from a torch that a shepherd has forgotten in a
field: at first it is little and appears to be biding its time; presently,
as it gathers strength, it rises up and victoriously lays waste the
harvest and the fields and the neighboring woods, tossing flames   50
up to heaven. Far off some distant thicket, sacred to Jove, begins to
roar, and for miles around the sky and the fields are aflame.

But if indeed observable phenomena are to be believed, the
truth lies elsewhere. There is no reason to think that this disease   55
reached us from abroad, that it came from across the seas. To be-
gin, I could name many who, with no such contact, still developed
the affliction spontaneously and were the first to suffer. Further-
more, no one disease could possibly traverse so great a space in   60
so short a time. Consider the people of Latium and those who live
in the fertile pastures of Sagra, in the Ausonian woods and on
the shores of Iapis. Consider too the land where the Tiber flows
and where the Eridanus, accompanied to the sea by a hundred

65   centum urbes rigat et placidis interfluit undis:
uno nonne vides ut tempore pestis in omnes
saeviit, ut sortem pariter transegimus unam?
Quin etiam externos eadem per tempora primum
excepisse ferunt, nec eam cognovit Hibera

70   gens prius, ignotum quae scindere puppibus aequor
ausa fuit, quam quos disterminat alta Pyrene
atque freta atque Alpes cingunt Rhenusque bicornis,
quam reliqui quos lata tenet gelida ora sub Arcto;
tempore non alio, Poeni, sensistis et omnes

75   qui laetam Aegyptum metitis fecundaque Nilo
arva, et palmiferae silvas tondetis Idumes.
Quae cum sic habeant sese, nempe altius isti
principium labi rerumque latentior ordo,
ni fallor, graviorque subest et maior origo.

80   Principio quaeque in terris, quaeque aethere in alto,
atque mari in magno natura educit in auras,
cuncta quidem nec sorte una nec legibus iisdem
proveniunt: sed enim quorum primordia constant
e paucis, crebro ac passim pars magna creantur;

85   rarius ast alia apparent, et non nisi certis
temporibusve locisve, quibus violentior ortus
et longe sita principia; ac nonnulla, priusquam
erumpant tenebris et opaco carcere noctis,
mille trahunt annos spatiosaque saecula poscunt.

90   Tanta vi coëunt genitalia semina in unum.
       Ergo et morborum quoniam non omnibus una
nascendi est ratio, facilis pars maxima visu est,
et faciles ortus habet et primordia praesto;
rarius emergunt alii, et post tempore longo

95   difficiles causas et inextricabile fatum
et sero potuere altas superare tenebras.
Sic elephas sacer, Ausoniis incognitus oris,

tributaries, waters a hundred cities and glides among them with its   65
peaceful waves. Do you not see that the disease has reached all of
them at the same time, that all of us have borne a common fate?
Indeed, it is said that at that time even foreign lands began to suf-
fer the affliction. Nor did the Spanish race, who had dared to sail   70
through unknown seas, contract the disease before other nations
that are bordered by the lofty Pyrenees, by the sea, the Alps and
the twin-horned Rhine, or before those who inhabit the broad
lands beneath the frigid Bear. And you as well felt it at the same
time, O Carthaginians, and you who till the lands of fecund Egypt   75
and the fertile plains of Nile and who prune the forests of Edom,
rich in palms. All of that being true, surely it follows that there is
a deeper cause to this disease, a more hidden design in nature (un-
less I am mistaken) and a graver and greater origin.

First, those things that nature has brought to light on earth, in   80
the lofty skies and on the great seas, have not all proceeded from a
single source, nor are they all governed by the same set of laws.
But because their component elements are few in number, a large
quantity of these ailments arise frequently and in many places.
Other diseases, however, appear more rarely, at specific times and   85
in specific places, and, because they emerge after long incubation,
they are more virulent. Some require a thousand years and many
ages before they burst forth from darkness and night's dusky
prison: so great is the violence with which the generative seeds of   90
such afflictions are joined. Therefore, since not all diseases have
the same process of generation, the great majority are easy to ob-
serve and emerge readily and promptly. Others arise more rarely
and after many years, having had to overcome more resistant   95
causes, intractable destiny and deep darkness. Thus the accursed
elephantiasis and lichen, unknown in Ausonian lands, long lay

sic lichen latuere diu, quibus accola Nili
gens tantum regioque omnis vicina laborat.
100   De genere hoc est dira lues quae nuper in auras
exiit, et tandem sese caligine ab atra
exemit, durosque ortus et vincula rupit.
Quam tamen, aeternum quoniam dilabitur aevum,
non semel in terris visam, sed saepe fuisse
105   ducendum est, quamquam nobis nec nomine nota
hactenus illa fuit, quoniam longaeva vetustas,
cuncta situ involvens, et res et nomina delet,
nec monumenta patrum seri videre nepotes.
      Oceano tamen in magno sub Sole cadente,
110   qua misera inventum nuper gens incolit orbem,
passim oritur nullisque locis non cognita vulgo est.
Usque adeo rerum causae atque exordia prima
et caelo variare et longo tempore possunt.
Quodque illic fert sponte aër et idonea tellus,
115   huc tandem annorum nobis longa attulit aetas.
Cuius forte suo si cunctas ordine causas
nosse cupis, magni primum circumspice mundi
quantum hoc infecit vitium, quot adiverit urbes.
Cumque animadvertas tam vastae semina labis
120   esse nec in terrae gremio nec in aequore posse,
haud dubie tecum statuas reputesque necesse est
principium sedemque mali consistere in ipso
aëre, qui terras circum diffunditur omnes,
qui nobis sese insinuat per corpora ubique,
125   suetus et has generi viventum immittere pestes,
aër quippe pater rerum est, et originis auctor.
Idem saepe graves morbos mortalibus affert,
multimode natus tabescere corpore molli,
et facile affectus capere, atque inferre receptos.

8

hidden, galling only the inhabitants of the Nile and its surrounding regions.

Of such a sort is the dire disease that lately emerged into the light, finally breaking free from dark mists and bursting the chains of its harsh birth. But we may assume that it was seen on Earth not once, but often in the eternal passing of the ages, though its name, until now, was unknown to us. For great antiquity covers everything in decay, erasing even the names of things, and distant descendants no longer recognize the monuments of their ancestors.

But in great Ocean, where the sun sets and a wretched race of men inhabits a newly discovered world, this disease can be found everywhere. There is no place where the people have not known it. But the causes and origins of the disease can change constantly over time, depending on the region. That which, over there, the air and a ready earth brought forth spontaneously, arrived here only after a multitude of years. And should you wish to know the history of this disease's emergence, look first at how much of the world it has attacked, how many cities it has reached. Since you understand that the seeds of so great a pestilence are not to be found in the lap of the earth or in the sea, it follows that its origin and dwelling place are in the very air, which circulates through every land and insinuates itself throughout our bodies, accustomed as it is to spread pestilence among the living. For air is the father of all things and the cause of their coming into being. And it often spreads diseases among mortals, since in many ways it has, by virtue of its native softness, a tendency to decay, and thus it can

100

105

110

115

120

125

130 Nunc vero quonam ille modo contagia traxit
accipe, quid mutare queant labentia saecla.
    In primis tum Sol rutilus, tum sidera cuncta
tellurem liquidasque auras atque aequora ponti
immutant agitantque, utque ipso sidera caelo
135 mutavere vicem et sedes liquere priores,
sic elementa modis variis se grandia vertunt.
Aspice ut, hibernus rapidos ubi flexit in Austrum
Phoebus equos nostrumque videt depressior orbem,
bruma riget, duratque gelu, spargitque pruina
140 tellurem, et gelida glacie vaga flumina sistit.
Idem, ubi nos Cancro propior spectavit ab alto,
urit agros: arent nemora et sitientia prata,
siccaque pulvereis aestas squallescit in arvis.
Nec dubium quin et noctis nitor, aurea Luna,
145 cui maria alta, omnis cui rerum obtemperat humor,
quin et Saturni grave sidus et aequior orbi
stella Iovis, quin pulchra Venusque et Martius ignis
ac reliqua astra etiam mutent elementa, trahantque
perpetuum, et late magnos dent undique motus,
150 praecipue sedem si quando plurima in unam
convenere, suo vel multum devia cursu
longe alias tenuere vias. Haec scilicet annis
pluribus et rapidi post multa volumina caeli
eveniunt, diis fata modis volventibus istis.
155 Ut vero evenisse datum est, numerumque diesque
exegere suos praefixaque tempora fatis,
proh quanta aërios tractus, salsa aequora quanta,
telluremque manent! Alibi quippe omnia late
cogentur spatia in nubes, caelum imbribus omne
160 solvetur, summisque voluti montibus amnes
praecipites secum silvas, secum aspera saxa,
secum armenta trahent; medius pater impete magno

easily contract infection and pass it on. Now I shall relate how the   130
air became infected, and how the course of centuries can trans-
form things.

In the first place the glowing sun and all the stars alter and
disrupt the earth, the clear air and the waters of the sea. Indeed
the stars in heaven itself have shifted in alternation and abandoned   135
their former abodes: thus, in various ways, great elements trans-
form themselves. Behold how, in winter, when Phoebus has turned
his swift horses to the south and views our earth from a lower
point, winter grows stiff and hardens with ice, spreading frost over
the earth and freezing the wandering rivers. Likewise, when Phoe-   140
bus looks down upon us from the heights of Cancer, he burns up
the fields, while the forests and meadows are athirst and parching
summer grows squalid in the dusty fields. Clearly the glory of the
night, the golden moon that guides the deep seas and all that flows   145
in nature; clearly the grave star of Saturn and Jove's star, with its
kindlier orb; clearly beautiful Venus and the fires of Mars and all
the other stars as well, can indeed affect matter, perpetually induc-
ing and provoking great changes. This is especially true when sev-
eral of them occupy the same position or, greatly deviating from   150
their wonted course, travel along very different paths. Surely these
events have come about over many years and after many revolu-
tions of the changeful heavens. For it is in this way that the gods
spin our destinies. But when these events have come to pass, when   155
they have completed the appointed number of days, as prescribed
by fate, what great changes will be visited upon the wide sky, the
salt sea and the earth! In some places the whole sky will condense
into clouds and the heavens dissolve in rain, while rivers rush   160
headlong from their mountaintops, carrying forests with them,

aut Padus aut Ganges, super et nemora alta domosque
turbidus, aequabit pelago freta lata sonante.
165   Aestates alibi magnae condentur, et ipsae
flumina speluncis flebunt arentia nymphae.
Aut venti cuncta invertent, aut obice clausi
excutient tellurem imam et cum turribus urbes.
Forsitan et tempus veniet, poscentibus olim
170   natura fatisque deum, cum non modo tellus,
nunc culta, aut obducta mari aut deserta iacebit,
verum etiam Sol ipse novum (quis credere possit?)
curret iter, sua nec per tempora diffluet annus,
ast insueti aestus insuetaque frigora mundo
175   insurgent, et certa dies animalia terris
monstrabit nova, nascentur pecudesque feraeque
sponte sua, primaque animas ab origine sument.
Forsitan, et maiora audens producere, tellus
Coeumque Enceladumque feret magnumque Typhoea,
180   ausuros patrio superos detrudere caelo,
convulsumque Ossan nemoroso imponere Olympo.
    Quae cum perspicias, nihil est cur tempore certo
admirere novis magnum marcescere morbis
aëra, contagesque novas viventibus aegris
185   sidere sub certo fieri, et per saecula longa.
    Bis centum fluxere anni, cum, flammea Marte
lumina Saturno tristi immiscente, per omnes
Aurorae populos, per quae rigat aequora Ganges,
insolita exarsit febris, quae pectore anhelo
190   sanguineum sputum exagitans (miserabile visu)
quarta luce frequens fato perdebat acerbo.
Illa eadem Assyriae gentes, et Persidos, et quae
Euphratem Tigrimque bibunt, post tempore parvo
corripuit, ditesque Arabas, mollemque Canopum;

and livestock and sharp rocks. With great force, Father Po or the
turbid Ganges will overrun deep woods and houses, resembling
the broad sea with its sounding waves. Elsewhere, great surfs will   165
rise up until the very nymphs in their grottos weep for their dried-
up streams. Either the winds will overturn everything in their
path or, blocked by obstacles, will strike the inmost earth as well
as cities with their lofty towers. Perhaps the time will come, at the
behest of both nature and the fate of the Gods, when the earth,   170
though now cultivated, will be submerged in water or become a
desert, and the sun itself—unbelievably—will change its course
and the year will abandon the sequence of its seasons. Unheard of
heat and cold will overrun the world, and on the appointed day   175
new creatures will be revealed upon the earth, cattle and wild
beasts will be born spontaneously and, as though through a new
creation, will take on souls. Perhaps the earth, daring to bring
forth greater things, will engender Coeus and Enceladus and great
Typhoeus, emboldened to drive the gods from their paternal   180
heaven and heap uprooted Ossa upon wooded Olympus.

Once you understand this, you need not marvel to see that, at
the appointed time, the vast air is weakened by new diseases, or
that new contagions, influenced by a specific star, arise among   185
sickened mortals and last for centuries.

It is two hundred years since Mars mingled his flaming torches
with melancholy Saturn and a strange fever afflicted all the peoples
of the East and all the plains watered by the Ganges. Its victims,
panting for breath, spat up blood, a horrible sight, and on the   190
fourth day this assiduous affliction slew them in a painful death.
Shortly thereafter, the same disease attacked the peoples of As-
syria and Persia and those who drink the waters of the Tigris and
Euphrates, as well as wealthy Arabia and effeminate Canopus.

195   inde Phrygas, inde et miserum trans aequora vecta
infecit Latium, atque Europa saeviit omni.
    Ergo age iam mecum, semper sese aethera circum
volventem superumque domos ardentiaque astra
contemplare, animumque agitans per cuncta, require
200   quis status illorum fuerit, quae signa dedere
sidera, quid nostris caelum portenderit annis:
hinc etenim tibi forte novae contagis origo
omnis et eventus tanti via prima patescet.
Aspice, candentes magni qua Cancer Olympi
205   excubat ante fores et brachia pandit aperta,
hinc dirae facies, hinc se diversa malorum
ostendent portenta; una hac sub parte videbis
magna coisse simul radiis ardentibus astra
et coniuratas sparsisse per aëra flammas:
210   flammas, quas longe tumulo sirenis ab alto
prospiciens senior vates, quem dia per omnes
caelicolumque domos duxit docuitque futura
Uranie, 'Miseras,' inquit, 'defendite terras,
o superi; insolitam video per inania ferri
215   illuviem, et magnos caeli tabesecre tractus:
bella etiam Europae miserae, bella impia, et agros
Ausoniae passim currentes sanguine cerno.'
Dixit, et illa etiam scriptis ventura notavit.
    Mos superum est, ubi saecla vagus Sol certa peregit,
220   ab Iove decerni fata et cuncta ordine pandi,
quaecumque eventura manent terrasque polumque.
Quod tempus cum iam nostris venientibus annis
instaret, rerum summus sator et superum rex,
Iuppiter acciri socios in rebus agendis
225   Saturnum Martemque iubet: bipatentia Cancer
limina portarum reserat diisque atria pandit.
Conveniunt quibus est fatorum cura gerenda:

From there it infected Phrygia and, crossing the sea, infected sad 195
Italy too and raged throughout Europe.

Now let us consider together the air that circulates without
cease, as well as the abode of the gods and the blazing stars. Driv-
ing your mind through all these things, consider what the position 200
of the stars was, what signs they gave, and what heaven foretold
for our time. In this way perhaps you will grasp the entire origin
of the new disease and the initial progress of so great a develop-
ment. Behold how Cancer stands guard before the flaming gates of
great Olympus and opens wide its claws. From here dire presenti- 205
ments and varied portents of evil will reveal themselves. In this
one region of the sky you will see great stars come together with
their burning rays, dispersing through the heavens their conspiring
fires; these are the flames that an older poet watched far-off from 210
the lofty tomb of the Siren, when divine Urania led him through
the abode of the gods and taught him of things to come. And he
said: "Defend, O gods, the imperiled earth, for I see a strange pes-
tilence carried through the empty air and the great plains of af- 215
flicted heaven. I see impious wars raging in sad Europe and all the
fields of Italy overrun with blood." So he spoke and committed
these predictions to writing.

It is the custom of the gods, after the wandering sun has tra-
versed a fixed number of centuries, for Jove to determine the des- 220
tinies that await the earth and the heavens and for all of them to
be set forth in order. When, with the passing of years, that time
had come, Jupiter, the supreme creator of the world and king of
the gods, bade his companions, Saturn and Mars, bestir them-
selves in the completion of these tasks. Cancer threw open the 225
twinned thresholds of his gates and revealed the halls to the con-
vening deities, whose task it is to bring destinies to fulfillment.

impiger ante alios, flammis ferroque coruscans,
bellipotens Mavors, animis cui proelia et arma
230   vindictaeque manent, et ovantes sanguine caedes.
Post placidus curru invectus rex Iuppiter aureo
insequitur (ni fata obstent), pater omnibus aequus.
Postremus, longaque via tardatus et annis,
falcifer accedit senior, qui haud immemor irae
235   in natum veteris, nato et parere recusans,
saepe etiam cessit retro, et vestigia torsit,
multa minans, multumque animo indignatus iniquo.
Iuppiter at solio ex alto, quo se solet uno
tollere, percenset fata, et ventura resolvit,
240   multum infelicis miserans incommoda terrae,
bellaque, fortunasque virum, casuraque rerum
imperia, et praedas, adapertaque limina morti,
in primis ignota novi contagia morbi:
morbi, qui humanae nulla mansuescat opis vi.
245   Assensere dei reliqui: concussus Olympus
intremuit tactusque novis defluxibus aether.
Paulatim aërii tractus et inania lata
accepere luem, vacuasque insuetus in auras
marcor iit, caelumque tulit contagia in omne:
250   sive quod, ardenti tot concurrentibus astris
cum Sole, e pelago multos terraque vapores
traxerit ignea vis, qui, mixti tenuibus auris
correptique novo vitio, contagia visu
perrara attulerint; aliud sive aethere ab alto
255   demissum late aërias corruperit oras.
     Quamquam animi haud fallor, quid agat quove ordine caelum
dicere et in cunctis certas perquirere causas
difficile esse: adeo interdum per tempora longa

Busiest was Mars, mighty in war and gleaming with fire and
sword, Mars who loves battles and arms, revenge and slaughter
that rejoices in blood. After him Jupiter, the peaceful king, fol-   230
lowed in a golden chariot, a father who is kind to all, fate permit-
ting. Finally, slowed by years and the long journey, came his aged
father, wielding a sickle. Hardly forgetting his ancient quarrel with   235
his son, he refused to obey him, and often looked behind him and
often turned back and made many threats, sore-vexed in his angry
soul. On a lofty throne that he alone had the right to occupy, Jupi-
ter now determined destinies and revealed what was to come,
greatly moved to pity by the sufferings of the doleful earth, by   240
wars and the fortunes of men, unstable empires, pillage and doors
open to death. But most of all he lamented the unknown pesti-
lence of a new disease that could be tamed by no force of human
art. The other gods gave their assent and, as stricken Olympus   245
trembled, the air was disturbed by unknown currents. Gradually
the pestilence reached the fields and broad expanses of the sky
and a new affliction suffused the empty air, spreading contagion
throughout the heavens. This occurred because, through the con-   250
junction of the stars and the burning sun, a fiery force had drawn
an abundance of vapors from the earth and sea: they, mixing with
the light breezes and stricken by a strange malady, produced this
contagion that was very rarely observed. Or perhaps something
else, descending from heaven, spread corruption abroad through   255
the fields of air.

Yet I am hardly unaware of the difficulties either in describing
what heaven ordained and how it played out, or in seeking with
certainty the causes of all these events: for sometimes heaven

effectus trahit, interdum (quod fallere possit)
260   miscentur fors et varii per singula casus.
     Nunc age, non id te lateat super omnia miram
naturam et longe variam contagibus esse.
Solis nam saepe arboribus fit noxius aër,
et tenerum germen florumque infecit honorem.
265   Interdum segetem et sata laeta annique labores
corripuit, scabraque ussit rubigine culmos,
et vitiata parens produxit semina tellus.
Interdum poenas animalia sola dedere,
aut multa aut certa ex ipsis. Memini ipse malignam
270   luxuriem vidisse anni, multoque madentem
autumnum perflatum Austro, quo protinus omne
caprigenum genus e cunctis animantibus unum
corruit. A stabulis laetas ad pabula pastor
ducebat: tum forte, alta securus in umbra
275   dum caneret tenuique gregem mulceret avena,
ecce aliquam tussis subito irrequieta tenebat,
nec longe mora mortis erat; namque acta repente
circum praecipiti lapsu, revomensque supremam
ore animam, socias inter moribunda cadebat.
280   Vere autem (dictu mirum!) atque aestate sequenti
infirmas pecudes balantumque horrida vulgus
pestis febre mala miserum paene abstulit omne.
Usque adeo varia affecti sunt semina caeli
et variae rerum species, numerusque vicissim
285   inter mota subest interque moventia certus.
Nonne vides, quamvis oculi sint pectore anhelo
expositi mollesque magis, non attamen ipsos
carpere tabem oculos, sed sese immergere in imum
pulmonem? Et pomis quamquam sit mollior uva,
290   non tamen iis vitiatur, at ipsa livet ab uva.
Nempe alibi vires, alibi sua pabula desunt;

achieves its results over many years and sometimes (which can
mislead you) chance and varied accidents account for each event.   260

Now it should not escape your notice that nothing is more
wondrous than nature and that it is infinitely varied in its conta-
gions. Often the air is noxious to trees alone, infecting their tender
buds and the beauty of their flowers. On occasion it has destroyed   265
harvests and fertile plantings and the labors of a year, parching the
stalks with scaly rust, till Mother Earth brings forth barren seeds.
At other times animals alone have paid the penalty, sometimes
many of them, sometimes only certain ones. I myself remember
seeing the year's harvest become strangely abundant, when the   270
damp autumn was buffeted by a southern wind: suddenly goats,
alone of all animals, were undone. The goatherd had led his happy
flock from their pens to pasture and, as it happened, he was sing-
ing without a care beneath the deep shade, beguiling the flock   275
with his slender flute, when a persistent cough suddenly took hold
of one of the goats and death soon followed. Suddenly the beast
tossed about and then fell down and, vomiting the last breath
from its mouth, dropped dead in the midst of its companions.
Strange to say, the following spring and summer, a contagion, with   280
its evil fever, carried off the sickened flocks and nearly all of the
pitiably bleating herd. So varied then are the seeds of the infected
air, so varied the forms of nature: and yet a fixed relation exists
reciprocally among those elements that move and those that are   285
moved. Have you not noticed how, even though one's eyes are
softer and more exposed to infection than one's panting chest,
consumption does not affect them none the less, but rather sinks
down into the depths of the lungs? And though a grape is softer
than an apple, it is bruised not by the apple, but rather by another   290
grape. Sometimes strength is lacking in a disease, sometimes nour-
ishment. Sometimes there is a fixed period of delay and the pores

ast alibi mora certa, nec ipsa foramina multum
non faciunt, hinc densa nimis, nimis inde soluta.
    Ergo contagum quoniam natura genusque
295   tam varium est, et multa modis sunt semina miris,
contemplator et hanc, cuius caelestis origo est,
quae, sicut desueta, ita mira erupit in auras.
Illa quidem non muta maris turbamque natantum,
non volucres, non bruta altis errantia silvis,
300   non armenta boum, pecudesve, armentave equorum
infecit, sed mente ingens ex omnibus unum
humanum genus, et nostros est pasta sub artus.
Porro homine e toto, quod in ipso sanguine crassum
et sordens lentore foret, foedissima primum
305   corripuit, sese pascens uligine pingui.
Tali se morbus ratione et sanguis habebant.
    Nunc ego te affectus omnes et signa docebo
contagis miserae: atque utinam concedere tantum
Musa queat, tantumque velit defendere Apollo,
310   tempora qui longa evolvit, cui carmina curae,
haec multas monumenta dies ut nostra supersint.
Forte etenim nostros olim legisse nepotes,
et signa et faciem pestis novisse iuvabit.
Namque iterum, cum fata dabunt, labentibus annis
315   tempus erit cum nocte atra sopita iacebit
interitu data: mox iterum post saecula longa
illa eadem exsurget, caelumque aurasque reviset,
atque iterum ventura illam mirabitur aetas.
    In primis mirum illud erat quod, labe recepta,
320   saepe tamen quater ipsa suum compleverat orbem
Luna, priusquam signa satis manifesta darentur.
Scilicet extemplo non sese prodit aperte
ut semel est excepta intus, sed tempore certo
delitet et sensim vires per pabula captat.

contribute greatly to the disease, being sometimes too constricted, sometimes too dilated.

And so, since the nature and type of contagious diseases are so   295
varied, since the seeds of affliction are so many and so strange, consider even this affliction, of celestial origin, that burst across the sky, as odd as it was wondrous. For it did not attack the silent schools of fishes swimming in the sea nor the birds nor the beasts that wander in the deep woods; neither did it harm herds of oxen   300
or sheep or horses. Rather it infected us humans alone, with our great minds, and feasted upon our limbs. Indeed, out of the entire body, this disgusting malady first seized on the element in the blood itself that is thick and filthy in its viscosity, thus feeding on   305
greasy moistures. For the disease is intimately involved with the blood.

Now I will describe the symptoms and effects of this dreadful illness. And I ask only that the Muse and Apollo — who has un-   310
furled the long centuries and cares for poetry — grant that my song might survive for many years. Perchance one day it will avail my descendants to read it and so learn the symptoms and nature of this disease. For there will come a time many years hence when, by   315
the decree of fate, this affliction, having disappeared and lain dormant in black night, once more will rise up after long centuries, and once more revisit the winds of heaven, and once more a future age will be moved to wonder at it.

First of all, it was strange that, once the disease had been contracted, often the moon would complete its cycle four times be-   320
fore the symptoms were manifested. For initially the disease does not betray itself, once it has been contracted internally: rather it hides for an allotted time, gradually gaining strength as it is fed.

325 Interea tamen, insolito torpore gravati
sponteque languentes animis, et munera obibant
aegrius et toto segnes se corpore agebant.
Ille etiam suus ex oculis vigor et suus ore
deiectus color haud laeta de fronte cadebat.

330 Paulatim caries foedis enata pudendis
hinc atque hinc invicta locos aut inguen edebat.
Tum manifesta magis vitii se prodere signa.
Nam, simul ac purae fugiens lux alma diei
cesserat, et noctis tristes induxerat umbras,

335 innatusque calor noctu petere intima suetus
liquerat extremum corpus, nec membra fovebat
obsita mole pigra humorum, tum vellier artus
brachiaque scapulaeque gravi suraeque dolore.
Quippe, ubi per cunctas ierant contagia venas,

340 humoresque ipsos et nutrimenta futura
polluerant, natura, malum secernere sueta,
infectam partem pellebat corpore ab omni
exterius; verum crasso quia corpore tarda
haec erat et lentore tenax, multa inter eundum

345 haerebat membris exsanguibus atque lacertis.
Inde graves dabat articulis extenta dolores.
Parte tamen leviore magisque erumpere nata,
summa cutis pulsa et membrorum extrema petebat.
Protinus informes totum per corpus achores

350 rumpebant, faciemque horrendam et pectora foede
turpabant: species morbi nova, pustula summae
glandis ad effigiem et pituita marcida pingui,
tempore quae multo non post adaperta dehiscens
mucosa multum sanie taboque fluebat.

355 Quin etiam erodens alte et se funditus abdens,
corpora pascebat misere: nam saepius ipsi
carne sua exutos artus squallentiaque ossa

In the meantime, the victims were weighed down by a strange   325
torpor and, their minds suddenly languishing, they sluggishly per-
formed their wonted business, though they were physically spent.
Also the native liveliness of their eyes and the native cast of their
complexion soon disappeared from their saddened countenances.   330
Gradually, an infection arose from their base private parts and here
and there unconquerably devoured their groin area and elsewhere.
Finally the symptoms of the disease revealed themselves openly.
For as soon as the pure and nurturing light of day had ceased,
yielding to the sad shadows of night, as soon as that native warmth   335
that usually seeks at night the innermost parts of the body had
deserted the extremities and no longer warmed those limbs, over-
come by the sluggish weight of humors, suddenly a sharp pain
swept over the torso and the arms, over the shoulders and legs.
Indeed, once the disease had spread through all the veins, it con-   340
taminated the bodily fluids and future nourishment. And nature,
accustomed to ward off disease, expelled the infected substance
from the entire body: but because this substance was sluggish and
tenacious, due to its thick and viscous nature, much of it remained   345
stuck in the bloodless limbs. From there it extended to the joints,
causing sharp pains. And with its lighter components, easier to
expel, it sought the surface of the skin and the extremities of the
body. At once disfiguring sores broke out over the entire body,   350
basely defiling the deformed face and the chest. Then the disease
took on the new appearance of a pustule that, resembling the
top of an acorn, was rotten with thick pus. Not long after, it
burst open, unleashing a multitude of phlegmlike blood and dis-
ease. Soon the affliction gnawed into the body and, hiding deep   355
therein, mercilessly consumed it. Often I myself have seen limbs

23

vidimus, et foedo rosa ora dehiscere hiatu,
ora atque exiles reddentia guttura voces.
360 Tum saepe aut cerasis aut Phyllidis arbore tristi
vidisti pinguem ex udis manare liquorem
corticibus, mox in lentum durescere gummi:
haud secus hac sub labe solet per corpora mucor
diffluere, hinc demum in turpem concrescere callum.
365 Unde aliquis, ver aetatis pulchramque iuventam
suspirans, et membra oculis deformia torvis
prospiciens foedosque artus turgentiaque ora,
saepe deos, saepe astra miser crudelia dixit.
Interea dulces somnos noctisque soporem
370 omnia per terras animalia fessa trahebant:
illis nulla quies aderat, sopor omnis in auras
fugerat, iis oriens ingrata Aurora rubebat,
iis inimica dies, inimicaque noctis imago.
Nulla Ceres illos, Bacchi non ulla iuvabant
375 munera: non dulces epulae, non copia rerum,
non urbis, non ruris opes, non ulla voluptas,
quamvis saepe amnes nitidos iucundaque Tempe
et placidas summis quaesissent montibus auras.
Diis etiam sparsaeque preces, incensaque templis
380 tura, et divitibus decorata altaria donis:
dii nullas audire preces donisve moveri.
Ipse ego Cenomanum memini, qua pinguia dives
pascua Sebina praeterfluit Ollius unda,
vidisse insignem iuvenem, quo clarior alter
385 non fuit, Ausonia nec fortunatior omni:
vix pubescentis florebat vere iuventae,
divitiis proavisque potens, et corpore pulchro;
cui studia aut pernicis equi compescere cursum,
aut galeam induere, et pictis splendescere in armis,

and ravaged bones shorn of their flesh, while the mouth and
throat, gnawed away and gaping in a sordid wound, could emit
only the feeblest sounds. It resembled the thick fluid that one of-   360
ten sees flowing from the moist bark of the cherry tree or the sad
almond tree of Phyllis and that quickly hardens into a dense gum.
Very similar indeed was the fluid that this disease spread over the
afflicted body and that then calcified into ugly scabs.

And so, a man would often lament the passing of the spring-   365
time of his life and of his beautiful youth: casting his disgusted
eyes upon his deformed limbs, his ravaged frame and swollen face,
he would sadly indict the gods and the cruel stars above. Mean-
while, throughout the land, all the wearied creatures enjoyed sweet   370
sleep and nightly repose: but for the victims of the disease there
was no peace, as sleep vanished completely into thin air. For them
the golden dawn shone unwelcome and for them both day and
shady night had become enemies. They took no joy in the gifts of
Ceres or Bacchus, in delicate meals and abundant riches, in the   375
wealth of the city or the countryside, in any pleasure whatever,
even though they often sought sunny streams and jocund valleys
and the pleasing breezes of mountain tops. They offered up scat-
tered prayers to the gods and burned incense in the temples and   380
adorned altars with rich gifts: but the gods heard no prayers, nor
were they moved by any gifts.

I myself once saw an outstanding young man among the
Cenomani, who lived where the rich Oglio flows past fertile mead-
ows nourished by the waters of Lake Sebinus. In all of Italy, no
man was more handsome or more affluent than he was. Scarcely   385
having attained the springtime of early youth, he was eminent in
wealth, ancestors and physical beauty. His constant loves were rac-
ing swift horses, donning helmets and shining in brilliant armor.

390　　aut iuvenile gravi corpus durare palaestra,
　　　　venatuque feras agere, et praevertere cervos;
　　　　illum omnes Ollique deae, Eridanique puellae
　　　　optarunt, nemorumque deae, rurisque puellae,
　　　　omnes optatos suspiravere hymenaeos.
395　　Forsan et ultores superos neglecta vocavit
　　　　non nequicquam aliqua, et votis pia numina movit:
　　　　nam, nimium fidentem animis nec tanta timentem,
　　　　invasit miserum labes, qua saevior usquam
　　　　nulla fuit, nulla umquam aliis spectabitur annis.
400　　Paulatim ver id nitidum, flos ille iuventae,
　　　　disperiit, vis illa animi: tum squalida tabes
　　　　artus (horrendum!) miseros obduxit, et alte
　　　　grandia turgebant foedis abscessibus ossa.
　　　　Ulcera (proh divum pietatem!) informia pulchros
405　　pascebant oculos et diae lucis amorem,
　　　　pascebantque acri corrosas vulnere nares.
　　　　Quo tandem infelix fato, post tempore parvo,
　　　　aetheris invisas auras lucemque reliquit.
　　　　Illum Alpes vicinae, illum vaga flumina flerunt,
410　　illum omnes Ollique deae, Eridanique puellae
　　　　fleverunt, nemorumque deae, rurisque puellae,
　　　　Sebinusque alto gemitum lacus edidit amne.
　　　　　　Ergo hanc per miseras terras Saturnus agebat
　　　　pestem atrox, nec saeva minus crudelis et ipse
415　　miscebat Mavors coniunctaque fata ferebat.
　　　　Quippe lue hac nascente, putem simul omnia diras
　　　　Eumenidas cecinisse fera et crudelia nobis,
　　　　Tartareos etiam barathro (dira omina) ab imo
　　　　excivisse lacus, Stygiaque ab sede laborem,
420　　pestemque, horribilemque famem, bellumque, necemque.
　　　　　　Dii patrii, quorum Ausonia est sub numine, tuque,
　　　　tu Latii Saturne pater, quid gens tua tantum

He hardened his youthful body through wrestling, hunting wild   390
beasts and outpacing the stag. All the goddesses of the Oglio, all
the daughters of the Po, all the dryads of the woods and all the
country girls longed for him and hoped to be his bride. Perhaps   395
one of these, having been rejected, prayed not in vain to the aveng-
ing gods and with her vows moved the pious spirits. For the piti-
able youth, too self-confident and heedless, was stricken by a dis-
ease more virulent than anything that had been seen before or that
will ever be seen hereafter. Gradually that splendid flower and   400
springtime of his youth vanished, together with all force of mind.
Soon a sordid infection — a horrid sight — covered his poor body
and, lodging deep within, caused his larger bones to swell up with
filthy abscesses. And O, for the love of god!, unsightly sores con-
sumed his beautiful eyes and his love of the blessed daylight and   405
his nose, corroded by an acrid wound! Finally laid low by this fate,
he soon departed the detested air and light of day. The neighbor-
ing mountains wept for him and the wandering streams. All the   410
goddesses of the Oglio wept for him and the daughters of the Po,
the dryads of the woods and the country girls. Even Lake Sebinus
sent forth its lamentation in a deep stream.

And so harsh Saturn drove this disease through the wretched
earth, and Mars himself, no less cruelly, joined with him in spread-   415
ing the savage death. Truly I do believe that, with the emergence
of this plague, the dread Furies foretold for us at the same time all
the cruelest and most savage afflictions; that they called forth
all the horrors from the depths of the Tartarean lake and from
the Stygian abode — a dire omen — pestilence and travail, hideous   420
hunger, slaughter and war.

Gods of our fathers, whose spirit stands guard over Italy, and
you, Saturn, father of Latium: what could your people have done

est merita? An quidquam superest dirique gravisque,
quod sit inexhaustum nobis? Ecquod genus usquam
425   aversum usque adeo caelum tulit? Ipsa labores,
Parthenope, dic prima tuos, dic funera regum,
et spolia, et praedas, captivaque colla tuorum.
An stragem infandam memorem, sparsumque cruorem
Gallorumque Italumque pari discrimine, cum iam
430   sanguineum, et defuncta virum defunctaque equorum
corpora volventem, cristasque atque arma trahentem,
Eridanus pater acciperet rapido agmine Tarrum?
Te quoque spumantem et nostrorum caede tumentem,
Abdua, non multo post tempore te pater idem
435   Eridanus gremio infelix suscepit, et altum
indoluit tecum, et fluvio solatus amico est.
     Ausonia infelix, en quo discordia priscam
virtutem et mundi imperium perduxit avitum?
Angulus anne tui est aliquis, qui barbara non sit
440   servitia et praedas et tristia funera passus?
Dicite vos, nullos soliti sentire tumultus
vitiferi colles, qua flumine pulcher amoeno
Erethenus fluit, et, plenis lapsurus in aequor
cornibus, Euganeis properat se iungere lymphis.
445   O patria, o longum felix, longumque quieta
ante alias, patria o divum sanctissima tellus,
dives opum, fecunda viris, laetissima campis
uberibus rapidoque Athesi et Benacide lympha,
aerumnas memorare tuas summamque malorum
450   quis queat, et dictis nostros aequare dolores,
et turpes ignominias, et barbara iussa?
Abde caput, Benace, tuo et te conde sub amne,
victrices nec iam deus interlabere lauros.
     En etiam, ceu nos agerent crudelia nulla,
455   nec lacrimae planctusve forent, en, dura tot inter,

to deserve such a plight? Or is there some other dire and terrible   425
affliction that awaits us that we have not already seen? Has any
other race known so hostile a heaven? And you, Parthenope, speak
first and tell of your travails, of the deaths of kings, of spoils and
plunders and the captive necks of your subjects. Or should I tell
of unspeakable carnage, of the blood of Frenchmen and Italians   430
spilled in equal measure, now that Father Eridanus has received
the Taro river, its rushing waters thick with blood, as it bears
crests and arms, as it churns up the lifeless cadavers of men and
horses? And soon thereafter, unhappy Father Eridanus received   435
you as well in his embrace, O Adda, foaming and swelling with the
blood of our sons. And deeply did he pity you and console you
with his loving streams!

Behold, sad Italy, to what condition discord has reduced your
ancient virtues and the far-flung empire of your ancestors! Is there
any corner of your land that has not suffered barbarous servitude,   440
plunder and lamentable death? Answer, you vine-rich hills, once
strangers to all upheaval, where the lovely Erethenus glides in a
gentle stream before it falls, overflowing, into the sea, the Erethe-
nus that hastens to mingle its waters with those of the Euganean
springs.

O land of my fathers, you who for so long were happier and   445
more peaceful than any other land, best loved by the gods, rich in
wealth, fecund in men and fertile in abundant fields, graced by the
rushing Adige and the waters of Benacus: who could recite all
of your travails, all of the ills that you have suffered? Who could   450
find words to equal our sorrows, the base ignominies we have suf-
fered, the barbarous dominion? Cover your head, Benacus, and
hide beneath your waves: no longer glide, a god, among victorious
laurels!

As though we had not suffered a cruel fate, as though we hadn't
known tears and lamentations, behold, amid all these calamities,   455

spes Latii, spes et studiorum et Palladis illa
occidit: ereptum Musarum e dulcibus ulnis,
te miserum ante diem crudeli funere, Marce
Antoni, aetatis primo sub flore cadentem
460   vidimus extrema positum Benacide ripa,
quam media inter saxa sonans Sarca abluit unda.
Te ripae flevere Athesis, te voce vocare
auditae per noctem umbrae manesque Catulli,
et patrios mulcere nova dulcedine lucos.
465   Tempestate illa Ausoniam rex Gallus opimam
vertebat bello et Ligurem ditione premebat.
Parte alia, Caesar ferro superabat et igni
Euganeos, placidumque Silim, Carnumque rebellem,
et totum luctus Latium maerorque tenebat.

: LIBER II :

Nunc age, quae vitae ratio, quae cura adhibenda
perniciem adversus tantam, quid tempore quoque
conveniat (nostri quae pars est altera coepti)
expediam, et miranda hominum comperta docebo.
5   Quippe nova cum re attoniti multa irrita primum
tentassent, tamen angustis sollertia maior
in rebus crescensque usu experientia longo
evicere, datumque homini protendere longe
auxilia, et certis pestem compescere vinclis,
10   victorem et sese claras attollere in auras.
Credo equidem et quaedam nobis divinitus esse
inventa, ignaros fatis ducentibus ipsis.
Nam, quamquam fera tempestas et iniqua fuerunt

the one hope of Latium, the hope of Pallas and the liberal arts, has died! For we have seen you, Marcus Antonius, torn before your time from the sweet embrace of the Muses, vanquished by a cruel death in the flower of youth, lying in state on the banks of Lake Garda, buffeted amid the rocks by the sounding waters of the Sarca. The banks of the Adige wept for you and at night the ghost of Catullus was heard calling for you, soothing his paternal groves with renewed sweetness. 460

At that time, the king of France overturned rich Italy in war and reduced Liguria to his sway. Elsewhere the Emperor, with fire and sword, vanquished the Euganean Hills, peaceful Silis and the rebellious Carnic mountains. And all of Italy was seized by sorrow and lamentation. 465

꞉ BOOK II ꞉

Listen now as I explain, in the second part of my poem, what regimen and care are to be taken against this great affliction, and what measures are suitable to each phase of the disease. I will also speak of the wondrous discoveries of men. For though at first they were thoroughly perplexed by this strange disease and tried many remedies in vain, yet great skill in trying circumstances and experience that grew with increased familiarity finally carried the day. It became possible for human beings to offer great assistance and to confine the contagion with effective bonds, so that they could raise themselves victorious into the clear air. Truly I believe that certain discoveries were made possible by divine help and that destiny itself led us on in our ignorance. For though it was a wretched time 5 10

sidera, non tamen omnino praesentia divum
15 abfuit a nobis, placidi et clementia caeli.
Si morbum insolitum, si dura et tristia bella
vidimus et sparsos dominorum caede Penates
oppidaque incensasque urbes subversaque regna
et templa et raptis temerata altaria sacris,
20 flumina deiectas si perrumpentia ripas
evertere sata, et mediis nemora eruta in undis
et pecora et domini correptaque rura natarunt,
obseditque inimica ipsas penuria terras:
haec eadem tamen, haec aetas (quod fata negarunt
25 antiquis) totum potuit sulcare carinis
id pelagi immensum quod circuit Amphitrite.
Nec visum satis extremo ex Atlante repostos
Hesperidum penetrare sinus, Prassumque sub Arcto
inspectare alia praeruptaque litora Rhapti,
30 atque Arabo advehere et Carmano ex aequore merces,
Aurorae sed itum in populos Titanidis usque est,
supra Indum Gangemque supra, qua terminus olim
Catygare noti orbis erat, superata Cyambe
et dites ebeno et felices macere silvae.
35 Denique et a nostro diversum gentibus orbem,
diversum caelo, et clarum maioribus astris
remigio audaci attigimus, ducentibus et diis.
Vidimus et vatem egregium, cui pulchra canenti
Parthenope placidusque cavo Sebethus ab antro
40 plauserunt, umbraeque sacri manesque Maronis,
qui magnos stellarum orbes cantavit, et hortos
Hesperidum, caelique omnes variabilis oras.
Te vero ut taceam atque alios, quos fama futura
post mutos cineres, quos et venientia saecla
45 antiquis conferre volent, at, Bembe, tacendus
inter dona deum nobis data non erit umquam

and the stars were averse, the gods were not entirely absent, nor   15
was the clemency of a peaceful heaven.

It is true that in this age we have seen the emergence of an un-
heard-of disease and have suffered sad and protracted wars. We
have seen houses scored with the blood of their owners, towns and
cities set aflame, kingdoms overturned, temples and altars pro-
faned, and sacred relics borne away. We have seen rivers burst   20
their low-lying embankments, destroying crops, and whole forests
torn up and floating in the waters, as flocks and shepherds were
submerged, together with the ravaged countryside. And a baleful
poverty has beset the earth. But this is also the age in which our   25
ships have cut a path across the entire immensity of the ocean
embraced by Amphitrite—something that fate denied to the an-
cients. And not satisfied with sailing past the Atlas Mountains and
penetrating the gulfs of the Hesperides to behold Prasum, beneath
a new arctic star, as well as the rocky coasts of Rhaptum—not sat-
isfied with bringing goods back from Araby and the Kerman sea,   30
we have even visited the people of Dawn, the Titan's daughter,
beyond the Indus and the Ganges, beyond Cattigara, once the
limit of the known world. We have sailed beyond Cyambe to
woods rich in ebony and fertile in macir. Finally, by rowing boldly,   35
and guided by the gods, we have reached a world that differs from
ours in its people and its sky, and that shines with brighter stars.
We have seen a great poet whose beautiful singing was applauded
by Parthenope and peaceful Sebethus in his hollow cave, as well as   40
by the shades and ghosts of sacred Vergil. He sang of the great
revolutions of the stars, the gardens of the Hesperides, and all the
corners of the moving heavens.

I do not mention you, Bembo, and many others who, once you
have become mute ashes, will be favorably compared to the an-   45
cients by fame and future ages; but among God's gifts to us, I can

magnanimus Leo, quo Latium, quo maxima Roma
attollit caput alta, paterque ex aggere Tybris
assurgit, Romaeque fremens gratatur ovanti,
50   cuius ab auspiciis iam nunc mala sidera mundo
cessere, et laeto regnat iam Iuppiter orbe
puraque pacatum diffundit lumina caelum,
unus qui aerumnas post tot longosque labores
dulcia iam profugas revocavit ad otia Musas,
55   et leges Latio antiquas rectumque piumque
restituit, qui iusta animo iam concipit arma
pro re Romana, pro relligione deorum,
unde etiam Euphrates, etiam late ostia Nili,
et tantum Euxini nomen tremit unda refusi,
60   atque Aegaea suos confugit Doris in isthmos.
    Ergo, alii dum tanta canent, dumque illius acta
inclita component, dum forte accingeris et tu
condere et aeternis victurum intexere chartis,
nos, quos fata vocant haud tanta ad munera, lusus
65   inceptos, quantum tenuis fert Musa, sequamur.
    Principio, quoniam affecti non sanguinis una
est ratio, tibi sit morbo spes maior in illo,
sanguine qui insedit puro: verum, quibus atra
bile tument spissoque resultant sanguine venae,
70   maior in iis labor est, pestisque tenacius haeret.
Quare operae pretium est validis atque acribus uti
omnibus hos contra, miseris nec parcere membris.
Quin etiam meliora sibi promittere cuncta
ille potest, qui principiis novisse sub ipsis
75   serpentem tacite valuit per viscera labem.
Namque, ubi pasta diu vires per pabula longa
auxerit, et iam se vitium firmaverit intra,
heu quanto tibi libertas speranda labore est!

never remain silent about great-hearted Leo, thanks to whom Italy
and its greatest city raise high their heads, while Father Tiber
overflows its banks and noisily congratulates triumphant Rome.   50
Under Leo's auspices, the opposing stars have now retreated at last
from the firmament, Jupiter reigns across the happy heavens, and
the sky, peaceful once again, pours forth its pure light. After so
much suffering and such long travails, Leo has recalled the exiled
Muses to their sweet leisure. Restoring Latium's ancient laws, as   55
well as rectitude and piety, he now considers waging a just war for
the sake of Rome and the religion of the gods. In consequence, the
Euphrates, the Nile with its wide delta, and the Euxine with its
backward-flowing waves all tremble at his great name, while Ae-   60
gean Doris takes refuge in its isthmus.

   And so, whereas others will sing of Leo's great exploits and his
illustrious deeds, and perhaps you too, Bembo, gird yourself to
compose an undying song and commit it to eternal pages, we,
whom the fates have hardly called to such great duties, will con-
tinue on with the lesser poem we have already begun, as our hum-   65
bler muse directs us.

   First, since not all blood is afflicted in the same way, the disease
is most benign when it infects pure blood. But those who suffer
from an inflammation of black bile, whose veins throb with thick
blood, are more grievously afflicted, and in them the disease is   70
more tenacious. Therefore it is worthwhile to use strong medicine
against the latter, and not to spare the afflicted body. Indeed, that
man's condition is most promising who has been able, from the
very beginning, to sense the disease snaking silently through his   75
internal organs. For when the affliction is well fed and has grown
in strength through an abundance of food, when the disease has
established itself within, how painful it is to break free of it!

Ergo omnem impendes operam te opponere parvis
80   principiis, memorique animo haec praecepta reconde.
      In primis ego non omni te assuescere caelo
exhorter: fuge perpetuo quod flatur ab Austro,
quod caeno immundaeque grave est sudore paludis.
Protenti potius campi mihi liber et agri
85   tractus et apricis placeant in collibus aurae,
et molles Zephyri, pulsusque Aquilonibus aër.
Hic, iubeo, tibi nulla quies, nulla otia sunto.
Rumpe moras, agita assiduis venatibus apros
impiger, assiduis agita venatibus ursos.
90   Nec tibi sit labor, aërii cursu ardua montis
vincenti, rapidum in valles deflectere cervum,
et longa lustrare altos indagine saltus.
      Vidi ego saepe malum qui iam sudoribus omne
finisset, silvisque luem liquisset in altis.
95   Sed nec turpe puta dextram summittere aratro,
et longum trahere incurvo sub vomere sulcum,
neve bidente solum et duras proscindere glebas,
et valida aëriam quercum exturbare bipenni,
atque imis altam eruere ab radicibus ornum.
100   Quin etiam, exercere domi quo te quoque possis,
parvam mane pilam versa mihi, vespere versa.
Et saltu et dura potes exsudare palaestra.
Vince malum: nec te fallat, quod desidis otii
assidue desiderium lectique sequetur.
105   Tu lecto ne crede, gravi ne crede sopori:
his alitur vitium, et placidae sub imagine pacis
decipit, e dulcique trahit fomenta quiete.
      Nec non interea effugito quae tristia mentem
sollicitant: procul esse iube curasque, metumque
110   pallentem, ultricesque iras, omnemque Minervae
addictum studiis animum; sed carmina, sed te

Therefore, make every effort to attack it in its inception and al- 80
ways remember the following advice.

First, I would exhort you not to go out in all weather. Avoid the
air that is perpetually blown hither by the south wind, that is
heavy with mud or the filthy sweat of a polluted marsh. Rather I
would advise you to seek the open tracts of meadows and broad
fields and the breezes of sunlit hills, as well as the soft western 85
winds and the winds of the north. While you are outdoors, I
strongly urge you to enjoy no rest or relaxation. Shake off idleness
and hunt boars, hunt bears relentlessly. Nor should you spare any 90
effort, as you conquer the cliffs of lofty mountains, to chase the
swift stag down into valleys and to traverse deep forests as you try
to entrap it. Often have I seen men rid themselves of their afflic-
tion with much sweat, leaving the disease in the deep woods. Do 95
not consider it beneath you to put your hand to the plow, to dig
long furrows with the hooked plowshare, to split the soil and hard
earth with a hoe, or with an ax to cut down the lofty oak and
thoroughly uproot the tall ash tree. In fact, even at home you can 100
take exercise, throwing a small ball around in the morning and at
night. And you can also raise a sweat by dancing and wrestling.
Defeat the disease, and be not deceived when there follows a nag-
ging desire for sleep and indolent rest. But do not go to bed or give 105
in to deep sleep. For through such means, and through the sem-
blance of peaceful repose, the illness deceives us, drawing strength
from gentle rest. Meanwhile avoid sad thoughts that trouble the
mind; keep cares and pallid fears far off, as well as vengeful anger
and a mind too much drawn to the pursuits of Minerva. Rather 110

delectent iuvenumque chori, mixtaeque puellae.
Parce tamen Veneri, mollesque ante omnia vita
concubitus: nihil est nocuum magis, odit et ipsa
pulchra Venus, tenerae contagem odere puellae. 115
    Quod sequitur, victus ratio tibi maxima habenda est,
nec sit cura tibi neve observantia maior.
Principio, quoscumque amnes, quoscumque paludes,
quosque lacus liquidi pascunt, quosque aequora pisces,
omne genus procul amoveo. Sunt quos tamen usus 120
liberius, cum res cogit, concedere possit.
Omnibus his est alba caro, non dura tenaxque,
quos petrae et fluviorum adversa marisque fatigant:
tales nant pelago phycides, rutilaeque per undas
auratae, gobiique, et amantes saxea percae; 125
talis dulcifluum fluviorum scarus ad ora
solus saxa inter depastas ruminat herbas.
Sed neque quae stagnis volucres, quaeque amnibus altis
degere amant, liquidisque cibum perquirere in undis
laudarim: tibi pinguis anas, tibi crudior anser 130
vitetur, potiusque vigil Capitolia servet,
viteturque gravi coturnix tarda sagina.
Tu teneros lactes, tu pandae abdomina porcae,
porcae heu terga fuge, et lumbis ne vescere aprinis,
venatu quamvis toties confeceris apros. 135
Quin neque te crudus cucumis, non tubera captent,
neve famem cinara bulbisve salacibus exple.
Non placeat mihi lactis amor, non usus aceti,
non fumosa mero spumantia pocula Baccho,
qualia Cyrnaei colles campique Falerni 140
et Pucinus ager mittunt, aut qualia nostris
Rhetica dat parvo de collibus uva racemo.
Nempe Sabina magis placeant, dilutaque tellus
quae tulit et multo domuerunt Naiades amne.

you should seek diversion in the songs and choruses of young men and women mixed together. But forgo the pleasures of Venus and, above all, avoid soft dalliances. Nothing is more harmful. Beautiful 115 Venus herself and all lovely maidens beside hate disease.

Next you should pay great attention to your diet: you should have no greater care or concern. First, whichever fishes live in rivers and ponds, in clear lakes and in the sea, I would have you avoid. There are others, however, which, when necessity compels 120 it, experience can more liberally allow. All of these have white flesh, but not hard or tough. They are wearied by the rocks and shallows of rivers and streams. Of such, in the sea, are the wrasse and shining gilthead, gobies and perch that live among the rocks. 125 Such as well is the scarus that all alone feeds on plants that grow at the mouths of freshwater streams. But I would not suggest such fowl as love to live in marshes and deep streams or that seek their sustenance in clear waters. Avoid the rich duck or the juicier 130 goose, which would better serve to protect the Capitol. Avoid as well the lethargic quail heavy from having been force-fed. Avoid tender tripe and bacon from a plump sow, as well as its ham and the loin of boars, however many you may have felled in the hunt. 135 Be not enticed by raw cucumber or truffles, nor satisfy your hunger with artichokes or lusty onions. Nor would I suggest milk or vinegar, nor cups frothing with old and undiluted wine, such as 140 come from the Cyrnaean Hills, the Falernian fields or the plains of Pucinum, or such as the Rhaetian grapes of our hills put forth in small clusters. Better by far are the Sabine grapes, born of the wet earth and conquered by the Naiads with their abundant streams.

145 At, tibi si ex horto victus mensaeque deorum
sunt animo atque olerum simplex et inempta voluptas,
non mentae virides, non laeta sisymbria desunt,
intybaque, et toto florentes frigore sonchi,
et sia fontanis semper gaudentia rivis,
150 et thymbrae suaves, et odoriferae calaminthae;
laeta meliphylla et riguo buglossus ab horto
carpantur, plenisque ferax erucula palmis,
atque olus, atque rumex, et salsi gramina chrithmi.
Ipsa lupum dumeta ferent: hinc collige primos
155 asparagos, albae asparagos hinc collige vitis,
cum nondum explicuit ramos, umbracula nondum
texuit, et virides iussit pendere corymbos.

Singula sed longum est, nec percensere necesse,
iamque aliud vocor ad munus: iuvat in nova Musas
160 naturae nemora Aoniis deducere ab umbris,
unde mihi, si non e lauro intexere fronti
serta volent tantaque caput cinxisse corona,
at saltem ob servata hominum tot milia dignum
censuerint querna redimiri tempora fronde.

165 Vere novo, si quem morbus tenet, aut et in ipso
autumno, si firma aetas, si sanguis abundat,
regalem mediamve lacerti incidere venam
proderit, atque extra foedatum haurire cruorem.
Praeterea, quocumque habeat te tempore pestis,
170 corruptum humorem et contagem educere turpem
ne pigeat, facilique luem deponere ab alvo.
Ante tamen ducenda para, concreta resolve,
et crassa attenua, et lentore tenacia frange.
Ergo Coryciumque thymum sit cura thymumque
175 Pamphylium, thymbrae similis qui durior exit,
prima tibi coxisse, lupique volubile gramen,
foeniculumque, apiumque, et amari germina capni.

But if you have a taste for a garden's fare and for the feasts of the   145
gods, for the free and simple pleasures of herbs, there is always
green mint and pleasant sysimbrium, endives and sowthistle that
flourishes even in cold weather, watercress that always delights in   150
spring streams, sweet savory and fragrant calamint. You should
also pluck florid balm and borage from a well-watered garden, and
fertile rocket with its large leaves, potherbs, sorrel and grass of
salty samphire. Thornbushes too will bring forth hops: from these   155
gather the first shoots of white briony, when it has not yet spread
out its branches to provide shade, nor bidden its green clusters
hang down.

But to enumerate every one of these would be tedious and un-
necessary. For I am called to another duty. Now I wish to lead the
Muses down from their Aonian bowers into new groves of natural   160
science. And if therefore they chose not to wreathe a laurel for my
forehead and gird my head with so great a crown, at least may
they see fit, in light of my saving the lives of so many thousands,
to adorn my temples with an oak leaf.

If the disease is contracted at the beginning of spring, or even   165
in the depths of autumn, and if the patient is in good health and
has an abundance of blood in him, then you should make an inci-
sion in the basilic or middle vein of the arm and extract the in-
fected blood. But no matter the season in which the disease takes   170
hold, do not hesitate to draw out the corrupted humor or base
contagion, or to discharge the sickness from loosened bowels. But
beforehand you must ready those elements that are to be removed
by loosening what has hardened, thinning out the fatty parts, and
breaking up what has grown tenacious in its viscosity.

And so your first concern should be to boil Corycian or Pam-   175
phylian thyme, which grows more powerfully, like savory, as well
as the winding shoots of hops, fennel, parsley and seeds of bitter

His polyporum hirtos imitata filicula cirros
additur, et nymphis tangi renuens adiantus;
180   his sterile asplenum, his pictam phyllitida iunge.
Quorum ubi decoctum permultis ante diebus
ebiberis crudumque humorem incoxeris omnem,
tum scilla medicare acri, et colocynthide amara,
helleboroque gravi, nec non quae in litore surgens,
185   qua ludit maris unda, ter evariata colorem,
ter flores mutata die (rem nomine signat),
herba potens radice, suum cui zinziber adde;
adde etiam anguineum cucumin, Nabathaeaque tura,
myrrhamque, bdelamque, hammoniacique liquorem,
190   et lacrimam panaceam, et dulci Colchica bulbo.
    His actis, si forte tibi frigentia corda
et molles animi fuerint, nec acerba placebit
in primis tentare brevique exstinguere pestem,
sed placidis agere et per tempora lenibus uti,
195   tum superest tibi cura animum ad fomenta relicta
vertere contagisque ad tenuia semina caecae,
illa quidem consueta modis inserpere miris.
Profuerint igitur quaeque exsiccantia, quaeque
marcori resinosa solent obsistere putri.
200   Tales sunt myrrhae lacrimae, sunt talia tura,
cedrusque, aspalathusque, immortalisque cupressus,
et bene cum calamo spirans redolente cyperus.
Ergo nec desint casiae, nec desit amomum,
macerve, agalochumve tibi, nec cinnama odora.
205   Est etiam in pratis illud iuxtaque paludes
scordion, omnigenis quod tantum obstare venenis
contagique solet, parvo quaerenda labore
herba tibi: viret ipsa comis imitata chamaedryn,
flore rubens, referensque alli cum voce saporem.
210   Aurora nascente huius frondemque comantem

fumitory. To these add fern that imitates the polypus's shaggy ten-
tacles, and maidenhair, which refuses the touch of water, as well as   180
sterile spleenwort and parti-colored harts tongue. And when you
have drunk what you prepared over many days, and absorbed all
of the untreated moisture, then treat it with sharp squill and bitter
gourd and grave hellebore, as well as the plant that grows upon the
shore, where the sea's waves disport, the plant that changes its   185
color and its flowers thrice in a day and takes its name from that
fact, an herb of potent root. To this add an equal measure of gin-
ger, as well as the serpentine cucumber and Nabatean incense,
myrrh and bdellium and gum ammoniac, tear-shaped all-heal and   190
saffron with its sweet bulb.

If, after all of this, your heart is still chilled and your spirit
droops, if you do not wish to begin by using harsh remedies that
expel the disease swiftly, but rather choose softer, pleasanter rem-
edies over time, then give no thought to cures and rather turn your   195
attention to what nourishes the minute seeds of blind contagion,
which tend to steal into the body in marvelous ways. To this end
use dry and resinous herbs that can obstruct putrescent decay. Of   200
such are tears of myrrh and incense, cedar and aspalathus and cy-
press that never dies, as well as galingale, fragrant with its sweet-
scented reed. Also use cassia and cardamom, macir or aloes' wood
or fragrant cinnamon. And in the fields and beside ponds is   205
the renowned scordium which is wont to impede all poisons
and contagions, an herb you can find with little effort. As it
blooms, its foliage imitates the germander, produces a red flower
and recalls the flavor of garlic, as well as its name. At break of day,   210

radicesque coque, atque haustu te prolue largo.
Sed neque carminibus neglecta silebere nostris,
Hesperidum decus et Medarum gloria, citre,
silvarum, si forte sacris cantata poëtis
215   parte quoque hac medicam non dedignabere Musam:
sic tibi sit semper viridis coma, semper opaca,
semper flore novo redolens, sis semper onusta
per viridem pomis silvam pendentibus aureis.
Ergo, ubi nitendum est caecis te opponere morbi
220   seminibus, vi mira arbor Cithereïa praestat.
Quippe illam Citherea, suum dum plorat Adonim,
munere donavit multo et virtutibus auxit.

    Quorundam inventum est vitrei intra concava vasis,
cui collum oblongum est, venter turgescit in orbem,
225   aut hederae folia, aut Ida mittente maniplos
dictamni, Illyricamve irim, thamnive nigrantem
radicem, aut inulas coquere: in sublime solutus
effertur vapor, et tenuis vacua omnia complet.
Ast, ubi frigenti occursavit ab aëre vitro,
230   cogitur, et rorem liquidus densatur in udum,
decurritque vagis per aperta canalia rivis.
Destillantis aquae cyathum sub lumina prima
Luciferi potare iubent, stratisque parare
sudorem; nec certe ab re: vis utilis olli est
235   relliquias morbi tenues dispergere in auras.
    Interea, si membra dolor convulsa malignus
torqueat, oesypo propera lenire dolorem,
mastichinoque oleo, lentum quibus anseris unguen,
emulsumque potes lini de semine mucum,
240   narcissumque, inulamque, liquentiaque addere mella,
coryciumque crocum, et vilem componere amurcam.
At fauces atque ora malus si eroserit herpes,

boil the roots and luxuriant foliage of this plant, and drink it
down in great gulps. But you, lemon, will not be passed over in
silence by our poem, you honor of the Hesperides and glory of the
Median woods: if you have been praised by divine poets, perhaps   215
here as well you will not disdain the medical arts. So may your
leaves remain forever green, forever dark and fragrant with new
flowers, and so may you be weighted, throughout your lush foli-
age, with golden fruit that hangs down. For when one needs to
defend against the blind seeds of sickness, the Cytherean tree will   220
prove most excellent: when Venus bewept her beloved Adonis, she
endowed this fruit with great gifts and abundant strength.

Some natural philosophers, using a hollow glass vase with elon-
gated neck and rounded belly, have discovered how to boil the   225
leaves of ivy or handfuls of dittany sent from Mount Ida, as well as
Illyrian iris, root of black briony or elecampane: converted to a fine
steam, it rises skyward and fills all the empty spaces. But as it flies
through the air and encounters the cold glass, it condenses and,   230
turning into water, forms a damp dew whose meandering streams
descend through the open channels. Then one should drink, at the
very onset of day, a pint of this distilled liquid in order, with blan-
kets, to induce sweating. And with good reason, surely: for it has
the useful power of dispersing into thin air the remains of the   235
disease.

Meanwhile if a malignant pain torments your convulsed body,
hasten to alleviate it with wool grease and oil of mastic, to which
you can add thick goose fat and greasy extract of linseed, narcissus   240
and elecampane, flowing honey and Corycian crocus. Then form a
mixture resembling the cheap lees of oil. But if an evil herpes

tange nitro, et viridi medicata aerugine lympha
semina inure mala, et serpentem interfice pestem.

245   Verum ipsos ope non alia consumere achores
urentum quam vi poteris; quibus addere debes
pingue aliquid, quod secum intus siccantia portet.
Haec eadem, et miseros artus si qua ulcera pascunt,
tollere concretosque valebunt solvere callos.

250   Si vero aut haec nequidquam tentasse videbis,
aut vires animique valent ad fortia quaeque,
nec differre cupis quin te committere acerbis
festines diramque brevi consumere pestem,
hinc alia inventa expediam, quae tristia quanto

255 sunt magis, hoc tanto citius finire labores
aerumnasque mali poterunt: quippe effera labes,
inter prima tenax et multo fomite vivax,
nedum se haud vinci placidis et mitibus, at nec
tractari sinit et mansuescere dura repugnat.

260 Sunt igitur styracem in primis qui cinnabarimque
et minium et stymmi agglomerant et tura minuta,
quorum suffitu pertingunt corpus acerbo,
absumuntque luem miseram et contagia dira.
At vero et partim durum est medicamen et acre,

265 partim etiam fallax, quo faucibus angit in ipsis
spiritus, eluctansque animam vix continet aegram.
Quocirca totum ad corpus nemo audeat uti,
iudice me: certis fortasse erit utile membris,
quae papulae informes Chironiaque ulcera pascunt.

270   Argento melius persolvunt omnia vivo
pars maior. Miranda etenim vis insita in illo est:
sive quod id natum est subito frigusque caloremque
excipere, unde in se nostrum cito contrahit ignem
quodque est condensum, humores dissolvit, agitque

275 fortius, ut candens ferrum flamma acrius urit;

46

gnaws at your mouth and throat, apply soda and, using water
tinged with verdigris, burn away the malignant seeds and slay the
insidious disease.

For truly there is no other way to remove sores than cauteriza- 245
tion, to which you must apply some fatty ointment that has within
it elements that can dry them out. The same remedy has the
power both to remove any ulcers that afflict the ailing body and to
soften hard calluses.

But if you find that you have tried these remedies in vain, and 250
if you have strength and spirit enough to attempt something
stronger, and if, in order to be more quickly rid of the dread pesti-
lence, you would not put off harsher expedients, I will now reveal
other discoveries that, in proportion as they are harsher, are also 255
able to terminate more quickly the travails and anxieties of the af-
fliction. For this raging disease is one of the most tenacious there
is: strengthened by an abundance of nourishment, it cannot be
easily and lightly vanquished or tamed and in its harshness it dis-
dains to be conquered. And so, some physicians begin by mixing 260
styrax and cinnabar, minium, antimony and small parcels of in-
cense, in whose bitter fumes they immerse the body and thus re-
move the baleful illness and dire disease. But in truth this medica-
tion is not only somewhat painful and harsh, but also somewhat 265
treacherous, for the breath is constricted in the throat itself and, as
it labors, it scarcely holds the sick spirit. For that reason I would
not advise applying it over the entire body: rather it is useful only
on certain parts that are prey to ugly pustules and Chironian
ulcers.

Most doctors would more wisely treat the entire body with 270
quicksilver, for it possesses an admirable power. In fact, by nature
it immediately attracts warmth or cold, instantly feeding upon our
bodily heat and, being very dense itself, it dissolves the humors,
having strongly stirred them up, just as glowing iron burns more 275

sive acres, unde id constat compagine mira,
particulae nexuque suo vinclisque solutae
introrsum, ut potuere seorsum in corpora ferri,
colliquant concreta et semina pestis inurunt;
280   sive aliam vim fata illi et natura dedere.
      Cuius et inventum medicamen munere divum
digressus referam: quis enim admiranda deorum
munera praetereat? Syriae nam forte sub altis
vallibus, umbrosi nemora inter glauca salicti,
285   Callirhoë qua fonte sonans decurrit amoeno,
fama est cultorem diis sacri agrestibus horti,
cultorem nemorum sectatoremque ferarum,
Ilcea labe gravem tanta, dum molle cyperum
et casiam et silvam late fragrantis amomi
290   irrigat, haec orasse deos et talia fatum:
     'Dii, quos ipse diu colui, tuque optima tristes,
Callirhoë, quae sancta soles depellere morbos,
cui nuper ramosa ferens ego cornua cervi
aëria victor fixi capita horrida quercu,
295   dii, mihi crudelem misero si tollere pestem
hanc dabitis, quae me afflictat noctesque diesque,
ipse ego purpureas, ipse albas veris et horti
primitias, vobis violas, ego lilia vobis
alba legam, primasque rosas, primosque hyacinthos,
300   vestraque odoratis onerabo altaria sertis.'
Gramen erat iuxta viridans: sic fatus, ut aestu
fessus erat, viridi desedit graminis herba.
Hic dea, vicino quae sese fonte lavabat,
Callirhoë liquido ex antro per lubrica musco
305   saxa fluens, iuveni dulci blandita susurro,
lethaeum immisit somnum sparsitque sopore
graminea in ripa et salicum nemus inter opacum,
atque illi visa est sacro se flumine tollens

fiercely than fire. Furthermore, the sharp particles that make up quicksilver's remarkable structure, having dissolved their internal bonds and connections and transferred themselves variously into the body, liquefy solid matter and burn up the seeds of the disease. Or perhaps fate and nature have bestowed upon it some other power. 280

Allow me to digress and relate how this cure was discovered through a gift of the gods. For who would pass in silence over the admirable gifts of the gods? They say that once, deep in the Syrian vales, among the pale groves of a shady willow, where babbling Callirhoe descends in a pleasant stream, it happened that Ilceus, who tended the groves and garden sacred to the rustic gods and hunted wild beasts, fell prey to this disease; and as he watered the soft galingale and cassia and the grove of cardamom that exhales its incense abroad, he prayed to the gods with these words: 290

"You gods whom I have long worshipped and you, holy Callirhoe, who, better than any other, are wont to dispel sad diseases, you to whom I lately offered the branching horns of a hart and victoriously fixed its bristling head upon the lofty oak, O gods, if 295 you will grant that I be relieved, in my misery, of this cruel pestilence, which afflicts me night and day, then I myself will pluck for you the first red and white flowers of the garden and of the spring, as well as violets and white lilies, primroses and hyacinths, and I 300 will burden you altars with fragrant chaplets."

It happened that there was a grassy field nearby. Having thus spoken, Ilceus, wearied by the heat, sat down in the green grass. The goddess Callirhoe, who was bathing in a nearby stream, flowed forth from her gleaming cave over stones slippery with 305 moss. Charming the youth with sweet words, she lulled him into Lethean sleep, scattering drowsiness across the grassy banks and the dark groves of willows. And in a dream it seemed as though she arose from the sacred river and stood before him, speaking

in somnis coram esse, pia et sic voce locuta:
310 'Ilceu, in extremo diis tandem audite labore,
cura mei, tibi nulla salus, quacumque videt Sol,
speranda est terram magnam super. Hoc tibi poenae
dat Trivia, et precibus Triviae exoratus Apollo,
ob sacrum iaculo percussum ad flumina cervum
315 et nostris affixa tibi capita horrida truncis.
Nam, postquam illa feram exanimem per gramina vidit
abscisso capite et sacro sparsa arva cruore,
omnibus ingemuit silvis, dirumque precata est
auctori. Oranti Latous tanta sorori
320 affuit et pestem misero immisere nefandam
durus uterque tibi; quin et quacumque videt Sol,
interdixit opem. Quare tellure sub ima,
si qua salus superest, caeca sub nocte petenda est.
Est specus arboribus tectum atque horrore verendum
325 vicina sub rupe, Iovis qua plurima silva
accubat et raucum reddit coma cedria murmur.
Huc, ubi se primis Aurora emittet ab undis,
ire para, et nigrantem ipsis in faucibus agnam
mactato supplex, atque, "Ops, tibi, maxima," dic, "hanc,"
330 dic, "ferio." Nigram tum Noctem, umbrasque silentes,
umbrarumque deos, ignotaque numina nymphas
et thya venerare atrae et nidore cupressi.
Hic tibi narranti causam auxiliumque vocanti
haud aberit dea, quae caecae in penetralia terrae
335 deducat te sancta et opem tibi sedula praestet.
Surge age, nec vani speciem tibi concipe somni.
Illa ego sum, quae culta vago per pinguia fonte
dilabor, dea vicinis tibi cognita ab undis.'
Sic ait, et se caeruleo cita condidit amne.
340 Ille autem, ut placidus cessit sopor, omina laetus
accipit, et nympham precibus veneratur amicam:

thus in a pious voice: "Ilceus: in your utmost labors, the gods have   310
finally heard you. Though you are a care to me, yet may you ex-
pect no cure under the sun or over the broad earth. This penalty
has been imposed upon you by Trivia, and by Apollo who has
heard her prayers, to punish you for killing a sacred stag with a
spear beside the waters and for placing its bristling head among   315
our trees. For when she saw the lifeless beast in the grass, with its
head cut off and the fields covered in sacred blood, her lamenta-
tions filled the entire forest and she dreadfully cursed the author
of the deed. Latonian Apollo seconded his sister's imprecation and   320
both of them harshly sent you, in your misery, this unspeakable
affliction. And so, wherever the sun shines, Apollo has forbidden
you to find any succor. Therefore, if any help is to be found, it
must be sought in the blind night of the underworld. Under a
neighboring cliff is a grotto covered with trees, a place of religious   325
awe, where Jove's woods grow in abundance and the leaves of ce-
dars make a raucous sound. When dawn first rises from the wa-
ters, prepare to go there, a suppliant, and slaughter a black ewe at
the very mouth of the cave, saying, 'Great Ops, I slaughter her for   330
you.' Then, with the fragrant wood of citrus and black cypress,
you are to worship dark night and the silent shades, the gods of
the dead and the Nymphs, those unknown spirits. As you plead
your cause and ask for help, hardly will the infernal goddess refuse
to lead you down into the sacred depths of the earth and offer   335
prompt aid. Arise then, and do not suppose that this is an empty
dream. For I am she who glides, a meandering stream, through
the fertile croplands, a goddess known to you from the neighbor-
ing waters." Thus she spoke, and hid herself swiftly in the blue
waters.

    As peaceful sleep receded, he gladly received these omens and   340
worshipped the kindly nymph in his prayers: "Callirhoe, loveliest

'O sequor, o quocumque vocas, pulcherrima fontis
vicini dea, Callirhoë.' Tum, postera primum
exsurgens Aurora suos ubi protulit ortus,
345 monstratum Iovis in silva sub rupibus altis
antrum ingens petit, et nigrantem tergora primo
vestibulo sistit pecudem, magnaeque trementem
mactat Opi, 'Tibique,' inquit, 'ego hanc, Ops maxima, macto.'
Tum Noctem noctisque deas, ignota precatur
350 numina. Iamque simul thyan atramque cupressum
urebat, cum vox terrae revoluta cavernis
longe audita sacras nympharum perculit aures,
nympharum, quibus aera solo sunt condita curae.
Extemplo commotae omnes ac coepta reponunt,
355 sulphureos forte ut latices et flumina vivi
argenti, mox unde nitens concresceret aurum,
tractabant, gelidoque prementes fonte coquebant.
Centum ignis spissi radios, centum aetheris usti,
bis centum concretorum terraeque marisque
360 miscuerant, nostros fugientia semina visus.
    At Lipare, Lipare, argenti cui semina et auri
cura data et sacrum flammis adolere bitumen,
continuo obscurae latebrosa per avia terrae
Ilcea adit, firmansque animum, sic incipit ipsa:
365 'Ilceu (namque tuum nec nomen, nec mihi labes
ignota est, nec quid venias) iam corde timorem
exue. Nequidquam non te huc carissima mittit
Callirhoë. Tibi parta salus tellure sub ima est.
Tolle animos, et me per opaca silentia terrae
370 insequere: ipsa adero, et praesenti numine ducam.'
    Sic ait, et se antro gradiens praemittit opaco.
Ille subit, magnos terrae miratus hiatus,
squallentesque situ aeterno et sine lumine vastas
speluncas, terramque meantia flumina subter.

goddess of the neighboring stream, I follow wherever you call me."
Then, as soon as the following Dawn arose and began ushering in
the new day, Ilceus sought the great cave, as indicated, in the forest   345
of Jove, under the lofty cliffs. He placed a sheep with swarthy
fleece at the entrance to the cave and, trembling, sacrificed it to
great Ops. "This ewe," he said, "I sacrifice to you, supreme Ops."
And then he prayed to Night and to the goddesses of night, those
unknown spirits. As he was burning the wood of the citrus and   350
black cypress trees, his voice was heard echoing far and wide in the
earth's caverns and it struck the sacred ears of the nymphs who
keep a care for metals buried in the earth. At once all bestirred
themselves, setting aside their chores. It happened that they were
treating the sulfurous streams and rivers of quicksilver, from which   355
would soon form the gleaming gold that they were tempering in
the cool waters. They mixed together one hundred rays of dense
fire, one hundred of burning air, and of earth and water twice one
hundred particles that elude our sight.   360

Then Lipare, in whose charge were placed the seeds of gold and
silver and the task of burning sacred bitumen, at once approached
Ilceus through the hidden recesses of the dark earth and, to give
him courage, began thus:

"Ilceus—for I know you name, your malady and the reason for   365
your coming—set aside your fears, for dearest Callirhoe has not
sent you here in vain. You have found your cure in the entrails of
the earth. Raise up your spirits and follow me through the dark
and silent spaces of the underworld. I will remain at your side, and   370
lead you with my divine spirit."

So she spoke, as she stepped out ahead through the dark cave.
He followed, marveling at the great gorges in the earth, the vast,
lightless caves covered in immemorial decay, and the rivers that

375 Tum Lipare: 'Hoc quodcumque patet, quam maxima terra est,
hunc totum sine luce globum, loca subdita nocti,
dii habitant: imas retinet Proserpina sedes,
flumina supremas, quae sacris concita ab antris
in mare per latas abeunt resonantia terras.
380 In medio dites nymphae, genera unde metalli,
aerisque, argentique, aurique nitentis origo:
quarum ego nunc ad te miserans ipsa una sororum
advenio, illa ego quae venas per montis hiantes,
Callirhoae haud ignota tuae, fumantia mitto
385 sulphura.' Sic ibant terra et caligine tecti.
Iamque exaudiri crepitantes sulphure flammae,
conclusique ignes, stridentiaque aera caminis.
'Haec regio est late, variis ubi foeta metallis,'
virgo ait, 'est tellus, quorum vos tanta cupido
390 exercet, superas caeli qui cernitis auras.
Haec loca mille deae caecis habitamus in antris,
Nocte deae et Tellure satae, queis munera mille,
mille artes: studium est aliis deducere rivos,
scintillas aliis rimari et sparsa per omnem
395 semina tellurem flammarum ignisque corusci,
materiam miscent aliae, massamque coërcent
obicibus multa et gelidarum inspergine aquarum.
Non procul eruptis fumantia tecta caminis
Aetnaei Cyclopes habent, versantque, coquuntque
400 Vulcano stridente, atque aera sonantia cudunt.
Laeva haec abstrusum per iter via ducit ad illos.
Dextera sed sacri fluvii te sistet ad undam,
argento fluitantem undam vivoque metallo,
unde salus speranda.' Et iam aurea tecta subibant,
405 rorantesque domos spodiis, fuligineque atra
speluncas varie obductas et sulphure glauco.

passed under the earth. Then Lipare spoke: "This vast expanse   375
that you see, extending as wide as Earth itself, this great lightless
sphere and these regions subservient to night, all of it is the abode
of the gods. Proserpina occupies the lowest dwellings, while the
highest belong to the rivers that, issuing from the sacred caves,
pass noisily through broad lands into the sea. The middle realm   380
belongs to the wealthy nymphs, the source of such metals as
bronze and silver and gleaming gold. I am myself one of these
sisters: now taking pity on you, I, a friend of your dear Callirhoe,
send forth smoking sulfur through the gaping veins of the moun-   385
tain." So they passed under cover of darkness and earth. Already
they could hear the roaring sulfurous flames, the enclosed fires and
bronze hissing in the furnaces. "This is the broad region," the
nymph explained, "where the earth is rich in those many metals
that arouse such desire in you men who behold the air of heaven   390
above. A thousand goddesses inhabit the dark caves of this land,
goddesses born of Night and Earth, who have a thousand tasks
and arts. Some strive to draw down the streams, others to examine
the sparks and seeds of flame and of gleaming fire that are strewn   395
across the earth. Others stir up the matter and then force the mass
into bars, dousing them with an abundance of water. Not far off
the Cyclopses of Aetna have their huts, made smoky by belch-
ing furnaces: there, amid the hiss of Vulcan, they turn and smell   400
and strike the sounding brass. This road on the left leads, by a
secret path, unto them. But the path on the right will bring you to
the waters of the sacred stream flowing with quicksilver, wherein
consists your hoped-for health." And now they approached a
golden palace, houses bedewed with ash, and caves variously cov-   405
ered in black soot and grayish sulfur. Presently they reached

Iamque lacus late undantes liquidoque fluentes
argento iuxta astabant, ripasque tenebant.
'Hic tibi tantorum requies inventa laborum,'
410   subsequitur Lipare, 'postquam, ter flumine vivo
perfusus, sacra vitium omne reliqueris unda.'
Sic fatur, simul argenti ter fonte salubri
perfundit, ter virgineis dat flumina palmis
membra super, iuvenem toto ter corpore lustrat,
415   mirantem exuvias turpes et labe maligna
exutos artus pestemque sub amne relictam.

    'Ergo age, cum primum caeli te purior aër
accipiet, nitidamque diem Solemque videbis,
sacra para, et castam supplex venerare Dianam
420   indigenasque deos et numina fontis amici.'

    Sic virgo, et iuvenem tanto pro munere grates
solventem e nocte aetherias educit in oras,
dimittitque alacrem, atque optata in lumina reddit.

    Accepit nova fama fidem, populosque per omnes
425   prodiit haud fallax medicamen: coeptaque primum
misceri argento fluitanti axungia porcae,
mox etiam Oriciae simul adiuncta est terebinthi
et laricis resina aëriae. Sunt qui unguen equinum
ursinumve adhibent, bdelae, cedrique liquorem.
430   Nonnulli et myrrhae guttas et mascula tura
adiiciunt, miniumque rubens, et sulphura viva.
Haud vero mihi displiceat, componere si quem
trita melampodia atque arentem iuverit irim,
galbanaque, et lasser grave olens, oleumque salubre
435   lentisci, atque oleum haud experti sulphuris ignem.

    His igitur totum oblinere atque obducere corpus
ne obscenum, ne turpe puta: per talia morbus
tollitur, et nihil esse potest obscenius ipso.
Parce tamen capiti, et praecordia mollia vita.

the lakes that flow abroad with liquid silver, and they stood upon
the shore. "Here you will find rest from such great labors," Lipare   410
continued, "after you have thrice bathed in the vital stream and left
all illness behind in the sacred waters." Thus she spoke, and at
once she steeped him three times in the salubrious stream of sil-
ver; three times her virginal hands covered his body with water
and three times she doused the body of the young man, who mar-   415
veled at his ugly sores, at his body now free of the malign disease
and at the affliction abandoned beneath the stream.

"And so, when once again you taste the purer air of heaven and
see the sun and shining day, perform a suppliant's rites and wor-
ship chaste Diana, the local gods and the spirits of the friendly   420
fountain."

So the maiden spoke, and then she led the youth, grateful for
such favors, out of darkness into the upper earth, where she sent
him speeding forth, as she returned him to the longed-for light.

Word of his experiences won credit and brought to all people   425
news of this trustworthy remedy: first they began mixing the
grease from a sow with quicksilver; then they added the resins of
the Orician terebinth and lofty larch. Some doctors would include
the grease of horses or bears, as well as the oil of bdellium and
cedar. Others include drops of myrrh and strong incense, reddish   430
minium and live sulfur. Nor would I quarrel with those who in-
clude ground hellebore, dried iris, galbanum, harshly scented sil-
phium, the mastic's salubrious oil and sulphuric oil untouched by   435
fire.

Do not consider it filthy or base to smear or cover the entire
body with them: for through such remedies the body is cured, and
nothing could be filthier than the disease itself. Spare only the

440 Tum super et vittas astringe, et stuppea necte
vellera: dein stratis tegmento imponere multo,
dum sudes foedaeque fluant per corpora guttae.
Haec tibi bis quinis satis est iterasse diebus.
Durum erit, at, quidquid tulerit res ipsa, ferendum est.
445 Aude animis. Tibi certa salus stans limine in ipso
signa dabit: liquefacta mali excrementa videbis
assidue sputo immundo fluitare per ora,
et largum ante pedes tabi mirabere flumen.
Ora tamen foeda erodent ulcuscula; sed tu
450 lacte fove, et cocto cytini viridisque ligustri.
Tempore non alio generosi pocula Bacchi
annuerim sumenda tibi, purumque Falernum,
et Chia, et pateris spumantia Rhetica largis.
  Sed iam age vicinae victor gratare saluti:
455 ultima adest tibi cura, eadem et placidissima, corpus
abluere, et lustrare artus, ac membra piare
stoechade, amaracinisque comis, et rore marino,
verbenaque sacra, et bene olentibus heracleis.

⁝ LIBER III ⁝

Sed iam me nemora alterius felicia mundi
externique vocant saltus: longe assonat aequor
Herculeas ultra metas, et litora longe
applaudunt semota. Mihi nunc magna deorum
5 munera et ignoto devecta ex orbe canenda
sancta arbos, quae sola modum requiemque dolori,
et finem dedit aerumnis. Age, diva, beatum,
Uranie, venerare nemus, crinesque revinctam
fronde nova, iuvet in medica procedere palla

head and avoid the soft organs near the heart. Then wrap the   440
anointed parts with bandages and dressings made out of tow;
next, cover yourself with an abundance of blankets until you begin
to sweat and sordid drops flow down your body. You should repeat
this for ten days. It will be difficult, but you must bear whatever
the treatment requires. Take heart, for salvation, standing before   445
you, will reveal itself through these unmistakable signs: you will
see the liquefied refuse of the disease flow abundantly from your
mouth in the form of ugly spit, as you marvel at the abundant flow
of pestilence at your feet. Ugly sores will grow at your mouth,
which you should treat with milk and the boiled juice of the   450
pomegranate's flower and green privet. At no other time would I
advise you to drink cups of noble wine, pure Falernian and Chian,
and Rhetic wine frothing up in broad beakers.

    But rejoice now, victorious in your approaching health: your last   455
task, and also the most pleasant, is to bathe your body and wash
your limbs, purifying them with lavender, leaves of marjoram and
rosemary, sacred vervain and sweet-smelling lilies.

: BOOK III :

But now the happy groves and distant thickets of another world
call to me; far off the sea resounds beyond the Pillars of Hercules
and the distant shores echo in response. Now must I sing of that
great gift of the gods, brought hither from an unknown land, the   5
sacred tree that alone grants solace and relief from pain and an end
to anguish. Divine Urania, honor this blessed tree. And may it
please you, your head crowned with a new chaplet, to go forth

10 per Latium et sanctos populis ostendere ramos,
et iuvet haud umquam nostrorum aetate parentum
visa prius, nullive umquam memorata referre.
   Unde aliquis forsan, novitatis imagine mira
captus et heroas et grandia dicere facta
15 assuetus, canat auspiciis maioribus ausas
Oceani intacti tentare pericula puppes,
nec non et terras varias et flumina et urbes
et varias memoret gentes, et monstra reperta
dimensasque plagas, alioque orientia caelo
20 sidera, et insignem stellis maioribus Arcton,
nec taceat nova bella, omnemque illata per orbem
signa novum, et positas leges, et nomina nostra;
et canat (auditum quod vix venientia credant
saecula) quodcumque Oceani complectitur aequor
25 ingens omne una obitum mensumque carina.
Felix, cui tantum dederit Deus. At mihi vires
arboris unius satis est usumque referre,
et quo inventa modo fuerit nostrasque sub auras
advena per tantum pelagi pervenerit aequor.
30   Oceano in magno, ardenti sub sidere Cancri,
Sol ubi se nobis media iam nocte recondit,
hac ignota tenus, tractu iacet insula longo
(Hispanam gens inventrix cognomine dixit),
auri terra ferax, sed longe ditior una
35 arbore: voce vocant patrii sermonis Hyacum.
Ipsa, teres ingensque, ingentem vertice ab alto
diffundit semper viridem semperque comantem
arbuteis silvam foliis; nux parva, sed acris,
dependet ramis, et plurima frondibus haeret.
40 Materia indomita est, duro et paene aemula ferro
robora, quae resinam sudant incensa tenacem.
Dissectae color haud simplex: in cortice lauri

through Latium in the robes of a healer, and reveal the sacred 10
branches to the people. May it please you as well to sing of things
never before seen by earlier generations, and never before related
by anyone else.

Some other poet, therefore, dazzled perhaps by marvels and
accustomed to tell of heroes and great deeds, should sing of those 15
ships that, under auspicious omens, dared to brave the perils of
the uncharted ocean. Let him also tell of varied regions, rivers and
cities, of varied peoples and wonders discovered, of strands tra-
versed and constellations rising in a different sky and Arctos re- 20
splendent with its greater stars. Nor let him pass in silence over
the new wars, and our standards, our laws and our names that
have been sent forth throughout the new world. And even though
future generations will scarcely credit the report, let him tell of
how the great expanse of Ocean was entered and traversed in a 25
single ship. Blessed is the man on whom God has bestowed such
powers. But for me it will suffice to tell of a single tree, of its uses,
and of how it was first discovered and brought, a newcomer, to
our shores over such a great expanse of the sea.

In the middle of the vast ocean and under the burning star of 30
Cancer, where the sun hides when midnight is upon us, there lies
an island of vast extent, hitherto unknown. It is named Hispaniola
after the race that discovered it. Though rich in gold, it is far
richer in a single tree, called Guaiacum in the native tongue. This 35
is a smooth tree of huge dimension, which, from its lofty summit,
spreads out large branches whose ever-green leaves resemble those
of the strawberry tree. The nut, small but bitter, hangs abundantly
amid the leaves of its branches. Its wood is almost unworkable 40
and, when burned, its trunk, which rivals hard iron, exudes a vis-
cous resin. Split open, it reveals many colors: its outer bark shines

exteriore viret levor, pars altera pallet
buxea, at interior nigro suffusca colore est,
45   iuglandemque ebenumque inter: quod si inde ruberet,
iam poterat variis aequare coloribus Irim.
    Hanc gens illa colit, studioque educere multo
nititur: hac late colles, campique patentes,
hac omnis vestitur ager, nec sanctius illis
50   est quidquam aut potiore usu, quippe omnis in illa
spes iacet hanc contra pestem, quae caelitus illic
perpetua est. Validos abiecto cortice ramos
multa vi tundunt aut in segmenta minuta
elimant, puroque scobes in fonte reponunt,
55   dum bibulas noctemque diemque emaceret humor.
Inde coquunt, nec non illos ea cura fatigat,
Vulcano ne forte furens erumpat aquae vis,
et superundantem spumam proiectet in ignes.
Spuma quippe linunt, si quidquam e corpore toto
60   abscedit, si quidquam aegros depascitur artus.
Dimidia absumpta, superest quodcumque reponunt
divini laticis. Quin et segmenta relicta
rursus, ut ante, coquunt, addentes suaveliquens mel.
Scilicet hunc unum mensis accedere potum
65   et lex ipsa iubet gentis mandatque sacerdos.
Servatum at laticem et decocti pocula primi
bina die quaque assumunt, cum surgit ab ortu
Lucifer, et sero egreditur cum Vesper Olympo.
Nec prius absistunt potu, quam menstrua cursum
70   Luna suum, et totum peragrans perfecerit orbem,
fraternasque iterum convenerit aemula bigas.
    Interea caecis sese penetralibus abdunt,
quo neque vis venti, non halitus aëris ullus
insinuet sese, et gelidis afflatibus obsit.

with the smoothness of the laurel, while its inner bark recalls the
pallor of the box tree; but within it is suffused with a blackish
color, somewhere between walnut and ebony. If red were added, it   45
would rival the rainbow in its varied hues.

   The local people cultivate this tree, striving mightily to grow it.
Far and wide, every hill, every field and open plain is covered with
it. Nothing is held in higher regard or is of greater use. For in it-   50
self it holds all hope against the affliction that, heaven-sent, rages
perpetually in these lands. With much effort the people, removing
the bark, beat the sturdy branches and file the wood into small
pieces, placing the thirsty shavings in pure water until it saturates   55
them for a night and a day. Then they boil the wood, working tire-
lessly so that the force of the water, as it rages over the fire, does
not spill over and toss the billowing froth into the flames. For with
this froth they anoint the body, if perchance it has anywhere an
abscess or if some growth feeds upon its weary limbs. When half   60
has been consumed in this way, they store what remains of the
divine liquid. Then once again they cook the shavings that remain
as before, adding honey's sweet liquid. For the very law of the   65
people enjoins, and the priest commands, that this potion alone
accompany their meals. Then every day they drink two cups of the
first potion, which had been stored: one when Lucifer arises in the
morning and one when Vesper goes forth at night from Olympus.
And they do not leave off drinking until the moon has run her   70
monthly course and moved through all her phases, once again
meeting her brother's steeds in rivalry.

   In the meantime, the patients hide themselves in the dark-
est corners of their homes, where no force of wind or current of
air can insinuate itself, and where one needn't fear cold blasts.

75 Quid mirandum aeque memorem super omnia victum
quam tenuem, quam magna sibi ieiunia poscant?
Quippe solet satis esse, ipsum dum corpus alatur,
dum superet vita, et tantum ne membra fatiscant.
Ne tamen, ah ne tanta time: sacer ilicet haustus
80 ille, modo ambrosiae, vires reficitque fovetque,
inque occulta gerit ieiunis pabula membris.
Nectare ab epoto binas, non amplius, horas
imponunt sese stratis, medicamen ut intro
large eat et calido sudorem e corpore ducat.
85 Interea vacuas pestis vanescit in auras
et (dictu mirum!) apparet iam pustula nulla:
iamque nomae cessere omnes, iam fortia liquit
membra dolor, primoque redit cum flore iuventa;
et iam Luna suum remeans nova circuit orbem.
90   Quis deus hos illis populis monstraverit usus,
qui demum et nobis casus aut fata tulere
hos ipsos, unde et sacrae data copia silvae,
nunc referam. Missae quaesitum abscondita Nerei
aequora in occasum Solisque cubilia, pinus,
95 litoribus longe patriis Calpeque relictis,
ibant Oceano in magno pontumque secabant,
ignaraeque viae et longis erroribus actae.
Quas circum innumerae properantes gurgite ab omni,
ignoti nova monstra maris, Nereïdes udae
100 adnabant, celsas miratae currere puppes,
salsa super pictis volitantes aequora velis.
      Nox erat et puro fulgebat ab aethere Luna,
lumina diffundens tremuli per marmora ponti,
magnanimus cum tanta heros ad munera fatis
105 delectus, dux errantis per caerula classis,
'Luna,' ait, 'o, pelagi cui regna haec humida parent,

Above all else, what can I mention more admirable than how little   75
food is needed to sustain them, and what great fasts they take
upon themselves? Indeed, it is enough simply to keep the body
going, as long as life remains in it and the limbs do not grow wea-
ried. But do not let this thought frighten you; for the sacred draft,   80
like ambrosia, immediately fosters and restores one's strength and
brings hidden sustenance to fasting limbs. After the patients have
drunk it, they lie down in bed not longer than two hours, so that
the medicine can spread, drawing a sweat from their feverish bod-
ies. Meanwhile, the disease vanishes into thin air and, astonish-   85
ingly, no more pustules can be seen. All sores have disappeared, all
pain has left the reinvigorated body, and youth returns in its first
blush. And already the new moon has passed through the circuit
of its phases.

   I shall now reveal which god first taught the people about this   90
cure, what chance or destiny at last brought it to us, and whence
an abundance of such wood is to be found. Once some ships of
pine were sent forth into the west, into the resting place of the set-
ting sun, to seek the hidden waters of Nereus. Having left far be-   95
hind them Calpe and their paternal shores, they entered upon
great Ocean and cut through the waves. They did not know their
way and were often pushed off course. From every direction wet
Nereids beyond number, the newfound marvels of this unknown   100
sea, hastened around them, swimming up to them and admiring
their tall ships, which floated over the salt sea, their painted sails
aflutter.

   It was night and the moon was shining in the cloudless sky,
pouring its light over the marbled surface of the tremulous sea.
Then it was that a noble hero, chosen by fate to take up such great
tasks, the captain of the fleet that wandered through the waters,   105
spoke thus: "O Moon, whom these wet realms of the sea obey, you

quae bis ab aurata curvasti cornua fronte,
curva bis explesti, nobis errantibus ex quo
non ulla apparet tellus, da litora tandem
110   aspicere, et dudum speratos tangere portus,
noctis honos, caelique decus, Latonia Virgo.'
    Audiit orantem Phoebe, delapsaque ab alto
aethere, se in faciem mutat, Nereïa quali
Cymothoë Clothoque natant, iuxtaque carinam
115   astitit, et summo pariter nans aequore fatur:
'Ne nostrae dubitate rates: lux crastina terras
ostendet, fidoque dabit succedere portu.
Sed vos litoribus primis ne insistite: dudum
ultra fata vocant. Medio magna insula ponto
120   est Ophyre: huc iter est vobis, hic debita sedes
imperiique caput.' Simul haec effata, carinam
impulit: illa levi cita dissecat aequora cursu.
    Aspirant faciles aurae et iam clarus ab undis
surgebat Titan, humiles cum surgere colles
125   umbrosi procul et propior iam terra videri
incipit. Acclamant nautae terramque salutant,
terram exoptatam, tum portu et litore amico
excepti, diis vota piis in litore solvunt,
quassatasque rates defessaque corpora curant.
130   Inde, ubi quarta dies pelago crepitansque vocavit
vela Notus, remis insurgitur, altaque rursum
corripiunt maria, et laeti freta caerula sulcant.
Linquitur incerto fluitans Anthylia ponto,
atque Hagia, atque alta Ammerie, exsecrataque tellus
135   cannibalum, et ripa Gyane nemorosa virenti.
Protinus innumerae panduntur turribus altis
insulae Oceano in vasto; quas inter opacis
undantem silvis unam cursuque sonantem

who twice have curved the horns of your gleaming face, and twice
have filled them up again, without any land appearing to our wan-
dering ships, grant that we may finally behold the shore and reach   110
the port we have so long hoped to see, O beauty of night, orna-
ment of heaven, chaste daughter of Leto!"

Phoebe heard his prayer and, gliding down from high heaven,
she assumed a form like that of the Nereids Cymothoe and Clotho.
Remaining beside the ship as she swam along the surface of the   115
water, she spoke thus: "Doubt not, my ships. Tomorrow's light will
reveal land and allow you to reach a safe port. But do not settle
upon the first shores you see. For destiny has long summoned you
further. In the middle of the sea is a great island, Ophir, the goal   120
of your voyage and the due seat and capital of your empire." Hav-
ing thus spoken, she drove the ship, which swiftly parted the wa-
ters at a light clip.

The winds blew favorably, and already the radiant Titan was
rising from the waves when, far off, low hills began to appear,   125
shaded with trees, and already land was spotted nearby. The sail-
ors cried out and greeted the land, the land they had hoped to see.
Once arrived at this port and friendly shore, they offered up
prayers to the pious gods on the beach, then repaired their dam-
aged ships and their wearied bodies.

From there, on the fourth day a strong south wind called them   130
back to the sea. They took to their oars and once again raced
across the deep waters, joyously parting the blue waves. In time
they sailed past Anthylia, which floated in the uncertain sea, past
Hagia, lofty Ammeria, and the loathsome land of cannibals, as   135
well as Gyana, rich in thickets, with its virid coast. Soon islands
numberless, with lofty peaks, dotted the vast ocean. They found
one of these, abounding in shady forests and echoing with a rush-

fluminis aspiciunt, magno qui spumeus alveo
140 in mare fulgentes auro subvectat arenas.
Huius in ora placet pronas appellere puppes.
Invitant nemora, et dulces e flumine lymphae.
Iamque solo viridante alacres ripaque potiti,
in primis terram ignotam nymphasque salutant
145 indigenas, geniumque loci, teque, aurifer amnis,
quisquis in ora maris nitida perlaberis unda.
Tum duram Cererem et patrii carchesia Bacchi
aggere in herboso expediunt; dein quaerere, si qui
mortales habitent; pars fulvam fluminis undam
150 mirari, mixtamque auro disquirere arenam.
      Forte per umbrosos silvarum plurima ramos
assidue volitabat avis, quae, picta nitentes
caeruleo pennas, rostro variata rubenti,
ibat nativo secura per avia luco.
155 Has iuvenum manus ut silvas videre per altas,
continuo cava terrificis horrentia bombis
aera et flammiferum tormenta imitantia fulmen
corripiunt, Vulcane, tuum, dum Theutonas armas,
inventum, dum tela Iovis mortalibus affers.
160 Nec mora, signantes certam sibi quisque volucrem,
inclusam, salicum cineres sulphurque nitrumque,
materiam accendunt, servata in reste favilla.
Fomite correpto, diffusa repente furit vis
ignea circumsepta simulque cita, obice rupto,
165 intrusam impellit glandem: volat illa per auras
stridula, et exanimes passim per prata iacebant
deiectae volucres; magno micat ignibus aër
cum tonitru, quo silva omnis ripaeque recurvae
et percussa imo sonuerunt aequora fundo.
170 Pars avium nemus in densum conterrita et altos
se recipit scopulos: quorum de vertice summo

ing stream. It bubbled up in a large channel and carried to the sea   140
its sands that gleamed with gold. Happily they drew their ships
into the river's mouth, enticed by the forests and the river's sweet
water. As soon as the eager mariners reached the shore and the
green earth, they hailed this unknown land and the local nymphs,   145
the genius of the place and you, gold-bearing river, who glide into
the sea on a clear stream. Then upon a leafy sward they spread sea
biscuits and jars of their native wine, before inquiring whether
any human beings inhabited the place. Some admired the river's
gleaming waters, while others examined the sands mixed with   150
gold.

   It happened that an abundance of birds flew repeatedly about
the leafy branches of the trees. Their wings were a shimmering
blue while their necks were bright red. They flew, free of fear,
through the recesses of their native woods. A group of young men,   155
having spied them through the deep vegetation, at once took up
their firearms of hollow brass that bristle with a hideous noise,
and bullets that imitate the flamed lightning that you invented,
Vulcan, to arm the Teutons and bring Jove's bolts to mortal men.
Without delay each man chose a bird and then they ignited the   160
enclosed matter — the charcoal of willows, sulfur and saltpeter —
with a spark kept in tow. Once the tinder caught, suddenly the
enclosed force of the fire raged abroad. Immediately the bar was
removed and the bullet within was discharged. This volleyed   165
screeching through the air and suddenly everywhere dead birds lay
scattered on the ground. The air was singed with fire and a terrible
thunder resounded through every grove and curving riverbank, as
the very waters shook to their furthest depths. Some of the birds   170
fled, terrified, into the deep woods, while others flew up to the

horrendum una canit (dictu mirabile!), et aures
terrificis implet dictis, ac talibus infit:
    'Qui Solis violatis aves sacrasque volantes,
175   Hesperii, nunc vos, quae magnus cantat Apollo,
accipite, et nostro vobis quae nuntiat ore.
Vos, quamquam ignari, longum quaesita secundis
tandem parta Ophyrae tetigistis litora ventis.
Sed non ante novas dabitur summittere terras
180   et longa populos in libertate quietos,
molirique urbes, ritusque ac sacra novare,
quam vos, infandos pelagi terraeque labores
perpessi, diversa hominum post proelia, multi
mortua in externa tumuletis corpora terra.
185   Navibus amissis pauci patria arva petetis,
frustra alii socios quaeretis magna remensi
aequora; nec nostro deerunt Cyclopes in orbe.
Ipsa inter sese vestras Discordia puppes
in rabiem ferrumque trahet; nec sera manet vos
190   illa dies, foedi ignoto cum corpora morbo
auxilium silva miseri poscetis ab ista,
donec paeniteat scelerum.' Nec plura locuta,
horrendum stridens, densis sese abdidit umbris.
    Ollis ossa rigor subitus percurrit, et omnis
195   palluit ac gelida fugit formidine sanguis.
Tum vero sacras volucres divosque precati,
in primis Solem et sanctum servantia lucum
numina supplicibus venerantur agrestia votis:
pacem orant, rursumque Ophyren fluviumque salutant.
200   Interea e silvis nigrum genus ora comasque
ad naves, nova turba virum, concurrit inermis,
pectora nudi omnes, evincti frondibus omnes
paciferis. Tanta qui celsas mole carinas
mirati vestesque virum fulgentiaque arma

lofty cliffs. Astonishingly, one of them, from the summit of a cliff, uttered a terrible prophecy. Filling their ears with terrifying words, it thus began:

"You men of the West, who have done violence to the sacred birds of the Sun, hear now the oracle that great Apollo addresses to you through my mouth. Thanks to favorable winds, you have finally arrived, though unawares, at the long sought shores of Ophir. But you will not be permitted to subdue these new regions and a peaceful people long accustomed to freedom, nor to found cities and establish rites and religion, before you have suffered unspeakable calamities on sea and land, before you have battled many nations and laid high your dead bodies in a strange land. You will lose ships and few of you will return to your native fields. In vain will others scour great Ocean seeking your companions. Cyclopses will not be absent from these lands, and Discord will cause your crews to rage and draw swords against one another. And that day is nigh when an unknown affliction will defile your bodies and, in your misery, you will seek remedy in these woods, until you come to repent of your crimes." The bird said nothing more and, with a shrill sound, hid itself in the thick shade.

A sudden shiver ran through their bones and all of them went pale as sheer terror drained the blood from their faces. They prayed to the gods and the sacred birds and then raised suppliant vows to the Sun and to the rustic spirits who guarded the sacred grove. They prayed for peace and once more hailed Ophir and the river.

Meanwhile a strange group of men, their hair and bodies black, emerged unarmed from the forest and approached the ships. They were barechested and covered in peaceable fronds. They marveled at the enormous size of the tall ships, as well as the clothes and

205 vix satis expleri possunt et, ab aethere missi
sive homines sive heroes sint sive deorum
numina, adorantum ritu precibusque salutant,
ante alios ipsum regem: cui munera laeta,
e ripis collectum aurum et Cerealia dona
210 et patrios fructus et mella liquentia, portant.
Vestibus ipsi etiam nostris et munere multo
donati exceptique mero nova gaudia miscent:
non aliter quam si, mensis dapibusque deorum
mortalis quisquam adscitus felixque futurus,
215 hauriat aeternum, caelestia pocula, nectar.
    Ergo, ubi amicitiae securos foedere utrimque
firmavere animos, habita et commercia gentis,
ipsi inter sese reges in litore laeti
complexu iungunt dextras et foedera firmant.
220 Alter gossipio tenui pectusque femurque
praecinctus, viridi limbum pingente smaragdo,
ora niger, iaculo armatur cui dextera acuto,
squamosi spolium sustentat laeva draconis.
Alter at intexto laenam circumdatus auro,
225 quam subter rutila arma micant, capiti aerea cassis
insidet, et pictae volitant in vertice cristae,
fulgenti ex auro torques cui candida colla
cingunt, atque ensis lateri dependet Hiberus.
Et iam commixti populi hospitioque recepti,
230 hi tectis domibusque, altis in navibus illi,
laetitia ludisque dies per pocula ducunt.
    Forte loco lux festa aderat, Solique parabant
Ultori facere umbroso sacra annua luco.
Hesperiaeque Ophyraeque manus convenerat omnis.
235 Hic convalle cava, ripae viridantis in herba,
selectorum ingens numerus, matresque virique
confusi, plebs atque patres, puerique senesque,

dazzling weapons of our men. They could scarcely get their fill of   205
looking, and they greeted the newcomers with prayers and rites of
adoration, uncertain whether these newcomers were heaven-sent
men or a race of heroes or gods. Most of all they hailed the cap-
tain himself, bringing him delightful gifts of gold collected from
the riverbank, of grain, local fruits and gleaming honey. In turn   210
they received our apparel and many gifts and, welcomed among us
with wine, they experienced new joys. They were like some mortal
who, destined for happiness and chosen to share in the feasts and
banquets of the gods, quaffs eternal nectar from celestial cups.   215

And so, with each side confident of the others good intentions,
now that relations had been established between them, the two
leaders gladly joined hands upon the shore and secured their
friendship. The legs and chest of the native chieftain were clad in   220
a light cotton garment, bordered with a bright emerald hem, and
his face was black. In his right hand he held a sharp spear and in
his left the skin of a scaly dragon. Our leader wore a cloak inter-
woven with gold, beneath which his shining armor gleamed. His   225
head was covered in a brass helmet with a crest of many colors.
Around his pale throat he wore a collar of bright gold and at his
side was a Spanish sword. And so the two peoples mingled and
received one another in friendship, one in their covered huts, the   230
other in tall ships, and they passed the days in drinking, amid
much sport and good cheer.

As it happened, there was just then a holiday in those parts, as
the natives prepared to perform their annual rites in honor of the
Avenging Sun, within the shady forest. All the Hesperian people
and all the people of Ophir gathered together. In a hollow cave,   235
upon a green riverbank, a large crowd of select people, all mingled
together, men and women, nobles and commoners, young and old,

adstabant, animis tristes, et corpora foedi,
squallentes crustis omnes, taboque fluentes.
240 Quos circumfusos albenti in veste sacerdos
pura lustrat aqua et ramo frondentis hyaci.
Tum niveum ante aras caedit de more iuvencum,
et iuxta positum pastorem sanguine caesi
respergit, pateraque rigat, Solique potenti
245 ad numeros paeana canit, nec cetera turba
non sequitur. Mactantque sues, mactantque bidentes,
visceribusque veru tostis epulantur in herba.

Obstupuit gens Europae ritusque sacrorum
contagemque alio non usquam tempore visam.
250 At dux, multa animo tacitus secum ipse volutans,
'Hic erat ille,' inquit, 'morbus (dii avertite casum)
ignotum, interpres Phoebi quem dira canebat.'
Tum regem indigenam (ut sermo fandique facultas
iam communis erat) cui sint sollemnia divum
255 scitatur, quid tanta adstet convalle sub alta
languentum miseranda manus, quid pastor ad aras
sacra inter caesi respersus sanguine tauri.

Quem contra, 'Hesperiae o heros fortissime pubis,'
rex ait, 'hi gentis ritus, haec sacra quotannis
260 Ultori de more deo celebramus: origo
antiqua est, veteresque patrum fecere parentes.
Quod si externorum mores hominumque labores
audivisse iuvat, primaeva ab origine causam
sacrorum et pestis miserae primordia pandam.
265 Forsitan Atlantis vestras pervenit ad aures
nomen, et ex illo generis longo ordine ducti.
Hac et nos, longa serie, de stirpe profecti
dicimur, heu quondam felix et cara deum gens,
dum caelum colere et superis accepta referre
270 maiores suevere boni; sed, numina postquam

74

stood in sadness, their wretched bodies covered in scabs and
oozing pus. As they lay about, a priest, clad in white vestments,   240
touched them with pure water and the wood of the leafy guaiacum
tree. Then, according to prescribed ritual, he slaughtered a pure
white bullock before the altar. From a bowl he next spilled its
blood over a shepherd who lay nearby and he sang a paean in me-   245
ter to the potent Sun. The others in attendance followed suit, as
they slaughtered pigs and lambs. Sitting on the grass, they feasted
on meat that they cooked upon a spit.

The Europeans were astonished at these rites and at a disease
they had never seen before. But for a long time the captain medi-   250
tated in silence and then he said: "This is the strange affliction
(may the God avert such a calamity) that the dire augur of Phoe-
bus foretold." Then he asked the tribal king—for already they
were able to communicate with one another—to which god these
honors were paid, why a great multitude of diseased souls was   255
standing in the hollow cave, and why that shepherd lay before the
altars, amid the sacred rites, covered in the blood of a slaughtered
bull.

To whom the king replied, "O bravest leader of the Hesperian
people, these are the native rites and rituals that each year we
make, according to custom, to the Avenging God. It is an ancient   260
ritual practiced by our forefathers. And if it behooves you to learn
the customs and travails of another race, I shall relate to you the
ancient causes of these rites, as well as the origins of this terrible
pestilence.

Perhaps the name of Atlas has reached your ears, and the race   265
that, through many generations, is descended from him. We as
well are said to be his progeny. Alas, how happy a race we once
were, how dear to the gods, in the days when our noble ances-
tors worshiped heaven and acknowledged its gifts. But then, their   270

contemni coeptum est luxu fastuque nepotum,
ex illo quae sint miseros quantaeque secutae
aerumnae, vix fando umquam comprendere possem.
Insula tum prisci regis de nomine dicta
275 ingenti terrae concussa Atlantia motu
corruit, absorpta Oceano, quem mille carinis
sulcavit toties, terrae regina marisque.
Ex illo et pecudes et grandia quadrupedantum
corpora, non ullis umquam reparata diebus,
280 aeternum periere, externaque victima sacris
caeditur, externus nostras cruor imbuit aras.
Tum quoque et haec infanda lues, quam nostra videtis
corpora depasci, quam nulli aut denique pauci
vitamus, divum offensis et Apollinis ira
285 de caelo demissa, omnes grassatur in urbes.
Unde haec sacra novo primum sollemnia ritu
instituere patres, quorum haec perhibetur origo.
    Syphilus, ut fama est, ipsa haec ad flumina pastor
mille boves, niveas mille haec per pabula regi
290 Alcithoo pascebat oves. Et forte sub ipsum
solstitium urebat sitientes Sirius agros,
urebat nemora, et nullas pastoribus umbras
praebebant silvae, nullum dabat aura levamen.
Ille, gregem miseratus et acri concitus aestu,
295 sublimem in Solem vultus et lumina tollens,
"Nam quid, Sol, te," inquit, "rerum patremque deumque
dicimus, et sacras vulgus rude ponimus aras,
mactatoque bove et pingui veneramur acerra,
si nostri nec cura tibi est, nec regia tangunt
300 armenta? An potius superos vos arbitrer uri
invidia? Mihi mille nivis candore iuvencae,
mille mihi pascuntur oves: vix est tibi Taurus
unus, vix Aries caelo (si vera feruntur)

offspring, through their wanton profligacy, ceased to honor the
gods. I can scarce find words to express the great and manifold
sufferings that have afflicted our miserable race since that time.
The island of Atlantis, whose name derives from its first king, was   275
struck by a massive earthquake and swallowed up by the ocean,
which she, as queen of sea and land, had so often furrowed with a
thousand keels. From that day, cattle and other large beasts were
lost forever, never to be restored. And so a foreign victim is slaugh-   280
tered in our rituals and foreign blood stains out altars. From that
time as well, our cities have been overrun by the unspeakable af-
fliction that you see devouring our bodies, an affliction that few or
none of us escape, sent down from heaven through the vengeance   285
of the gods and the anger of Apollo. Therefore our ancestors first
instituted this strange annual rite, whose origin is told thus:

"It is said that the shepherd Syphilus used to bring the thou-
sand oxen and snow-white sheep of King Alcithoos to feed beside   290
these very streams. It happened that, at the height of summer,
Sirius was parching the thirsting fields and groves. The woods of-
fered no shade to shepherds, nor did any breeze afford relief.
Syphilus took pity on his flocks and, maddened by the scorching
heat, raised his glance to the lofty Sun and spoke thus: 'Why, O   295
Sun, do we call you the father of nature and the gods, why do we,
a rustic tribe, raise sacred altars to you and honor you with slaugh-
tered oxen and rich incense, if you have no concern for us or the
kingly flocks? May it be that you gods are consumed by envy? I   300
take to pasture a thousand snowy oxen and a thousand sheep,
while you have scarcely one bull, scarcely one ram in heaven (if
there is truth to the report) and a raging dog to guard that great

unus, et armenti custos Canis arida tanti.
305 Demens quin potius regi divina facesso,
cui tot agri, tot sunt populi, cui lata ministrant
aequora, et est superis ac Sole potentia maior?
Ille dabit facilesque auras, frigusque virentum
dulce feret nemorum armentis, aestumque levabit."
310 Sic fatus, mora nulla, sacras in montibus aras
instituit regi Alcithoo, et divina facessit.
Hoc manus agrestum, hoc pastorum cetera turba
exsequitur: dant tura focis incensa, litantque
sanguine taurorum, et fumantia viscera torrent.
315 Quae postquam rex, in solio dum forte sederet
subiectos inter populos turbamque frequentem,
agnovit, divum exhibito gavisus honore,
non ullum tellure coli, se vindice, numen
imperat, esse nihil terra se maius in ipsa:
320 caelo habitare deos, nec eorum hoc esse quod infra est.
Viderat haec, qui cuncta videt, qui singula lustrat,
Sol pater, atque animo secum indignatus, iniquos
intorsit radios, et lumine fulsit acerbo:
aspectu quo terra parens correptaque ponti
325 aequora, quo tactus viro subcanduit aër.
Protinus illuvies terris ignota profanis
exoritur. Primus, regi qui sanguine fuso
instituit divina sacrasque in montibus aras,
Syphilus ostendit turpes per corpus achores.
330 Insomnes primus noctes convulsaque membra
sensit, et a primo traxit cognomina morbus,
Syphilidemque ab eo labem dixere coloni.
Et mala iam vulgo cunctas diffusa per urbes
pestis erat, regi nec saeva pepercerat ipsi.
335 Itur ad Ammericen silva in Cartheside nympham,
cultricem nemorum Ammericen, quae maxima luco

flock! Fool that I am, would I not do better to worship the king,   305
who has so many territories and subjects, whom the broad seas
obey and whose power is greater than the gods and the sun? He
will provide my flocks with a fair breeze and the pleasant coolness
of greening groves. He will mitigate the heat.'

   "Thus speaking, he did not delay in raising altars in the hills to   310
King Alcithoos and in performing sacred rites. His example was
followed by the rustic population and by the other shepherds.
They placed incense upon the fire, brought libations of ox blood
and they roasted the smoking innards. Then one day, as the king   315
was sitting enthroned amid a multitude of his subjects, he learned
of these deeds: delighted to receive these honors due to the gods,
he ordered that no god be honored on earth or be held higher
than himself, lest it incur his anger. The gods, he said, held sway   320
in heaven, but not here below. Father Sun, who sees and illumines
all, saw this and, with an indignant soul, hurled his dire rays and
poured down an angry light. At his glance, Mother Earth and the
smooth sea were struck, and the air, touched by contagion, grew   325
hotter. At once an unknown pollution arose in the offending
lands. First Syphilus, who had spilled blood while establishing
rites and raising mountain altars to the king, discovered disfigur-
ing sores throughout his body. He was the first to pass sleepless   330
nights and to feel his body being convulsed. From this first victim
the disease took its name and so the people called it Syphilis.

   "Soon the evil affliction had stricken every city, savagely attack-
ing even the king himself. It was decided to visit the nymph Am-   335
merice in the Carthesian wood, Ammerice, dweller of the groves

interpres divum responsa canebat ab alto.
Scitantur quae causa mali, quae cura supersit.
Illa refert: "Spreti vos o, vos numina Solis
340 exercent: nulli fas est se aequare deorum
mortalem. Date tura deo, et sua ducite sacra,
et numen placate: iras non proferet ultra.
Quam tulit, aeterna est, nec iam revocabilis umquam
pestis erit. Quicumque solo nascetur in isto,
345 sentiet. Ille lacus Stygios fatumque severum
iuravit. Sed enim, si iam medicamina certa
expetitis, niveam magnae mactate iuvencam
Iunoni, magnae nigrantem occidite vaccam
Telluri: illa dabit felicia semina ab alto,
350 haec viridem educet felici e semine silvam,
unde salus." Simul obticuit: specus intus et omne
excussum nemus, et circum stetit horror ubique.
Illi obeunt mandata: sua ipsi altaria Soli
instituunt; niveam, Iuno, tibi, magna, iuvencam,
355 nigrantem, Tellus, mactant tibi, maxima, vaccam.
Mira edam, at divos iuro et monumenta parentum:
haec sacra, quam nemore hoc toto vos cernitis, arbor,
ante solo numquam fuerat quae cognita in isto,
protinus e terra virides emittere frondes
360 incipit et magna campis pubescere silva.
Annua confestim Soli facienda sacerdos
Ultori nova sacra canit. Deducitur ipse
sorte data, qui pro cunctis cadat unus ad aram,
Syphilus. Et iam, farre sacro vittisque paratis,
365 purpureo stabat tincturus sanguine cultros:
tutatrix vetuit Iuno, et iam mitis Apollo,
qui meliorem animam miseri pro morte iuvencum
supposuere feroque solum lavere cruore.

and greatest interpreter of the gods, who sang their responses
from the depths of the forest. The people wished to know the
cause and cure of this disease. She answered them thus: 'You are
sore vexed by the divine power of the Sun, whom you have de-   340
spised. It is not right for any man to hold himself equal to the
gods. If you placate him by burning incense and observing his
rites, he will abate his anger. The plague he has sent is eternal and
cannot be recalled. Whoever is born in this land will know it, for   345
the god has sworn it by the Stygian lakes and cruel fate. But if you
seek a sure remedy, offer a slaughtered heifer to great Juno, and a
black cow to the great Earth. For Juno will send fertile seeds from 350
heaven and, from them, Earth will grow a flourishing tree that will
restore health.' At once she fell silent. The cave was stricken
within and the forest as well, and fear arose everywhere. The men
carried out her commands, raising altars to the Sun and sacrificing
a white heifer to you, great Juno, and a black cow to you, supreme   355
goddess of Earth. Though I shall now relate astounding things, I
vouch for them by all the gods and by the graves of our forefa-
thers. This sacred tree that you see throughout the woods, entirely
unknown here before that time, suddenly began to shoot forth its
green foliage out of the earth and grow into a large forest through- 360
out this land. The priest instructed that new rites be established at
once and that they be annually observed in honor of the avenging
Sun. After lots had been drawn, Syphilus was brought forth to be
sacrificed before the altar for the good of all. Garlands and sacred
grain had already been prepared and Syphilus was standing, ready
to stain the priest's knives with his purple blood. But Juno the   365
protector and Apollo, now appeased, forbade the sacrifice. In place
of the death of the poor man, they found a more fitting victim, a
bullock, and bathed the ground with the blood of this beast.

Ergo eius facti aeternum ut monumenta manerent,
370   hunc morem antiqui primum statuere quotannis
sacrorum. Ille tuum testatur, Syphile, crimen,
victima vana, sacras deductus pastor ad aras.
Illa omnis, quam cernis, inops miserandaque turba
tacta deo est, veterumque luit commissa parentum,
375   cui votis precibusque piis numerisque sacerdos
conciliat vates divos et Apollinis iras.
Lustrati ingentes ramos et robora sanctae
arboris advectant tectis, libamine cuius
vi mira infandae labis contagia pellunt.'
380   Talibus atque aliis tempus per multa trahebant
diversis populi commixti e partibus orbis.
Interea, Europae fuerant quae ad cara remissae
litora, iam rursus puppes, freta lata remensae,
mira ferunt: late (proh fata occulta deorum!)
385   contagem Europae caelo crebrescere eandem,
attonitasque urbes nullis agitare medelis.
Quin etiam gravior naves it rumor in omnes,
illo eodem classem morbo iuvenumque teneri
haud numerum exiguum, et totis tabescere membris.
390   Ergo haud immemores, diras cecinisse volucres
affore cum silva auxilium poscatur ab illa,
continuo faciles nymphas Solemque precati,
intacti nemoris ramos et robora ab alto
convectare parant luco, medicataque sumunt
395   pocula, pro ritu gentis: quo munere tandem
contagem pepulere feram. Quin dona deorum,
haud patriae obliti, et felicem ad litora silvam
nostra iubent ferri, caelo si forsitan isto
assimilem pellant labem; nec fata secundos
400   ipsa negant Zephyros, facilisque aspirat Apollo.
Munera vos divum primi accepistis, Hiberi,

As a lasting monument to that deed, our forefathers first estab- 370
lished these annual rites, and a shepherd, led to the sacred altars as
a fictitious victim, attests to your crime, Syphilus. This luckless
and miserable crowd that you see has been afflicted by god, aton-
ing for the misdeeds of their ancestors. For them the sacred priest, 375
with vows and songs and pious prayers, conciliates the gods and
mitigates Apollo's wrath. After purification, they carry into their
homes the large branches and wood of the sacred tree. Using
drafts made with it, they expel, thanks to its wondrous power, the
contagion of the dread disease."

With such stories and more, the two peoples intermingled, 380
though they were from very different parts of the world, and they
whiled the time away amid many occupations. Meanwhile the
ships that had been sent back to the dear shores of Europe, and
then had crossed the broad ocean once again, brought marvelous
report. Alas for the cryptic oracles of the gods! Far and wide be- 385
neath the European sky the selfsame affliction was spreading, and
dumbstruck cities chafed for want of a cure. An even graver rumor
had spread to all the ships, that the fleet and no small number of
its young men were prey to the disease and that their bodies were
wasting away. And so the crew, hardly forgetful that the baleful 390
birds had sung of a time when the woods would yield a remedy,
prayed at once to the Sun and the yielding nymphs. They began to
bring from the deep woods the branches and timber of the un-
spoiled forests, and they drank the healing potion, according to 395
the customs of the natives. In this way, finally, they warded off the
disease. Indeed, remembering the fatherland, they ordered that the
marvelous wood, a gift of the gods, be brought to our shores, in
case it might serve to ward off a kindred ailment under this sky.
The very fates did not withhold a favorable wind, and Apollo blew 400
auspiciously upon this crowd. You Spaniards first received this
gift of the gods, marveling at the succor as it was given. But now

praesens mirati auxilium; nunc cognita Gallis
Germanisque Scythisque, orbe et gavisa Latino,
iam nunc Europam vecta est huyacus in omnem.

405   Salve, magna deum manibus sata semine sacro,
pulchra comis, spectata novis virtutibus arbos,
spes hominum, externi decus et nova gloria mundi,
fortunata nimis, natam si numina tantum
orbe sub hoc, homines inter gentemque deorum,
410   perpetua sacram voluissent crescere silva.
Ipsa tamen, si qua nostro te carmine Musae
ferre per ora virum poterunt, hac tu quoque parte
nosceris, caeloque etiam cantabere nostro.
Si non te Bactra et tellus extrema sub Arcto,
415   non Meroë, Libycisque Ammon combustus arenis,
at Latium, at viridis Benaci ad flumina ripa
audiet et molles Athesi labente recessus.
Et sat erit, si te Tiberini ad fluminis undam
interdum leget et referet tua nomina Bembus.

guaiacum is known in France and Germany and among the Slavs, and, delighting in Italy, already it has been carried throughout Europe.

Hail to you, great tree, sown by the gods from a sacred seed, splendid in your foliage and conspicuous in your medicinal powers, you hope of men, you honor and newest glory of a distant world. You would have been most blessed if only fate had allowed you to grow in our hemisphere, among the men and people who belong to the gods, a sacred tree in a perpetual wood. But if somehow, through my song, the Muses succeed in scattering your name among the mouths of men, then will you be known in these parts as well and sung beneath our sky. Though Bactria and the northern edge of the world may know you not, nor Meroe and Ammon scorched by the Libyan sands, yet will Latium and the virid banks of Benacus hear of you and the gentle glens watered by the Adige. And it will be enough if, beside the streams of the Tiber, your name, now and then, is read and recalled by BEMBO.

405

410

415

IOSEPH
AD ALEXANDRUM FARNESIUM
CARDINALEM AMPLISSIMUM

JOSEPH
TO ALESSANDRO FARNESE,
MOST EMINENT OF CARDINALS

Quae veterum heroum, divae, facta inclita, Musae,
et monumenta aevi longis obscura tenebris
illustrare novis numeris, et carmine sacro
ferre per aetates omnes perque ora nepotum
5 gaudetis, famamque virum proferre sub auras,
nunc, o, nunc populi illius, quem maximus unum
delegit Deus, et generis longo ordine ducti
principe ab Abramo veteres evolvite fastos,
et iuvenem cantate pium, quem magnus Iacob
10 Isacides genuit, dederat cui nosse futura
per somnos monstrata Deus. Vos dicite quanta
ille tulit, Phariis tandem dum victor in oris
imperium gereret magnum, populumque beatum
conderet, unde salus hominum, spes unde futura
15 vitae erat et clausi reserandum limen Olympi.
    Nec minus Italiae iuvenis decus (omnia quando
quae canimus, tua, Farnesi, sunt maxima iussa)
ipse ades et, plenum scopulis dum currimus aequor,
da faciles in vela auras, da numine dextro
20 (namque deus mihi semper eris) tua grandia vota
posse sequi, pelagique omnes superare labores.
En primas sulcantem undas me litora Ioppes,
me iuga Samariae, nemorosaque pascua Sichen
Iordanisque vocat. Curvis en vallibus Hebron
25 applaudit, caeloque simul tua nomina tollit,
responsatque Tabor voces, et sidera pulsat.
    Noverat infernus Pluton, cui multa futuri est
scire datum, in fatis Abrami e sanguine sacram
progeniem terris promitti, Tartara per quam
30 evertenda forent. Metuenti talia pastor
rexque idem Sichenus erat suspectus Iacob

: BOOK I :

Muses divine, who delight in illumining through new verse the
famous deeds of heroes old and monuments darkened by the long
shadows of time, you who, with sacred song, rejoice in preserving
for posterity the fame of men beneath the heavens, now, O now,   5
relate the ancient acts of that one race beloved of the highest God,
the many generations of Abraham; and sing of the pious youth
whom great Jacob, the son of Isaac, begot and whom God en-   10
dowed with the power to see the future through dreams: tell of all
that he suffered so that in the end, victorious, he might attain
great power in the land of Egypt and create a blessed nation,
through whom would come the salvation of men, the future hope
of life, and the opening of heaven, once closed.   15

And you assist my song as well, glory of Italy's youth, (since all
that I sing, Farnese, I sing at your behest). As I embark upon a sea
full of shoals, be a favorable wind in my sails and (since you will   20
always be a god to me) grant through your auspicious will that I
might follow your grand commandments and overcome all the la-
bors of the sea. For as my bark begins to divide the waves, the
shores of Jaffa call to me, the cliffs of Samaria and the leafy mead-
ows of Sichen and of Jordan. From within its hollow valleys, He-
bron cheers me on and raises your name to heaven, while Mount   25
Tabor echoes my words and with them strikes the stars.

Infernal Pluto, endowed with the power to foresee the future,
knew that, through destiny, a sacred race born of Abraham's blood
had been promised to these lands, a race that would vanquish the   30
Tartarean realms. Fearing such things, he looked with suspicion
and great loathing upon Jacob, alike a shepherd and the king of
Sichen. For no other man preserved the justice and law of God

invisusque nimis: tum quod nec sanctius alter
iustitiam legemque Dei servaret et aris
tura daret, tum quod, bissena prole beatus
35 natorum, populum in sanctum concrescere solus
posse videbatur. Quare hanc intentus in unam
progeniem, dabat omnem operam quo perdere posset,
praecipue insignem puerum, cui sidera fausta
nascenti et late felix arriserat aether.
40 Quem forma egregium Charites studia inter alebant
ingenua et leges patrias rectumque docebant.
Illi autem mens alta inerat divina futuri
nescio quae, atque animus summi admirator Olympi,
et pia relligio, et puero prudentia maior.
45 Ergo, et ob has dotes, et quod per vota parenti
longaevo hic fuerat Rachele e coniuge cara
natus, erat patri ante alios dilectus Ioseph.
    Ex his non parvam invidiam tacitumque serebat
fratribus in reliquis odium et letale venenum
50 Alecto, Eumenidum una, imis emissa tenebris
in genus invisum, totis quae adnixa colubris
dissidium furiasque ferat bellumque necemque.
Nec tantis non ipsa malis Fortuna fovendis
affuit augendisque odiis. Nam forte per aestum
55 cum fraterna cohors pecudes ad pabula nota
lanigeras una silvas duxisset in altas,
iliceaque umbra resident, primus Ioseph
in fratres conversus ait: 'Mea somnia, fratres,
audite, illa quidem mira et, nisi me mea fallunt
60 auguria, haud vani speciem referentia somni.
Namque sub auroram, cum sese sidera condunt
casura iam nocte et solus nuntiat ortum
Lucifer, ipse meas spicas offerre videbar

more piously or offered more incense at His altars. Also, Jacob was
blessed with twelve sons, through whom his one family could   35
found a sacred race. Therefore Pluto eyed them closely and sought
every means to destroy them, and most of all that noble youth
upon whose birth the stars and the rejoicing heavens smiled auspi-
ciously abroad. In this handsome child the Graces nurtured noble   40
studies, teaching him justice and the law of his ancestors. His
deep mind had a certain divine sense of the future, and his spirit
displayed an abiding love of highest heaven. He possessed a piety
in religious matters and an uprightness that were beyond his years.
Therefore, because of these endowments and because, after many   45
prayers, he had been born to his aged father, through his beloved
wife Rachel, Joseph was dearer to Jacob than all his other sons.
    In response, the Fury Alecto sowed great envy, silent rancor and
deadly bane among the other brothers: crowned with many snakes,   50
she went forth from the deepest darkness against that hated race,
to bring them conflict, fury, war and death. Nor did Fortune fail
to play a part in fostering such great ills and inciting hatred. For it
happened one summer that, when the brothers together had led   55
their wooly flocks into the deep woods to their wonted pasture
and were resting under the shadow of an ilex tree, Joseph turned
to them and said, "Hear, brothers, my dreams. For they are mar-
velous and—unless my skill in prophecy deceives me—they hardly   60
resemble false dreams. At the approach of dawn, when the stars
began to conceal themselves and night was giving way, and the
morning star alone foretold the rising sun, I seemed to offer my

sacras ante aras, pariter vos ponere vestras.

65   Sed nostri caelum fasces se tollere in altum
et rutilam insignes late diffundere lucem;
vestri autem obscuri atque humiles summittere sese,
utpote adorantes nostros.' Cui grandior annis
atque odio in puerum non parvo accensus Iudas:

70   'Vane puer, quid mira vocas tua somnia? Numquid
illa aliquis tibi forte deus demisit ab alto?
Credo equidem; nam vina deum dicuntur habere,
qui miranda facit nobis oblata videri.
Augurium quodnam somno tibi fingis ab isto?

75   Num forsan rex noster eris? Tibi sume coronam
e lauro, noceant regi ne vina futuro.'
Talia dicenti fratrum quoque cetera turba
adclamant, dominumque vocant, regemque salutant,
ac puero illudunt; tum patri haec somnia narrant.

80   At senior, cui non aberat Deus, omnia mente
evolvit tacita atque, in nato grande futurum
nescio quid spectans, aliis tamen omnia natis
dissimulat puerumque monet nos ludere somnos.
     Ille autem, cui fata Deus maiora parabat,

85   post paulo in somnis aliud quid pondere maius
perspexit: nam se sublimi in sede locatum,
sub pedibus Solem ac Lunam stellasque minores
undique adorantes divinos reddere honores.
Ergo horum interpres (talem nam numina mentem

90   indiderant) rursus fraternas omnia ad aures
detulit. Illi autem subito nova somnia fratris,
et spes illicitas regnandi, animumque superbum
exposuere patri, atque offensae signa dedere,
internique odii, atque accensae in pectore flammae.

95   Obstupuit primum genitor puerumque vocatum
his, velut interpres somni, duro increpat ore:

stalks upon the sacred altars, as you did yours. My bundles lifted 65
themselves to high heaven and, resplendent, spread abroad a
golden light. Yours, on the other hand, were dark and bowed
down low, as though making obeisance unto mine." At which his
older brother Judas, inflamed with no small hatred against the
youth, replied, "Foolish child: why do you say your dreams are 70
marvelous? Do you suppose that some God has perhaps sent
them to you from high heaven? I can believe it, for a God is said
to dwell in wine and makes us see wonders. What augury do you
think to find in this dream? That you will become our king? Give 75
yourself a crown of laurels, lest the wine do harm to our future
king!"

After Judas had spoken thus, the other brothers, as well, joined
in cozening Joseph and acclaiming him their new lord and king.
Then they related his dreams to their father.

But the old man, with God by his side, pondered these things 80
in the silence of his mind; and though he sensed some vague and
future greatness in the boy, he dissimulated these feelings before
his other sons, and he warned Joseph that dreams can deceive us.

But because God had prepared a loftier destiny for Joseph,
shortly thereafter he saw in dreams something of greater moment: 85
he seemed to be placed upon a high throne while, everywhere be-
neath his feet, the sun, the moon and the lesser stars prayed to
him and made divine obeisance. After interpreting these dreams,
as the divine spirit induced him to do, he yet again related them to 90
his brothers. At once they revealed these new dreams to their fa-
ther, as well as Jacob's unrighteous hopes of ruling them and his
arrogant spirit. And they showed their resentment and deep-
rooted anger and the flame that burned in their hearts.

At first Jacob was astonished: he summoned the boy and, 95
as though interpreting the dream, thus harshly berated him: "So

'Tene igitur pater ac mater fratresque,' ait, 'et plebs
omnis adorabit? Tu sede locabere in alta,
nos infra viles humilesque precabimur? Ah te
100   si malus hic error tenet et spes impia nutrit,
pone animum hunc, atque his falsis et inanibus umbris
deme fidem, teque his fallacibus eripe monstris:
quae dii, si mala sunt et iniqua, immittere nobis
non suevere boni, at potius mala numina, manes
105   inferni, exitium in nostrum ludibria fingunt.
Sic falsa ex adytis referunt oracula, sic et
auguria ex avibus, dissectis omina ab extis:
omnia quae directa Deo lex nostra profanat.
Vade age et haec nobis posthac ne somnia perfer.'
110   Sic ait, et natos alios per dulcia mulcens
dicta pater iubet in Sichen saltusque virentes
ducere molle pecus, puerum consistere Ioseph
se penes. Expediunt iuvenes mandata paterna,
felicesque Hebron valles et amoena vireta
115   invisunt; sed non virides in vallibus herbae,
non umbrae nemorum, non gratae e collibus aurae,
non volucrum cantus inimica insomnia possunt
ex animis delere: eadem per singula versant,
exacuuntque odia, atque irae laxantur habenae.
120   Nec non Alecto diris serpentibus instans
corda urit, tantumque odii, tantum excitat ignis,
ut iam immane nefas animis meditentur iniquis
perdendi puerum et sese in scelus omne parandi.
Ergo, dum iuvenes exercent talia, iam Sol
125   condiderat geminos ortus, cum luce sequente
castra movere parant Dothainque in pascua laeta
ducere oves, quo plus patriis ab ovilibus absint
invisoque a fratre, pater quem diligat unum,
quem sibi, quem reliquis regem haud detrectet habere.

will your father and mother, your brothers and all the peoples bow
down to you? Will you sit on high while we, base and humble,
pray to you? O, if this evil error has taken hold of you and if you   100
have been nourished by impious hope, let go of such notions.
Cease to believe in these vain and empty shadows, and free your-
self from such false fantasies. For if they are evil and base, then it
is not the gods, who are good, who are wont to send them to us.
Rather evil spirits, the gods of the underworld, devised these illu-   105
sions to our peril. Thus they produce false oracles from within
their shrines, auguries from birds and omens from dissected en-
trails. All of this is forbidden by our law, which descends from
God. Come now, do not bring me any more of your dreams." So   110
speaking Jacob allayed the feelings of his other sons with sweet
words. Then he ordered that they bear a wooly sheep into Sichen
and its greening groves and that young Joseph remain with him.
The young men carried out their father's will, by going to the fer-
tile vales and pleasant woods of Hebron. But neither the green   115
meadows of the valleys nor the shade of the groves, neither the
pleasing breeze from the hills nor the song of the birds could erase
the hateful dreams from their hearts. Rather they kept recalling
each grievance and, sharpening their hatred, let go the reins of
their anger. And raging Alecto, with her evil snakes, seared their   120
hearts, kindling so much hate and conflagration in them that al-
ready their wicked minds began to conceive a monstrous plan
against the boy, as they readied themselves for the most heinous
crimes. After two days had passed in this condition, on the third   125
the brothers prepared to move their encampment and lead their
flocks to the fertile meadows of Dothain, where they would be
farther away from their father's sheepfolds and from the loathed
boy whom their father loved most, and whom he would have been
content to see as king over himself and the others.

130   Ergo aliam atque aliam solito plus forte morati
cum traherent cum nocte diem, miratus abesse
hos tantum genitor, confestim accersit Ioseph:
'Ique,' ait, 'o mihi care puer, fratresque require
in Sichen, patrique refer quae causa morandi.
135   Nam timeo ne quid male faustum evenerit illis
aut pecori.' Ille viam, nulla est mora, corripit et iam
advolat in Sichen; sed fratribus et grege nusquam
compertis, quid agat dubius, huc spectat et illuc,
omnia collustrans oculis; modo nomine fratres
140   magna voce vocat: tantum nemora alta vocanti
respondent vallesque cavae. Forte ilicis altae
frondator ramorum aderat, qui, ut vidit anhelum
ancipitemque sui puerum, noto obvius illi,
'Quid quaeris, puer?' inquit, 'Oves si forte paternas,
145   si fratres, ne quaere istis in vallibus illos,
quandoquidem audivi dicentes: "Saltibus ex his
in Dothain cedamus." Ibi fratresque pecusque
invenies.' Dein monstrat iter, qua tramite recto
ocius inveniat laetissima pabula: namque
150   plurima pars exusta aret, nec gramina nutrit.
    Ille datum festinat iter. Iamque, ultima Sichen
emensus, Dothain laetus propiora tenebat,
cum specula longe venientem vidit ab alta
plena odii fraterna cohors, ac protinus, 'En rex
155   noster,' ait, 'quem Sol, quem Luna et sidera adorant.
Nos, famuli viles ad pastoralia nati,
per deserta die rabido sub Sole vagamur,
nocte in speluncis patulave sub arbore somnos
captamus, tecti rude lana et pellibus hirtis,
160   despecti, et vili polenta et flumine pasti.
Ille patris mensa virgata in veste recumbens
lactibus haedorum et lumbo pinguescit ovili,

Now when they had passed several days and nights in this way   130
and delayed more than usual, their father was struck by the length
of their absence and promptly summoned Joseph. "Go, dear son,"
he said, "and seek your brothers in Sichen, and then come back
and tell me why they tarry. For I fear that something bad has hap-   135
pened to them and to the flocks." Joseph departed at once and
soon arrived in Sichen. But, not finding his brothers or the flock
anywhere, he looked here and there, casting his glance in all direc-
tions, uncertain what to do. He called to them by name at the top   140
of his voice, but only the deep woods and the hollow vales reech-
oed to him. It happened that a forester was pruning the branches
of a lofty oak when he saw the breathless youth running distract-
edly. He recognized the boy and went to him. "What are you seek-
ing here? If perchance you are looking for your brothers and for
your father's flocks, do not seek them in these valleys. I heard your   145
brothers say that they were leaving these woods for Dothain.
There you will find them and the flocks." Then he indicated to
Joseph how to go and showed the straightest path by which he
might find those fertile pastures; in fact most of the area was   150
parched and sere and there was no grass. So Joseph departed upon
the prescribed course.

Soon he had reached the outskirts of Sichen and rejoiced to
approach Dothain, when he was spotted from afar by his malevo-
lent brothers atop their lofty lookout. At once they said, "Here
comes our king, whom the sun, the moon and the stars obey. We   155
lowly shepherds, born to drive the flocks, wander by day through
the desert under the blazing sun and by night we sleep in caves or
under the spreading foliage of a tree, covering ourselves in rough
wool and shaggy hides, contemned as we eat base porridge and   160
drink from streams. But he, reclining at his father's table in a
striped coat, is fattened on goat's milk and lamb shank and sated

repleturque mero, tum stertens impia nobis
somniat. Huncne igitur, fratres, atque ista feremus
165   opprobria? Anne adeo caeci exspectabimus ut iam
grandior atque animis fidens et patris amore
nos premat, et ditionem omnem et benedicta paterna
surripiat, sic vera nimis sua somnia reddens?'
(Heu fratrum ignarae mentes, et pectora caeca!)
170   'Cur potius, dum testis abest dumque omnia nobis
dant animos, non hunc capimus? Cur protinus istis
confossum gladiis puteo non condimus illo,
qui prope contegitur dumis et sentibus atris?
Dicemusque fame rabidis ursove lupove,
175   qui multi deserta habitant haec, dente peremptum.'
      Talia iactabant inter sese effera fratres
consilia. At cunctis aderat, qui maior et annis
et maior pietate, Ruben: 'Dii talia nobis
avertant,' ait, 'ah vestras ne sanguine, fratres,
180   fraterno maculate manus, neve ira deorum
hoc velit, ut scelus ob tantum nos, et domus, et grex
una omnes pereamus. Abest si testis, at ipse
est testis Deus: ipse Deus, quem nulla latere
facta queunt, quique hic et nos nunc spectat et audit.
185   Si tamen est animus vobis secludere prorsus
hunc puerum, sine caede eius, sine sanguine in illum
trudite vicinum puteum, et dimittite fatis.'
Haec vero suadebat, uti iam caede remota
mox ipse ad puteum sera iam nocte rediret,
190   extraheretque illum, et misero sua pignora patri
redderet, ac fratrum tandem componeret iras.
Verba omnes movere. Placet sine caede prehensum
proiicere in puteum et miserum dimittere sorti.
Tum Ruben: 'A vobis fuerint quaecumque peracta,
195   horum me insontem videat Deus.' Ac procul inde

with wine. Then, while he sleeps in luxury, he snores out impious
things about us. O brothers, can we bear him and his insults? 165
Shall we blindly wait until he grows greater and, confident in his
mind and in his father's love, he oppresses us and, seizing power
and our father's blessing, makes his dreams all too true? O foolish
brothers, how blind are your hearts! Why not seize on him now, 170
when there is no witness, and when everything gives us courage?
Why not drive him through with these knives right away and hide
his body in that well, concealed by brambles and harsh briars? We
will say that he was eaten by some rabid bear or wolf that abounds 175
in this desert."

Such were the mad designs that the brothers discussed among
themselves. But Reuben, who was older and more pious than the
others, came forward. "May the gods keep us from such acts," he
said. "My brothers, stain not your hands with fraternal blood, lest 180
God in his anger requite this crime by destroying us, our home
and our flocks together. Though there be no witness, yet God
Himself bears witness, who notices every deed and even here and
now can see and hear us. But if you are determined to be rid of 185
the boy, then without violence or blood fling him into this nearby
well and leave him to his fate." Reuben persuaded them in this
way so that, once the murder was averted, he could return to the
well alone, late at night, and pull the boy out: then he would re- 190
turn him to their wretched father and finally try to allay the anger
of his brothers. His words moved all of them. They resolved,
without violence, to seize the poor youth, throw him into the well,
and leave him to chance. Reuben added, "Whatever is done by
you, may God see that I am innocent." Thereupon he departed 195

discessit silvisque latens se condidit altis,
visurus rerum eventum. Et iam laetus Ioseph
festinans aderat; contra fratrum impia turba
circumfusa ruit minitans, manibusque revinctis,
'Nunc,' inquit, 'tua vana tibi quid somnia prosint
aspicies: numquid regi parebimus omnes?'
Ille, pavens stupidusque rei novitate, precari
talia ne insonti facerent, superosque vocare,
nequidquam, quando impatiens magis et magis urget
crescens corde furor, facibus furialis Erynnis
instat atrox, daemonque malus, qui, obsistere fatis
posse putans, cunctorum aciem vertebat in unum.
At puer, ut nullis precibus nullisve moveri
fratrum corda videt lacrimis, sed iam impete multo
compelli in foveam, quod restat, lumina tollens
in caelum, tales fundebat ad aethera questus:
'Dii Abrahae, dii magni Isac, dii patris Iacob,
vos ego si sancte colui, si iussa paterna
semper obii, semperque pie et sine crimine vixi,
aspicite, et si fata mihi nunc ultima pendent
ut moriar, miserum saltem servate parentem.
At vos o, tenere, fratres, quos semper amavi
maioresque habui, curate haec tristia ad aures
ne patris adveniant; sed me rapuisse latrones
dicite, quo saltem spe se soletur inani
viventis nati, Stygias nec tendat ad umbras
ante diem. Deserta ipse intumulatus arena
emoriar.' Lacrimae dicenti talia fusae
ex oculis cecidere, simul voxque ipsa repressa est.
Et iam etiam fratrum sedari pectus et ira
coeperat, Isachar cum, 'Ne desistite, fratres,'
dixit, 'ab incepto: quin vinctum et fune ligatum
in foveam mittamus, ibi suspensus in imo

some distance and hid himself in the deep woods, to watch what
happened. Presently Joseph appeared, walking happily at a brisk
pace. The impious band of his brothers ran toward him and men-
acingly surrounded him. Then they tied his hands and said, "Now   200
you will see what your empty dreams are worth. Or shall we all
obey you as our king?" He became frightened and was struck
dumb by the strangeness of their threat. He besought them to
spare him in his innocence and he called upon the gods in vain. In
fact the brothers were urged on by a mounting madness, growing
ever greater in their hearts, and the repulsive Erynnis goaded them   205
with her fires, and the evil Demon, thinking he could stand in the
way of destiny, drew the attention of all of them toward Joseph
alone. But when the boy saw that his brothers' hearts could be
moved neither by entreaties nor by tears and that he would now
be thrown violently down a well, there remained nothing for him   210
but to raise his eyes to heaven and fill the air with these laments:
"You Gods of Abraham, great Gods of Isaac and of Jacob, my fa-
ther: If ever I did reverently honor you, if ever I obeyed my fa-
ther's orders and lived piously and without offense, behold me   215
now. If fate wills it that I am now to die, at least protect my be-
reaved father. As for you, my brothers, whom I always loved dearly
and held greater than myself, take care that no word of this sad
deed should reach the ears of our father. Say rather that I was   220
taken by thieves, so that, at the very least, he can console himself
with the vain hope that I am still alive and not descend into the
Stygian shades before his time. For my part, I shall perish and lie
unburied in the desert sands." As he spoke, tears fell from his eyes
and his voice was stifled within him. And already the rage and   225
anger of his brothers had begun to abate when Isachar said, "Do
not fail in the act, brothers. Let us shove him into the well, bound
and tied with a rope. There let him remain at the base of the well

sistatur fundo, donec meliora parent dii
230 consilia, atque cibum interea capiamus in herba,
quandoquidem iam Sol invitat et altior hora.'
Assensere omnes dictis, puerumque revinctum
ad puteum flentem ducunt. Hic, fune ligata
arboris ad truncum pendentis desuper altae,
235 demittunt pavitantem intro, fundoque relinquunt
suspensum. Ast ipsi, circum per gramina fusi,
implentur vili Cerere et cariotide pingui.
At Deus, aetherio terras qui spectat ab axe,
insontem aspiciens, illo et miseratus amore
240 quo mare, quo terras, quo caelum condidit altum,
unum ex aligeris qui circum mille ministris
exspectant mandata vocat, 'Fidissime,' et inquit,
'vade age, Samariamque, tibi notissima dudum
arva, pete, et, quem scis fatis ad magna vocari
245 Isacidae puerum, qui caeco poscit ab antro
auxilium, et fraterna odia et facta impia plorat,
hunc inopem solare; nec est mandare necesse
quae referas, cui nota mea est et aperta voluntas.'
Sic ait et nutu placido, quo sidera cursu
250 perpetuo ducit, iuvenem dimittit. At ille
aetherias humeris accingit tenuibus alas,
queis caelum illaesum penetrat, queis nubila tranat
praevertitque fuga Zephyros. Iamque, aethera scindens,
aërios tractus et inania lata secabat.
255 Qualis, ubi in liquidis stagnis aut ardea longe est
aut albus conspectus olor, sacer accipitrum rex,
post varios gyros sublimis ab aethere lapsus,
immotis secat alta ruens oculo ocius alis,
impete non alio volucer caelestis adibat
260 Samariae terras; primus quem vertice summo
excepit Tabor, insuetum frondescere silvas

until the gods have some better idea. Meanwhile let us eat in the   230
grass, since the sun and the rather late hour bid it." All of them
agreed and led the youth, bound and weeping, to the well. Here
they tied a rope to the trunk of a tall tree that hung down and
then they lowered their frightened brother into the well and left   235
him hanging there. Meanwhile they lay strewn upon the grass, fill-
ing themselves with cheap grain and fat dates.

But God, who watches the earth from his heavenly summit,
saw the innocent youth and pitied him with that same love with
which he created the sea, the earth and high heaven. He called   240
upon one of the thousand winged messengers who surround him
and await his bidding, and he said, "Faithful servant, go to Sama-
ria and seek the fields that you have long known well. Console the 245
bereaved son of Isaac, whom you know to have a great destiny and
who now seeks help in that dark pit and laments the hateful and
impious deeds of his brothers. I do not need to tell you what to
say, since my will is clear and well known already." So speaking He
dispatched the angelic youth with that serene nod with which He   250
guides the stars in their perpetual courses. The angel placed upon
his delicate shoulders airy wings by which he could pass through
the inviolate sky, swim among the clouds and outrun the zephyrs.
Now parting the air, he furrowed the tracts of sky and the empty   255
expanses of heaven. As when in some clear pond a heron or white
swan is spotted far off, the fierce king of hawks circles round sev-
eral times and then rapidly drops from the height of heaven with-
out moving his wings, rending the air faster than the eye can fol-
low. With no less speed did the celestial messenger reach the lands 260
of Samaria. The first place to receive him on its summit was
Mount Tabor, which marveled to find its groves blooming with

miratus, terramque nova vestirier herba,
et varios praeter solitum summittere flores.
Excepere illum prognatae monte Napeae
265   et divina Deo cecinerunt; omnia rupes
responsant; ipsa antra Deum silvaeque salutant.
At sacer interpres divorum, ut vertice ab alto
lumina deflexit terris ac gramine fusos
vescentesque videt fratres, ast inde camelos
270   mercatorum Arabum spectat (Iovis omnia facta
imperio), hinc animum ad miserum convertit Ioseph
descenditque celer; puteique in margine summo
ut stetit, extemplo nova lux effulsit in antro,
miratum et subitus puerum circumstetit horror.
275   Quem pius interpres placida sub imagine et ipso
ore puer puerum dictis solatur amicis:
'Pone metum, diis care, patrum Deus ille tuorum,
qui caelum regit, huc alto me ex aethere mittit,
qui referam mandata tuos solantia luctus.
280   Hinc primum mittere foras, sed venditus auro,
nomine mancipii; tum Nili in regna fereris,
atque iterum vendere illic, multosque per annos
servus eris. Tunc ne vetita atque iniusta libido
te alliciat, neu dii alieni et falsa, caveto,
285   numina decipiant. Vestrum si semper habebis
corde Deum, ipse aderit semper tibi, te bona semper,
quicquid ages, quocumque ieris, fortuna sequetur.
Quin, magis ut fidas animis, tibi magna parantur
imperia et tempus veniet cum vera videbis
290   somnia visa tibi, cum te fratresque paterque
supplice adorabunt fletu; misereberis illis,
neve perire fame miseros patieris iniqua.
Quin ipsos, natosque illorum, ipsosque nepotes
in partem imperii atque in tua regna vocabis,

unusual abundance, while the earth was mantled in new grass and
brought forth more varied flowers than was its wont. Next he was
received by the nymphs of the wooded valleys, who raised to God   265
a divine hymn that was echoed by the cliffs, and the very caves and
groves greeted him. But as the sacred minister of God looked
down upon the land from on high, he saw the brothers feasting in
the grass and then the camels of some Arab merchants, all of it   270
arranged by the will of God. Next he turned his attention to piti-
able Joseph and swiftly descended. As the angel came to rest at the
utmost rim of the well, all at once it was filled with a weird light
and fear seized the astonished youth. The holy angel, himself a   275
youth, consoled the young man with kindly mien and kind words.
In his own voice he said, "Be not afraid, beloved of God. For the
God of your fathers, who reigns in heaven, sent me down from his
airy abode to relate to you his commands, which will console you
in your sorrow. First you will be sent from here, but sold for gold   280
and called chattel. Then you will be borne into the realms of Nile.
There you will be sold once again and for many years you will be
a slave. While there, take care that no forbidden or unjust desire
lead you astray, that no foreign gods or false spirits deceive you. If 285
you keep your God ever in your heart, He will always stand beside
you and, whatever you do, wherever you go, good fortune will fol-
low. Verily, so that you might take heart, know that great domin-
ion awaits you, that a time will come when you will see your   290
dreams realized, when your father and your brothers will beseech
you with suppliant tears. You will pity them and suffer no evil
famine to destroy them in their affliction. Indeed, you will wel-
come them, their sons and even their grandsons into your realms

295   ingens ut tandem populus concrescat, arenae
        instar; quem Deus Aegypti de parte superba
        deducet tandem et pedibus super aequora siccis
        pertransisse dabit; mox haec in regna reducet,
        lacte novo quae regna fluent et melle perenni.
300   Mox (anni, properate) diem felicia saecla
        aspicient, saecla illa diem, quam tanta futuram
        vatum oracla canunt, cum demittatur ab alto
        magna Dei soboles, vestro de sanguine creta,
        quae scelus antiquum tollat, quae limina caeli
305   clausa diu magnique fores praepandat Olympi.'
        Nec plura effatus caelum se tollit in altum.

          At iuvenis, quamquam stupefactus numine tanto
        restitit et rerum confusus imagine multa,
        laetatur tamen, atque animum per singula versat,
310   speque futurorum praesentem corde dolorem
        discutit, atque oculos in caelum et sidera tollens
        sic fatur: 'Rex terrarum, rex aetheris alti
        omnipotens, patrum Deus et tutela meorum,
        respice nos et, nostra tuo sub numine si spes
315   est omnis, super his primum miserere parentis.
        De me autem quidquid statuet tua recta voluntas,
        seu laetum seu triste pares, nihil ipse recuso.
        Unum oro, si Parca mihi vidisse negabit
        his oculis felicem illam semperque beatam
320   optatamque diem, qua tandem ex aethere summo
        descendet tua progenies, da cernere saltem
        in speculo, atque umbram monstra mihi, speque fideque
        noscere da puroque eius de fonte lavari.'
        Dixit et ex imo traxit suspiria corde.
325   Interea, e Madian stacten bdelamque ferentes
        cinnamaque et liquidam styracem et pinguia tura,
        transibant Arabes, qua stabant gramine laeto

to share in your power, so that from them a great nation will arise   295
as numerous as the sands. Finally God will lead this nation from
the proud land of Egypt. Allowing them to cross the sea dry-shod,
he will guide them back into these realms, which will flow with
fresh milk and unabating honey. And then (may the years pass   300
quickly) happy ages hence will see the day, the blessed day, which
so many prophecies have foretold, when the great son of God,
descended from your blood, will be sent down from on high to
wash away the ancient stain and throw open the gates of heaven,
long closed, and the posterns of great Olympus." Without another   305
word, the angel flew back to heaven.

   Though astonished by this divine apparition, the youth re-
sisted, confused by all he had seen. But he also rejoiced to recall
each thing he had heard and he drove the present sorrow from his   310
heart in hopes of things to come. Raising his eyes to the sky and
to the stars he spoke thus: "Omnipotent God of heaven and earth,
God of my fathers and guardian of my people, look upon us: and
if all our hope lies with you, before all else, take pity on my father.   315
As for me, whatever your upright will should decide, whether you
have prepared good or ill for me, I do not rebel. I ask only that, if
fate prohibits me from seeing with these eyes the happy, ever
blessed and ever hoped for day when finally your son descends   320
from high heaven, at least let me see some image, some foreshad-
owing of it, that I might see him through hope and faith and
bathe in his pure stream." So he spoke and a sigh escaped from his
heart.

   At that time, some Arab merchants from Midian, bearing   325
myrrh and aromatic gums, cinnamon, clear styrax and rich frankin-
cense, were passing beside where the brothers lay in the abundant

vescentes iuvenes simul et diversa loquentes.
Qui ut primum videre viros, 'Deus,' inquit Iudas,
'o fratres, meliora parat quam nostra ferebant   330
consilia: his etenim si mercatoribus ipsum
vendamus puerum, cum lucro auroque piati,
fraterna a morte immunes reddemur et ad nos
posthac nec fama adveniet nec nomen Ioseph,
sive Arabes isti Aegyptum, seu barbara regna,   335
Marmaricam, Libyamve petant. Ergo unus ad illos
mittatur, qui mancipii sub nomine merce
proposita pretium statuat, responsa reportet.'
Dicta placent; qui pacta ineat, iam mittitur; ipsi
interea speluncam adeunt, funemque ligatum   340
arboris ad truncum solvunt, et in aethera sursum
suspensum educunt puerum; qui talis in auras,
qualis mane rosa aut riguo narcissus in horto,
prodiit, et formae servato vera decore
signa dedit certumque Dei praesentis amorem.   345
Iamque aderat mercator Arabs et nuntius una,
vile satis pacti pretium. Proh Iuppiter! Ille,
quem tanta in fatis promissa et tanta manebant
imperia, argenti bis deno venditur asse,
mancipium infelix. Iam curvo terga camelo   350
excipitur, Nili ignotas iam fertur in oras.
At quadrupes, ceu divino sub pondere, vector
insolitos dedit hinnitus et signa recentis
laetitiae, iamque et grato facilisque levisque
sessori tergum sellamque accommodat aptam,   355
agglomeransque pedes retro socia agmina linquit.
   At fratres, puer ut cessit, mala nuntia patri
quis ferat et quo infanda tegant facta impia pacto
ambigui, tandem statuunt praemittere vestem
a puero ereptam, caprino sanguine tinctam,   360

grass, eating and speaking of divers things. As soon as Judas saw
them, he said, "O brothers, God has contrived an even better fate   330
than we could have planned. Indeed, if we sell the boy to these
merchants, then, enriched with money and gold, we will be inno-
cent of shedding a brother's blood, and hereafter we will hear nei-
ther report nor even the name of Joseph, whether these Arabs are   335
destined for Egypt, for barbarous realms, for Marmarica or Libya.
Therefore one of us should go to them and, as regards selling him,
name a price for our wares and return with their response." The
brothers liked the plan and dispatched one of them to strike a
bargain. Meanwhile the others went to the well, and, untying the   340
rope from the tree trunk, hauled up the suspended youth. Like the
morning rose or narcissus in a well-watered garden, he emerged
into the air, and his unscathed beauty gave proof of God's pres-   345
ence and His constant love. Soon one of the Arab merchants ap-
peared together with the brother who had been dispatched, and
they announced that they had agreed on a price, a rather low one.
By Jupiter, he for whom fate had reserved such promise and such
empire was sold into slavery for twenty pieces of silver, a sad chat-   350
tel. Soon he was placed on the curved back of a camel and carried
into the unknown land of Nile. But his four-footed mount, as
though sensing his divine burden, whinnied in a new way and
seemed suddenly happy. Gladly and swiftly, he offered his back to
the grateful rider and made the saddle more comfortable; then he   355
picked up his pace until he had left the rest of the caravan be-
hind.

Once the boy was gone, his brothers were at first uncertain who
should bring the bad news to their father and how they should
conceal their impious and unspeakable deeds. Finally they decided
that someone should take the coat that had been ripped from the   360

qui ferat, inventamque inter nemora avia dicat;
Danque placet commissa dari. Qui, instructus abunde
omnia, longaevum non haec miseranda parentem
exspectantem adit et, monstrato sanguine et ipsa
365   veste, ait: 'Hanc nostrae nemora inter devia primae
invenere canes: cuius sit vestis et unde
hic cruor ignari, patrem primum esse monendum
duximus, ut te, si quid agendum est, consule agatur.'
      At pater, ut notam maculisque et sanguine vestem
370   conspersam vidit, 'Quis te, carissime Ioseph,
quis divum, ut tecum morerer, spes una senectae,
nate, meae, quis casus,' ait, 'tam durus ademit?
Heu mala te silvae fera sustulit. Ite per alta
vos nemora et, si quid misero de corpore restat,
375   omne afferte mihi, saltem ut suprema sepulcri
dona feram, vel et ipse feris laniandus in altas
proripiar silvas: dabitur natoque patrique
mors eadem. Haec dicens, foedatos pulvere canos
vellebat lacerosque sinu exscindebat amictus.
380   Et famuli tandem collapsum in tecta reportant.
      Parte alia Ruben, ut serum se vesper in orbem
intulit, ad caulas pecudes pecudumque magistri
cum redeunt saltusque vacant pastoribus omnes,
desertum ad puteum solus redit, atque ibi Ioseph
385   terque quaterque vocat. Non respondente vocanti
ullo, sollicitus puerum ne forte necassent,
rem spectare parat, caesaque ex ilice conto
scalam aptat, solersque imum se mittit in antrum,
omnia collustrans. Verum, postquam omnia dudum
390   rimatus, puerum quaesitum haud repperit usquam,
ambiguus tandem reliquos perquirere fratres
destinat, ac pecoris vestigia nota secutus
per noctem, demum inventos de fratre quid actum est

boy and covered in goat's blood and say that it had been found in
some distant woods. It was decided that Dan should do this. So,
having conned his part, he went to his aged father, who had not
expected all of these sad tidings. Dan showed him the bloodied
coat and said, "Our hounds, running ahead of us, found this in the   365
deep woods. We didn't know whose it was or why it was covered
with blood, so we decided to bring it to you first, to find out what
should be done."

But when Jacob saw the familiar coat covered in dirt and blood,   370
he said, "Dearest Joseph, what god or fate was so harsh as to take
you from me and cause me to die with you, only hope of my old
age? Alas, the wild beasts of the forest have eaten him. Go now
into the woods and, if anything remains of his wretched body,
bring it to me so that, at least, I might bestow upon him the final   375
burial offerings. Or rather I myself will race to the deep woods to
be torn apart by beasts! Let father and son suffer the same fate!"
So speaking, he pulled at his white hairs, covered with dust, and
ripped the torn cloak from his body. Finally he fell to the ground   380
and his servants carried him back into his house.

As evening descended upon the twilit world, at the hour when
the masters return the flocks to their pens and no more shepherds
haunt the groves, Ruben returned alone to the deserted well and
repeatedly called after Joseph. When he received no response he   385
began to worry that the boy had been killed. He decided to inves-
tigate, and using a pole made of oak wood in place of a ladder, he
cleverly lowered himself to the bottom of the well and looked all
around. But in truth he sought long and hard and still he could   390
nowhere find the missing boy. Finally, uncertain what to do, he
decided to question his brothers. It was night and he followed the
known paths of the flocks. Finally he found his brothers and

inter multa rogat. Rem totam ex ordine pandunt.
395 At Ruben, ut puerum audivit superesse nec ullis
affectum damnis, 'Hinc, fratres,' inquit, 'eamus
ad miserum genitorem, et spe viventis et auras
spirantis gnati saltem (quod nunc datur unum)
solemur: rapuisse Arabes de more, relicta
400 veste levi pueri fugientis vulnere tincta,
pastores ita ferre. Aliquemque adducere testem
expediet; neque enim deerunt qui dicere possint
se vidisse Arabes.' His ergo rite paratis,
patrem adeunt et, quae possunt, solatia iungunt.
405 Ille autem, quamvis aliqua spe forte levatur,
non tamen aeternas lacrimas planctusque perennes
comprimere aut tristi meditari gaudia mente
ulla potest, sed vitam aegram noctesque diesque
in tenebris, hominum fugiens consortia, ducit.
410   Interea puerum laetus deportat Ioseph
mercator, plenis miratus cedere votis
omnia. Non illis terrae exarsere diebus,
non ventis agitatae ullae tolluntur arenae
ex solito: puerum Charites comitantur euntem,
415 et Caeli favor, et faustis Spes dextera pennis.
Iamque pererratis Iudaeae finibus, altae
incipiunt turres et moenia Osiridis urbis
apparere procul, campis ubi fusa iuventus
munera militiae exercent: hi vincere cursu
420 contendunt pedibus, hi fulvo in pulvere sudant
luctantes, alii duro sub pondere cestus,
pars volucres exercet equos cursuque fatigat,
aut inferre hosti versas post terga sagittas
discit equo currente, aut hastam tollere campo.
425 Ergo Arabes postquam accessere et pulcher Ioseph,
mirati pugnas placidi et praeludia Martis,

asked, among many other things, what had become of Joseph. They related the whole event from start to finish. But when Ruben heard that his brother was alive and had sustained no harm, he said, "Come brothers: We should go to our grieving father and at least console him — it is all we can do now — with the hope that his son yet lives and breathes the air, that the Arabs took him, as they are wont to do, and that his cloak was left behind, stained by some light wound as he tried to escape. Let some shepherds say this. We should find some witness — it can't be so difficult — who will say that he saw the Arabs." Once that had been duly arranged, they went to their father and offered such consolation as they could. But although Jacob was perhaps relieved to find any hope, still he could not suppress his endless tears and perennial laments, nor could he meditate, in his sad mind, upon any joy: rather he passed his aggrieved days, morning and night, in darkness, fleeing the company of men. 395 400 405

Meanwhile, the merchant happily carried Joseph off and marveled at how all his prayers had been fully answered. For in that season, the earth was not too hot, nor were the sands stirred up by the winds, as is their wont. As he went, the boy was accompanied by the Graces, the favor of heaven and auspicious hope with its propitious wings. When they had crossed the borders of Judaea, they began to see the walls and lofty towers of the city of Osiris, throughout whose fields the local youth were engaged in military exercises. Some competed in foot races. Others sweated as they wrestled in the golden dust or under the harsh blows of the pugilist's glove. Still others exercised their swift horses, wearying them in races, or learned how to strike the enemy by shooting their arrows behind them as they rode, or how to raise their spears in the field. After the Arabs arrived together with the handsome Joseph, they stood marveling at the bouts and the games fought in the name of a peaceful Mars, and scarcely could fill their eyes and 410 415 420 425

consistunt, oculisque intenti et pectore toto
vix satis expleri possunt. Quos forte magister
militiae, eunuchus regis, cui summa potestas
430   et duri data erant Mavortia munera belli,
ut vidit, confestim ad sese accedere iussos
compellat: 'Geritisne ullas quas vendere merces
optetis?' 'Quaedam,' dixere, 'et aromata et istum
gestamus puerum, domino qui si placet, ultro
435   munus habe, aut emptum si mavis, pro indole tanta
da quodvis: pretium est magnum tua gratia nobis.'
Ille autem: 'Haud umquam ingratum, mercator, habebis
Fetifarum. Accipiam puerum: at tu munere largo
speque tua maiore mihi donabere multo.'
440   His dictis recipit puerum, quem veste decora
induit et sagulum donat, quo purpura limbo
fulva nitet; tum donat equum. Laetissimus ille
altior it iuvenes inter pulcherrimus omnes.
Quem custode dato laetus praemittit ad urbem
445   Fetifar et carae uxori commendat habendum.
Interea seras invexerat Hesperus horas,
et iuvenum campis cedens manus omnis apertis
ibat ovans comitata ducem, ac iam pulcher Ioseph,
ut dominam invisit, thalami et cognovit herilis
450   officia, ipse humilis servorum se agmine miscens,
obvius it domino. Media se qualis arena
monstrat gemma nitens radiisve micantibus aurum,
talis et ipse puer multis in milibus ibat.
Quem matres populusque omnis mirantur, ut ipso
455   incessu, gravis ore, pedes non dimovet usquam
a duce, non oculos, sed semper totus in illo est.
Nec minus, intra aedes ut ventum, epulaeque paratae,
ulli ipse officio deest, seu corpore opus sit,
seu celeri ingenio. Sed enim super omnia mira est

minds with watching. They happened to be spotted by the royal
eunuch, who held supreme power and military authority in mat-   430
ters of harsh war. As soon as he saw them, he ordered that they be
brought to him. "Have you brought anything, merchants, that you
wish to sell me?" he asked. And they replied, "We have brought a
variety of aromatic herbs, as well as this youth. If he pleases you,
take him as our gift. Or if you prefer to buy him, give whatever   435
you wish for such a fine person. We lay great store by your good-
will." To which the eunuch answered, "You will find, merchant,
that Potiphar is hardly ungrateful to you. I will take the boy and
requite you far beyond your expectations." With these words he   440
received the boy, dressed him in fine clothes, and bestowed upon
him a horse and a cloak hemmed with bright purple. Delighted,
Joseph rode proudly, more handsome than all the other youths.
Potiphar gladly sent him, together with an escort, into the city and
commended him to the keeping of his dear wife. Now Hesperus   445
had brought on the evening, and the entire band of youths, leaving
the open fields, accompanied their commander, cheering him as
they went. When the handsome Joseph saw his new mistress, and
understood the duties of his lord's chamber, he humbly joined the   450
other servants and approached his lord. He shone like a gem in
the sand or like gleaming gold. Such was Joseph as he walked
among thousands of others. Mothers admired him, as did the en-
tire populace, even though he, with his grave manner and expres-   455
sion, stood close by his lord, his eyes fixed upon him, a totally
devoted servant. And when they went into the house for the pre-
pared meal, Joseph never shirked his duty, whether it required
physical strength or a sharp mind. But what people most admired

460 grataque sedulitas apta et prudentia cana.
     Quo factum est, parvo post tempore, Fetifar illum
     non thalamo ut tantum ipse suo praefecerit unum,
     sed domui, et rerum summam commiserit omnem.
     Scilicet auspiciis et diis cuncta ire secundis
465 Fetifaro sunt visa: agri producere fruges
     uberius, sobolem armentum, sibi crescere honores.
     Omnia quae, ostento quodam permotus, Ioseph
     attribuit puero, vatumque oracula suadent.
         Arbor erat Persaea, deo sacrata Camesi,
470 aedibus in mediis, quam vectam e Perside fertur
     orbe pererrato, monumentum insigne futurum,
     ipsa suis manibus plantasse nepotibus Isis.
     Hanc apis externis veniens insedit ab oris,
     insignis fulgore et versicoloribus alis,
475 pulcher apis, quem mox examen grande secutum
     pendentem ramo longum traxere racemum.
     Protinus ostentum ad vates defertur. At ipsi
     venturum externis aliquem portendere ab oris
     declarant, ingens populus quem deinde sequatur,
480 ipsum qui fortunae opibus super aethera tollat
     Fetifarum largosque simul promittat honores.
     Ergo his auguriis tantis censetur Ioseph
     monstrari. Hinc maiore illum dignatur honore
     Fetifar, hinc omnes adamant; sed maxime Iempsar,
485 pulchra ducis coniunx, prae cunctis diligit unum,
     nescia adhuc quanto iam sit devota furori,
     quis deus insideat miseram. Suspiria nondum
     emittit, nondum lacrimas: sunt omnia laeta
     dulciaque et nondum quicquam persentit amari.
490 Quae deus infernas sedes Cocytia regna
     qui regit, humani generis turbator et osor,
     ut vidit Pluton, semenque accrescere felix

was his pleasing diligence and a prudence that was resourceful 460
beyond his years. And so, in short order Potiphar placed Joseph in
charge not only of his chamber but of his house, and he placed all
his belongings in the young man's care. For the gods' favor and
good auspices seemed to accompany all of Potiphar's affairs: as he 465
grew in rank, the fields yielded more abundant crops and herds.
As though moved by a sort of heavenly sign, he attributed all of
his good fortune to young Joseph, and the priestly oracles con-
firmed this.

For in the middle of the house was a Persian tree, sacred to
Camesis. Legend had it that it came from Persia, a world away, 470
and that Isis had planted it with her own hands to serve as a mar-
vel for future generations. In time a bee, a beautiful bee, came
from afar and settled there, dazzling in its sheen and parti-colored
wings and followed soon after by a large swarm that clustered in 475
its branches. At once news of this was brought to the priests, who
declared that it portended that someone would come from abroad,
followed by a great multitude, and that this person would vastly 480
enrich Potiphar, while promising him great rank. Thus it was
thought that these auguries had foretold the coming of Joseph,
and in consequence Potiphar increased Joseph's standing in the
house and everyone loved him. But no one admired him more
than Iempsar, Potphar's beautiful wife, who did not yet realize 485
how great her passion was already growing or what god had
lodged within her, poor woman. She had not yet begun to sigh or
weep. As yet all was pleasant and sweet and she sensed no bitter-
ness. This was perceived by evil Pluto, the troubler and enemy of
the human race, who rules the underworld and the kingdom of 490
Cocytus. He also observed the growth of the fertile seed of Isaac's

Isacidum, invisam sobolem, vocat ocius unum
servorum, quibus insidiae fraudesque dolique
495   sunt animo, queis mille artesque viaeque nocendi,
'Ique,' ait, 'et pulchram circum insinuatus Iempsar
falle dolo, et primas escas quas sensit amoris
tu flabris accende, imis illum ossibus ignem,
illam immitte facem quam nec vis ulla deorum,
500   non hominum exstinguat; mox ipsum accendere Ioseph,
si possis, omni arte stude. Quod vincere si qua
non dabitur, tu perge tamen, pete rursus Iempsar,
acrius ure, furorem adde, inspiraque venenum:
queis monstris agitata domum permisceat omnem,
505   inque odium furiasque omnem convertat amorem.
I celer et nihil ipse doli scelerisque relinque.'
     Ille, hilaris promptusque malis, sumptam e Styge lympham
miscet Acidalio latici; tum ex anguibus unum
Tisiphones capit atque sinu mala semina condit.
510   Fetifari dein tecta petens, nutricis Iempsar
induit Iphicles formam, dominamque salutans,
'Audi,' ait, 'o mihi cara, miser quis casus Ioseph
torquet ad extremum vitae: vidi ipsa gementem
nuper et optantem supremae munera vitae.
515   Quaerenti mihi quae tanti sit causa doloris,
"o mater, ne quaere," inquit, "nam, sive tacebo,
sive edam, omnino moriar, praestatque tacendo
et vitam et nostri causam finire doloris."
Cui ego: "Non sic, o fili; nam vulnera saepe
520   auxilium patefacta et opem invenere salubrem.
Dic audacter: amasne? Haec si tibi causa doloris,
spera et fide, puer; namque ipsum vel tibi amorem
eripiam magicis, vel tu potiere cupito."
Erubuit; tum dixit: "Amo. Dii sunt mihi testes

race, a detested clan. At once he called on one of his servants who
delight in stratagems and tricks and deceit, who know a thousand   495
arts and a thousand paths of harm. "Go," he said, "ingratiate your-
self with the fair Iempsar. Deceive her by guile. Blow upon the
new embers of her love until they catch fire. Then send that flame,
that brand, down into the marrow of her bones, so that no force
of god or man can put it out. Next seek by every art to enflame   500
Joseph as well, if you can. If you cannot vanquish him, don't give
up. Seek Iempsar once again and burn her still more sharply, add-
ing rage and filling her with venom. Goaded by these wiles, may
she convulse the entire house, converting all her love into fury and   505
hate! Go quickly now, setting aside no treachery or crime!"

   Rejoicing in evil and skilled in it, the servant took a draft from
the Stygian lake and mixed it with Acidalian waters. Then he
plucked one of the many adders of Tisiphone and hid this seed of
evil in the folds of his garment. Hastening to the house of Po-   510
tiphar, he assumed the form of Iphicle, Iempsar's nurse, who sa-
luted her lady. "Listen, my dear one, to the lamentable occurrence
that tortures Joseph nearly to death. I myself lately saw him groan,
hoping to end his life. When I asked him the cause of his great   515
sorrow, he replied, 'O, mother, do not ask, since I will surely per-
ish, whether I remain silent or reveal it. I prefer, through silence,
to end my life and the source of my suffering.' 'Be not like that, my
son,' I said, 'for often have wounds, once laid bare, found succor   520
and a cure. Be bold and tell me, are you in love? If this is the cause
of your suffering, take hope and confide in me, son. For either I
will cure you of your love through magic, or you will attain what
you desire.' He blushed and then he said, 'I am in love. The gods

525   hunc quantum eluctans cepi, quam invitus, amorem,
infidum in dominum qui me facit. At mihi sit mors
exoptanda magis. Fidum periisse iuvabit."
Sic ait et fusis lacrimis pulchra ora rigabat.
Ut video, puer hic dominam te deperit: at ni
530   opportune adsis, nimio moriturus amore est.'
Cui virgo: 'O nutrix, quam dura et tristia portas!
Namque et amo hunc puerum et vellem succurrere posse,
sed me iura deum, sed vincla iugalia primum
obsistunt: tum me tanto male sana periclo
535   obiiciam et duri haud formidem coniugis arma?'
Et nutrix: 'O nata, ipsorum crimina amantum
dii ridere solent. Solvendi iura mariti
causa potens et iusta tibi est depellere mortem
a puero, qui nec crimen commiserit umquam,
540   ni crimen sit amare nimis vel amore perire.
Audendum est in amore, pericla nec ulla timenda
prudenti: dii deinde ipsos tutantur amantes,
queis amor et pietas est prima et maxima cura.
Est mihi aqua, in dubiis rebus quae assumpta videre
545   vera facit, dubiique omnis pars utra legenda est.
Hanc dabo, si hac in re ancipiti stat cernere verum.'
Ac Stygiam demonstrat aquam medicataque fonte
pocula Acidalio. 'Placet, o carissima nutrix,'
virgo inquit, totumque manu capit ipsa venenum
550   intrepida, atque uno craterem exhauriit haustu.
     His actis puerum Iphicle se vertit ad ipsum,
et gressu ad thalamum illius contendit anili,
qui laudes superum regi et divina legebat.
Ut vero in thalami mentitus limine daemon
555   constitit, et puero caelestem assistere Ioseph
custodem vidit minitantem ensemque coruscum
vibrantem, extemplo subita formidine captus

are my witnesses that I fought against and unwillingly conceived 525
this love that has made me unfaithful to my master. I would rather
die and still be faithful.' So he spoke and his handsome face was
filled with tears. As I can see, this boy is perishing for his mistress,
and unless you help him he will die from an excess of love!" To 530
whom the young lady thus replied, "O nurse, how hard and sad are
the things you relate. For I love the boy and wish to help him. But
first the laws of the gods and my conjugal bonds forbid it. Then
should I, maddened, place myself in such peril, heedless of my 535
stern husband's might?" The nurse replied, "O child, the gods
smile upon the crimes of lovers. To save the young man's life is a
just and potent cause for you to disregard the laws of marriage.
This youth has committed no greater crime than to love too much 540
and to risk dying from it. One must be bold in love, and no peril
is to be feared as long as you are careful. For lovers are protected
by the gods, whose greatest concern is love and piety. I have a po-
tion which, when drunk, allows one to see clearly in doubtful cir- 545
cumstances and to choose correctly among two options. I shall
administer this potion, if you wish to learn the truth in this dan-
gerous matter." At this she revealed the Stygian water and the
beaker treated with the Acidalian stream. "Dearest nurse, I like the
plan," Iempsar said, and fearlessly seizing the entire cup of poison
in her hand, she emptied the beaker in a single gulp. 550

That done, Iphicle went to Joseph himself, hastening to his
chamber with aged step. He was singing praises to the king of
angels and reciting his prayers. But when in truth the disguised
Demon stood upon the threshold of the chamber and saw himself 555
threatened by the divine spirit who protected Joseph and bran-
dished a gleaming sword, he was suddenly struck with fear. He

horruit, et retro gressusque animumque reduxit,
aufugitque celer, nocturnaeque alitis oti
560 effigiem capit, et tecto se sistit in alto.

: LIBER II :

At misera ut Stygios latices desumpsit Iempsar
solaque permansit, totis ardere medullis
visa sibi est, tota in subitum convertier ignem,
suspiransque gemensque unum deposcit Ioseph.
5   Et modo se imponit stratis, paulumque morata
assurgit, modo mutat et hunc, modo mutat et illum,
fastiditque locum infelix, nec se capit usquam,
non secus ac solet ille, acris praecordia causus
cui torret, vel quem dipsas sitibunda momordit.
10   Tandem ait: 'Heu quidnam est quod me tam saeviter urit?
Estne amor, an sumpti latices? Nempe est amor iste,
quo moriar, nisi formosus succurrat Ioseph.
Tu mihi nunc succurre, puer; succurrere namque
ipsa etiam tibi constituo. Moriemur amando
15   insontes ambo. Dii tanti criminis haud me
auctorem videant, non haec Aegyptia tellus.
Dum licuit potuique, tori concordia iura
servavi; nunc maior agit me visque deusque,
imperioque premit. Sic sit mihi numen amicum,
20   ut nosco experiorque deum, cui femina non est
contra stare potens. Deus hic custodiet ambos;
quin et, suetus amare, teget solatia nostra.'
Dixerat impatiensque morae vocat ocius Efren,
unam ex ancillis, dominae quae fida solebat
25   ferre vigil mandata, vigil responsa referre.

stepped back, disheartened, and swiftly fled. Then assuming the
form of a nocturnal bird, he sat himself upon the lofty roof of the   560
house.

: BOOK II :

As soon as sad Iempsar had drunk the Stygian drafts and found
herself alone, she felt as though she were burning up inside, as
though she were bursting into flame. As she sighed and groaned,
all she asked for was Joseph. She threw herself upon her bed and   5
then, a few moments later, she got up again, constantly changing
positions and disdaining all of them in her unhappiness. She
could not contain herself. In this she was no different from some-
one who has felt a sharp fever that inflames his heart, or who has
been bitten by a thirsting serpent. Finally she said, "What is this   10
thing that burns me so savagely? Is it love or the drafts that I
drank. Surely it is love, and it will slay me unless handsome Joseph
comes to my aid. Help me now, boy, for I have decided to help
you as well. Innocent both, we will perish through love. May the   15
gods attest that I was hardly the author of this great crime. Let all
of Egypt avow it as well. While it was allowed, and while I was
able, I preserved the honor of my marriage bed. But now a greater   20
force, a greater god, drives me on and compels me. So may the god
be kind, as I have already found him to be, he whom no woman
can withstand. This god will protect us both. Accustomed to love,
he will conceal how we console ourselves." So she spoke. Then,
impatient of delay, at once she called upon Efren, one of her hand-
maidens, whom she trusted faithfully and promptly to convey her   25

'Vade,' ait, 'et puero dic huc accedat Ioseph,
si vacat, et domini si nulla negotia nostri
impediunt.' Abit illa cita et mandata facessit.
Nec longe post iussus adest formosus Ioseph.
30   Quem solum admissum virgo, mutata colore,
iuxta astare facit: tum corde et voce tremente,
'Care,' inquit, 'puer, atque oculis mihi gratior ipsis,
verane tu dominae dices, quaecumque rogabit?'
'Vera equidem (an fallam dominos?),' ait ille, 'fatebor.
35   Tu quodvis pete.' Et illa: 'Puer, te perdite amare
audio: si verum est, debent me nulla latere,
nec si sim quam perdite amas; nam (vera fatebor)
ipsa etiam te perdite amo. Tu nec mihi amanti,
nec tibi ego crudelis ero; da iungere dextram:
40   qualis eris, quantoque a me donaberis auro!'
Sic ait et summis puero dedit oscula labris.
Ille, pudore rubens et secum mente revolvens
quae divum interpres puero mandaverat olim
in puteo, neu dii alieni aut iniusta libido
45   alliceret, taciteque Deum sibi adesse precatus,
haec tandem responsa dedit: 'Quod perdite amare
audis me, domina, illicitum si forsan amorem
audis, non ullam fateor me perdite amare;
nec sic ipse etiam a quoquam peramarier opto,
50   praecipue a domina. Scis rebus me omnibus unum
praefecisse ducem, seclusa coniuge tantum.
Anne igitur legisque meae dominique mei sim
proditor? Ah Stygias potius detrudar ad umbras,
esca vel alitibus media intumulatus arena
55   mittar!' Et haec dicens dominam thalamumque reliquit.
Illa autem, ut sese illusam et spe funditus omni
deiectam vidit, tamquam qui fulminis ictu
percutitur, primum stupefacta immotaque paulum

messages and to return with a response. "Go," she said, "and tell young Joseph to come here, if he is not busy and if the business of my lord does not prevent it." The woman quickly went off to do as she was bidden. Soon thereafter, the handsome Joseph dutifully appeared. When he entered alone, youthful Iempsar blushed and 30 bade him stand next to her. Then, with trembling heart and voice, she said, "Dear youth, dearer to me than my very eyes, will you answer your mistress truly, whatever she should ask?"

"I will answer truly," he replied. "Could I deceive my masters? Ask whatever you wish." "I hear, young man, that you are deeply 35 in love. If this be true, hide nothing from me, not even if I should be the woman you deeply love. For, to speak truly, I love you deeply too. You must not be cruel to me in my love, nor I to you. Come, give me your hand. Whatever the truth may be, I will re- 40 ward you with an abundance of gold." So speaking, she kissed him on the lips.

He blushed and then recalled the angelic messenger who had come to him in the well when he was a child, warning him not to be led astray by any foreign gods or any sinful or unjust desire. 45 Silently praying for God's help, he finally responded thus: "My lady, as regards your hearing that I am desperately in love, and that perhaps it is some forbidden love, I insist that I am in love with no one. Nor should I wish anyone to love me in that way, especially 50 my mistress. You know that my lord has placed me in charge of all his belongings, with the exception of his wife. Should I then be- tray my own laws and my master? Rather might I be thrown to the Stygian shades or, a pray of birds, lie unburied in the sand!" 55 So speaking he left his lady and her bedchamber. For her part, when she perceived that she had been deceived and fully disap- pointed in her hopes, she seemed thunderstruck and for a time

125

constitit; inde, imo ducens suspiria corde
60   astringensque manus, sese resupina cubili
stravit, inops animi desertaque sanguine pallens.
    At malus haec summo tecti de culmine daemon
aspiciens, ave deposita, se rursus anilem
vertit in Iphiclen, miseramque revisit Iempsar,
65   atque ait: 'O, quinam casus te, nata, malignus
insequitur? Quid cor cecidit? Quid pallor in ore est?
Ah ne animum assuetum, ne te ipsam desere, nata.
En adsum auxilio nutrix tua: pone timorem.
Respice me.' Audito nutricis nomine, paulum
70   erexit sese in cubitum; tum lumina torquens,
'O nutrix, quondam nutrix, nunc dira noverca,
occidisti,' inquit, 'miseram me: nec puer ille
perdite amat, nec se (quod longe est peius) amari
sustinet, aut ullis precibus donisve movetur.
75   Proieci memet, genus, et decus omne pudore
foedavi amisso, fractae spes, foedera rupi
coniugii. Tu causa mali, tu criminis huius
principium. Quid restat ad haec, nisi cetera ferro
conficere et meritam hanc animam demittere ad Orcum?'
80   Cui dictis falsa Iphicle respondet amaris:
'Heu, mulier rerum ignara et male conscia amorum,
quid mirum, puer insuetus plenusque pudore,
ceu virgo intacta, ad primos si expavit amoris
aggressus, de te dubius metuensque pericli?
85   Non ita res tractanda fuit. Nec tu tamen omnem
spem depone; rudem puerum nam rursus adibo,
arguam, et ignarum, quae sint facienda, docebo.
Tu tantum triduo exspecta: lux quarta benignum
sidus habet, miseros sidus quod spectat amantes
90   coniungitque. Sub hoc Hymenaeus sidere primum
natus et ipse puer Venere enitente Cupido.'

remained dumbfounded and motionless. Then, sighing from the
depths of her heart, she wrung her hands and, blanching, threw   60
herself back upon her bed in utter despair.

But the evil demon watched her from atop a roof, and having
shed his avian disguise, he transformed himself once again into
the old woman Iphicle and went again to see mournful Iempsar.
"What untoward thing has befallen you, child? Why do you look   65
so crestfallen and so pale? Do not lose heart or abandon yourself.
Look! Your old nurse is here to help. Don't be afraid. Look at me."
Hearing the name of her nurse, Iempsar slowly raised herself in   70
her bed, and looking at her, spoke thus: "O nurse, or rather my
former nurse, now a baneful stepmother, you have destroyed me in
my sorrow, for the youth is not desperately in love with me—and
what is far worse—he will not allow me to love him and cannot be
moved by any gifts or entreaties. I threw myself at him, besmirch-   75
ing my family and all my honor, having lost all shame and hope
and having broken my marriage vows. You are the cause of this
harm and the initiator of this crime. What else is there for me to
do than to take my own life and commit my deserving soul to the
hell?"

To whom the false Iphicle responded with these bitter words: 80
"Foolish woman, ignorant in the ways of love! What wonder
if, like an untouched virgin, this bashful and inexperienced boy
should doubt you and fear danger, taking flight at the first on-
slaughts of love? That is not how to proceed in these matters. Nor   85
should you give up hope. I will go once more to this innocent boy,
and talk to him and show him, in his innocence, what is to be
done. Only wait for three days. The fourth day is under an auspi-
cious star which shines down upon sad lovers and unites them. It   90
was under this star that Hymenaeus was first born, as was Cupid
himself from the laboring Venus.

His dictis sese paulum solatur Iempsar
erexitque cadentem animum. 'Meliora ferant dii,
vade,' ait, 'interea sacras venerabimur aras,
95   fundemusque preces, et amica vocabimus astra.'
     Ergo, ubi luce nova rutilum Sol aureus orbem
implevit, visura deos sese ornat Iempsar,
pulchra auro, spectanda ostro, spectanda pyropo,
sed forma spectanda magis, proprioque decore;
100   quam matrum numerosa cohors comitatur euntem,
nec non et famulis praeses formosus Ioseph,
lumina deiectus dominaeque suique misertus,
it comes. Ipse tamen sanctas procedere ad aras
patronam putat, ut commissi criminis oret
105   exposcatque deos veniam et deponat amorem.
Contra autem illa rogat divosque et sidera cuncta
ut faveant votis et sint in amore secundi.
Haec eadem celebrat demens et luce sequenti
atque alia, donisque etiam maioribus aras
110   accumulat, pecudumque fibras rimatur et exta.
Verum, ubi quarta dies rediit, Solque igneus orbi
illuxit, 'Lux sancta,' inquit, 'lux optima, salve,
sidera vos, salvete, quibus coniungere amantes
est amor et sobolem mundo servare perennem.'
115   Tum puerum acciri carum iubet. Ocius ille,
nulla timens et iam dominae securus amorum,
advenit. Illa itidem sperans fore prospera cuncta,
nutricis decepta dolis, ut vidit amatum
in manibus puerum, 'Meus es, meus,' inquit, 'et ipsa
120   sum tua: quid prohibet ne nos iungamur amantes?
Iste torus communis erit: ne gaudia differ,
neu sortem contemne tuam.' Tum pallia captat
et trahit ad sese puerum. Stupet ille pudorem
in domina amissum, tandemque his vocibus infit:

At these words, Iempsar gradually consoled herself and lifted her spirits. "May the gods be more auspicious," she said. "Come. In the meantime, we will go to the sacred altars and pray and call upon the propitious stars."

And so, on the next day, when the golden sun had filled its flaming orb, Iempsar dressed herself to visit the altars of the gods. She was resplendent in gold and bronze and purple robes, but most resplendent in her own beauty and native bearing. As she went, she was accompanied by an abundant train of matrons. With downturned eyes the handsome Joseph, who was in charge of the household, accompanied her as well, sad for his mistress and himself. He supposed that she was going to the sacred altars, having set aside her love, to beg and implore the gods to forgive her for the sin she had committed. Instead, she besought the gods and all the stars to second a lover's prayers. Then she foolishly celebrated the same rites on the next two days as well, loading the altars with still greater gifts, as she examined the guts and entrails of sheep. When the fourth day had come and the fiery sun shone down upon the earth, she said, "Hail to you, sacred day, best of all days, and you stars that love to join lovers, bestowing perennial generations upon the world." Then she summoned the dear youth, who came promptly, suspecting nothing and unconcerned about his mistress's amorous ambitions. She meanwhile, deceived by her nurse's tricks, hoped that her ambitions would be realized. When she perceived that the beloved youth was within her grasp, she said, "Now you are mine, mine! And I am yours! What is to stop us from uniting in love? Let us share this bed. Don't defer pleasure or spurn your destiny." Then she grabbed at his cloak and pulled him toward her. Astounded to find his mistress so shameless, he

95

100

105

110

115

120

125 'Quis furor aut quaenam mala mens, olim inclita coniunx
Fetifari, nunc haec suadet te talia posse
moliri? Certe Eumenidum nunc te una sororum
exagitat; nam, quam reris, non est tua nutrix
Iphicle, sed de Stygiis emissa tenebris

130 Dirarum una, dolis quae te decepit et astu.
Illa eadem me aggressa malis conatibus ausa est,
sed vetuit tentare Deus. Vidi ipse retrorsum
cedentem, et formam mentitam, et fumida novi
sulphura, nidoremque atrum post terga relictum.'

135 Talia dictabat puer. At post ostia daemon
qui stabat clausos magno conamine postes
impulit, intravitque ferox, et lumine torvus
Tartaream effudit vocem, qua terruit omnes:
'En ego mentita Iphicle, en sum una sororum

140 Eumenidum, una e Stygiis emissa tenebris!
Nunc faxo experiare.' Sinuque cita eripit anguem
pestiferum, qui secreta sub veste latebat,
in puerumque iacit. Custos caelestis at illum
reppulit atque omnes conatus fecit inanes.

145 At coluber, sibi ut in puerum sublata potestas,
in miseram insidias omnes molitur Iempsar,
perque solum tacite irrepens ventremque retorquens
lubricus, in vestem insinuans se illabitur; inde
interiora petens et viscera cuncta pererrans,

150 Tartareum virus iaculatur ad intima cordis.
     His monstris puer interea pavefactus, amictus
immemor aufugit seque in sua tecta recepit.
Quem virgo ut fugisse videt, utque acre venenum
sensit, in insanum subito conversa furorem,

155 clamorem immensum tollit, quo ipsa atria et omnis
intremuit domus et timuit vicinia tota,
non secus ac si Vulcanus penetralia cuncta

finally spoke: "What madness or malignity, once honorable wife of 125
Potiphar, compels you to attempt such things? Surely one of the
Furies has driven you to this, for Iphicle, your nurse, is not whom
you believe her to be, but rather one of the dire sisters sent forth
from the Stygian shades, deceiving you with trickery and wiles. 130
She even dared to approach me with her base plots, but God
would not allow it. With my own eyes I saw her fall back and I
recognized her disguise and the smell of smoky sulfur and the
black soot that she left behind her."

Such were the youth's words. But the demon, who stood before 135
the entrance to the room, pushed open the closed doors with great
effort. Entering ferally and wild-eyed, he emitted these hellish
words that frightened everyone: "Am I then disguised as Iphicle?
Am I one of the Furies, sent forth from the Stygian shades? Now 140
I will prove it to you!" Forthwith the creature produced the pestif-
erous serpent that was hidden in a fold of its garment, and threw
it at the young man. But a celestial guardian repelled it, rendering
all attacks useless. When the serpent saw that it had no more 145
power against the youth, it turned all its wiles upon the distraught
Iempsar. Crawling silently upon the ground, and coiling its slip-
pery belly, it easily insinuated itself into the folds of Iempsar's gar-
ment. As it explored her body and wandered inside of her, it filled 150
her heart with its tartareous poison.

Frightened by such marvels, the youth forgot his cloak as he
fled, hiding himself in his chamber. When the young woman, feel-
ing the poison within her, saw that he had fled, she suddenly be-
gan to rage, creating a great noise that shook the chamber, the 155
whole house and the entire neighborhood, as when a volcano

involvat caeloque furens incendia iactet:
'Currite io, matres, scelus atque audite nefandum
160 mancipii Hebraei, qui nunc — proh Iuppiter! — ausus
Fetifari est magni sacrum violare cubile
vimque inferre mihi, nisi nutrix tempore in ipso
prompta tulisset opem et sceleratum veste relicta
eiecisset. Io fugitivum apprehendite, servi,
165 ite citi, properate, viarum claudite cuncta
effugia, et domini scelus hoc afferte sub aures.'
Talia vociferans misera effundebat Iempsar.
Omnia quae falsa Iphicle confirmat et auget,
dignum morte fore, hoc sceleris qui admittere tantum
170 audeat, exacuitque animos. Clam deinde recedit
nulli visa, et avi similis se immiscuit atris
nubibus, et Stygias sedes atque impia Ditis
regna petit, laetoque refert crudelia facta.
    Interea miser a servis comprensus Ioseph
175 ducitur, et nemo est qui, dicere multa volentem,
auscultare velit miserum, non Fetifar ipse,
quem iam res audita acri compleverat ira,
non tamen ut morti damnet; sed turre sub ima,
carceris esse locus miseris ubi sueverat, illum
180 intrudi iubet et vigili custode teneri,
tantum olyra vili, limoso et flumine pasci.
    At iuveni caelestis erat custodia maior
aliger aetherius, summo qui missus ab axe
carceris intrarat portas, ubi proxima terras
185 nox omnes caecis tenebris obduxit et umbra:
ergo, alias puero notus, solatur amico
ore illum, firmatque animum, tollitque timorem
luce nova, excussa noctisque et carceris umbra.
Omnia quae postquam custos Aegyptius alta
190 prospexit de turre, 'Deus, deus,' inquit, 'in illa

132

churns up its entrails and in its fury spews fire into the heavens.
"Come here, women," she cried, "and hear of the outrage at-
tempted by this Hebrew slave, who now, by Jupiter, dared to vio-   160
late the sacred marriage bed of great Potiphar and would have
raped me had not my nurse rushed to my aid and thrown out the
wretch, who left only his cloak! You slaves, quickly! Catch the   165
runaway! Close off all paths of escape and go inform my master
of this crime." Such were the words that the wretched Iempsar
shouted. All of which were confirmed by the false Iphicle, who
added that any man who would attempt so great a crime was wor-
thy of death. Thus she goaded their spirits. Then, when no one   170
was looking, she secretly retreated and, in the form of a bird, as-
cended into the dark clouds, seeking the Stygian abodes and the
impious realms of Dis, to whom she eagerly reported her cruel
deeds.

Meanwhile poor Joseph was caught and lead away by servants,
and though he greatly wished to speak, no one was willing to lis-   175
ten, surely not Potiphar, who had already been greatly angered by
the rumor of what had happened. He ordered that Joseph, rather
than being condemned to death, should be incarcerated in the
bowls of the prison, the usual dwelling of wretches, to be kept   180
under constant vigil and fed stale bread and filthy water.

But Joseph had a more powerful guardian, an ethereal angel,
dispatched from the height of heaven, who entered the doors of
the prison when night covered all the earth with impenetrable   185
darkness and shadow. Having been previously known to the youth,
the angel consoled him with friendly conversation, encouraging
him and removing fear, as his miraculous light chased away the
darkness of night and prison. When the Egyptian jailor beheld all
of this from atop the tower, he said, "A god, surely, dwells within   190

luce viget. Nosco splendorem et verba notavi.
Nec deus est illic, nisi et huius criminis insons
est puer. Insontem servabit Iuppiter aequus.'
Ex illo custos iuvenem veneratur Ioseph,
195   et pascit meliore cibo quam dura iubebant
Fetifari mandata, et duri carceris omne
tollit onus ferrumque pedum, visitque frequenter
solaturque, et saepe in caelum educit apertum.
    Iamque quater binos Phoebe compleverat orbes,
200   cum duo, quorum alter pincerna Pharaonis, alter
pistor erat regis, prae suspicione veneni
in Cerere inventi, conclusi carcere eodem
cum puero Isacide fuerant. Hi tempore parvo
post utrique una viderunt somnia nocte,
205   somnia quae mox mane novo dum mutua versant,
ignari quid portendant monstrentve futurum,
sollicitis stabant animis. Quod pulcher Ioseph
conspiciens, 'Quidnam, iuvenes, tam pectore tristes
vos hoc Sole novo video?' 'Nos somnia facta
210   nocte hac sollicitos reddunt, quae exponere nemo est
qui sciat hic,' dixere. Quibus sic pulcher Ioseph:
'Somnia vos narrate, Deus dignoscere forsan
illa dabit.' 'Dicemus,' ait pincerna, 'priorque
ipse edam. Nam vitis erat pulcherrima ternis
215   laeta propaginibus: gemmas turgescere primum
palmitibus, mox et flores exire videbam,
post flores gravidis uvas pendere racemis;
quos ego maturos manibus premere ipse videbar,
vinaque diffundens pateris spumantia plenis
220   regi larga dabam, solito rex more bibebat.'
    Cui puer interpres: 'Quidnam tua somnia monstrent,
expediam. Vitam illa tuam pulcherrima vitis
ostendit: gemmae, flores, uvaeque secutae

134

this light. I recognize him in his splendor and in his words. And surely God would not be here with the youth unless he were innocent of this crime. For Jupiter, in his justice, protects the innocent." From that moment forth the jailor held young Joseph in great reverence, giving him better fare than was required by the 195 harsh mandates of Potiphar, and removing his fetters and all the burdens of incarceration. Frequently he visited the youth, consoling him and often taking him outside.

Already Phoebe had eight times completed her course when two men, one the Pharaoh's butler, the other his baker, were sus- 200 pected of having poisoned his food and were sent to the same prison as the descendant of Isaac. Shortly thereafter, on the same night, these two men had dreams that, the following day, they 205 discussed with one another. Ignorant of what future events these dreams might indicate or portend, the two men were very uneasy in their souls. When the handsome Joseph saw this, he said, "Why, young men, do I find you so sad this morning?" "We have both had dreams this past night," they said, "that have worried us. 210 And there is no one who knows how to explain them." The handsome Joseph replied, "Tell me your dreams. Perhaps god will grant me the power to understand them." And the butler said, "We will tell you. I will go first. I saw a beautiful vine fertile in threefold shoots. At first I saw buds sprout from its branches, then flowers 215 grow and, after the flowers, grapes hang down from the heavy vines. I seemed to press the ripe fruit with my hands. Then I filled the cups with frothing wine and gave them in abundance to the 220 Pharaoh, who drank them according to his custom."

Joseph responded thus: "I will tell you the meaning of your dream. The beautiful vine represents your life. The buds, flowers

sunt fructus quos tu peperisti temporis huius
225   curriculo; dabitur merces, et honoribus ipse
restituere tuis, et pristina pocula regi
consueto de more dabis; terna illa propago
tres luces, quibus haec veniant tibi prospera, monstrant.
Tu vero, cum te carum gratumque Pharaon
230   accipiet, nostri, si qua huius gratia facti est,
sis memor, immeritumque isto dic carcere claudi.'

    Tum pistor simul ac vidit dicta omnia recte
congruere, 'Ipse etiam,' dixit, 'mea somnia pandam.
Nam capiti imposita ipse meo tria plena canistra
235   spectabam: duo farinae inferiora, supremum
omni opere plenum, omni illo pistoria quod scit
ars facere et nostrum ingenium; sed cuncta volucres
exesse et secum latas deferre per auras.'

    Cui bonus interpres: 'Divum est novisse futura,
240   falli hominum est. Dicam quidnam tamen augurer ipse
his super. Illa, quibus vidisti plena canistra,
sunt opera et vitae fructus: duo prima, ubi simplex
farina est, vitae monstrant duo tempora prima,
in quibus et simplex vita et sincera peracta est;
245   summum opere infido plenum est, et fraude, dolisque
omnibus, ingenium quae aut ars pistoris iniqui
extudisse valet, quae sunt iam cognita regi.
At merces horum meritorum et praemia foedae
sunt volucres, corvi immundi, milvique rapaces,
250   vulturiique, caput qui effossaque lumina pascent
in cruce suspenso; tribus haec ventura diebus
terna canistra notant. Tamen haec me fallere possunt,
si tu animo possis mutari; nam et Deus ipse
saepe solet mutare mala et convertere fata.'

255   Talia tractabant iuvenes. Et tertia iam lux
orbi invecta aderat, cum custos carcere aperto

and grapes that followed are the fruits that you have earned in the span of your life. The time will come when a pardon will restore 225 your honors and once more, as is your custom, you will serve pure drafts of wine to the Pharaoh. The threefold branches mean that in three days these prosperous events will befall you. I ask only that, if you feel any gratitude for this interpretation, you remember me when you are restored to the Pharaoh's favor, and tell him 230 that I am unjustly confined in this prison."

When the baker perceived that all of these words seemed to make sense, he said, "Now I will tell my dream as well. I seemed to be carrying three full baskets on my head. The two lower ones 235 held flour, while the top one contained every sort of pastry known to the baker's art and to my own skill. But all of it was devoured by birds who carried it off into the broad heavens."

To him the honest interpreter said, "It is the part of the gods to know the future and the part of men to err. But I shall tell you 240 what I think is the meaning of your dream. What you saw filling the baskets were the deeds and fruits of your life. The first two indicate, with their simple flour, the first two ages of your life, which you led simply and honestly. The third, however, is filled 245 with faithless works, fraud and all manner of deceit that your own skill or the art of a dishonest baker can achieve. And these are already known to the Pharaoh. The prize and recompense of these merits are the vile birds, filthy crows and rapacious bitterns and 250 vultures that pluck at a man's head and eyes as he hangs on the cross. The three baskets signal that this will happen in three days. But perhaps they deceive me; perhaps you can change your heart. For God himself often changes and converts bad destinies."

These were the words that the young men exchanged. And 255 already the third day had arrived, when the jailor opened the

pincernam insontem, noxa poenaque solutum
declarat; miserum regis decreta severi
pistorem damnare cruci. De carcere uterque
260   ducitur haud aequa sorte et longe impare fato:
hic ad tigna, ille ad regem stipatus ovantum
et laetus clamore virum et clangore tubarum.
    Vertitur interea ter Solis cursus in alta
solstitia, atque novum mundo portaverat annum,
265   forteque rex dulcem prona iam nocte quietem
ducebat, Deus ex alto cum somnia in illum
immisit, miranda adeo, ut cedente sopore
attonitus rex magnum aliquid portendere visa
crederet. Ergo omnes iubet e regione vocari
270   Chaldaea Aegyptoque, quibus cognoscere cursus
metirique vias caeli, et momenta minuta
astrorum, casusque hominum, et praenosse futura est
cura audax, nec non magicis qui incumbere sacris
consuevere, et qui ex adytis oracula divum
275   consulere, et caesarum oviumque boumque per exta
rimari secreta solent, qui noscere flammae,
qui fluitantis aquae motus, qui iungere arenae
fatalem numerum, et cognoscere fulminis iras,
quique vias servare avium, et dignoscere cantus,
280   denique divini rerum quicumque vocantur.
Quorum ingens numerus magni plena atria regis
intrarant, alii longis capita alta tiaris
induti, ast alii spectandi cornibus hirtis,
auratis alii strophiis: longissima mento
285   cunctis pendet barba, ipso stat pallor in ore.
Quos simul ac ad se rex alta a sede vocavit,
somnia visa docet primum, dein munera larga
promittit largosque illis proponit honores,
somni qui interpres fuerit; noctemque diemque

doors of the prison and declared that the butler was innocent and would be spared any harm or penalty, but that the decrees of the harsh Pharaoh had condemned the pitiable baker to death. Both men were led from the prison, but to a very different lot and destiny. One was destined to be crucified, the other, at the Pharaoh's side, to be gladdened by the noise of cheering men and roar of trumpets. 260

In the meantime, the Sun's course had brought a new year to the world and was reaching the summer solstice for the third time: it once happened that, as the Pharaoh was enjoying sweet sleep as night was ending, God sent down to him from on high a dream so marvelous that, when the Pharaoh waked, he believed it to have great import. Therefore he summoned from every part of Chaldea and Egypt those whose bold care it was to know and measure the courses and paths of heaven and the minutest movements of the stars, as well as to predict the destinies of men and things to come. Also he summoned those who busied themselves with magical rites or who, in the temples, consulted the oracles of the gods or studied the hidden entrails of slaughtered sheep and cows, or gauged the motions of fire and flowing water. Also those who computed the fated number of the sands or understood the rage of thunder, or could interpret the flight and song of birds: in short all those who were called prophets. A great gathering of such entered the swelling palace of the great Pharaoh. Some of them wore a tall crown on the top of their heads. Others were conspicuous for shaggy horns, others for golden chaplets. All of them had long beards and pale complexions. As soon as the Pharaoh, seated upon a lofty throne, bade them approach, he first told them what he had dreamed and then promised generous gifts and honors to anyone who could interpret his dream. He instructed that they would 265 270 275 280 285

290 responso tempus statuit. Sed noxque diesque
venerat et nemo apparet qui somnia regi
enodare queat: nulli sua sidera, nulli
ars magica aut quaesita aris oracula prosunt,
non artes aliae, non barbae, altaeque tiarae.
295 Ergo hinc irasci, et tristis maerere Pharaon,
nec quemquam audire, at solo in conclave latere.
    Hic regis pincerna, memor quae in carcere Ioseph
fecit et ipsorum quam verus somnia vates
exposuit, subito regem petit atque ita fatur:
300 'Peccavi, rex magne, tibi quae in carcere vidi
non referens. Nam scis, ut mecum pistor iniquus
carcere damnatus fuerit sub turre magistri
militiae, eunuchi. Forte illo carcere eodem
Fetifari puer Hebraeus, puto crimine falso,
305 missus erat. Duo nos (ita suasi) somnia quaedam,
nocte habita a nobis, iuveni narramus. At ille,
divino quodam afflatu visa omnia nobis
exponens, "Mihi te," dixit, "lux tertia ab isto
carcere deducet, multis et honoribus auctum
310 restituet primo officio; te, pistor inique,
lux eadem in cruce consistet, te immunda volucrum
agmina depascent, corvi, milvique rapaces,
vulturiique, nisi ipse animum convertere possis
in melius: sic namque Deus mutatur et ipse."
315 Omnia quae evenisse vides. Tua somnia certe
hic puer exponet: magnum nam numen in illo est.'
    Auditis rex laetus ait: 'Vade ocius ergo,
duc puerum, et nostro iussu de carcere solve.'
Ille celer mandata facit, puerumque parumper
320 ornat, detondetque comas, vestemque ministrat;
tum regi adducit timidum. Rex omnia lustrat
in puero: sibi cuncta placent; sic denique fatur:

have a day and a night to divine its meaning. But a day and a night   290
passed and no one came forth able to explain the Pharaoh's dream.
They derived no help from their stars or magic arts or the oracles
they sought upon the altars, no help from any other art, nor from
their beards and lofty chaplets. And so the Pharaoh, angered and   295
sad, would hear no one, but hid himself in his solitary study.

Then the butler, remembering what Joseph had done in jail,
how he had revealed himself to be a true interpreter of their
dreams, immediately sought out the Pharaoh and spoke thus: "I   300
have sinned, great king, in not acquainting you with what I saw in
jail. For you know that the wayward baker was condemned with
me to prison, in the tower of your eunuch, the master of the army.
As it happened, Potiphar's Hebrew slave was sent there as well,
having been falsely accused, as I think. I persuaded the youth to   305
hear some dreams that the baker and I had had one night. At
which the youth, through some divine inspiration, explained all
our visions, saying, 'In three days you will be freed from prison,
and restored to your previous position with great recompense. But   310
you, evil baker, will be condemned, on the very same day, to death
and devoured by filthy flocks of birds — crows, vultures and rapa-
cious kites unless you change your ways for the better, for only
thus can God himself change toward you.' All of this, as you   315
know, came to pass. Surely the young man will be able to explain
your dreams, for there is a divine intelligence in him."

Delighted by this report, the Pharaoh said, "Go, then, at once.
Release the youth from prison upon my orders and bring him to
me." The butler quickly did as instructed, hastily adorning the   320
youth, cutting his hair and providing him with suitable clothes.
Then he led him, all timid, into the Pharaoh's presence. The Pha-
raoh looked the young man over thoroughly and was pleased with

'Te, puer, hi dicunt exponere somnia: numquid
vera ferunt?' Ast ille: 'Deus, rex optime, solus
325 somnia nosse potest, et si cui maximus ille
hoc dederit. Potero ipse meo pro rege precari
atque orare Deum: forsan dabit, omnia quando
quae regum sunt, ipse solet curare deum rex
atque hominum.' Dein paulum animoque et mente moratus,
330 'Nunc' inquit, 'rex magne, mihi tua somnia pande.'
     'Fluminis ad ripas Nili stare ipse videbar,'
rex ait, 'et septem ecce boves e flumine pulchrae
exire et late errantes per litora pasci
florentes herbas, loton, medamque virentem,
335 et suavem mynianta; quibus pinguescere, quantum
plena solet sacras quae ducitur hostia ad aras.
Vix oculos verti, ecce aliae per litora septem
deformes aegraeque, quibus vix pellis adhaeret
ossibus, apparere boves, quae carice summa
340 vix pastae et dura paliuro et sentibus hirtis,
corpora macra, suis nervis vix ducta, trahebant.
Obstupui: nam dira fames atque ardor edendi
improbus exegit tantum has, ut pinguia septem
corpora prima boum congressae tota vorarent.
345 Mox iterum dulcis me habuit sopor alter, et ecce
rursus septem uno spicae consurgere culmo,
pulchraeque gravidaeque et onustae pondere multo.
Mox septem prodire aliae tenuesque et inanes
exili e stipula, scabraque urigine tostae,
350 quae succum et decus omne aliarum absumere visae
sunt mihi. Miratus, postquam sopor ille recessit,
somnia proposui multis; sed dicere nemo
scit sensum et portenta horum; te si manet ista
gloria, si te unum e tantis haec somnia poscunt,
355 toto animo laetare, puer: te fama sequetur

what he saw. Finally he said, "These men say that you can inter-
pret dreams. Do they speak the truth?" To which Joseph replied,
"Great king, dreams may be interpreted by God alone and by him   325
to whom God has given this power. I can pray to him and beseech
him, in behalf of my sovereign, to bestow it upon me. And per-
haps he will, for all that concerns kings also concerns the king of
gods and men." For a moment he prayed and then he said, "Now   330
tell me your dreams, great king."

    "I seemed to stand on the banks of the river Nile," the Pharaoh
said, "and, lo, seven beautiful cows emerged from the river and
wandered far and wide along the banks, grazing on such flowering
plants as the lotus, green meda and sweet mynians. Whereat they   335
grew fat like victims led to the sacred altars. But scarcely had I
turned my glance when I saw seven other cows upon the shore,
these misshapen and sick, the flesh hardly sticking to their bones.   340
They had scarcely fed themselves upon the tips of sedge and sharp
thorns and shaggy brambles and scarcely had strength to carry
their emaciated bodies. I was astonished. For dire hunger and an
unsightly compulsion to eat drove them to gather and devour the
large bodies of the seven fat kine. Then once again I resumed my   345
peaceful sleep, and, lo, once again seven stalks arose from a single
plant and they were beautiful and full and weighed down with
their heavy grain. Then I saw seven other stalks appear, weak and
hollow, upon a thin stem, seared with scaly smut, and it seemed to   350
me as though they consumed the sap and loveliness of the seven
healthy stalks. As sleep left me, I was amazed and told my dreams
to many people, but none of them was able to discern their sense
or import. If, however, the glory of divining my dreams is des-
tined to be yours, if, out of all these interpreters, my dreams await
your interpretation alone, then rejoice with all your heart, young   355

perpetua et tantis a me ditabere donis,
ut te non videat maiorem Aegyptia tellus.'
    Cui iuvenis: 'Rex magne, Deus te diligit: ipse est
somnia qui immisit, nec quae illa intelligat esse ars
360   ulla potest, quae auctore Deo non utitur; unde
nec vates potuere tui, quibus omnibus est ars
absque Deo. Primum septem felicibus annis
largius undantem solito maioreque Nilum
flumine rumpentem ripas, secumque trahentem
365   felicem limum fecundaeque aequora arenae,
fortunata nimis tellus Aegyptia cernet.
His annis tantum messis, tantum uberis illa
colliget, ut non sufficiant solita horrea messi.
Ubertatem istam pingues nimiumque nitentes
370   monstravere boves septem, quae e flumine Nili
exivere, herbas pingues per litora pastae.
Hanc etiam et spicae septem, quas pondere onustas
laetasque plenasque uno consurgere culmo
vidisti, pariter monstrant: nam somnia visa
375   non duo sunt, sed idem ostendunt. Nunc porrige mentem,
optime rex: nam septem annos, qui deinde sequentur,
infelix steriles durosque Aegyptus habebit.
Ipse intra ripas demisso flumine Nilus
curret iners, supraque caput limumque feracem
380   non tollet; sicca arebunt arva omnia, sicca
solstitia, et nulli descendent montibus amnes,
consueti pluviarum amnes sub sidere Cancri,
Aethiopum populis nec hiems aestiva redibit.
Agricola infelix nullo versabit aratro
385   arva, nec arenti mandabit semina terrae,
sed miseros edet annona cogente iuvencos.
Haec septem docuere boves per litora siccae,
deformes, macraeque, quibus vix ossibus haerens

man! For you will win eternal fame and I will shower you with
abundant gifts, such that Egypt will not behold a greater man
than you.

The young man replied thus, "Great Pharaoh: God loves you.
He himself has sent these dreams to you, and there is no art that
can divine their meaning that does not rely upon God, their au-
thor. And so it was that the meaning of your dreams was obscure
to all of your soothsayers, who are versed in art, but do not know
God. At first, the land of Egypt, abundantly favored for seven
auspicious years, will see the Nile overflow its banks with a broader
and larger flood than is its wont, bringing with it fertile mud and
washing the earth in its nourishing sands. During these years, the
ripe harvest will garner so much crop that the usual granaries will
not be able to contain it all. The seven fat and splendid kine that
emerged from the waters of the Nile and that fed upon the ripe
grasses of its banks reveal this abundance. The same is proved by
the seven stalks that you saw arise, weighed down, fertile and full
upon a single stalk. For in fact, the dreams do not reveal two dif-
ferent things, but rather one and the same thing. Now take heed,
great king, for seven years will follow that will be sere and hard
for unfortunate Egypt. The Nile itself, with a meager stream, will
run listlessly among its banks, without raising its head and its
fertile mud above them. All the fields will be arid and parched.
The summers will be dry and no rivers will descend from the
mountains, those rivers of rain that always appear under the sign
of Cancer. Nor will summer storms relieve the Ethiopians. The
forlorn farmer will ply his plow over no field or commit any seed
to the parching earth, but rather, compelled by poverty, will con-
sume his pitiable cattle. Such is the lesson of the seven kine that

360

365

370

375

380

385

pellis erat; haec septem illae rubigine tostae,
390 squallentesque situ spicae, et sine pondere turpes
ostendunt: duplici exemplo te commonet ipse,
qui novit ventura, Deus, quo tu quoque solers
commoveare magis damnoque occurrere possis.
Quod facere ut valeas, si me fortasse requiris,
395 sic habeas: maiora para primum horrea, et omne
quod superat segetum his septem felicibus annis
coge illic, servaque vigil; dein multa talenta
aurique argentique in fruges undique emendas
impende, annorum quantum penuria septem
400 exposcet ventura fami campisque serendis.'
    Talia narrabat iuvenis, quae singula mente
rex volvit tacita, tandem et sic voce profatur:
'Hoc certe deus in puero: nec talia dici
absque deo potuere, nec illi Aegyptia tellus
405 aut Chaldaea videt similem.' Tum amplectitur illum,
laetitia illacrimans: 'Post me tota ista secundum
te aspiciet regio, Servatoremque vocabit.'
Sic ait, et chlamydem gemmis ostroque nitentem
ferre dat, atque auri torquem circumdare collo.
410 Mos erat, ut gemma caelata insignis et auro
anulus, antiquo regum de more vocatus
regius, a nullo, nisi rege Pharaone, posset
gestari, aut siquis foret ipso ab rege secundus:
hunc sibi rex digito detractum imponit Ioseph,
415 quo populus post regem illum sciat esse secundum.
Praeterea, qua se sollemnibus ipse diebus
invectum mula populis urbique solebat
ceu quendam monstrare deum, sic mandat et ipsum
urbe vehi mulaque eadem procedere Ioseph,
420 praeclamante tuba: 'Regi inclinate secundo
quisque caput sanctoque novos conspergite flores

stood upon the shore, dry, misshapen and drawn, the skin scarcely
clinging to their bones. And such is the lesson of the seven stalks   390
ravaged by rust, sordid with infection, baseless and deformed.
God, who sees into the future, has warned you through this two-
fold example, that you might be especially industrious and ward
off any harm. If perchance you would ask me what you can do, I
would give this advice: First, make ready larger granaries. There   395
gather together and vigilantly guard all the excess harvests of the
seven abundant years. Then spend many talents of silver and gold
to buy, where you can, as many crops as the approaching seven
years of hunger will demand, in order to fend off famine and to   400
sow crops."

Such were the young man's instructions, and the Pharaoh si-
lently considered each of them in his mind. Finally he spoke thus:
"Surely God dwells within this youth. Surely such words could
not come from him without God's willing it. Nor in Egypt or   405
Chaldea is there anyone like him." Weeping tears of joy, he em-
braced the young man. "This entire land will esteem you second
only to me, and look upon you as its savior." So speaking, he be-
stowed on Joseph as a gift a cloak that gleamed with jewels and
finery and he placed a gold pendant about his neck. It was an an-   410
cient custom that a certain ring, time out of mind called royal, and
conspicuous for its gold and curved gemstones, was to be worn
only by the Pharaoh or by his second in command. Taking this
from his finger, the Pharaoh gave it to Joseph, that the populace   415
might know that he was second only to the Pharaoh himself. Fur-
thermore, on certain holy days, the Pharaoh was carried around
on a mule to be shown, like some god, to the people and to the
city. Thus he commanded that Joseph too be carried around the
city by the same route on a mule, while a trumpet preceded him,   420
declaring: "Let each man bow his head before your second king
and bestrew this sacred savior of men with newly blown flowers,

Servatori hominum, solus qui somnia regis
exposuit, qui plena deo praecordia gestat.'
Talibus ornatus donis et honoribus auctus
425   Isacides iuvenis, cuncto acclamante senatu,
praeficitur toti Aegypto. Qui sedulus omni
ingenio curaque in primis horrea ubique
magna parat, mox frugum ingentibus undique acervis
collectis, partim terra Memphitide natis,
430   partim emptis aliunde, implet stipatque, nec ullum
dat rebus spatium: regionem lustrat, equorum
comminuit numerum atque hominum. Dii cuncta secundant.
    Urbs erat Helipolis, Solis de nomine dicta,
cuius rex, idem et templi Phoebique sacerdos
435   supremus, natam formae et virtutis habebat
insignem, quam saepe deus consultus Apollo
dixerat haud ulli indigenae thalamo esse locandam:
coniugium externum fato maiore parari,
quo genus et clari tollantur in astra nepotes.
440   Ergo istaec iuvenem monstrare oracula Ioseph
censet et antistes templi et rex ipse Pharaon.
Quocirca, cum iam septem felicibus annis
Aegypto in tota ubertas atque omnia ubique
laeta forent, placuit regi dignis hymenaeis
445   et thalamo Isacidem iuvenem sociare iugali,
laetitiamque augere, diesque inducere festos.
    Ergo haec per ludos, dum per convivia laeta
ducuntur, septem fecundi messibus anni
iam finem, ubertasque omnis, iam copia habebat.
450   Iamque, pererratis Geminis per sidera Cancri,
Sol altos ducebat equos, Aegyptia cum gens
miratur Nili nulla incrementa videri,
sed purum et nulla permixtum flumen arena
ipsum inter ripas tristi procedere cursu.

for he alone could explain the dreams of Pharaoh and he alone has
a heart filled with divinity." And so, endowed with great gifts and
enhanced rank and acclaimed by the entire senate, the youthful   425
scion of Isaac was placed in charge of all of Egypt. First, with great
intelligence and care, he readied all the great granaries, and filled
them with crops, massed together, some of them from the Mem-
phian land itself, others purchased abroad. He was not idle for   430
a moment: he traveled throughout the kingdom, wearing out an
array of horses and men. And the gods helped him in all his en-
deavors.

There was a city named Heliopolis, taking its name from the
sun. Its ruler, who was also the supreme priest of Phoebus and his   435
temple, had a daughter eminent in beauty and virtue. Often the
oracle of Apollo had declared that she was not to be placed in the
bridal chamber of any local man of that region. Rather a higher
destiny awaited her, marriage to a foreigner through whom her
race and illustrious progeny would be exalted to the stars. That   440
the man foretold by the oracles was none other than young Joseph
was clear to the priest of the temple and to the Pharaoh himself.
And so, during the seven fertile years, when there was abundance
throughout Egypt and everything flourished, the Pharaoh decided   445
to join the scion of Isaac in marriage through a worthy ceremony
and to increase the common happiness by decreeing several feast
days.

And so, amid games and happy banquets, the seven years of
fertile harvests came to an end, and with them abundance and
wealth. Already the stars of the Gemini had come and gone and   450
now the Sun had driven his horses high across the stars of Cancer,
when the Egyptian people were astonished to observe that there
was no rise in the Nile, that its pure stream, mixed with no sand,

455 Iam tellus, fecunda prius, nunc aret hiatque
usta siti, nec spes Cereris promittitur ulla.
Semina quin etiam siqua immittuntur in arvis,
aut nullos edunt foetus, aut protinus omne
enatum foedae vitio rubiginis aret,
460 aut abit in lolium infelix fluidumve papaver.
Vivitur ex annis lapsis retroque coacto
foenore, quod primo sterili vix sufficit anno.
Verum ubi dira fames homines se vertere ad herbas
et pecus immeritum atque immunda animalia adegit,
465 regem urbes et rura adeunt, subsidia poscunt.
Rex ad praefectum cunctos dimittit Ioseph,
Servatorem hominum. Populis hinc horrea aperta
et iustum indictum pretium: gaza undique et omnes
congestae portantur opes, aeraria regis
470 complentur; nec adhuc quartus se verterat annus.
Quid facerent miserae gentes? Sola arva supersunt
quae vendant, si emptorem habeant; nam solus Ioseph
esse potest pro rege emptor. Ergo ille rogatur
arva emat, et miseris det opem, nec pacta recuset.
475 Reddituum cuiusque agri quintam dare regi
promittunt: sic pacta ineunt, sic foedera firmant.
    Interea, externas quoniam penuria terras
haec eadem affligit, populos it fama per omnes
Aegyptum sat frumenti quod vendat habere.
480 Ergo et Sichenus natos affatur Iacob:
'Cur non Aegyptum, nati, cur regna beata
non petitis? Cur non nobis alimenta paratis?
Num perimat nos ista fames?' Mandata capessunt
natorum deni; fratrum natu ultimus astat.
485   Ut vero Aegyptum petiere et Osirida terram,
frumentis praefectum adeunt et supplice cultu
aere dato frumenta rogant. Cognovit Ioseph

flowed miserably between its banks. Despite its former fertility, 455
the earth was now parched and burned and the ground cracked
with thirst, and there was no hope of harvesting grain. If any seeds
were placed in the fields, either nothing grew or, if anything did, it
was immediately ravaged by base rust, or came up as useless tares 460
or swaying poppies. All one could live on were the gains of earlier
years, which scarcely sufficed for the first year of hardship. Truly,
when dire famine had reduced men to eating grass, unworthy live-
stock and baser animals, the cities and the countryside both came 465
to the Pharaoh, seeking help. He sent all of them to Joseph, his
prefect, the savior of men, who opened the granaries to them at a
fair price. From all sides, wealth and treasure accrued and the royal
fisc overflowed. But when the fourth year had not yet past, what 470
were the miserable people to do? All that they had left to sell were
their fields, if only they could find a buyer. For Joseph alone could
purchase them in the king's name. Thus he was asked to buy the
fields and help the poor, without refusing any agreement. Promis- 475
ing to give the king the fifth part of their profit from any field,
they accepted the terms and signed a compact.

Meanwhile, because this same famine afflicted other lands as
well, news spread to all peoples that in Egypt they had enough
grain to sell. And so Jacob of Sichen addressed his sons thus: 480
"Why do you not go to the wealthy kingdom of Egypt and bring
back food. Will this famine kill us?" Ten of his sons did his bid-
ding, while the youngest remained at his side.

And so, entering into Egypt and the land of Osiris, they ap- 485
proached the prefect of the granaries and, as suppliants, asked if
they might purchase some grain. Through God's guidance, Joseph

germanos, statuente Deo, non cognitus illis;
praeteritique memor, quamvis iniuria multum
490 facta potest, tamen et patris fratrisque misertus
Beniamin, his etiam parcit; tum fatur ad illos:
'Unde et quinam hominum ad nostras acceditis oras?'
Illi autem: 'E terra Canaam, de sanguine Iacob,
venimus huc cogente fame, quae plurima perdit
495 Samariam. Domus est nobis plenissima, primus
est pater, undeni nati, parvique nepotes,
pastorumque manus, vernarum est plurima turma.
Venimus ergo ad te, nobis alimenta rogantes,
ne pereat gens tanta: tibi iusta aera dabuntur.
500 Nec nos immemores erimus. Pater optimus urbem
ipse regit Sichen, pastor cui milia multa
sunt pecudum: quovis pretio da vivere tantum.'
His verbis quamquam frater commotus et aegre
abstinuit lacrimis, ficto tamen omnia vultu
505 dissimulans, 'Quid verba mihi datis?' inquit, 'an ipse
eludar? Nisi me os fallit vultusque loquentum,
exploratores puto. Cur mandata paterna
non geritis? Cur nec frater huc venit et alter?'
Ast illi: 'Minime. Tales ne rere precamur.
510 Per patrem patrisque Deum iuramus, adire
nos iussit nos dira fames; natu ultimus unus
cum patre Benïamin adolescens restitit et spes
solamenque senis; nos, qui sufferre laborem
possumus atque moras longarum auferre viarum,
515 venimus orantes vitam, mandata putantes
nulla opus esse istuc ferri. Miserere precantum,
et miserere patris, pueri miserere relicti,
parvorumque, potest pietas si in te ulla, nepotum.'
    Hic lacrimas vix continuit, convertit et ora,
520 toto animo et vultu multum commotus, Ioseph.

recognized his brothers without their recognizing him. Though he
well remembered what they had done to him, and though earlier
injury can still have great force, nevertheless, taking pity on his   490
father and on his brother Benjamin, he pardoned the others as
well, and he addressed them thus: "Who are you and whence do
you come into our land?"

To which they responded: "From the land of Canaan and of the
blood of Jacob, we have come hither driven by the great famine
that has laid waste to Samaria. Our household is numerous. First   495
there is our father, then his eleven sons and young grandchildren,
as well as a cohort of shepherds and an abundance of servants.
And so we have come to you seeking food, so that our large family
should not perish. We will pay a good price. Nor will we forget   500
your benefaction. Our dear father is the leader of Sichen, a pastor
with an abundant flock. Name your price and only let us live."

Though their brother was moved by these words and struggled
to withhold his tears, still he dissimulated his feelings under a de-   505
ceptive countenance. "Would you cozen me, then? Do I look like
a fool? Unless your language and appearance deceive me, I think
you are spies. Why have you not brought your father's orders?
Why has the other brother not come here as well?"

And they replied, "We are not spies at all. You must not think
that, we pray you. By our father, and by the god of our father, we   510
swear that we were compelled to come here by dire famine. Only
our youngest brother, Benjamin, remained with his father, the
hope and solace of his old age. We, who can bear the burden and
withstand the length of the journey, have come begging for our   515
lives. We did not think it necessary to come bearing orders. Pity
us as we beseech you. Pity our father and the young brother we
left behind. Pity—if there is any piety in you—his grandchil-
dren."

Hardly able to contain his tears, Joseph turned away from
them. In his face and his entire soul he was greatly moved. He   520

Inde ait: 'Est mihi firma, viri, sententia menti,
frater ut huc alius veniat. Vestrum hic erit unus
obses: vos alii ad patrem frumenta feretis
interea. Haud aliter (per regem et numina iuro)
525 ulla potest vobis cedendi hinc esse potestas,
neu faciem spectare meam, aut audire loquentem.
Consulite et ternis dentur responsa diebus.'
Sic ait et custode dato victuque remittit.
  Illi, inter sese postquam diversa locuti
530 viderunt praefecti animum, praestare putarunt
ferri multa domum frumenta, loco obsidis unum
dimitti, properare alios, iterumque reverti
emptum alias fruges, alium et conducere fratrem.
Ergo nominibus scriptis sors ducitur, obses
535 extrahitur Simeon. Et iam lux tertia mundo
clara aderat, responsa petit praefectus, at ipsi
enarrant decreta. Igitur frumenta parari
imperat accepto pretio; clam deinde ministros
admonet ut summis saccis aera omnia ponant,
540 quod fuerit cuiusque datum. Custodibus obses
traditur; at fratres oneratis tergora asellis
Aegyptum et multo fratrem maerore relinquunt,
Samariamque petunt. Quo postquam denique ventum est,
et genitor numero natorum unum abfore vidit,
545 clamat: 'Ubi Simeon meus est? Cur cernere natum
non datur? Estne aeger?' 'Minime, pater,' inquit Iudas,
'sed valet: Aegypti est obses tellure relictus,
dum rursus redeamus et hinc ducamus et istum
Beniamin. Nam qui frumentum vendidit, ut nos
550 vidit, vir magnus et ab ipso rege secundus,
quaesivit multa a nobis, numquid pater esset,
an frater nobis alius; quae cum omnia recte
diximus, "Vos certe istas venistis ad oras

spoke thus: "I am determined, men, that the other brother should come here. He will remain here as security while you bring the grain back to your father. By the Pharaoh and the gods I swear that there is no other means of your going hence, of looking upon my face or hearing me speak. Consider this and give me your response in three days." So speaking, he sent them back with an escort and provisions.

After they had severally discussed the matter and understood the prefect's thoughts, they deemed it best to carry home an abundance of grain: they would leave one of their number behind as security while the rest hastened away, returning to purchase more grain and to bring their brother. Therefore they wrote down all their names and drew lots: it was decided that Simeon should remain as security. On the third day, when the prefect sought their response, they told him what they had decided. And so, having received their payment, he ordered that the grain be prepared. Secretly he bade his servants place in each sack the coins that had paid for it. After Simeon was handed over to the guards as security, the brothers loaded the backs of their mules and then, with a heavy heart, they left Egypt and their brother behind as they headed for Samaria. When at last they arrived, their father saw that one of them was missing. "Where is Simeon? Why can't I see my son? Is he unwell?" "Not at all, father," Judas said. "He is well. He was left behind as security in the land of Egypt, until we return, bringing Benjamin with us. For when the great man, who is second only to the king and is in charge of selling the grain, beheld us, he asked many things about our family, whether our father still lived and whether we had another brother. When we had answered all of these questions truthfully, he said that we had surely

525

530

535

540

545

550

exploratores," inquit, "mandata paterna
555 cur non huc geritis? Cur non alium quoque fratrem
huc duxistis?" Ad haec respondimus omnia. Tandem
summa fuit frumenta dari, nos deinde reverti,
adduci puerum, interea obses detur et unus
e nobis maneat. "Per regem et numina caeli
560 iuro," inquit, "nec vos aliter frumenta feretis
posthac, nec me audire umquam, aut spectare licebit.'"
      At pater, haec postquam audivit, 'Proh Iuppiter,' inquit,
'estne adeo infelix alius pater? Occidit unus
natorum, est obses alius, subducitur alter
565 cum reliquis, simul ut cuncti moriantur, et ipse
exspectem, ferat haec nostras crudelis ad aures
nuntius: o prius hanc miseram, dii, demite vitam.'
Talia fundebat lacrimans. Circum undique nati
solantur tam adversa bonos non numina habere.
570 Mox, ubi depositis solverunt vincula saccis,
in summis aes omne datum pretiumque repostum
inveniunt. Stupuere omnes, sed tristis Iacob,
'Hoc deerat, nati, hoc,' inquit, 'quod funditus omnem
spem raperet. Nam si vobis Aegyptia ad arva
575 sit reditus, qui vos primum vir maximus ille
exploratores dixit, nunc nomina furum
imponet, causam inquirens qua perdere possit.
Nempe ego Benïamin puerum, spem patris et unum
solamen, non huic tradam fidamque periclo.
580 Vos alii, si fata urgent divumque voluntas,
ite rei fidei promissae: ego, quicquid apud me est
aurique argentique dabo, quo vos redimatis
et fratrem et, si fors aderit, frumenta feratis.'
      Quem contra illacrimans iuvenis sic fatur Iudas:
585 'Care pater, nos primum audi, dein consule nobis,
atque tibi. Nam quo pacto continget adire

come as spies and he demanded to know why we had not brought 555
your orders along with our other brother. We responded to each
question and finally it was resolved that we should be given the
grain, and that we should return with Benjamin, while one of us
remained there as security. For he swore, by the Pharaoh and the
gods in heaven, that this was the only way we would receive grain 560
hereafter, or be allowed to hear or see him."

When he heard this, Jacob cried out: "By Jupiter, is there any
father as unhappy as I am? One of my sons is dead. Another is
held hostage, while a third must go away with all the remaining 565
brothers so that all may die at once, while I wait for a cruel mes-
senger to bring me the news. Before that happens, you gods, end
my miserable life." So he spoke, weeping. His sons stood all
around him and consoled him, saying that God was not so ma-
levolent toward good men. Then, as soon as they undid the cords 570
of the sacks that lay about, they found therein all the coins they
had paid, restored in full. They were astonished. But sad Jacob
spoke thus, "This was the only thing still needed to deprive me of
all hope. For if you return to the Egyptian fields, the powerful 575
man who called you spies will now call you thieves, seeking a rea-
son to put you to death. Verily I will not send Benjamin, my hope
and only consolation, and place him in such peril. The rest of you 580
can go, if fate and divine will impel you, guilty as you are of having
made this promise. I shall give you all the gold and silver I have to
ransom your brother and, if possible, to purchase more grain."

Weeping, young Judas responded thus: "Dear father, first hear 585
me out and then consider what is best for us and you. For how

157

illum hominem, qui iuravit per regia sceptra,
per superos, nisi Beniamin duxerimus ipsum,
ille quidem nec nos, nec qui est in carcere fratrem
590 dimittet, faciemve eius spectare licebit?
Verum, ut de nobis sint dura et tristia quaeque,
vos miseri quonam pacto vivetis, et unde
tanta domus? Capiti, quaeso, pater optime, tandem
fide meo: puer iste omnes servabit, et ipsum
595 te patrem. Mihi praeterea duo pignora cara
sunt nati, tu illos (concedo) interfice, si quid
adversi puero eveniat: depone timorem,
atque omnem defende domum. Quod pondera saccis
sint aeris posita in nostris, iussisse ministris
600 id dominum certum est, incertum fraude dolove,
an pietate magis. Nos certe audivimus illum
insignem virtute omni, nos vidimus illum
nobiscum flevisse famem atque incommoda nostra,
dum teque et parvum fratrem parvosque nepotes
605 commemoramus. Age, o genitor, ne tempora differ
neu plures innecte moras.' Et talia dicens
adiecit lacrimas. Victus pater, 'Ibitis ergo,'
tandem ait, 'et puerum, et regionis dona feretis,
stactenque, et lacrimas terebinthi, et roscida mella,
610 et gummi, et liquidam styracem, et amygdala amara.
Insuper et duplex pretium portabitis: et quod
inventum fuit in saccis et quod data poscent
frumenta. Interea faciemus sacra parentum
nostrorum nostrique Deo, quo cuncta secundus
615 dirigat et servos caelo prospectet ab alto.'
 Postera Phoebeos currus Aurora vehebat,
cum pater et nati sacris de more peractis
cuncta viae opportuna parant, et munera, et ipsum
Beniamin; quem iam genitor complexus euntem

shall we even speak with that man who swore, by the royal scepter and by the gods, that unless we brought Benjamin himself, he would not release us or our imprisoned brother, or even allow us to see his face. Truly, if things should go hard and ill for your remaining sons, how will you and this great house survive? I implore you, dearest father, trust me: Benjamin will save us all, and even you, his father. I have besides two dear sureties, my sons. Kill them — I allow it! — if something should happen to the boy. Set fear aside and protect this entire house. It is certain that the prefect ordered his ministers to place those coins in the sacks, but it is uncertain whether he did so through fraud and treachery or rather through kindness. Surely we have heard that he is a man conspicuous in every virtue, and we saw him taking pity on our hunger and adversity, when we spoke of you, our young brother and our little children. Come, father. Do not postpone our going or create any delays." So speaking, he began to weep. His father was won over. "You will go then," he said at last, "and you will bring the boy together with the varied gifts of this region, oil of myrrh and tears of terebinth, dewy honey and aromatic gum, as well as liquid styrax and bitter almonds. Beyond that you will bring twice the required money to cover both what was found in the sacks and what the new grain will cost. In the meantime, I will offer unto God the rites of my fathers and myself, so that he, propitiated, may guide your steps and look down upon us, his servants, from high heaven."

When the next dawn brought forth the chariots of Apollo, Jacob and his sons performed the accustomed rites and made the necessary preparations for the trip, readying their gifts and Benjamin as well. As the boy was about to leave, his father embraced

590

595

600

605

610

615

620   et lacrimans, 'I, care puer, felicibus,' inquit,
        'auspiciis: si te rediturum fata reservant,
        vitam oro.' Lacrimae vetuerunt dicere plura.
        Tum simul et reliquos natos complectitur omnes
        commendatque Deo. Ast illi, bona verba precati,
625   durum iter et longum capiunt, camposque relinquunt
        Samariae, Solymenque sacram. Iam consita Idumes
        praetereunt palmeta, Gerar, et Tartara vasta
        Syrbotis, tandemque vident Aegyptia regna,
        optatamque petunt Memphim. Quos laetus Ioseph
630   suscipit atque una fratrem de carcere solvit.
            Ut vero admissis coram data copia fandi,
        sic Ruben: 'Hinc postquam discessimus, optime princeps,
        venimus ad genitorem, illi tua maxima iussa
        narramus, fratrem duci te velle minorem
635   Beniamin huc istum; tum saccis ordine apertis
        — res mira! — in summis pretium atque aes omne quod ante
        exhibitum fuerat se offert: quis miserit et cur
        ignotum est, Deus est testis. Verum, ut pater istaec
        audivit viditque, imo suspiria corde
640   traxit, et "Heu, nati," dixit, "male numen amicum
        nos aliquod nunc insequitur, fortuna recessit
        illa bona: e bis sex natis amisimus unum,
        in vinclis alius longinquis exsulat oris,
        nunc spes et miserae solamen dulce senectae,
645   Beniamin, abduci petitur, vos rursus abitis
        nescio quo et vereor furum ne nomine eatis,
        omnes ut tandem fato pereatis ab uno."
        Nos contra miserum solari: "Fide parentum,
        nostrum et fide Deo, genitor: iustissimus ille,
650   ille vir est, regio quem tota Aegyptia dicit
        Servatorem hominum, sanctumque piumque fatetur
        et colit: hinc nihil adversum durumque timendum est."

him and, weeping, said, "Go, dear child, under good auspices. If   620
fate grants that you return, I hope to live." Tears prohibited him
from saying more. Then he embraced his other sons and com-
mended them to God. After praying auspiciously, they undertook
the long and hard journey. Having left behind the fields of Sa-   625
maria and sacred Jerusalem, they soon passed the planted palm
groves of Edom, Gerar and the vast tartareous regions of Syrbos,
until at last they saw the realms of Egypt and sought the wished-
for Memphis. Joseph received them gladly and at the same time he   630
released their brother from jail.

Once they were admitted into his presence and given leave to
speak, Ruben thus began: "After leaving you, great prince, we went
to our father and related your high commands, that you wished
that our youngest brother, Benjamin here, be brought to you.   635
Then, as bidden, we opened the sacks and, astonishingly, at the
top of each was revealed the entire amount that we had just paid
for them. Who had placed it there, and why, was unknown, as
God is our witness. When our father heard and saw these things,
he sighed from the depths of his heart and said, 'My sons, a bad   640
spirit for some reason now pursues us, and fortune has withdrawn
its former favors. Out of twelve sons we have lost one. Another,
bound, has been exiled in a distant land. And now the one hope
and solace of my sad old age, Benjamin, is to be led away. You   645
yourselves are returning I know not where, and I fear that you will
be accused of theft and, at last, all of you will perish by the same
fate.'

In response, I tried to console him. 'Have faith, father, in our
god and the god of our ancestors: for the man is just whom all of   650
Egypt has proclaimed the savior of men, whom it honors and calls
holy and pious. Thus there is no reason to fear some harsh or

His victus cessit tandem. "Vos ibitis ergo,
et ducetis," ait, "puerum, atque haec parva feretis
655   munera, quae regio fert haec: stactam, et terebinthi
resinam, et liquidam styracem, et amygdala amara,
mellaque; dein duplex pretium portabitis: et quod
impositum fuerat saccis et quod data poscent
frumenta; et demum iusto natumque patremque
660   commendate illi, pueri miserescat et huius,
atque senis natos nimium miserescat amantis."
    Talia dictabat iuvenis, cum lumina princeps
vix lacrimis cohibens tali est sic ore locutus:
'Este bonis animis, iuvenes, ego munera grata
665   accipio regionis et hunc, qui adductus ab omni
suspicione puer vos omni a fraude piabit.
Ite, et fessa via foeda et sudore lavate
membra, viri; mox luce bona discumbite mecum.'
    Haec princeps. Famulorum alii in conclave lavacrum,
670   vasa alii mensasque parant. Haec inter Ioseph
multa super regno et populis disponit alendis.
Dein redit ad fratres magnamque educit in aulam,
regales ubi monstrat opes, vasa aurea signis
caelata, argentumque abacis, stratosque tapetas,
675   nec non parietibus circum pendentia longis
aulaea, intextis auro et bombyce figuris,
quas dicas spirare. Illic, divina secutus
iussa, Abraham puerum in silvas ducebat Isaac
mactandum; puer ilignis onerabat asellum
680   fascibus, ipse pyram genitor vittasque parabat.
Ille idem dextram vicina in parte levabat
crudelemque ensem; demissus lumina Isaac
et flexis genibus ferituro colla parenti
praebebat; caeli demissus ab axe vetabat
685   nuntius, et dextram sublatam ensemque tenebat.

adverse treatment.' Finally he relented. 'You will go then,' he said,
'and take the boy, and take these meager gifts that our land brings   655
forth, oil of myrrh and resin of terebinth, liquid styrax and bitter
almonds and honey too. And you will bring twice the amount,
both for what was placed in the sacks and what is needed to pur-
chase more grain. Finally commend to that just man both the son
and the father, and may he take pity on the boy, and may he take   660
pity on an old man who loves his sons excessively.'"

So the young man spoke. At which the prince, hardly with-
holding his tears, spoke thus: 'Be of good cheer, young men.
Gladly do I accept the gifts of your land and this boy who absolves   665
you of all suspicion and all fraud. Go and wash your bodies, wea-
ried from the voyage and covered in dirt and sweat. Then, on this
auspicious day, you will dine with me."

So spoke the prince. At which some of the servants prepared
the baths in a private room, while others prepared cups and meals.   670
In the meantime Joseph tended to the kingdom and the task of
feeding the population. Then he returned to his brothers and led
them into a great hall, where he showed them royal wealth and
golden vases chased with images, silverware for the tables and car-
pets strewn everywhere, as well as tapestries hanging upon large
walls, their figures woven with gold and silk, such that you would   675
say they breathed. Depicted therein was Abraham who, in obedi-
ence to divine command, led Isaac into the forest to be slaugh-
tered. The boy loaded an ass with bundles of oak wood, while his
father, with his own hand, prepared the fire and sacred chap-   680
lets. In an adjoining scene, he raised his hand and the cruel knife,
while the kneeling Isaac looked down and offered his neck for his
father to cut; but an angel sent down from heaven stopped him,
and stayed his raised hand and knife.   685

Parte alia, fratrem fugiens, tendebat Iacob
in patris antiquas sedes cognataque regna,
Euphratem Tigrimque inter; patruelibus inde
virginibus hauribat aquas; tum pastor ad undas
690   Euphratis, dum pascit oves per litora Laban,
Rachelem vocat et dulces decantat amores.
    Talia dum laeti spectant Israele nati
spemque aliquam sibi promittunt, tum magnus Ioseph,
'Iam genio libemus,' ait, 'date flumina palmis,
695   vos famuli.' Tum sede altus discumbit eburna.

MORTE PRAEVENTUS, HOC ITEM, QUOD SERO INCEPERAT,
ABSOLVERE NON POTUIT.

In another scene, Jacob, fleeing from his brother, hastened to
the ancient seat of his ancestral dwelling, between the Euphrates
and the Tigris. There he drank water offered to him by maidens
who were his cousins. Then, as Jacob the shepherd was tending
the flocks of Laban by the waters of the Euphrates, he called forth   690
Rachel and sang his sweet love.

As the sons of Jacob beheld these works with delight, they be-
gan to take hope, and Joseph said: "Let us now pour a libation for
our guardian spirits. Bring us water, servants, to wash our hands."   695
Then he sat down upon a lofty ivory throne.

THE AUTHOR WAS PREVENTED BY DEATH FROM
COMPLETING THIS POEM, WHICH HE HAD
UNDERTAKEN IN OLD AGE.

CARMINUM LIBER

BOOK OF POEMS

: I :

Alcon sive
de cura canum venaticorum

Assiduis nuper fessus venatibus Alcon,
falleret aestivi ut fastidia longa diei,
Corvini qua se nemora excelsissima caelo
extollunt, viridi dum captat frigus in umbra,
5   dicitur ad iuvenem senior sic fatus Acastum:
'Me segnes artus defectaque viribus aetas,
et superare iuga, et latis discurrere campis,
et torquere leves hastas, et ferre pharetram,
nate, vetant, densaque indagine cingere silvas;
10   sed te pulvereum cursu transmittere campum,
ferre aestum frigusque, leves agitare Molossos,
et pinguem silvis ad tecta avertere praedam
nunc decet, ac validam pro me exercere iuventam.
En arcum, pharetramque tibi, iaculumque relinquo.
15   Ne tamen usque adeo plenae confide pharetrae,
ut postrema canum interea tibi cura putetur,
quorum ope veloces poteris praevertere cervos,
aut aprum ingentem aut fulvum superare leonem.
Ergo age, et haec tecum semper mandata reserva.
20   Principio, ut generosa canum tibi copia numquam
desit quae certam valeat promittere praedam,
elige degeneri nequaquam semine natos,
sed quos assidue silvis exercuit altis
et labor indomitus, saevarum et praeda ferarum.
25   Nec vero parvi formamque genusque putaris:
nam neque sunt animi neque mores omnibus iidem,
et variae diversa canum dant semina gentes.
Nam rabidas si forte feras te cura tenebit

: I :

Alcon, or
On the care of hunting dogs

Weary of his assiduous hunts, Alcon recently decided to beguile
the lengthy tedium of a summer's day in the land where the lofty
forests of Mount Corvinus rise toward heaven. Enjoying the cool-
ness of the green shade, the older man supposedly addressed   5
young Acastus thus: Son, my wearied body and old age, deficient
as it is in strength, prohibit me now from climbing hills and run-
ning through broad fields, from hurling swift javelins or sporting a
quiver or ensnaring beasts in the deep woods. For you, however,   10
this is the time to tear through the dusty fields, enduring heat and
cold. It is time to impel the swift Molossian hounds and carry off
the fatted game from the woods into the house, as you exert your
strenuous youth in my place. Here, then: I leave you my bow, my
quiver and my spear. But do not place so much trust in the full   15
quiver that you pay scant attention to your hounds. For with their
help you will be able to overtake swift stags, to vanquish the huge
boar and the tawny lion. Come then, remember what I will tell
you.

   First, always have an abundance of hounds of good stock that   20
can assure you of catching worthy prey: never choose those that
are born of a degenerate seed, but rather choose those sharpened
by strenuous exercise in the deep woods and by chasing after fierce
beasts. Do not suppose that the appearance and race of hounds   25
are unimportant. Not all of them have the same drive and char-
acter, and the varied races of dogs bring forth varied offspring. If,
for instance, you mean to hunt after raging beasts and expose

venari, et variis caput obiectare periclis,
30   Spartana de stirpe tibi, de stirpe Molossa
quaere canes; Libycos illis, acresque Britannos,
Pannoniosque truces, et amantes proelia Celtas
adde, nec Hircanos, nec Seras sperne feroces.
Si vero parvos lepores, capreasque fugaces
35   malueris, timidosque sequi per devia cervos,
delige Paeonios agiles volucresque Sicambros.
Quod tibi si latebras abstrusaque lustra ferarum
rimari certa catulorum indagine cordi est,
hunc usum implebit Perses et Saxogelonus.
40   At genere ex omni praesertim delige quae nec
corpore sit gracili, nec densis aspera villis;
sed sublime caput, vivacia lumina, et amplam
ostentet frontem, atque ingentes oris hiatus;
cui rectae surgant aures, cui pinguia terga
45   dividat in caudam descendens spina reflexam;
sint armi lati, sint aeque pectora lata,
lata alvus, quae sic costis adiungitur imis,
ut tamen in spatium sensim se colligat artum,
ut cava diductis succedant ilia costis,
50   excipiant siccis quas fortia crura lacertis;
ima pedum parva signent vestigia planta.
Huic similem coniunge marem, cum vere tepenti
tangit amor genus omne avium, genus omne ferarum.
Bis quinos tamen ante dies accensus uterque
55   in venerem, venere abstineant: sic plena libido
acrius exstimulat, viresque ad semina praebet.
Hinc maior soboles, atque inde valentior exit.
Quae simul ac sese numeroso protulit ortu,
selige de multis quos iam praestare videbis
60   pondere, vel stipulae flammis include sonoris
ingentem turbam: prolis nam mota periclo

yourself to danger, seek dogs of the Spartan and Molossian race. 30
Add to these Lybian hounds as well as sharp Britannic and fierce
Pannonian hounds and Celtic hounds that love battle. Nor should
you reject the ferocious hounds of Hircania and China. But if you
prefer to hunt small rabbits, fleeing goats and timid deer through 35
their twisting paths, then choose agile Paeonian and swift Sicam-
brian hounds. And if you want to root about in coverts and hid-
den dens with the help of a reliable cordon of whelps, then Persian
and Saxogelonian hounds will answer to your need.

But the most important thing in breeding is to chose from the 40
entire race the bitch whose body is not too slender and whose coat
is not too dense: rather you should seek one whose head is held
high, with darting eyes, a broad forehead and a wide bite. Her ears
should stand up straight and the spine should run down her mus- 45
cular back, ending in a backward-curving tail. Her shoulders
should be broad, as well as her chest. Her broad belly should be
joined in such a way to the lower ribs that it gradually constricts
itself into a narrow space, that the thin loins should descend from 50
the chiseled ribs and themselves be followed by muscular limbs,
whose tracks should be marked by narrow paws. You should mate
her with a male of similar build, and when, in the warmth of
spring, love strikes every race of bird and beast, both of them,
though eager to mate, should abstain from doing so for ten days. 55
For then the full force of desire will urge them more forcefully,
giving strength to their seed and producing larger and stronger
offspring.

As soon as they have brought forth abundant brood, choose
from the numerous litter the heaviest puppies, or place the whole 60
lot of them in a pen surrounded by roaring flames. Moved by the

egregiam sobolem melioraque pignora mater
ocius eripiet flammis, et inertia linquet.
    Illi igitur plenis ubi nondum viribus aetas
65   accessit, parvum cursu conscendere collem
et molli assuescant sese demittere clivo.
Hinc tenerum leporem vel crura infirma trahentem
sectari capream et facilem percurrere campum
incipiat, verbisque viri parere vocantis.
70   Nulla mora est, ipsis crescant cum viribus anni.
Iam potes hos tuto densis committere silvis,
perque altos montes, per lustra agitare ferarum,
nec minus aut apro aut fulvo obiectare leoni,
si modo vel capreas vel dedignabere cervos.
75   Immodicis tum parce cibis, tum cursibus illos
exerce assiduis, ac mox ad tecta reverti,
vincla pati discant: ita demum libera colla,
cum res ipsa ususque vocat, maiore feruntur
impete, nec cursum remoratur pigra sagina.
80   Hactenus in silvis catulos eduximus altis:
nunc quae morbosis sit cura adhibenda, docebo.
Insomnes cum forte canes occulta fatigat
vimque adimit febris, putrem tunc ore cruorem
ferro emitte levi; dein Bacchica dona rosarum
85   misce oleo, et rapidis simul omnia concoque flammis,
terque die inserto demitte in guttura cornu.
Si vero nimio venandi langueat aestu,
butyro lapathi succos, Siculique Lyaei
pocula, contusumque piper, simul omnia miscens,
90   prosubige ut, certi simul ac commixta liquoris
praetulerint speciem, cupido canis hauriat ore.
Immodicam sed forte sitim dum sublevat atro
fonte canis, lymphae mala si successit hirudo,
cimiceo suffire canem nidore licebit,

danger to her offspring, the mother will first seize from the flames
the noblest scion and the most precious, and will leave the lesser
brood behind. Before they have grown to their full strength, they   65
should be accustomed to climb up small hills and descend a
modest incline. Thereafter let them begin to chase the timid hare
and the goat that drags its weak legs, to run through untrammeled
fields and heed the words of their master when he calls. There is   70
no delaying: let their years grow with their strength. Soon you can
be confident in sending them out into the dense woods or letting
them loose on mountain tops and in the dens of beasts. You can
even unleash them against the boar or lion if you disdain goats
and stags. Then feed them sparingly and run them hard. They   75
should learn to return swiftly home and yield to the leash. Then
loosen the collar as need or custom requires and they will run with
greater force, and no sluggish meat will stay their course.

   Thus far we have exercised the whelps in the deep woods. Now   80
I shall teach you how to care for sick hounds, when some hidden
fever happens to weary the sleepless creatures and steal their
strength. First, wipe the base froth from their mouths with the
light touch of a knife; then mix the gifts of Bacchus with essence
of rose and boil both at a high flame. Three times a day, pour it   85
down their throats, using a tube. But if they languish from an ex-
cessive love of hunting, mix butter with the juice of sorrel, drafts
of Sicilian wine and ground pepper and knead it, so that, as soon   90
as the ingredients start to resemble a familiar liquid, the dog will
consume it with an eager mouth. But perhaps if the dog happens
to slake his great thirst from a dirty pond, infested by some evil
worm, breathe on the dog with an exhalation of crushed bedbugs,

95   aut oleo ptisanam et spumanti melle subactam
        incoquere, offensoque cani praebere vorandam.
        Aut cum taetra lues (clavos dixere) palatum
        afficiet misere, silvestria sesama, nec non
        Bacchi acidos latices, et chartam sume perustam,
100   atque ammoniaci frustum: dein singula in unum
        confundens, taetrae causam superilline pestis.
        Tum vero ardentes oculos inimica perurit
        cum tabes, crebraeque fluunt a lumine guttae,
        iam frondes sacrae myrti, silvestris et uvae,
105   arentesque rosas diluto concoque Baccho,
        hisque affecta levi citus ablue lumina dextra;
        inde oleum atque ovi niveos immitte liquores.
        Quod si nativo stimulatur coxa dolore,
        lemiulum lapidem (meditem nomine dicunt)
110   urina semel atque iterum demerge recenti;
        cui Bacchi dulces acidosque adiunge liquores,
        quaque latet pestis sumpta circumline penna.
        Ast ubi rupta novo manabit sanguine vena,
        tum murem geminum ac telam pendentis Arachnes
115   ure foco, cineremque undanti impone cruori;
        proderit et ferro candenti tangere vulnus.
        Obstructo vero lotii cum forte meatu
        vexari aspicies catulum, Cerealia dona
        obiice, lacte prius simae perfusa capellae.
120   At contra venis si quando sanguis apertis
        pro facili urina terram madefecerit atram,
        conveniet lente ferventi lactis aheno
        mollire, et tenues coriandri immittere succos,
        infractumque piper, laticemque undantis olivi,
125   insertoque cani paulatim infundere cornu.
        Quid? Taceam nimio cum decidit ungula cursu?
        Frangere namque iuvat pallentis grana cumini

or you can boil groats lightened with oil and frothing honey, and   95
give it to the ailing hound to devour. But when a cruel ailment—
which some call "clavi" or "warts"—painfully afflicts their palate,
use sesame seeds gathered in the woods, as well as vinegar, burned
paper and a morsel of sal ammoniac. Then mix them all together   100
and smear the ointment over the source of the dire disease. But
when a painful ailment afflicts the dog's burning eyes, and abun-
dant tears flow from them, boil leaves of sacred myrtle and sylvan
grapes, together with dried rose petals in diluted wine. With a   105
light touch, quickly wipe the residue over the afflicted eyes. Then
apply oil and egg whites. And if the hound should have an internal
pain in its hip bone, then steep a Lemiulum stone (which some
call Medis) twice in fresh urine, adding wine and vinegar and ap-   110
ply it with a feather to the afflicted area. And when fresh blood
issues from a broken vein, then place two mice and the web of a
dangling spider in the fire and apply the ashes to the oozing   115
wound. It would also help to cauterize the wound with a burning
iron. If you find that the whelp has trouble passing urine, then
give him grain that has been cooked in the milk a snub-nosed
goat. If, by contrast, a vein has broken and blood rather than urine   120
dampens the dark earth, it will be useful to soften the wound
with a slowly boiling pot of milk, placing therein the tender juice
of coriander, uncrushed pepper corns and olive oil, and gradu-   125
ally inserting it with a tube. And how can I leave out the treat-
ment for a nail that has been lost through excessive running?
You should break grains of pale cumin with your teeth and then

dentibus, admotaque pedem lenire saliva:
incipientque novi subcrescere protinus ungues.
130 Fit quoque ut immundo catulus iuguletur ab oestro:
at tu silvestrem crepitantibus urere rutam
ignibus, et fumo pariter mulcere salubri
disce, dehinc acri perfundere vulnus aceto.
Quin aures etiam muscarum turba molesta
135 impetit usque adeo, mutilatum appareat alte
ut caput: ipse autem venienti occurre periclo,
et prius has nucibus viridique putamine tinge.
Quid cum dura canes inter se proelia miscent,
alter ut alterius percussus dente laboret?
140 Tunc etenim cervi flammae subiecta voraci
ossa teres, oleo subigens frondentis olivae
unguinis in morem, ac vulnus letale perungens,
quamquam etiam possis ramenta inducere ferri.
Namque venenifero serpentis saucius ictu,
145 quo valeat scit sponte sua reperire salubre
gramen, et ipse sibi nullo auxiliante mederi.
Senserit at rabidos ubi morsus, protinus ipse
Idaeam rutae foliis acrique Lyaeo
iunge picem, laesaeque adhibe haec medicamina parti.
150 At mala cum scabies miseros depascitur artus
latrantum, et foede miserabile corpus adurit,
cerussam, abdomenque bovis, resinamque tenacem,
butyrumque recens viridantibus incoque sensim
lentisci foliis, infectaque membra perunge.
155 Sed tunc praecipue sollerti mente cavendum est,
cum rabie accensus nunc hos, nunc impetit illos,
ipsi infensus hero datque insanabile vulnus.
Ergo illum primo valida compesce catena;
inde rosae agrestis radicem pondere saxi
160 contusam vivi fontis consperge liquore,

176

cover the paw in saliva. Soon new nails will start to grow. And it   130
sometimes happens that a puppy is lanced by a foul horsefly.
Learn to boil rustic rue over a crackling fire and then to soften it
with salubrious smoke, then cover the wound with vinegar. For a
taxing swarm of flies can so goad the ears of a dog that its entire   135
head appears to have been mutilated. To prevent this danger from
occurring, anoint the ears before hand with nuts and green stalks.
And what should you do when dogs have been fighting fiercely
among themselves and one has been sorely bitten by the other?
Then smooth the bones of a deer by placing them in the voracious   140
flame and, kneading it with the oil of young olives to form a kind
of unguent, besmear the baleful wound. You can even place therein
shavings of iron. When wounded by the poisonous bite of a ser-
pent, a dog instinctively understands to seek the salubrious grass,   145
by which it can cure itself without your help. But if he receives a
rabid bite, you should immediately mix pitch from Mount Ida
with vinegar and leaves of rue and apply them to the wounded
part. But when the evil mange consumes the miserable limbs of   150
the barking race, basely scoring their pitiable bodies, slowly cook
white lead, cow's tripe, viscous resin and new butter, together with
the green leaves of the mastic tree, and anoint the affected parts.

But you must be especially vigilant when a dog, having con-   155
tracted rabies, attacks others indiscriminately, even his master, and
in his madness delivers an incurable wound. First you must re-
strain him with a strong leash. Then, after you have ground the
root of a wild rose with the weight of a stone, sprinkle it with   160

ut potus speciem lino colata nigranti
praeferat: hac sumpta, revocari ad pristina tradunt
sensa canem, ac posita rabie mitescere rursum.
Sunt qui silvestres ficus adipemque vetustum
165   contundant; hederas alii ferventibus undis
emollire iubent, donec pars una supersit
e tribus, atque ipsis foliis tepidoque liquore
pascere quadrupedem, aurora surgente, furentem.
Nil tandem usque adeo prodest ac prima sub ipsum
170   principium morbi rescindere semina ferro.
Nam qua parte imo coniungi lingua palato
cernitur, et fauces nativo concolor auro
occupat in rabiemque feros agit usque Molossos
vulnificus vermis, suffunditque ora veneno.
175   Quem si quis potuit ferro resecare, potentem
is tanti abstulerit causam stimulumque furoris.
    Quae superant, olim; nunc praedam ad tecta iacentem
ferre monet praesens fugientis temporis hora,
quandoquidem calamos posuit Coridallus acutos,
180   et iam sublustres invectat Luna tenebras.'

: II :

In obitum Marci Antonii Turriani Veronensis
ad Ioannem Baptistam Turrianum fratrem

Etsi egomet tanti casu perculsus amici
    solamen nostris discuperem lacrimis,
ne mea perpetuo manarent lumina fletu,
    pergeret aut tantus urere corda dolor,
5   attamen, ut mi animi valuit concedere amaror,

178

fresh water, so that, strained through a dark cloth, it may acquire
the aspect of a potion. Once he has drunk this, it is said that he
returns to his good senses and, the rabies having subsided, he be-
comes gentle again. There are those who would use wild figs and
aged grease, while others choose to soften ivy in boiling water,   165
until only a third of it remains. And then, with the leaves and
lukewarm water, they feed the raging quadruped at break of day.
Finally, nothing succeeds better than to cut away the seeds of the   170
affliction at the very outset. For at the point where the tongue is
joined to the base of the palate, a wounding worm, similar in color
to raw gold, occupies the dog's palate and can induce rabies even in
Molossian hounds and bathe their mouths in poison. If you can   175
cut away that part with a knife, you will have removed the power-
ful cause and stimulus of this great rage. The rest I will relate
some other time: now the fleeting hour bids us return home with
our felled prey. For Coridallus has set aside his shrill pipe and al-   180
ready the moon brings on the glimmering darkness.

∶ II ∶

*On the death of Marcantonio della Torre, a citizen of Verona,
to his brother, Giovanni Battista della Torre*

Stricken as I am by the loss of my dear friend, I wish that I might
console my own tears, lest a perpetual stream flow from my eyes
and lest this great sorrow continue to consume my heart: still, to   5

istaec maesta tibi carmina persolui,
quo fortasse meis consolarere Camenis,
  si miseros quicquam Musa levare potest,
ac ne tu in lacrimas paulatim totus abires,
10   liquitur ut pluvio tacta pruina Noto.
Quandoquidem cari fato te fratris acerbo est
  rumor in extrema vivere tristitia,
nec iam posse quietis habere aut commoda somni,
  sed cedente die, sed redeunte queri,
15 maerentemque, vagumque, et turpem fletibus ora
  amissum totis quaerere litoribus,
fertur ut Eridani ripas errasse per omnes,
  anxia fraterno funere, Lampetie,
septem quam perhibent somni sine munere noctes,
20   ieiunam septem continuasse dies,
et, quoties longo defessa errore viarum
  umbrosi in ripa concidit Eridani,
'Reddite vos Phaetonta mihi,' clamabat ad undas,
  'o quaecumque sub hoc flumine nympha latet.'
25 Te tamen, ullius si cuiquam morte dolendum est,
  iusta quidem tanti causa doloris habet,
quandoquidem immatura morte tibi omnia frater
  commoda, teque ipsum perdidit, atque tuos:
perdidit hei misero carus tibi frater ademptus,
30   quo tibi non ullus carior alter erat.
Ille amor, ille tuae solamen dulce iuventae,
  ille tuae fuerat spes, columenque domus,
quicum versari semper, quicum esse solebas,
  atque animi arcana dicere consilia,
35 unum mirari atque unum praeponere cunctis,
  ambrosiae e cuius effluere ore lepos.
O nimium miseri nos, et genus aerumnosum,
  deterius quorum est conditione nihil:

the extent that my grieving soul allows, I have composed for you
this sad poem. Perhaps you will find solace in my song, if poetry
has any power to console the bereaved. Thus may you not lose
yourself in tears, like hoarfrost melting under the rainy southern   10
wind.

I have heard that you are living in greatest sorrow at the bitter
death of your dear brother, that you have found no comfort in rest
or sleep as you mourn day and night, wandering, lamenting along   15
the shore, your face sullied with tears, while you seek the one you
lost. It is said that Lampetia wandered as well along the banks of
the Eridanus, distraught at her brother's death. Seven days and   20
seven nights, they say, she fasted without the boon of sleep. And
as often as she lay down on the shady banks of the river, wearied
by her long wanderings, she would cry out, "Bring back my Pha-
eton to me, O waves, or any nymph who dwells within these wa-
ters."

But if the death of any man is worthy of another's tears, then   25
surely this occasion is a just cause for your sorrow. For the un-
timely death of your brother has vanquished you, your family and
all your comforts, that dear brother who was stolen from you and   30
was dearer to you than anyone else. He was the love, the solace of
your sweet youth, the hope and bastion of your house. You were
inseparable from him and used to share with him all the inmost
councils of your heart. Him alone you admired and set before   35
all others. From his mouth flowed ambrosial charm. Alas for us
and for our careworn race, whose misfortune is greater than any

in nos saevitum est bello, quo durius umquam
40   vidit nulla aetas, nec feret ulla dies;
servitium tulimus crudele, et barbara iussa,
      parsque domos caras liquimus et patriam;
relliquias miserosque absumpsit tabida cives
      pestis, et huc illuc saevit Erinnys adhuc.
45   Nec sat erat: miseri crudelia funera Cottae
      flevimus. O indigna Cotta perempte nece,
o Cotta infelix, quae te fata impia nobis
      tam subito ante tuos abripuere dies?
Iam neque finierant gemitus, et lumina siccis
50   non bene cessarant tristia flere genis,
cum tu, Marce, cadis, cum nos tot tristibus actos
      deseris, heu falsos credulitate tui.
Non hoc vivida nos tua iam sperare iuventa,
      hoc tua non virtus, non benefacta dabant,
55   exanimem ut nos te iuvenem nec iam ulla loquentem
      externa miseri contegeremus humo,
sed fore, quem fama virtus aequaret Olympo,
      unus qui multos instrueres populos,
qualis ab aërio decurrens monte iugi fons
60   communes multis sufficit unus aquas.
Nam quid ego aut laudes memorem, aut tua maxima laudum
      praemia, quam humano profueris generi,
aut quam saepe animas positas iam sedibus Orci
      ad sua Apollinea membra vocaris ope?
65   Vos testes, Ticine, et qui inter pascua laeta,
      Medoace, antiquos abluis Euganeos,
illo quos fama est naturae arcana docente,
      saepe inter nymphas obstupuisse suas,
at nunc amisso turbatis flesse sub undis,
70   inque mare assuetas non habuisse vias.

other's. Our land is ravaged by a harsher war than any age has
seen thus far, than any future day will know. We have borne cruel
servitude and barbarian rule. Many of us have abandoned the dear
homes of our fatherland. As for those who remained, a rabid pes-
tilence has consumed them, and this Fury still rages everywhere.
But there is more: for we mourned the harsh end of sad Cotta,
dear Cotta, who died an unworthy death. Unhappy Cotta, what
lamentable fate stole you from us so suddenly before your time?

But even before we could cease to mourn you, Cotta, before our
eyes stopped weeping and we had the chance to dry our cheeks,
you too have perished, Marco, abandoning us to sorrow, deceived
in our hopes for you. Surely this is not what we expected from
your vibrant youth, your virtue or your good deeds, that we should
sadly bury you in a foreign land, a lifeless, voiceless youth. Rather
we expected that the fame of your virtue would raise you to
heaven, that you, one man, would instruct many peoples, as a
mountain stream, rushing downward from lofty peaks, is able by
itself to distribute its waters to many. What would it avail me to
recite your praises, or the great benefits of that praise? Or the
benefits you bestowed upon the human race? Or how often, when
souls were already sent to the house of Orcus, you summoned
them back to their bodies with your Apollonian art? You are wit-
nesses, Ticino and Brenta, who, among fertile pastures, water the
ancient Euganean Hills. I have heard how, when he taught the se-
crets of nature, these rivers would stand dumbfounded among
their very nymphs. And now, beneath the rough waters, they weep
for the one they have lost, without flowing into the sea as they are

40

45

50

55

60

65

70

Non tamen aut soli, nec vos magis omnibus, amnes,
    indoluistis acerbo illius interitu.
Illum etiam Graiae et nymphae flevere Latinae,
    illum etiam Tuscis Calliopea modis.
75   Quin etiam silvae et montes gemuisse feruntur,
    et vos extremi flestis Hyperborei.
Sed mage Benacusque senex et Sarca, sepulti
    qui prope vicinum praetereunt tumulum.
Sed magis ipse Athesis, olim qui corpus humandum,
80   condendum caram perferet in patriam,
ne extra cognatos cineres Turriensiaque ossa
    illum perpetuo terra aliena tegat.
Tunc vos, o patrio prognatae Naiades amne,
    spargite odoratis plena sepulcra rosis.
85   Tempus erit cum posteritas mirata nepotum,
    'Quantum isti,' dicent, 'attribuere dei!'
Atque aliquis, monumenta legens et scripta iacentis,
    devota ad mutos serta feret cineres.
Interea, o vos, Benaco centum patre nymphae,
90   Sarcaque ab Alpinis edite verticibus,
et vos, o Naci rupes et saxa Briani,
    et nemora umbrosis densa cacuminibus,
ferte aliqua, o nunc ferte meo solatia Batto,
    et tantam ex animo demite tristitiam.
95   Quem neque sancta potest Sophie complexa levare,
    Musa nec assuetis sedula carminibus.
Batte, tamen vates, longum ut quaesisset ademptam,
    et longum flesset Thracius Eurydicen,
nullo solatus blando quam carmine curas,
100   nullo quam Sophia dicitur esse magis.

wont. But you rivers are not alone, nor are you loudest, in lament-
ing his bitter death. For he was mourned by the nymphs of Greece
and Rome, and Calliope wept for him as well in a Tuscan strain.
Indeed, it is said that the woods and mountains wept for him, and   75
you wept too, O utmost Hyperboreans! But louder in lamentation
were old man Benacus and the Sarca that flows hard by the tomb
of the buried man, and louder was the Adige, which one day will   80
carry his body back to be buried in his fatherland, so that no for-
eign earth may cover his body forever, far from the bones and
ashes of his family. Then, O Naiades, born of the paternal spring,
bedew his grave with fragrant roses. The time will come when his   85
distant progeny will marvel and say, "Look at how much the gods
bestowed upon this man." And someone, reading the memorials
and the gravestone of the deceased, will lay devoted flowers before
his mute ashes.

Meanwhile you hundred nymphs, born to father Benacus, and   90
Sarca, who rise in the Alpine summits, and you rocks of Nago and
cliffs of Briano and forests dense with shady treetops: bring solace
to my friend Battus, and drive the great sorrow from his heart. For 95
neither can the embrace of sacred Wisdom allay his sorrow, nor
the muse who plies her wonted songs. But Battus, know that
nothing consoled the Thracian bard more, in his long search for
Eurydice, in his long lamentation and his sorrows, than wisdom   100
and sweet song. Whether he wandered through the deep forests of

Illi, seu Rhodopes silvis erraret in altis,
    sive in deserti Strymonis aggeribus,
semper Musa comes, semper pendebat eburna
    ex humero numeris docta sonare lyra.
105   Ille orbem immensum semper spectabat, et orbis
    ornatum, puris sidera luminibus,
et maria, et montes vastos, atque irrequieta
    flumina, tum quicquid denique terra parit.
Quorum animadvertens certa sub lege tenorem,
110   paulatim caram senserat Eurydicen
deleri, et tristem mutari in gaudia mentem:
    tantum animos rerum forma levare potest.
Aspice lucentem Lunae Titanidis orbem,
    et cum Sole suo quae super astra micant.
115   Omnia sunt aeterna, et vitae iuncta perenni,
    quae loca felices diique animaeque colunt.
Inferior Leti regio est, sedesque malorum,
    in qua est quod felix intueare nihil.
Quippe solum hoc ventique, imbresque, et cuncta fatigant
120   quaecumque aëria de regione cadunt.
Adde aestusque, hiemesque, et morborum genus omne.
    Tum natura aliqua est indiga semper ope.
Nos porro desideriis mala plurima nostris
    iunximus. O praeceps in sua damna genus!
125   Hinc odia, et timor, et lites, et bella cruenta,
    et via non uni plurima aperta neci.
Attamen in tantis aerumnis est animi spes
    unica, quem melior vita beare potest.
Quippe, ubi praefulgens ulla virtute reliquit
130   corporeum, sedes advolat aetherias,

Rhodope or among the embankments of deserted Strymon, the
muse was ever his companion and the ivory lyre, versed in song,
hung ever from his shoulder. He was forever gazing upon the im-   105
mense heavens, the order of the universe, and the stars with their
pure light, as well as the seas, the barren mountains and the never-
silent streams, and all that the earth brings forth. When he per-
ceived that their courses followed specific laws, he sensed that the   110
pain of losing his dear Eurydice was gradually fading, as his mind
turned from sadness to joy. Such power has the beauty of nature
to console the mind.

Behold the lucent orb of the Titan-born Moon, and the brighter
sun and stars. Eternal and graced with never-ending life are those   115
regions inhabited by the prosperous gods and the souls of men.
But below are the regions of Death and the seats of evil men,
where no happiness will be found. For this ground is buffeted by
wind and rain and whatever else falls from the sky. Add to that the   120
heat of summer and the chill of winter, and all manner of disease,
since nature is ever wanting some aid. Furthermore, our race has
earned much pain in the pursuit of pleasure. O race prone to ruin!
From this fact come enmity and fear, quarrels and bloody wars   125
and many paths to many kinds of death. But amid all these cares
the soul has one hope for a better life: that when, shining with
some virtue, it has left its body, it flies to the airy abodes, the   130

semideumque domos, et divum morte carentum:
    hic ubi non aestas, nec fera saevit hiems,
nec dolor, aut desideria infelicia nostri,
    nec sors partem aliquam nec rude vulgus habet,
135   at sancti heroes habitant, gens inclita bello,
    ingenuique, novem qui coluere deas,
quique pii, iustique, deum praecepta secuti,
    et sancta insignes qui fuerunt Sophia.
Quos inter tuus ipse recens a funere frater
140   miratur caelum, caelicolumque domos,
aeternamque diem, et felicem ex ordine gentem,
    inter quos gaudet se quoque dinumerans.
Quem circum illustres animae, proavique, paterque
    intentos oculos ore nepotis habent,
145   et pulchram effigiem agnoscunt: miratur et ipse
    egregiam stirpem magnanimumque genus,
agnoscitque suos, et facta et nomina discit,
    tum quantum sit adhuc terra habitanda tibi.
O fortunatum nimium, tristem ante senectam
150   carpere iter caeli cui potuisse datum est!
Quas Syrtes, quos et scopulos post terga relinquis,
    Marce! Tibi a quanto est salva carina mari!
Fortunate iterum: tu non incommoda vitae
    passus adhuc, non quae plurima habet senium,
155   sed dulces inter Musas et Apollinis artes
    fortunata nimis vita peracta tibi est.
I, decus Ausoniae iuvenis, numeroque deorum
    te immisce: culta est iam tibi terra satis.
Illa tuum, dum sidera erunt, dumque aequora current,
160   nomen in astra memor et benefacta feret.

home of the undying gods and the demigods. Here neither sum-
mer nor winter rages. Here there is no sorrow or sad longing for
what is ours, and neither fate nor the vulgar crowd has any part of
it. Rather it is the dwelling of saintly heroes, a race splendid in   135
war, as well as those wise men who have cultivated the nine muses,
and those pious and just men who followed the precepts of the
gods and achieved eminence through holy wisdom. Among such
men your brother, recently interred, admires the heavens and the   140
angelic abodes, the eternal day and the blessed beings in their hi-
erarchy, and he rejoices to count himself, as well, one of their
number. All around him illustrious souls, including those of his
father and his ancestors, look intently upon the face of their off-
spring. They recognize his handsome form, while he himself ad-   145
mires his eminent lineage and his noble race. He acknowledges his
ancestors and learns their names and deeds as well as the great
amount of land that you, his brother, still possess. How very
happy is that man who, before sad old age sets in, has been al-   150
lowed to journey up to heaven. What wildernesses, what rocky
waves you leave behind, Marco. From what a troubled sea your
bark has sailed on to safety. How doubly favored you are, no
longer to suffer the tribulations of life and old age. Rather among   155
the muses and the arts of Apollo you have come to the end of your
days. Go then, glory of Italian youth, and take your place among
the gods, for you have already done enough to enhance the earth.
But as long as the stars exist, as long as waters flow, so long will
the earth remember you and raise your name and your good deeds   160
to the heavens.

: III :

Ad Ioannem Baptistam Turrianum Veronensem
in obitum Pauli et Iulii, ipsius Fracastorii filiorum

Batte, animos quando tristes curasque levare
Musa potest, ego nunc sortem casusque supremos
ipse meos tristi solabor carmine tecum.
Et tecum dulces natos, quos funus acerbum
5   abstulit, aeterna et pariter caligine texit,
conquerar, ut saltem tenebris et nocte perenni,
quantum opis est nostrae, miserorum nomina demam.
Quae potui, dum vita illos auraeque fovebant,
exhibui genitorque gubernatorque duorum
10   infelix. Primas alter vix fingere voces,
alter adhuc teneris iam tum decerpere ab annis
prima rudimenta, atque omen praebere parenti.
Quos ego (sed Zephyri spes portavere paternas)
censueram, si fata darent, cum posceret aetas
15   fortior, ad dulces tecum traducere Musas
assiduos, citharamque humeris suspendere eburnam.
Inde, ubi iam caelum, ac Solem, fulgentiaque astra,
terramque, et liquidos ignes, aequorque profundum
mirari inciperent, latisque animalia campis,
20   te monstrante viam, te rerum arcana docente,
mens fuerat dulces Sophiae deducere ad hortos:
hortos quos ver perpetuum, quos aura Favonii
semper alit, semper caelesti nectare pascit.
Hic tremulo et longa confecto aetate parenti
25   purpureos legerent flores, seniique levamen,
Threïcia canerent cithara quae plurima quondam
audissent, te populea meditante sub umbra,

: III :

To Giovanni Battista della Torre of Verona
on the death of Paolo and Giulio, Fracastoro's sons

Battus, since the Muse has the power to lift up ailing spirits and to
relieve cares, I will sing you a sad lament and so console myself in
spite of fate and the extreme calamities of my family. In your pres-
ence I will weep for my dear sons, whom harsh death has stolen   5
away and steeped in everlasting darkness. Thus, at the very least, I
will rescue the names of these poor boys — to the extent of my
powers — from darkness and perennial night. While they lived and
breathed, I did all I could for them as their unhappy father and   10
teacher. One of them could hardly speak, as yet; the other was al-
ready at the tender age when he could pluck the first fruits of in-
struction, and he showed great promise in his father's eyes. Though
the winds have now scattered a father's hopes, I had thought, if
fate allowed it when they were a little older, to join with you in   15
leading them to the dear Muses and in hanging an ivory lyre from
their shoulders. Then they would begin to marvel at the heavens,
the sun and the shining stars, the earth and the bright fires, the
deep sea and the animals that roam the broad plains. You would   20
show them the way and teach them the secrets of nature. At the
same time I would bring them into the sweet gardens of wisdom,
gardens nourished by perpetual springtime and by the Favonian
breeze that would feed them eternally on heavenly nectar. There
they would gather beautiful flowers for their aged and infirm fa-   25
ther, and then — a solace to my old age — they would sing to the
Thracian lyre what once they had heard you recite under the shade

divino mirantem Athesim dum carmine mulces,
et rerum canis et teneri primordia mundi.
30   Fortunate senex, si natorum ore referri
fata sinant, ut nata chao antiquissima rerum
materies, visi correpta cupidine pulchri,
arserit, atque, deum thalamo complexa, iugarit
corpora prima. Quibus discordia nata hymenaeis
35   et divisa locis: suprema petiverit ignis
purior, et nitidis vicinus sederit astris;
quem iuxta per inane amplum se fuderit aër;
ima autem tellus vasto circum obruta ponto
constiterit; quam dudum hinc inde agitantibus undis
40   substerni late campi, deformiaque arva
paulatim apparere supra, et concrescere montes
coeperunt, procul et nudas ostendere cautes,
mox nemora, et virides undis mirantibus ornos.
Montanis tum speluncis et rupibus altis
45   exsiluere udae formoso corpore nymphae,
in viridi flavos siccantes litore crines.
         O fortunatum nimium, si numina tantum
haec mihi servassent, si non casura dedissent.
Verum aliter Lachesi visum est, quo tempore primum
50   natorum coepit producere fila duorum.
Quippe auram miseris et dulcem noscere vitam
spemque sui dederat praebere: alia omnia, ventis
tradita, nocte atra et tenebris involverat Orci.
Non licuit firmos annis viridesque iuventa
55   inspicere, et carae ad metam deducere vitae.
Nec potui votis nec ope adiuvisse paterna
clamantes, frustraque patris suprema petentes
auxilia, et nota nequicquam voce vocantes.
Heu mortem invisam! Quis te mihi, Paule, deorum

of a poplar tree, when you enchanted the marveling Adige with your divine song, as you sang the origins of nature and of this delicate world.

Happy the old man whom fate allows to see in the faces of his children, how elementary nature was anciently born out of chaos and how it burned with love as it beheld beauty and embraced it in the chambers of the gods, thus begetting the first corporeal forms. From this union discordant elements were born in divers places, as a purer fire rose to the heavens and sat, a neighbor, among the gleaming stars. And hard by, the air rolled forth through the great emptiness. The earth stood below, overrun by the vast sea. While the waves churned all around for a great age, gradually the fields began to spread out and shapeless plains appeared. And the waters looked on astonished as mountains arose, revealing rough and naked cliffs and woods and leafy ash trees. Then the watery nymphs, with their graceful forms, began to emerge from their mountain caves and lofty cliffs, drying their golden hair by the verdurous shore.

O how happy I should have been if fate had reserved these things for me, rather than giving them, only to take them away! But truly Lachesis thought otherwise when first she began to spin out the destinies of my two sons. Indeed, all she granted was that these poor souls should taste the air and sweet life and offer great promise of themselves. The rest, scattered to the winds, she covered in black night and in the darkness of Orcus. But she did not allow me to see them attain a firmer age, rife with youth, nor did she allow them to reach the natural limit of dear life. Neither through prayers nor any resources of a father was I able to help them as they called to me, as they called out in vain for a father's final aid, as they called to me in vain with those voices I knew well. O cruel death! Which of the gods stole you from me, Paolo,

60   arripit, et miserum complexibus abstrahit istis?
        Tu, prior immiti correptus morte, parentem
        deseris, et dulces auras et lumina linquis.
        Quod te si tali dederant sub lege futurum
        fata mihi, non iam fuerat maeroris abunde?
65   Non gemitus? Quid me tantis e patribus unum,
        caelicolae, lacrimisque novis et morte recenti
        opprimitis, caroque etiam spoliatis Iulo?
        Heu, miserande puer, quanto plena omnia luctu
        liquisti abscedens! Quem non vesana deorum
70   incusavit inops, cum te complexa iacentem
        aspiceret, laniata comas et pectora mater?
        Ah misera, ah male fausta parens, quid numina fletu
        sollicitas? Iacet ille, velut succisus aratro
        flos tener, et frustra non audit tanta gementem.
75   Ah misera, ah quid sublatum complexa moraris?
        Ille tuus non iam est. Vos illam in funere, matres,
        collapsam accipite, exanimemque reponite tectis.
           At vos, insontes animae, carissima nuper
        pignora (quod misero superest optare parenti)
80   semper avete mei, ut licuit, semperque valete.
        Seu dulce Elysium functos umbraeque tenebunt
        sanctorum nemorum, puro seu sidera caelo,
        ipse ego vos semper lacrimis, vos carmine tristi
        prosequar, et vestris persolvam iusta sepulcris,
85   donec me vobis tenuem coniunxerit umbram
        summa dies, natis aequat quae sola parentes.
           Interea curas numeris Musaque levemus,
        Batte, animos, quando rerum mortalis origo est,
        quando etiam vitae norunt vasta aequora finem.
90   Scilicet et quondam veniet, labentibus annis,
        illa dies, cum iam curvo sub vomere taurus
        insudet terramque gravis praevertat arator,

tearing you, poor soul, from my embrace? Seized by an untimely 60
death, you predeceased your father, leaving behind the sweet air
and light of day. But if fate required that I have you under such
conditions, would that not have been sufficiently sad and tearful?
Why, ye gods, do you oppress me, alone out of so many fathers, 65
with fresh tears and a recent death and then rob me of my dear
Giulio as well? Alas, poor child, how much sorrow you have be-
queathed in leaving us! Which of the gods did your maddened 70
mother not assail when, helpless, she embraced you, as you lay
there, after she had torn her hair and beat her breast? Ah, sad and
ill-fated mother, why do you trouble the gods with your lamenta-
tion? Like a tender flower cut down by the plow, here he lies, un-
able to hear his mother weeping in vain. Poor woman, why do you 75
waste your time embracing him who has been taken away? No
longer is he yours. And you matrons, receive her, overcome with
loss, and take her lifeless into the house.

But you blameless souls, you who but lately were my dearest
possessions, all that remains for me is to wish you, as is fitting, a 80
fond and eternal farewell. Whether sweet Elysium will hold your
departed souls or the shades of the sacred woods or the stars in
the pure sky, I will always follow you with tears and sad songs, and
perform the wonted rites upon your graves, until my dying day 85
unites me, a weightless shade, with you, which day alone makes
fathers equal to sons.

Until such time, Battista, let us lighten our sorrows with poetry
and our souls with song, seeing that the origin of nature is mortal,
that even the vast seas will know an end to life. For that day will 90
come, in the course of years, when the ox will sweat under the
curved plow and the heavy plowman will fend the earth, where

nunc ubi caeruleae rostris spumantibus undae
sulcantur, verruntque citae freta longa carinae.
95   Nec vos, o liquidi fontes, aeterna manebunt
saecula, se tanto quamvis pater efferat amne
Eridanus, tumidusque fluat tot cornibus Hister.
Quin etiam aërii montes (mirabile dictu!)
Taygetus, Syphilusque, iugo et Cymbotus opaco,
100   ingentes post aestates ac saecula longa,
senserunt seniumque suum supremaque fata,
ex quo materies thalamos primosque hymenaeos,
atque elementa novus sensit discordia mundus.

: IV :

Ad Danielem Rhainerium, Veronae praefectum,
senatorem amplissimum

Rhaineri venerande, uno quo sospite, nondum
iustitia et virtus terris antiqua recessit,
multa quidem monumenta tuis sub fascibus urbis,
multa cadunt antiqua piorum et templa deorum,
5   et Bromii vites, et amicae pacis olivae.
Verum haec ex urbis re dilabuntur, et ipsi
ultro etiam sua sacra volunt procumbere divi.
Ah, saltem antiquo medicorum parcere ritu
fasque, et suetus amor pietatis et inclita virtus
10   magna tui valeant. Valeant hoc more vetusto,
quo nostri vixere atavi, vixere parentes,
te duce venturi longum superare nepotes.
Sanctior hic templis, hic divum est sanctior aris,
quem neque tempus edax potuit, nec saecula tanta,

now the blue waves are plied by churning prows and swift ships
sweep the distant seas. Not even you, clear streams, will know   95
eternal life, though Father Eridanus rouses himself in an abundant
stream and swollen Hister flows with its many branches into the
sea. Indeed — though it is strange to say it — even the lofty moun-
tains, Taygetus and Syphilus and Cymbotus with its dark ranges,
after countless summers and long centuries, felt the approach of   100
age and death, since that first moment when nature and a new
universe experienced their wedding night and the birth of the dis-
cordant elements.

: IV :

*To Daniele Rainieri, prefect of Verona,
eminent senator*

Most worthy Rainieri, as long as you are alive, justice and ancient
virtue have not yet left the earth: but during your time as leader
many of the city's monuments and many of the ancient temples of
the pious gods have fallen down, together with the vines of Bac-   5
chus and the vines of the peace-loving olive. Truly they vanish
from the city and the gods themselves gladly see their temples fall
to earth. If only it were permitted to spare the ancient arts of
medicine, and if only your long-standing love of piety and your
great and famous virtue could do it. Would that, following your   10
lead, future generations could insure their long survival, in ac-
cordance with the ancient customs by which our fathers and fore-
fathers lived. For this art of medicine is more sacred than any
temple, more sacred than the altars of the gods, this art which
neither all-devouring time can assail, nor the course of centuries

15 non belli rabies, non ipsum infringere ferrum:
   tantum est iustitiam violari et foedera rumpi!
   Scilicet et sacra est medicina vetusque deorum
   inventum, et sacri medici, quibus auctor Apollo,
   qui revocare animas iam caligantibus Orci
20 faucibus impositas ad carae munera vitae,
   aetheriosque haustus, et dulcia lumina possunt,
   qui genus innocuum, vitaeque ad publica nati
   commoda, divinas tantum didicere per artes
   exercere aevum, atque humanae praeesse saluti.
25 Hos aequum est te praecipue longeque tueri,
   Rhaineri, ante alios, idem cui cessit Apollo
   ipse suas artes et munera nobilis otii,
   quemque domos divum docuit, perque omnia duxit
   sidera, quem Graio insignem Latioque cothurno
30 secretas dedit Aonidum percurrere silvas,
   et calamos citharamque humeris suspendit eburnam.
   Idem te dulces Sophiae deduxit ad hortos:
   hortos quos ver perpetuum, quos aura Favonii
   semper alit, semper caelesti nectare pascit.
35   Salve, magne parens, qui tot virtutibus auctus
   urbem iustitia et divis in pace secundis
   egregiam moderare, Athesis qua flumine pulchro
   labitur, et placido secat arva virentia cursu.
      Tu quoque, magna virum genitrix, urbs inclita, salve,
40 cura deum, Verona: tui cessere labores,
   aerumnaeque graves, atque horrida Martis imago,
   sanguinis et vesana sitis, et tristis Erinnys.
   Barbara iam cessit rabies, et in Alpibus atrox
   saevitiam miles gelidumque exercet ad Albim.
45 Iam duros nimium servitus et fera iussa
   desuemus perferre, ullos non iam urbe tyrannos
   conspicimus, sed te, Rhaineri maxime, sed te,

nor raging war nor even the sword. To harm it would be as much   15
as to violate justice and to breach a treaty. For medicine is sacred,
having been discovered by the ancient gods, and doctors are sacred
too, since Apollo was the first of them: doctors have the power to
rescue souls from the black jaws of death, restoring to them the   20
gifts of dear life, the breath of heaven and the sweet light of day.
The members of this unoffending profession, born to enhance the
lives of all men, have learned to pass their days practicing these
divine arts and to take charge of human health. It is fitting, Rain-   25
ieri, that you in particular should long protect them before all
others, since Apollo himself has shared with you his arts and the
rewards of noble study and has taught you about the dwellings
of the gods and guided you amid all the stars. He has enabled
you, conspicuous in your knowledge of Greek and Latin, to course
through the secret groves of the Muses, and has suspended from   30
your shoulders his pipes and ivory harp. He has led you, as well,
through the delightful gardens of wisdom, gardens forever fostered
by eternal springtime and the Favonian breeze, and nourished
with celestial nectar.

Hail, great father, who, through your many virtues, justly gov-   35
ern this great city that the gods have graced with peace, this city
through which the Adige flows with its lovely stream, dividing the
fertile fields in its tranquil course.

And hail to you as well, renowned Verona, great mother of
men, dear to the gods. Gone are your travails, your grave cares, the   40
horrid specter of Mars, the mad thirst for blood and sad ven-
geance. Gone is the barbarous rage, and now the amoral merce-
nary carries out his madness in the Alps and against cold Albis.
Now we are no longer accustomed to endure harsh servitude and   45
cruel commands, no longer do we see any tyrants in the city, but
rather we see you, supreme Rainieri, you through whom, as long

magne pater, uno tandem quo sospite nobis
iam bona Libertas rediit, Pacemque per agros
50   laeta Ceres Bacchique chorus comitantur ovantes.
Gaudete, o quicumque boni speratis agrestes,
quorum amor est sobolis, studiumque nepotibus arva
incolere, et parvas ulmis attollere vites.
Tempus io, nunc tempus adest quo saecula Parcae
55   aurea nent, tandem quae nunc te praeside laeta
incipiunt; sed erunt nobis tunc maxima, cum te,
insignem sceptro Venetum sanctaque tiara,
regna salutabunt terris diffusa, tuumque,
qua Sol exoriens visit, qua deserit orbem
60   occiduus, late clarum feret Hadria nomen.

: V :

Ad Ioannem Matthaeum Gibertum
episcopum Veronensem

Ille tuus, Giberte, sacras qui in montibus aras
Melsineis tibi constituit, qui teque tuumque
per nemus omne canit perque omnia litora nomen,
haec enata suis mittit tibi poma sub hortis
5   aurea, quae quondam Medorum e finibus Atlas
transtulit, et magno servabat tuta dracone.
Mox victor sacra exspolians pomaria Perseus,
dum levibus nostrum talaribus aëra tranat,
donavit Charitae Benaci ad flumina nymphae.
10   Insuper hos, Giberte, tibi dat munera pisces,
qui quondam Etrusci nautae nostraque fuere

as you live, noble liberty is restored to us, while fertile Ceres and   50
the chorus of Bacchus, rejoicing, accompany peace through the
fields. Rejoice then all good rustics who wish for children, who till
the fields for your grandchildren, engrafting the small vine upon
the elm. For lo, the time has come when the Fates spin out the   55
Golden Age that now, finally and happily, begins under your guid-
ance. But for us they will have reached their summit when king-
doms throughout the earth salute you, adorned with the scepter
and sacred tiara of the Venetians, when the Adriatic carries your
great name abroad, from the lands of the rising sun to where it   60
sets and leaves the world behind.

: V :

To Giovanni Matteo Giberti,
bishop of Verona

Giberti, your friend who raised sacred altars to you in the Melsin-
ian hills, who has spread your name through every grove and to
every shore, now sends you these golden fruits that grew in his
garden, fruits that Atlas once brought from the lands of Media   5
and kept safe from the great dragon. Then victorious Perseus, hav-
ing pilfered the groves of sacred fruit, swam through our skies on
the swift wings at his ankles, and bestowed these apples upon
Charita, a nymph who inhabits the waters of Benacus. In addition   10
to them I send you the gift of these fish, once Etruscan sailors and

effigie, nunc per Benaci marmora nantes
caerula converrunt sinuatis aequora caudis.
Quod si forte iuvat tanti miracula facti
15   atque hominum quondam versas audire figuras,
ipse edam, Saloi quae quondam ad litora Battus,
Battus amor Dryadum, cecinit, mihi rettulit Aegon.
     Forte senex Cretae patriis Saturnus ab oris
ab Iove depulsus regnum sedesque quietas
20   quaerebat Latio in magno fataliaque arva.
Iamque diem medio Sol inclinabat ab axe,
cum fessus, longaque via siccatus et aestu,
ad vada Benaci viridi prospectat in herba
vescentes nautas et puri grandia Bacchi
25   pocula miscentes. Placido quos ore salutans,
'Ecquis,' ait, 'vestrum, pueri, succurrit egenti
defessoque seni? Quis pocula parva ministrat
exstinguitque sitim?' Poscenti illudere nautae,
et ridere senem: 'Nam quis praesentibus undis
30   possit habere sitim? Tu flumine largius illo
ebiberis, gelidaque aestum solabere lympha.'
Illusus deus immissis in flumine palmis
haurit aquas, pronusque bibit; dein versus ad illos:
'Quo tamen, o pueri, pretio ducetis ad illas
35   remigio cautes, quae fluctibus undique circum
clauduntur, mediisque iacent, parva insula, in undis?'
Ostenditque locum. Pretium gens impia iniquum
postulat. At pactus senior tamen omnia firmat,
adiuratque deos testes, scanditque phaselum.
40   Illi autem, dum nave cita liquida aequora tranant,
ignari quisnam sedeat deus: 'Eia age nobis
fare, senex, quonam latebras pro crimine quaeris?
Anne fugam subrepto auro dominoque relicto

shaped like us, though now, swimming through the marbled sur-
face of Benacus, they sweep the blue waters with their sinuous
tails. If perchance you would like to hear about this miraculous   15
event, of men changing shape, I will relate what Battus, beloved of
the Dryads, once sang upon the shore of Salò, a tale that Aegon
repeated to me.

   It happened that old man Saturn, expelled by Jove from the
paternal shores of Crete, sought in great Italy a kingdom and a   20
peaceful dwelling and his allotted fields: the Sun had already
passed the midpoint of the day when Saturn, weary and parched
from the heat and the long journey, encountered some sailors eat-
ing in the lush grass beside the shallows of Benacus, mixing great
goblets of pure wine. Greeting them with a kindly aspect, he said: 25
"Will one of you youths help an old man, weary and in need?
Who will give me a bit of wine to quench my thirst?" But the
sailors mocked the old man in his request. "Why would anyone be
thirsty amid so much water?" they said. "If you drink abundantly   30
from this river, you will cool yourself with the fresh drink." Thus
mocked, the god stretched out beside the water, placed his hands
in the stream and drank. Then he turned to them again. "For what
price, young men, will you row me over to those banks, which are   35
shut off by water, a small island, in the middle of the waves?" He
pointed to the place, and the impious men demanded an extor-
tionate price. But the old man agreed to all their demands, and
calling the gods to witness, he boarded their ship. But as they   40
plied the clear waters in their swift ship, unaware of the god
among them, they said, "So tell us, old man, what crime did you
commit that you seek this hiding place? Do you seek to fly to a
safe place, having stolen money from your master and abandoned

in loca tuta paras? Sed te tua fata sequuntur,
45   demens, quem nullae poterunt servare latebrae.'
Nomine Carpus erat, qui tam temeraria verba
dixerat; ingeminant comites, aurumque reposcunt
proferri: subreptum aurum ni proferat omne,
vi rapiant, pulsumque rate in media aequora turbent.
50   Quos placidus dictis senior demulcet amicis:
'Etrusci nautae, quae nunc mens impia suadet
nec servare fidem vos, nec meminisse deorum?'
Dicenti iam vis, iam dextra infertur. At ille,
qui tandem agnosci posset deus, 'Impia,' dixit,
55   'gens inimica deum, dabitur, quod poscitis, aurum:
hoc imo sub fonte aurum pascetis avari.'
Dixerat. Ast illis veniam poscentibus et vox
deficit, et iam se cernunt mutescere, et ora
in rictum late patulum producta dehiscunt,
60   in pinnas abiere manus, vestisque rigescit
in squamas, caudamque pedes sinuantur in imam.
Qui fuerat subita obductus formidine, mansit
pallidus ore color, quamquam, livoris iniqui
indicium, suffusa nigris sunt corpora guttis.
65   Carpus aquas, primus numen qui laesit, in amplas
se primus dedit, et fundo se condidit imo.
Inde alii celeri sese in media aequora saltu
praecipitant, vacuamque ratem et sine remige linquunt.
    Iamque deus super unus erat: subit ipse magistri
70   munus, et adductis pelagi petit ultima ripis.
Expositus ripa, liquidas conversus ad undas:
'Ecquid io, nymphae Benacides, ista supersit
navis, an haec sacrumque amnem male fausta carina
et vestras sulcabit aquas? En certe ita et huius
75   criminis hoc semper scopulo monumenta manebunt.'
Dixit, et in partem rupis conversa pependit

him? But Fate will catch up to you, crazy old man, and no hiding 45
place will protect you." The one who spoke these bold words was
named Carpus, and his companions seconded him, demanding
that the old man produce the stolen gold. Unless he did so, they
would take it from him and violently throw him from the ship into
the water. Calmly the old man tried to allay them with these 50
friendly words. "Tuscan sailors, what impious thought persuades
you now to break your promise and forget the gods?" No sooner
had he spoken than they violently struck him. But he, finally re-
vealing himself as a god, said, "O impious men, hateful to the 55
gods, you will have the gold you seek. Beneath this flood you
greedy men will feed upon gold!" So he spoke. But even as they
begged forgiveness, their voices failed them and they perceived
that they were becoming mute, as their mouths split and opened
into a broad rictus. Their hands became fins and their clothes 60
hardened into scales and their feet twisted into tails. Overcome
with sudden fear, their complexions became permanently pale,
even as their bodies were covered with black spots, a testament to
their wicked envy. Carpus, the first to insult the god, was the first 65
to leap into the broad surf, hiding in the deep sea. Thereupon the
rest jumped hastily into the waters, leaving the ship empty with no
one to row it.

Now the god was there alone. He quickly assumed the role of
steersman and came to the banks at the water's edge. Bending over 70
the shore, he turned to the clear waters and said, "Behold, nymphs
of Benacus, will this ship survive, this ill-omened bark, to ply this
sacred stream and your waters? Rather there will always be upon
these rocks a memorial to this crime." So he spoke and the ship, 75
with its very oars, was transformed into part of the rock, where

cum remis ratis ipsa suis, ubi cernere conchas
nunc etiam licet, extremo quas litore nautae
collectas miseri media imposuere carina.

80 Ex illo nant Benaci per caerula nautae
atque auri venis fundo pascuntur in imo,
nunc etiam a primo retinentes nomina Carpo.

: VI :

Ad Margaritam Valesiam Navarrae reginam
Caesaris Fregosii nomine

Dum me Cenomanos inter tenet Itala tellus
Zefredique arces, mens autem nescia claudi
libera trans gelidas Alpes Rhodanumque vagatur,
trans Ararim, caelumque beatum et Gallica semper
5 regna videt, regemque suum, tecumque moratur
assidue, versatque tuas sub pectore laudes.
Ecce mihi, celata auro gemmaque nitenti,
armipotens, galeaque ferox et Gorgone, Pallas
oblata est, seu fors tulerit, seu fata dedere.
10 Continuo visa ante oculos effulgere imago
magna tui, inque ipsa micuerunt Pallade vultus
virtutesque tuae, moresque, et facta, decusque.
Quippe illam e cunctis sic tu mortalibus una
assimilas, sic una refers, in Pallade ut et tu
15 noscare et Pallas in te. Sive illa Minerva,
seu dici Bellona velit, consensus utrimque
est idem, ora, animi genius, cognataque virtus.
Iure igitur tibi debetur, tibi convenit uni

even now it is possible to see shells which the luckless sailors had
placed on the ship, having gathered them on a distant shore. From   80
that time to this very day they swim through the blue waters of
Lake Benacus, feeding upon the veins of gold at the bottom, still
preserving the name of that first Carpus.

∴ VI ∴

To Marguerite Valois, queen of Navarre,
in the name of Cesare Fregoso

Though Italy holds me between the land of the Cenomani and the
forts of Castel Goffredo, my free and unimpeded mind, wandering
over the freezing Alps, the Rhone and the Arre, ever beholds the
king, the realms and the blessed skies of France. And it also lin-   5
gers attentively upon you and sings your praises in its heart. Here
I have an image, chased in gold and gleaming gems, of Pallas Ath-
ena, mighty in arms and terrifying in her helmet and gorgon head,
an image brought to me by either fate or chance. Constantly the   10
great vision of your person shines before my eyes; and in this im-
age of Pallas your face and virtues gleam, your character and deeds
and beauty. Truly, of all humans, you alone so resemble her and so
recall her to mind that you can be seen in her and she in you.   15
Whether she is called Minerva or Bellona, you are alike in face
and cast of mind and famous virtue. And so, by rights, her godly
form, her gems and her gold are fitting for you alone, whether

gemma, aurum, effigiesque deae. Sive est Polycleti,
20   sive Myronis opus, placeat tibi munus: imago
est tua. Sit gratus cum munere muneris auctor.

    Quod si digressus paulum et provectus amore
Pierio, dum me dulces per grandia Musae
facta tua et dum per monumenta heroica ducunt,
25   ipse tuas memorem laudes, quibus aethera ad altum
scandis, et illa simul referam per quae una Minervam
usque adeo assimilas, iuvet auscultare canentem,
si vacat et solitae sunt te oblectare Camenae.

    Illa parente deo Iove magno, fratre superbit
30   Gradivo. Tum forte acres in bella phalanges
si quando exacuit, late timor occupat urbes,
turbati tremuere hostes, ac terga dedere.
Ipsa hastam quatit, atque horrenti Gorgone saevit.
Ante deam dirae effigies, Terrorque, Minaeque
35   sanguineae, et dans terga Pavor, Visque impia, et Irae,
Vinclaque, Vindictaeque astant, et Mortis imago.
At vero positis armis atque aegide dira,
mollius humanas si demittatur ad artes
mansuetosque usus, tum dulcia carmina cantat,
40   et facilem exercet Musam, aut heroica gesta
describit, numerisve orbes metitur et astra.
Sin autem imperiis et maiestatis honore
gaudeat, aeternae ramis insignis olivae,
aut iustas sancit leges, aut iura ministrat,
45   aut arces struit, aut medias regina per urbes
incedit, matresque super longe eminet omnes.
Condensi agglomerant altis clamoribus Afri,
spectatumque ruunt, arasque et publica ponunt
templa deae: plausu resonat Tritonia ripa.
50   Tu pariter, magno Gallorum rege deoque
ac Iove nata simul, germano Marte superbis:

they are sculpted by Polycleitus or Myron. So may this gift please 20
you—for it is your image—and with the gift, he who sent it.

I digress awhile, drawn by my love of the dear Pierian Muses,
who lead me on through a review of your great deeds and heroic
monuments. And as I sing your praises, by which you ascend to 25
the heights of heaven, and also as I recall your great resemblance
to Minerva, may it please you to hear my song, if you have leisure
and if the Muses are wont to delight you.

Minerva is proud of her great father, divine Jove, and of her
brother Mars. For when she leads dread phalanxes into battle, fear 30
lays hold of cities, as terror-stricken enemies tremble and run
away. She herself brandishes the spear and rages, holding up the
fearsome Gorgon's head. Before the goddess stand dreadful shapes,
Terror and bloodthirsty Menace, Fear that turns its back, impious 35
Violence and Rage, Manacles and Vengeance and the image of
Death. But once she has set aside her arms and dire aegis, she
calmly turns to the humane arts and to gentler habits, singing
sweet songs and invoking the kindly Muse as she recalls heroic 40
deeds or measures the heavens and stars in verse. But if she de-
lights in power and pride of majesty, then, adorned with branches
of imperishable olive, she establishes fair laws, administers justice,
builds fortresses or passes through cities, a queen far above all 45
matrons: then crowding together with a great clamor, the Africans
hasten to see her, raising altars and public temples to her, while
the Tritonian banks reecho with her praise.

Even so do you, born of Jove, take pride in the great king and 50
god of the French, and your martial brother. For who would deny

nam Martem quisnam esse neget, seu fortia nudus
brachia praevalidosque artus atque Herculis armos
ostendit, taurumque uno prostraverit ictu,
55 sive acrem pictisque armis spectandus et auro
pressit equum, struxitve acies, et victor in hostes,
ceu torrens, signa atque viros sternitque fugatque,
fulmineove, Iovis tonitrus imitatus et arma,
tormento muros et magnas diruit urbes?
60 Te quoque tantorum comitem partemque secundam
bellorum, si quando acies atque arma movenda
perculsae tremuere urbes, horrorque pavorque
it campis, Mars germanam comitatur ovantem:
attoniti spectant populi, gaudentque tueri
65 nunc primum, nunc et medium, nunc agmen obire
postremum, nunc pellere equum, nunc tendere in hostem,
turbantem cuneos et abactis agmina signis.
Assistunt comites circum Sollertia et Astus
et magna audentes Animi et Tolerantia dura
70 Curaque Sedulitasque vigil Spesque alta Laborque
et divum Favor et ventis Fortuna secundis;
pone sequens magno graditur Victoria plausu.
    Nec minus horrenti a bello partisque triumphis,
si iuvat ingenii pacisque incumbere in artes,
75 nunc lauro redimita comas, imitata sorores
Castalias, plectis numeros, et carmina dictas,
carmina nec rerum fato subiecta, nec aevo.
Nunc magnos dimensa orbes in templa deorum
attollis animos, patrioque assuescis Olympo;
80 nunc tua describis vel regum gesta tuorum,
aut eadem depingis acu. Stant curribus altis
et pater, et proavus, cunctique ex ordine reges,
captivosque hostes et vinctos colla tyrannos

that he is like Mars when, naked, he displays the mighty limbs and muscular body and shoulders of Hercules, slaying a bull with a single blow; or when, resplendent in gold and bright armor, he mounts a horse, laying waste to armies, as he rushes victoriously like a torrent against his enemies, overturning standards and men and putting them to flight; or when, with his fulgurant cannon, he imitates Jove's thunders and his arms, as he overturns fortifications and great cities? And Mars has accompanied you as well, his cheering sister and auspicious partner in these great wars, when stricken cities fear arms and armies on the move and Horror and Dread run through the fields. The astonished populace watch with delight as he goes forth against the enemy's van, middle and rear guard, as he presses their cavalry and hastens against the foe, frightening their rank and file and scattering their standards. All around stand his lieutenants, Diligence and Craft, audacious Spirits and harsh Endurance, Care and ever vigilant Sedulity, Labor and lofty Hope, Divine Favor and Fortune with her auspicious winds. Behind them, to great applause, comes Victory.

And like Minerva as well, once she is far from horrid war and once victory has been achieved, you are pleased to incline to the arts of peace and of the mind: then, having adorned your hair with laurel leaves, and imitating the Castalian sisters, you weave rhymes and write songs that are impervious to fate or time. Sometimes you raise your spirits to the temples of the gods in heaven's great spheres, as you grow accustomed to your heavenly home. At other times you either describe the deeds of the kings your ancestors, or depict them with the needle. In lofty chariots your father and great-grandfather and all the kings in due order triumphantly lead

ante rotas longis ducunt in templa triumphis:
85 ipsa opus et textum stupet immortale Minerva.
Quam vero, o quam te dicam, cum legibus aequis
iustitiaque feros populos frenasque, regisque,
et divina doces iura et civilia ferre,
aut arces tollis, aut propugnacula condis,
90 aut matres inter medias populosque frequentes
incedis regina? Favor comitatur euntem,
Maiestasque, Pudorque, tamen qui Pallada possit
armatam et Martis gradientem in bella decere.
It dextra Pax laeta manu, et praetendit olivam.
95 Applaudunt Sequani, floresque et lilia passim
effundunt, gaudentque tuas attollere laudes,
reginamque deamque salutiferamque salutant,
et pace insignem et bello ferroque potentem.
     Fortunata nimis, magnus quam Caesar et omnis
100 suspicit exoratque orbis, cui lumine tellus
felici arridet, totus cui militat aether.
Diis quamquam visum aspectu tibi debita regna
paulisper privare tuo, seu crimine cives
id meruere aliquo, seu te tua fata reservant
105 ad maiora, viamque tuis virtutibus amplam
expediunt panduntque. Etenim iam tempora laeta
illa instant, cum post lacrimas, post publica vota
te tandem tua regna novis decorata trophaeis
accipiant, et iusta tibi sollemnia solvant.
110 Iam ludi, festique dies, iam sacra parantur,
iam placidus ripa gaudet Meniascus amoena,
in templis pueri impubes mixtaeque puellae
sacra canent, ortusque tuos ad sidera tollent,
ut nascentem ulnis primae excepere Camenae,
115 melleque et Aonio tetigerunt ora liquore,
ut Charites fovere deae, et decus omne dedere,

into the temples, before their chariot wheels, captive enemies and 85
tyrants bound at the neck. Minerva herself marvels at the labor
and the imperishable weaving! O how can I describe you when,
with just laws, you curb and rule savage peoples, teaching them to
obey divine and civil law? Or when you raise battlements and
build fortifications, or pass, a queen, in the midst of matrons and 90
an onrushing populace? Favor accompanies you as you pass, and
Majesty and such Modesty as would beseem armed Minerva as
she enters into the moils of Mars. On your right stands Peace,
who rejoices as she holds out an olive branch. The Sequani ap- 95
plaud you and strew lilies and flowers all about, rejoicing as they
praise you and rapturously hailing you as their queen, their god-
dess and the bringer of health, resplendent in peace and mighty in
the weapons of war.

How lucky you are to be admired by great Caesar and by the
entire world, while the earth smiles upon you with its prosperous 100
gaze and all of heaven fights for you. It matters little that the gods
have chosen temporarily to deprive your kingdoms of your protec-
tive gaze, whether because your subjects have deserved this for
some transgression or because the fates, reserving you for greater
things, breach a wider path for your virtues. In truth those happy 105
days are near when, after many tears and public prayers, your
realms, graced with new trophies, will finally receive you and per-
form your wonted rites. Already public games and holidays and 110
sacred ceremonies have been readied. Already placid Meniascus
rejoices in its charming banks. In temples, beardless youths, to-
gether with virgins, will sing sacred hymns and exalt your birth to
the stars: telling how, at your birth, the Muses were the first to
hold you in their arms, wetting your lips with honey and Aonian 115
drafts; how the Graces warmed you and bestowed every charm

ut parva in numerum pedibus cunabula divae
pellentes, manibus nentes fatalia pensa,
grandia concordes cecinerunt fata sorores.
120   Stabunt ingentes sublatis molibus arcus,
caelati gestisque tuis factisque tuorum.
    Supra omnes humeris exstans altaque corona
frater erit, senosque ferox ex hoste triumphos
ducet ovans. Mox Fortuna congressus iniqua,
125   cum dura bellare dea et decernere dudum
cogetur. Longe illa, Euris in bella vocatis,
obiicere adversos, et toto nubila caelo,
et casus, et monstra modis minitantia miris
cernetur; rex contra animis et fortibus ausis
130   et virtute nova tandem superare cadentem,
tendentemque manus; tum ferro et compede vinctam
protrahere, et campo captivam ducere aperto,
nubila diffugere, et turpi deformia monstra
victa fuga, vario bello consumpta fameque,
135   in caecas latebras obscuraque Tartara condi.
    O, mihi si tantum iuvenili in corpore vitae
et tantum det Parca mihi, haec ventura superstes
ut videam, comiterque tuos, regina, triumphos,
mox etiam spectare queam et maiora parari!
140   En erit, en umquam illa dies, cum Gallica signa
attolli et Sequanos compleri milite campos
conspiciam, fremere arma Rhemos, fremere arma Cadurcos,
Aulercosque, Heduosque, et pictis Lingonas hastis?
In mediis regem, secum cataphracta trahentem
145   agmina, sublimem sanctas procedere ad aras,
per caput et sacram regum de more coronam
iurantem, et Solymas repetentem debita sceptris
regna suis; te parte alia fortes Ituriscos,
Andelos, Biturasque feros in bella moventem,

upon you; how, with their feet, the fatal goddesses rhythmically
rocked your little cradle, while their hands spun out your destiny
as they sang, in concert, your great future. Triumphal arches will   120
be raised up on lofty mounds, carven with your deeds and those of
your family.

　　Standing head and shoulders above the rest, with his tall crown,
will be your brother. Fierce and joyous, he will lead his enemies in
a sixfold triumph. Soon, harassed by unjust fate, he will be com-   125
pelled to fight against the harsh goddess and decide the contest in
due time. She, having called the Eastern winds to war, will assail
her enemies, as clouds, catastrophes and strangely menacing mon-
sters occupy the heavens. But with spirit and bold deeds and rare
virtue, the king will vanquish her, a fallen foe, as she holds out her   130
hand in supplication. Then he will drag and lead the captive
woman, bound and fettered with irons, through the open field; as
the clouds dissipate and the deformed monsters are compelled to
beat an inglorious retreat, as they are consumed by war and hun-
ger, they will hide themselves in the darkest pits and hidden   135
realms of hell.

　　If only Fate would let me live in a youthful body long enough to
see such things, so that I might courteously behold your triumphs,
then, my queen, I could witness still greater things to come! Truly,   140
will that day ever appear when I shall see the Gallic standards
raised and the fields of the Sequani filled with soldiers, while the
Remi and the Cadurci clamor for their weapons, as well the Au-
lerci, the Hedui, and the Lingones with their painted spears? And
in their midst is the king who brings mail-clad ranks with him as   145
he proceeds, head held high, to the sacred altars and swears, ac-
cording to custom, on his life and his kingly crown, as he seeks the
kingdoms of Jerusalem that properly belong to his scepter. Else-
where you wage war against the powerful Turks, the Moors and

150   consiliis tantoque operi comitemque ducemque
        ascitam; nec non tanto sub rege coactam
        in ferrum ruere Italiam, et socia arma trahentem
        signa sequi. Mox o liceat, caeloque secundo
        et praesente Deo, tot sese addentibus una
155   prospicere immensum consterni puppibus aequor,
        Carmelique procul rupes et litora Ioppes
        laeta Dei classem et victricia vela vocare,
        et trepidum Euphratem et magni tremere ostia Nili.
        Tunc ego non alium Martem mihi, Pallada poscam
160   non aliam mihi: rex Mavors, tu maxima Pallas
        sola eris. O ego tunc, gemino sub numine tutus,
        per medios hostes videor densosque maniplos
        victor agi, videorque mea sub cuspide fractos,
        munera magna tibi, captivos ducere reges,
165   nec non et spolia ampla tuis addenda triumphis
        iungere, barbaricas vestes, regumque tiaras,
        armaque, Mygdoniosque arcus, Lyciasque pharetras,
        cernere et exanimem fuso cum milite portas
        Caucaseas atque Hircanos inquirere saltus
170   Maumethem, et sese extremis occludere Bactris.
        Haec, precor, haec propere eveniant felicibus astris,
        si qua fata dabunt, votis si Iuppiter adsit.
        Interea, sive haec te cura et gloria tangit,
        seu pacem Europae miserae moliris, et arma
175   in superum saevos hostes avertere tentas,
        magnanimo assistente tuis conatibus Anna,
        Anna spectato meritis, cui summa potestas
        tradita, quo rerum moles onerosa recumbit,
        quicquid agis, si quando animum convertis ad ipsam
180   Italiam (neque enim teneat non haec quoque cura),
        tunc dicas: 'Caelo ante alios mihi fidus in illo est,
        qui, nisi pro rege invigilans noctesque diesque

the wild Basques, for you have been chosen a leader and partner in
your brother's councils and grand emprise; and Italy, coming to-   150
gether under this great king, will take up arms in solidarity and
follow your standard. With heaven's favor and the help of God,
may I be allowed to see the broad sea strewn with so many ships,   155
while far off Mount Carmel and the port of Jaffa eagerly call upon
God's navy and its victorious sails, as the timorous Euphrates
trembles and with it the Nile delta. Then could I ask for no other
Mars or Pallas. The King is Mars and you alone are the greatest   160
Minerva. Protected by your twofold spirit, I shall be seen passing
safely and victoriously amid the dense battalions of my foes and
offering up captive kings, vanquished by my sword, as great gifts to   165
you. And to your triumphs will I add ample spoils, exotic vests
and kingly crowns and arms, Mygdonian bows and Lycian quivers.
And I shall behold Mohammed, crestfallen at the sight of his scat-
tered infantry, as he seeks the gates of the Caucasus and the Hyr-
canean forests and hides himself in utmost Bactria. I pray that   170
auspicious stars will bring this about soon, if fate allows it and
Jove is present to my prayers. Meanwhile, if you are moved by
such glory and such cares, if you seek peace for ailing Europe and
wish to repel the cruel enemies of God, with the assistance of   175
greathearted Anne, conspicuous in merit—Anne, to whom su-
preme power is given and whom great duties weigh down—then,
whatever you do, if ever you turn your mind to Italy itself (for this   180
as well should be a care to you), may you declare: "Under this
heaven I trust him more than all others. Were it not that, in the

illic res Italas et regia munera tractet,
Gallica suspiret regna et tabescat abesse.'

185   Praeterea, dea bellipotens, quae munera Caesar
Fregosus, parva illa quidem, sed congrua, mitto,
haud ingrata tibi Latiis accedat ab oris,
una eadem faciesque tui, faciesque Minervae.
Quin etiam, quoties divam spectare iuvabit,
190   te toties spectare puta. Sed, me quoque tanti
si facies, si me tali dignabere honore,
cum memor ipsa mei fueris, tum nomine nostro
longaevamque diem et felicia cuncta precata,
Diva, tuum salvere iube super omnia Martem.

: VII :

Ad Marcum Antonium Flaminium
et Galeatium Florimontium

Dum vos fatidicos vates arcanaque sensa
volvitis, atque, animum caelesti nectare alentes,
alloquiis magnoque Dei consuescitis ori,
felices, duce Giberto, Campense magistro,
5   quid dicam miserum me agere, et quam ducere vitam,
irrequietum animi et quaerentem indagine vana
naturam semper fugientem? Quae se ubi paulum
ostendit mihi, mox facies in mille repente,
ceu Proteus, conversa sequentem eludit, et angit
10   maerentem seniique horas cassumque laborem.
    Nuper enim tenues species simulacraque rerum,
quae fluere ex ipsis dicuntur perque meare
omnia, dum sector meditans, tacitusque requiro

king's behalf, he frets day and night for the fate of Italy and carries out his royal duties, he would be sighing for France and be sad to be away from it."

To conclude, warlike goddess, may this token that I, Cesare   185
Fregoso, send you, small though it is, but fitting, come as a wel-
come gift from the shores of Italy: it depicts you and Minerva as
one and the same. As often as it pleases you to look on the god-
dess, think that you see yourself. But if you esteem me enough, if   190
you deem me worthy of such an honor, then, O goddess, when
you think of me and have prayed for my long life and complete
success, hope that your Mars succeeds beyond all else.

∶ VII ∶

To Marcantonio Flaminio
and Galeazzo Florimonte

You two are poring over the fateful poets and their arcane mean-
ings, nourishing your souls upon heavenly nectar and happily ac-
quainting yourselves with the discourse and eloquence of God,
with Giberti as your guide and Van Kempen as your teacher. But   5
how shall I say I spend my time, leading a sad and restless life as I
vainly toil after nature that forever flees me? For no sooner has it
revealed itself to me than it takes on a thousand forms, like Pro-
teus, and so altered, it eludes me as I pursue it and galls me as I   10
lament my old age and empty labors.

Lately, as I sought in solitude the forest's hidden lairs and its
secret, silent places, as my mind pursued the elusive forms of na-
ture as well as those simulacra that are said to flow from them and

avia silvarum et secreta silentia solus,
15   cognovi tamen his spectris illudier ipsis,
ut sensus feriant nostros, semperque lacessant,
perque fores caulasque animae ludantque, meentque,
ac remeent, ipsamque nec inter somnia linquant.
    Ergo, hoc elusum studio fessumque labore,
20   tandem me miserata suos abduxit in hortos
Musa memor, tetricumque animum somno atque quiete
curavit, numerisque et blando carmine fovit.
Tum mihi: 'Quo tandem, o semper mortalia quaerens,
hanc colere usque voles terram? Numquamne relinques
25   has tenebras, numquamne in lucem lumina tolles?
An nescis, quaecumque hic sunt, quae hac nocte teguntur,
omnia res prorsus veras non esse, sed umbras,
aut specula, unde ad nos aliena elucet imago?
Terra quidem, et maria alta, atque his circumfluus aër,
30   et quae consistunt ex iis, haec omnia tenues
sunt umbrae, humanos quae tamquam somnia quaedam
pertingunt animos, fallaci et imagine ludunt,
numquam eadem, fluxu semper variata perenni.
Sol autem Lunaeque globus fulgentiaque astra
35   cetera, sint quamvis meliori praedita vita
et donata aevo immortali, haec ipsa tamen sunt
aeterni specula, in quae animus, qui est inde profectus,
inspiciens, patriae quodam quasi tactus amore,
ardescit. Sed enim, quoniam hic non perstat, at ultra
40   nescio quid sequitur secum, tacitusque requirit,
nosse licet circum haec ipsum consistere verum,
non finem: verum esse aliud quid, cuius imago
splendet in iis, quod per se ipsum est, et principium esse
omnibus aeternum, ante omnem numerumque diemque,
45   in quo alium Solem atque aliam splendescere Lunam
aspicias, aliosque orbes, alia astra manere,

to pervade all matter, I understood nevertheless that I was being   15
deceived by those spectral images: by the way in which they strike
our senses, ever provoking them, disporting about the gates and
doorways of the soul, passing and repassing through it and never
abandoning it, even in dreams.

Finally the appreciative Muse took pity on me, disappointed as   20
I was in my pursuit and wearied by the effort: she lead me into her
gardens and restored my embittered spirits with rest and sleep,
gladdening me with poetry and sweet song. Then she spoke to me
thus: "O you who ever seek after mortal things, how long will you
wish to till this land? Will you never abandon this darkness and   25
raise your eyes into the light? Or don't you know that all these
things that are covered in darkness are not real, but are mere shad-
ows, phantasms from which we perceive a borrowed reflection of
reality? Truly the earth, the deep sea and the air that flows around
us, as well as all things formed from them, are but fleeting shad-   30
ows that, like dreams, strike the souls of men and deceive them
with false semblance, shadows that are never the same and are al-
ways changing in a state of constant flux. The sun, globe of the
moon and all the other shining stars, though graced with a better,   35
an immortal life, are but images of something eternal that our
minds, which themselves derive from that eternity, look upon with
longing, as though touched by a desire to return home. But be-
cause the mind is not stable, here, but constantly and silently looks   40
for something beyond, it is possible to know that a truth exists
about these things, but not possible to know the end: for truth is
something else, whose reflection shines forth in these things,
something that exists through itself and is the eternal principle of
everything, preceding all quantity and all time. In this truth you   45
could see another sun and another moon shine forth, other planets

terramque, fluviosque alios, atque aëra, et ignem,
et nemora, atque aliis errare animalia silvis,
denique cuncta alia cernas vegetantia vita.
50 'Ergo, umbras cum iam satis et specula illa superque
spectaris, longa iamdudum in nocte pererrans,
fas tandem lucem atque ipsum perquirere verum.
Quod quoniam longe seiunctum est corpore ab omni,
nec nexus habet aut affinem sensibus ullis
55 naturam, scito esse animum tibi dissociandum
corpore, purgandumque omni contage recepta,
terrena labe, et mortalis luminis haustu,
quaerendaeque aliae silvae, callesque tenendi
sunt alii, meliorque Deum quae semita monstrat.'
60 Haec Musa. O si te comitem dent rura beata
Bardolena mihi, o qui nos propter amoenum
Benacum viridi silvis in litore sistat
atque olea lauroque tegat, detque abdita vatum
sensa et utramque Dei praeceptam evolvere legem!
65 Rura, oro, Giberte, tuo Benacea vati
da, viridesque oleas, et multa protege lauro.
Ille tuas laudes primum canet, et tua facta
inclita Maeoniis numeris ad sidera tollet:
ut puerum mirata sacro cum Tybride Roma
70 ante annos meritis titulis et honoribus auxit,
ut res Romana et sacrorum tradita iussu
pontificum tibi summa in te uno saepe resedit,
ut septem fremuere novis applausibus arces.
Macte animis, macte ingenio, tu traiicis aequor
75 barbaricum, et ferro reges in bella ruentes
alloquiis frenas, et coeptos ore tumultus,
armaque, et hostiles animos, et proelia sedas,

and other stars, another earth and other rivers, air and fire, and
forests and beasts that wander in the woods. Finally, you could see
all manner of plants growing with a different vitality.

"And so, after you have seen enough and more than enough of   50
these shadows and phantasms, after you have wandered through
the long night, it is finally time to seek the light and truth itself.
Since this truth is far removed from any bodily form, is not con-
nected with any physical sensations and has no nature akin to
them at all, know that your mind needs to be divorced from your   55
body, to be purged of any contagion it has received, any earthly
taint or taste of mortal light: other woods are to be sought and
other roads, a better path that leads to God."

So spoke the Muse. O would that the blessed pastures of Bar-   60
dolino might grant you to me as a companion who would set me
beside the delightful Benacus, on its shore green with woods, who
would cover me with laurel and wild olive, while allowing me to
explore the hidden meanings of the prophets and of both laws,
which are the teachings of God!

I beseech you, Giberti, to bestow upon your poet your fields   65
beside Benacus and your greening olive trees, and to cover him in
an abundance of laurel leaves. For he will be the first to sing your
praises, raising your famous deeds to the heavens in Maeonian
verse. He will tell how Rome, together with the sacred Tiber, mar-
veled at you when you were merely a boy; how it bestowed upon   70
you titles and honors that were merited, but well beyond your
years; how often, at the behest of the holy pontiffs, the supreme
governance of Rome fell to you alone; how the seven hills echoed
with this unwonted praise. Let us honor the mind and wit with
which you traverse barbarian seas and, through conversation, con-   75
strain kings who would rush into war with swords drawn. Through
your words, you pacify new riots and arms, hostilities and battles.

foedera amicitiasque feris, pacemque reportas
Italiae populisque Dei. Nec te tamen ingens
80 terra capit: toto iuvenem tot plausibus orbe
exceptum, tua te pietas, tua maxima virtus
in caelum vehit, et terrae dat spernere honores,
dat contemnere opes, unique incumbere Olympo,
ac solis divorum epulis et nectare pasci.
85   Haec ubi perpetuo cantavit carmine, et omnes
respondent late rupes, tunc concitus oestro
fatidico, plenusque Deo, Davidica vates
ipse etiam pater interpres oracula solvit,
dignus qui ante omnes citharam pertractet eburnam,
90 quam quondam Solymae stupuere arcesque Sionis.

: VIII :

Ad Franciscum Turrianum Veronensem

Turri, si aut mihi villa et lar sit laetior, aut tu
ferre domum tenuem possis parvosque Penates
urbe procul ruri sese abscondentis amici,
quantum ego te his mecum Caphiis in montibus optem,
5 montibus his, ubi, si querulae nemora alta cicadae
non rumpant, equidem vix norim aestatis adesse
tempora, tam leni mitescit Iulius aura!
Sed quid, si est angusta domus, dum pulvere et omni
munda situ, dum sit nullo turbata tumultu,
10 nescia curarum, nullius conscia culpae,
alta ubi per totum sit pax, et amica Camenis
otia, et integri per magna silentia somni?
Quid refert, alius minio laquearia rubra

You forge treaties and alliances, bringing peace to Italy and to the
people of God. But the great earth, by itself, cannot contain you. 80
As you, young man, are received throughout the world with ap-
plause, your piety and great virtue draw you into heaven, enabling
you to despise worldly honors and to hold wealth in contempt, as
you keep your sights on heaven alone and nourish yourself solely
on the food and nectar of the gods.

    As he sang this immortal song, all the hills echoed round. 85
Then, ravished by divine inspiration and full of god, the poet,
himself a father and an interpreter, revealed Davidic prophecies,
he being worthier than all others to take up the ivory lyre that
once amazed Jerusalem and the cliffs of Sion. 90

: VIII :

To Francesco della Torre of Verona

If my villa and its hearth seem at all pleasant to you, della Torre,
or if you could endure the modest house and humble penates of a
friend who has hidden himself in the countryside, far from the
city, how I could wish to have you here with me amid the moun- 5
tains of Incaffi! If the song of the cicada did not break the silence
of the deep woods, I would scarcely know that it was summer, so
gentle is July here, with its soft breezes. But what does it matter if
the house be small, as long as it is free of dust and decay, as long
as it is disturbed by no commotion, being free of all care and in- 10
nocent of all crime, and as long as everything is suffused with deep
peace, with leisure that is dear to the Muses and with sleep undis-
turbed amid great silence? What does it matter if someone else
wishes to see coffered ceilings dyed a brilliant red? I prefer to see

si inspicere, ipse velim fuligine nigra videre?
15   Si non deiectum caelo Iovis igne Typhoea
terrigenasque alios, spirantia signa, videbis,
admirans opus aeterni memorabile Iuli.
At bona Libertas aderit, quae rura beata
praecipue insequitur, simplexque incedit et exlex.
20   Hic tibi, si paulo digitus sit inunctior, aut si
potanti insonuit cyathus, vel si pede utroque
non steteris, nemo obiiciet, nemoque sedentem
arguet, hoc illi si fors super incubuit crus.
Stare, sedere, esse ex libito, et potare licebit.
25   Forsitan et mihi quid vitae, quid sit studiorum,
nosse optas, quo vel damnes, vel singula laudes.
Mane venit, iuvat Auroram Solemque videre
nascentem, qui non alio consurgit Eoo
pulchrior, unde nova laetantur singula luce,
30   et silvae, scopulique, et pictis nubibus aër.
Parte alia Benacum alto de colle saluto,
centum cui virides invergunt flumina nymphae:
ipse sinu magno genitor magno excipit amne.
Tum iuvat aut spectare boves mugitibus alta
35   complentes nemora, aut pulsas in pascua capras.
Prae caper it, cui barba iubat, cui cornua pendent
intorta, et grandes olido de corpore setae.
Pone gregem reliquum compellit arundine virgo
upilio, multo armantur cui baltea fuso.
40   Interea natos, discentes rustica amare
numina, vicini nemoris gelidam voco in umbram,
qui libros, qui secum horae solatia portent.
Hic legitur, viridique toro saxove sedetur
glandifera sub fago aut castanea hirsuta.
45   At variae circum silvis et frondibus altis
assuetae ludunt volucres, atque aethera mulcent.

ceilings darkened by grime! For though you will not find statues   15
here that seem to breathe, statues of Typhoeus and the others Ti-
tans thrown from heaven by Jove's fire, yet will you look with ad-
miration upon the remarkable labors of the eternal month of July.
And here you will encounter decent Liberty, who seeks the blessed
countryside above all else and walks simply, without the con-
straints of laws. Here no one will reproach you if your finger is a   20
bit greasy, if your goblet resounds as you drink, if you cannot
stand on two feet. Nor will anyone scold you if, by chance, your
leg touches his. You may sit or stand, you may eat or drink as
much as you choose. Perhaps, wishing to know how I am getting   25
on in my life or my studies, you will choose to praise or blame one
thing or another. At daybreak it is a delight to behold the dawn
and the newborn sun, which in no other region of the East rises
more beautifully, gladdening the woods, the cliffs and the air with   30
its colored clouds, indeed, gladdening all things with its lovely
light. Elsewhere, from a lofty hill, I hail the Lago di Garda, into
which the green-robed nymphs pour their hundred streams. These
Father Benacus himself receives as a great river in his abundant
lap. It is a pleasure as well to see the cows filling the deep woods   35
with their lowings, as goats leap to pasture. The billy goat leads
the way, with his shaggy beard, his twisting horns that hang
down, and the bristling coat of his pungent body. Behind him a
maiden goatherd, her girdle covered in threads, drives the rest of
the flock with her stick. Meanwhile, I call my children — who are   40
learning to love the rustic deities — into the cool shade of the
neighboring forest and I bid them bring books to beguile the time.
There they sit and read on a green mound or rock, under the
beach tree, rich in acorns, or the shaggy chestnut tree. And brightly   45
colored birds, accustomed to disport themselves amid these woods

Tum densum nemus atque umbrae per gramina laeta
ieiunas nos invitant spatiarier horas.
At fessi haec inter pueri sitiuntque dolentque
50   plus aequo retineri, et iam Musasque, librosque,
et Pana, et gelidi pinus odere Lycaei.
Ergo praecurrere, et aquas et vina pararunt
lucenti in vitro, et flores sparsere nitentes.
Advenio. Primas atro lita mora cruore
55   aut grossi mensas ineunt, cors cetera et hortus
sufficit. Interea crebro sonat area pulsu,
increpitat seges, et duri sub Sole coloni
alternis terram feriunt et adorea flagris;
fit clamor, resonat tellus rupesque propinquae,
60   et paleae sursum strepitu iactantur inanes:
laeta Ceres alto ridens despectat Olympo.
Umbra diem reliquum, somnus, librique, viaeque
producunt, dum siccam aestu Canis excoquit urbem.
Verum, ubi caeruleis serus sese extulit undis
65   Vesper et in caelum surgentia sidera vexit,
vicina e specula, magni admirator Olympi,
alta rupe sedens natis astra omnia monstro,
accendoque animos patriae caelestis amore.
Illi admirari et cognoscere sidera discunt
70   Cepheaque, Arctonque, et servantem plaustra Booten.
      Haec ergo praeferre urbi et contemnere magna
si possis, quid te teneat ne tu ocius ad nos
accurras? Etiam has sedes, haec limina magnus
Naugerus subiit, nec dedignatus adire est
75   Battus, amor Musarum, ipsum quo tempore primus
Pana atque antiquos cecinit Telluris amores.
Hic me etiam desueta deae, medicumque senemque,
carmina iusserunt canere, et ridere beato,

and tall trees, charm the air with their song. Then the thick forest
and the shade invite us to spend hours without eating in the pleas-
ant grass. But the boys, weary of these things and thirsty and un-
happy to be held back too long, have come to dislike poetry and   50
books, as well as Pan and the pines of cool Lycaeum. And so they
have run off and prepared water and wine in gleaming crystal, and
scattered dazzling flowers. Then I arrive: brought to the table first
are blackberries covered in black syrup and young figs, while the   55
yard and garden provide the rest. Then the threshing floor re-
sounds with a great clamor. That is the noise of the harvest, as the
hardened farmers, beneath the sun, thrash the earth and grain in
alternation. A noise is heard and the earth and the neighboring
banks resound, and with much commotion the empty husks are   60
tossed upward. In her happiness, Ceres looks down smiling from
high heaven. The rest of the day is spent in the shade or asleep,
reading or going on walks, while the heat of Sirius bakes the
parched city. Indeed, by the time evening has belatedly emerged
from the blue waters, and borne the rising stars into the sky, from   65
a nearby lookout I sit upon a lofty cliff and, admirer that I am of
the great heavens, I point out all the stars to my children. Thus I
inflame their minds with a love of their celestial home. They learn
to admire and recognize the stars, Cepheus and the Bear and   70
Boötes guarding his wagon.

　　If you are able to prefer such things to city life, and if you can
set aside luxuries, what is to stop you from running to join us
without delay? For the great Navagero has graced this home, nor   75
did Battus, beloved of the muses, disdain to come when first he
sang of great Pan and the ancient loves of Mother Earth. It was
here that the Muses commanded me, an aged doctor, to sing songs
unheard before and to smile in my blessings, forgetting city life

illudentem urbem et male sani murmura vulgi.
80 Verum, haec Gibertus ne viderit ipse, caveto,
ni forsan Bubulone animum curasque relaxans
propter aquam viridi laetus consederit herba,
qua placidus leni descendit Tartarus amne.
Scilicet hic numeros non aspernatur, et audit
85 nos etiam et nostram, quamvis sit rustica, Musam.
Verum, ubi se sibi restituit, mentemque recepit
illam alto intentam caelo, seu sacra sacerdos
munera obit, totum seu contemplatur Olympum,
tum supra et Musas et ruris numina supra est,
90 vitam agitans divum, diis se caelestibus aequans.

: IX :

In mortem Aliprandi Madrutii
fratris Christophori cardinalis Tridentini

Impositum cum te pheretro, miserande Madruti,
cerneret illacrimans Caesar, circumque videret
et spolia, et victis erepta ex hostibus arma,
et modo victrices iuxta maerere phalanges,
5 'Quantum,' inquit, 'tua mors nostris inimica triumphis
laetitiae decorisque adimit! Spes quanta futuri
tecum, Aliprande, cadit! Sed non tua vivida virtus,
ut te hunc aspicerem, tua non promiserat aetas,
sed fore qui, Solymis mecum atque Oriente subacto,
10 barbaricis regum spoliis et mille trophaeis
olim magna tui decorares templa Tridenti.
Invidit mors tanta tibi. Vos nobile corpus
ferte ducis vestri, iuvenes, et reddite matri

and the murmurs of the fevered crowd. Indeed, take care that   80
Giberti not hear about these things, lest, easing his mind and cares
in Povegliano, he should sit happily beside the waters on the green
grass where the Tartaro descends in a gentle stream. For he does
not disdain poetry and listens even to me and my country muse.   85
Truly, when he is his old self again and resumes his intent contem-
plation of high heaven (whether, as a priest, he approaches the
sacred offices or contemplates the immensity of the universe) then
is he superior to the Muses and the rustic sprites, leading as he
does the life of the gods and making himself their equal.   90

: IX :

On the death of Eriprando Madruzzo, brother of Christopher, cardinal of Trent

Sad Madruzzo, when Caesar, weeping, saw you placed in the
hearse, when he saw all around you the spoils and arms seized
from your vanquished foes, and your troops, recently victorious,
weeping nearby, he said, "How much joy and honor were stolen by   5
death, the enemy of our triumphs! How much hope for the future
has fallen with you, Eriprando! But neither your living courage
nor your tender age could have foretold that I would now see you
thus: far rather, I thought that, once you had joined with me to
conquer Jerusalem and the East, you would adorn the great tem-
ples of Trent, your home, with the barbaric spoils of kings and a   10
thousand trophies. But death has denied you that. Take up, young
men, the noble body of your general and bear it to his grieving

exanimi; sed et haec miserae solatia ferte,
15   se tantum peperisse virum, qui, Caesaris usque
et comes et bene gestarum pars maxima rerum,
Caesaris ex animo nullo delebitur aevo.

: X :

Ad Alexandrum Farnesium
cardinalem amplissimum

Priscae virtutis Romani et sanguinis haeres,
Farnesi, quoniam nec dii munuscula laeta
despiciunt hominum, spicas, ac serta rosarum,
libaque, et exigui devotum turis honorem,
5   tu quoque (si mores imitari ac facta deorum
praecipue heroum est) non dedignabere parva
Frastori quae dona tui, natusque paterque,
perpetui affectus monimenta ac pignora mittunt.
Hos tibi, patre Lyco, Scylla genitrice, gemellos
10   dat natus sua dona canes. Scyllae inclita origo
a Nilo est, Lycus a magno descendit Araxe.
Qui quondam Euganeas transmissi munus ad oras
praestabant cunctis, sive aprum figere morsu
esset opus, rapidum cursu seu vincere cervum.
15   Horum igitur sobolem natus tibi ab ubere matris
nutriit ablatam, et nostris exercuit arvis
venatu assiduo et vires durante labore,
nostrorum famam nemorum geminumque ferarum
terrorem, nunc ille tibi quam mittit habendam,
20   Romanis eadem in campis si forte sequetur
gloria et ignota fors in regione iuvabit.

mother. But solace her with these words, that she gave birth to a   15
great man who, as a companion to Caesar and a large part of his
successes, will never be forgotten by him."

: X :

To Alessandro Farnese,
the eminent cardinal

Farnese, heir to ancient virtue and to Roman blood: the gods do
not reject the pleasant little gifts of men, stalks and rosy chaplets,
votive cakes and the devout tribute of a bit of incense. And so, if   5
it is the defining mark of heroes to imitate the habits and deeds of
the gods, then you as well will not contemn the humble gifts that
Fracastoro, father and son, send as a warrant and proof of their
perpetual affection. The son sends you the gift of twin dogs, sired   10
by Lycus and born to Scylla. Scylla's illustrious origin is the Nile,
Lycus's the great Araxis. Dispatched as a gift to the Euganean
land, they far surpassed all other hounds in biting the boar or
outrunning the swift deer. Therefore the boy, on your behalf, has   15
nourished them, taking them from the side of their mother. He
has exercised them in our fields with strenuous hunts and labors
that have hardened their stamina, until they were the talk of the
woods and the twofold terror of the beasts. These hounds he
sends you to keep, so that perhaps the same glory will follow them
into the Roman countryside, and help them in an unfamiliar land.   20

At genitor, nati cum munere, carmina mittit
haec tibi: quae, quamquam tristi fugiente senecta
laetitias cantusque, tamen voluere Camenae
25   in te unum, dominaeque mei nimiumque potentes,
ut canerem, Musaque canes comitarer amica.
Ergo tot rerum curis ac pondere tanto
quo premeris, dum rem Romanam ac publica curas,
si quando defessum animum mentemque remittes
30   liber, et ad dulces poteris te vertere Musas,
haec quoque nostra leges, ea si dignabere tanti,
inter Romanas ut eant spectanda Camenas.
Quod si etiam recreare animum corpusque iuvabit
venatu, et latos saltus ac densa ferarum
35   lustra fatigare, et capreas agitare fugaces,
tum canibus miscere tuis tecumque vocare
ne pigeat nato missos. Hirsutior ille,
cuncta niger, tantum pedibusque et gutture canus,
non invitus herum Tiberonis voce sequetur.
40   Ast Athiso (namque hoc alter de flumine nostro
nomen habet), nec cursu impar, nec dente minaci
segnior, anguineo suffusus terga colore,
frontem albo pictus discrimine, pictus et albo
cervicem caudamque imam pectusque pedesque,
45   addictus lateri numquam discedet herili:
tantus amor domini, nisi forte cupidine praedae
conspectae impatiens etiam retinacula frangat.
Hic tu, vel pulchro Calai vel Tyndaridae alto
Polluci similis, silvas latratibus omnes
50   complebis rupesque hominum clamoribus altas,
vectus equo Haemonio et fulgenti clarus in ostro.
Attonitae visu discent nemora inter amare
rusticae Hamadryades: discetis amare, Dianae

But the boy's father sends you this poem, together with his son's
gift. For although sad old age is wont to flee from songs and ca-   25
rousal, yet the Muses, my overly strong mistresses, have wished
me to send it to you and so accompany the hounds with a friendly
song. For though you are weighed down by many cares and bur-
dens, as you tend to the affairs of the pope and the public, if ever
you are free to relax your weary spirits and mind, and can turn   30
your attention to the dear Muses, then you will read my verse, if
you should deem it worthy to be viewed among the Roman Muses.
And if you decide to refresh your mind and body with hunting, as
you weary the wide thickets and dense lairs of the beasts and chase   35
the swift goats, then perhaps it will not displease you to add to
your hounds the two sent by my son and call on them to accom-
pany you. The shaggier of the two is all black except for his paws
and throat and, eagerly following his master, he answers to the
name of Tybero. But Athiso (for the other takes his name from   40
our river) is his equal in speed and menacing bite. His back has
the color of a snake, while his forehead is marked by a white
stripe, and white are his neck, the tip of his tail, his chest and his
paws. In his devotion, he will never leave his master's side. His   45
love of his owner is great indeed, except when, through desire for
some prey that he has happened to see, verily he breaks the leash
that restrains him. With him you will be able, like handsome Ca-
lais or tall Pollux, the son of Tyndareus, to fill all the woods with
barking and the lofty cliffs with the cries of men, while, resplen-   50
dent in gleaming purple, you sit upon a Haemonian steed. Aston-
ished at the sight, the rustic hamadryads of the woods will learn to
love. You too will learn to love, companions of Diana, though now

insuetae comites; volucri sed concitus ille
55 fertur equo, vestrosque alio deportat amores,
insequiturque feras. Ah, ne illum accensa cupido
venandi excitos silvis impellat in ursos,
ne in saevos impellat apros: tibi cura, Dione
Aeneadum genitrix, sit custodire nepotem,
60 et iuvenem ilicea defessum sistere in umbra.
Sat silvis animoque datum est: illum sua Roma
poscit, et exspectat lati res publica mundi.
I, spes magna Urbis, rebusque vocantibus adsis.
    Interea, quando mihi divus habebere semper,
65 ipse tibi Caphiis sacras in montibus aras
instituam, qua se summo de vertice collis
tollit, et aequatum Benaci prospicit aequor,
et virides olea ripas, patriamque Catulli.
Hic tibi sollemnemque diem et renovanda quotannis
70 sacra tuo statuam semper de nomine dicta.
Tunc rosa, tunc violae, tunc purpurei hyacinthi,
verbenaeque senem deceant, tunc texere flores,
et viridem cano capiti imposuisse coronam,
laetitiaque diem et multo producere Baccho,
75 fallentem senium et curas de corde fugantem.
Forsitan et Musarum aliqua et tibi fautor Apollo
plectra mihi citharamque dabit. Deus ipse canentem
perque tuos annos perque acta illustria ducet:
infanti ut prima impellens cunabula Pallas
80 adcecinit cantu Graio cantuque Latino,
scilicet et fari lingua assuefecit utraque;
ut puerum Aonio perfusum labra liquore
per dulces Musarum hortos et amoena vireta
perduxit, nunc Uranie, nunc Calliopea,
85 nunc Clio monstrante viam, nullaque sororum
non donante rosas et serta virentia lauro.

yet strangers to love. But he is borne upon a swift horse, and car- 55
ries your loves far off, as he chases wild animals. O may his love of
hunting not impel him to encounter bears, roused out of the
woods, or wild boars. May it be a care to you, Dione, mother of
the race of Aeneas, to protect your descendant, and let the weary 60
youth rest under the shade of an oak tree. Enough honor has been
given to these woods and to bravery. His beloved Rome needs
him, and the republic of the wide world awaits him. Go then,
great hope of Rome, and see to the business that calls you.

Meanwhile you will always be divine to me and I myself will
raise sacred altars to you in the mountain of Incaffi, where it rises 65
to its highest point, and looks down on the watery plain of Bena-
cus, on banks green with wild olive, and on the home of Catullus.
Here will I establish, forever after in your name, a solemn day and 70
sacred rites. Then may it befit an old man to wear roses and vio-
lets, bright hyacinth and verveine, to gather flowers and place a
blooming crown upon his white hairs, while drawing out the day
amid revelry and abundant wine, a day that gladdens old age and 75
chases cares from the heart. Perhaps one of the Muses, together
with Apollo, who loves you, will give me a lyre and a harp. The
god himself will lead me as I sing of your life and your illustrious
deeds: how, when you were a child, Minerva first rocked your
cradle and sang to you the music of Greece and Rome, thus ac- 80
customing you to speak both languages; how, as a child whose
lips were moistened by the Aonian stream, you were guided
through the sweet gardens and pleasant groves of the Muses, as
Urania, then Calliope, then Clio showed the way, and all the sis- 85
ters showered you with roses and chaplets rich in laurel. Then

Tum mores animumque dedit sensumque senilem,
atque Urbem regere, ac sacro splendere galero.
Nec iam Roma capit, sed lata in regna vocatum
90   ad pacem Europae, non te maria alta fatigant,
non iuga, non toties superatis nubibus Alpes.
Te Poeninae arces celerem, te Norica saxa
spectarunt rapido montana per ardua cursu,
quantum Sol caeli, tantum telluris obire,
95   matre dea comitante et iter monstrante nepoti.
Nec satis haec: maiora urgent. Germania nuper
grata Deo, nunc ingeniis elata superbis,
detrectare iugum Imperii, et se opponere patrum
sanctorum placitis et sacris legibus audet,
100   nec iam pontificum nec iam ullos Caesaris audit
infelix monitus, sed laevo numine divum
arma parat: socium Caesar te poscit in hostes,
pro sceptro Imperii, pro relligione deorum.
Tunc primum stupidae gentes videre Latinae
105   te fratremque tuum, patria virtute animisque
invictis pariter, res duri et munera belli
tractantes, gemini quales duxisse feruntur
Tyndaridae pulchri Graias in bella cohortes.
Tunc primum Romana acies antiquaque virtus
110   visa fuit: ducibus tantis Mavortia pubes,
magnanimi Aeneadae, memores virtutis avitae,
bella cient: Italo pleni iam milite campi
densantur, iam procedunt longo ordine signa
sublata in ventos, lateque inimica minantur.
115   Nec mora, iam summis Romanus miles et arma
Alpibus apparent: concussae motibus illae
fuderunt gemitus, longe vagus audiit Oenus,
obriguitque gelu, riguerunt flumina Rheni,
et pavidus fluxit demissis cornibus Hister.

they bestowed manners and spirit upon you and an old man's wisdom, teaching you to govern Rome and to shine in your cardinal's cap.

But Rome cannot contain you: when you are called abroad to other kingdoms to broker the peace of Europe, no deep seas or lofty mountains can weary you, nor the Alps, that rise above the clouds. The Apennine summits and the cliffs of Noricum have seen you hastening across steep mountains, and covering as great an expanse of earth as the sun traverses in the sky, while the divine mother accompanied you, her descendant, and showed you the way.

But that was not all: greater deeds draw you on. For Germany, so lately beloved of God, but now puffed up with insolence, dares to reject the yoke of the Empire and to oppose the decrees and sacred laws of the Holy Fathers. No longer does this unhappy land heed any of the warnings of Caesar or the popes. Rather, against the will of the gods, it takes up arms. And so, Caesar seeks you as an ally to fight against his enemies, both for the imperial scepter and for the religion of the gods. Then for the first time the Italian people watched in amazement as you and your brother jointly bore the trials and arms of harsh war, with unvanquished spirit and the virtues of your ancestors, as the handsome twins of Tyndareus are said to have led the Greek forces into battle. Then for the first time, Rome's might and ancient virtue could be seen. With such generals, the warlike and greathearted children of Aeneas, remembering the prowess of their ancestors, marched into war. The fields thronged with Italian soldiers, as the standards raised into the wind proceeded in long defile, breathing hostility. Forthwith the Roman soldier and his arms were seen in the summits of the Alps, which groaned as they were struck by the movements of the troops. Far off the meandering Oenus heard and froze, as did the waters of the Rhine, while the frightened Ister

120   Romanum ad nomen planxerunt pectora matres,
       caraque in Hercynias traxerunt pignora silvas.
       Sed quo me rapitis, Musae? Quid facta revolvo
       Farnesi? Maiora animo iam concipe, teque
       impavidum invictumque aliis accinge triumphis.

∶ XI ∶

Ad eundem
illustrissimum et reverendissimum cardinalem
Alexandrum Farnesium,
cui libros De contagione et contagiosis morbis dedicavit

       Haec ego, florentes Sophiae digressus in hortos,
       Italiae decus o iuvenis, Farnesia proles,
       condebam, lectasque tibi de more sacrabam
       primitias, dum tu magni inter Caesaris arma
5   Gallorumque acies, recti pacisque sequester,
       res miserae Europae fractas componis, et omne
       robur et arma Dei Maumethen vertis in hostem,
       percurrisque omnem, veluti Sol aureus, orbem.
       Fortunate nimis! Quem cunctae applausibus urbes
10   excipiunt, pacisque vocant patremque deumque,
       inque caput, sacrosque sinus, humerosque, manusque
       et nigras violas et candida lilia iactant.
       Cui magna Italia et terrarum maxima Roma

flowed with humbler horns. On hearing the name of Rome, moth-   120
ers beat their breasts and fled with their dear children into the
Hercynian woods. But where are you taking me, Muses? Why do
I repeat, O Farnese, things that are already done? Now conceive
still greater things in your mind, and gird yourself, fearless and
unvanquished, for other triumphs!

: XI :

To the Same
The Most Illustrious and Most Reverend Cardinal
Alessandro Farnese,
to whom the poet dedicated his books on contagious diseases

Having wandered through the flowering gardens of wisdom, I
composed this song for you, scion of the House of Farnese, young
ornament of Italy; and I culled for you, according to custom, the
finest flowers of the new year, while you, amid the arms of great
Caesar and the battles of France, a mediator of peace and justice,   5
rectified the damaged state of sad Europe and turned all the
strength and arms of God against the enemy Mohammed as you
crossed the entire globe like the radiant sun.

How very fortunate you are when every city receives you with
an ovation, calling you the father and god of peace, and throwing   10
dark violets and pale lilies at your head and sacred body, your
shoulders and hands. For you, their son, great Italy and supreme

assurgit, festosque dies et sacra nepoti
15 sollemnesque agitat pompas. Densi undique circum
stant populi, et studio ingenti et clamore secundo
Farnensum genus omne, alto de sanguine ductum
Aeneadum longa serie, super aethera tollunt:
patres, atque duces, et partos mille triumphos;
20 assensu resonat Tybris, et Tyrrhena resultant
litora, septeni responsant gaudia colles.
  O nimium dilecta Deo praelataque longe
progenies, sive imperiis et Marte regendae
sint res Romanae, seu relligionis habenis.
25 Atque equidem e fracto imperio Romaque cadente
servatam hanc stirpem fato, statuentibus et diis,
crediderim, quo Romanum per saecula nomen
staret, et ara Dei, quae primum maxima magnis
auspiciis fundata fuit, sit maxima semper.
30   Quo me, Paule, rapis, quo tuque neposque vocatis
laudibus heroum insuetum? Tu maximus ille es,
uni cui regni triplicis capite alta tiara
consurgit, cui summa uni terna illa potestas
terrarum caelique data est vastique profundi,
35 illorumque aperire fores et claudere posse,
qui, Petri Christique ratem turbante procella
ventorum varia et remorum parte revulsa,
tempestatem omnem atque adversos discutis Euros,
nec sanctam sine honore sinis, sine remige certo,
40 fluctibus in tantis, agitari turbine cymbam:
macte animo Romano et macte ingentibus ausis!
  At tibi quas, iuvenis fortunatissime, dignas
attribuam laudes, generis spes altera tanti,
inclite Alexander, puerum quem plurima virtus,

Rome rise up, honoring you with festive days and sacred rites and   15
solemn pomp. All around stand the people in dense crowds; and
with great zeal and acclamation, they exalt to heaven the entire
race of the Farnese (descended through many generations from the
noble blood of Aeneas), the forefathers and generals of the race as
well as the thousand triumphs they have won. The Tiber resounds   20
in assent and the Tyrrhenian shores reecho the clamor, as the
seven hills resound with joy.

O race most beloved of God, race greatly preferred before all
others—whether Rome is to be governed by Mars and might or
by the reins of religion. Indeed, I could believe that, when the   25
empire perished and Rome fell, fate and the gods preserved this
one race so that the Roman name might last through the centuries
and so that the altar of God, originally built under the most auspi-
cious omens, might ever endure.

Whither, O Paul, are you leading me, whither do you and your   30
scion call me, unaccustomed as I am to sing the praise of heroes?
You are the great man on whose head alone sits the lofty tiara of
the triple kingdom; to you alone is given that supreme, threefold
power over the earth, the sky and the vast deep, together with the   35
power to open and close all access to them. And when some storm
buffets the bark of Peter and of Christ, with part of the oarage
undone, then do you shake off all tempests and adverse winds. For
it is you who do not allow the sacred ship to be buffeted, dishon-
ored and without certain steerage, amid great floods and whirl-   40
pools, thanks to the Roman spirit and to your great endeavors.

But what worthy praise shall I pay you, most fortunate youth,
famous Alexander, second hope of that illustrious line? You were

45   canaque consurgens teneris prudentia in annis,
        et spondens maiora astris felicibus aether
        ad summos meritum ante annos evexit honores,
        et sacri gestare dedit decora alta galeri?
        En quantum de te sacri sibi pastor ovilis
50   spondet avus tuus ille! Animo quae gaudia versat!
        Forsitan et proprio non tam gavisus honore,
        quam spe sublatus tanti et virtute nepotis,
        nescio quid maius praesaga mente volutat.
        Scilicet, et gnarus fatorum et praescius aevi
55   venturi, illa videt felicia tempora, cum tu
        sede sua solioque Dei, diis proximus ipsis,
        considas, cum pontifici tibi maximus orbis
        gratetur, supplexque tuis ferat oscula plantis.
           O mihi postremae tantum dent numina vitae,
60   ipse etiam ut tum te tremulus, confectus et annis
        aspiciam, sanctosque pedes prostratus adorem!
        O et si possim canere et tua dicere facta,
        et ventura novo tecum saecla aurea mundo!
        Nam video sub te victum longeque fugatum
65   Maumethen se Caucaseis includere portis,
        at Pacem viridi redimitam tempora oliva
        ire per Europam magnam atque invisere terras,
        quam pia Relligio et iunctis Concordia dextris
        et Probitas et Amor Recti comitentur euntem.
70   Salve, magne Tybri! Salve et tu, maxima rerum
        Roma parens! Salvete arces, collesque Latini,
        aurea qui primi longo meministis ab aevo
        saecula, cum nulli variarent iugera sulci,
        sponte sua sed terra ferax daret omnia, et ipsae
75   praeberent dulci victum de robore glandes,
        et nunc venturis eadem speratis ab annis.

only a boy when abundant virtue, and an aged prudence that arose   45
in youth, and heaven itself that promised greater things under its
auspicious stars, all raised you up, precocious but deserving, to the
highest honors and allowed you to wear the lofty ornament of
the sacred cap. Indeed, how much promise does your renowned
grandfather, the shepherd of the sacred flock, perceive in you,
what happiness does he nurture in his heart! Perhaps he does not   50
rejoice more in his own honor than in the hope and virtue of his
great offspring, from whom he imagines still greater things in his
prophetic mind. For surely he is aware of destiny and can foresee
the coming age and happy times when you, next to the gods them-   55
selves, will occupy his seat and the throne of God, and when the
entire world will rejoice in your pontificate and, a suppliant, kiss
your feet.

O may the gods grant that I might live long enough, so that,
trembling and overcome with years, I might look upon you and   60
bow down before your sacred feet. And I wish I could sing and
relate your deeds, and describe the golden ages that will descend
upon a new world! Now I see Mohammed, whom you have van-
quished and chased far off, imprisoned beyond the gates of the   65
Caucasus, while Peace, her head crowned with the green olive
branch, passes through great Europe and overwhelms the entire
earth, while pious Religion and Concord with joined hands and
Probity and Love of Justice accompany her as she goes.

Hail great Tiber! Hail great Rome, mother of all things, and   70
you hills and citadels of the Latins who can recall of old a golden
age, when no furrows marked the fields, but the fertile earth
brought forth all things spontaneously, and the very acorns of the   75
sweet oak provided sustenance. Even now may you hope for the
same in years to come!

: XII :

Ad Iulium III pontificem maximum

Maxime divini pastor gregis, inclite Iuli,
in terris cui summa uni est concessa potestas,
sceptra vicesque Dei gerere, et regna infera Ditis
caelorumque fores aperire et claudere posse,
5   si tu, dum magnae Italiae, dum prospicis omni
Europae, et vasta mundi sub mole laboras,
paulisper potes a tantis secedere curis,
et potes agrestes pastorum audire Camenas,
nunc aures adhibe placidas mihi. Namque ego quae Pan,
10   Pan magnus, cecinit nostros ventura sub annos,
nunc referam, tua, magne pater, pars maxima quorum est,
cuius ab auspiciis Parcae nova saecula volvunt.
Nec te paeniteat pastorem audire canentem,
quando etiam Admeti tauros formosus Apollo
15   pavit ad Amphrysi ripas, tenuique cicuta
non puduit cantare deum sub tegmine acerno;
et Veneri dilectus oves ductavit Adonis.
Scilicet et tu etiam, post grandia nomina, pastor
diceris, atque hoc in primis cognomine gaudes,
20   et pecudes curare soles pecudumque magistros.
    Forte ego, dum medio terras Sol excoquit aestu,
ipse Suessani pastor puer incola campi
ducebam pastas viridi de valle capellas
in nemorum secreta, umbras et frigora quaerens,
25   qua placidus cursu descendit in aequora Lyris.
Est lucus prisci quem sacravere Latini

: XII :

To Pope Julius III

Great shepherd of the divine flock, famous Julius, to whom alone
is granted supreme power on earth as well as the right to wield the
scepter in God's stead and to open or close the nether realms of
Dis and the gates of heaven: if, as you look upon great Italy and all 5
of Europe, if, as you labor under the vast weight of the world, you
can absent yourself a moment from such great cares and listen to
the shepherds' rustic muse, then hear me now with indulgence as I
relate what Pan, great Pan, prophesied for our time. For you play 10
a large part in those prophecies and under your auspices the Fates
spin out new ages. But feel no shame in hearing a shepherd sing,
since handsome Apollo once fed the flocks of Admetus beside the 15
Amphrisian banks and, though a god, he was not ashamed to play
the lowly flute beneath a maple tree. And Adonis too, the beloved
of Venus, once herded sheep. Even you, in addition to your grand
names, are called Pastor, and this name delights you most of all.
For you care for flocks and for the leaders of flocks. 20

It happened once, while the midsummer sun burned the land,
that I myself, a young shepherd of the Suessan fields, led my sated
goats from a green valley to some hidden woods, as I sought cool 25
shade where the calm Liris descends into the sea. There I found a

Silvano, in cuius medio densa ilice cinctum
est pratum, agrestes ubi dii persaepe videri
audirique solent: hic capripedes satyriscos
30   pastorumque manum, iunctis per mutua palmis,
in gyrum canere et laetas agitare choreas
invenio admirans. Medius Pan magnus ovantem
ad calamos cantusque regit ducitque coronam.
Dumque deus canit ipse, silet tum cetera pubes;
35   dum silet ille, alii thiasos cantusque sequentes
instaurant, repetuntque dei postrema canentis:
ingeminat postrema nemus, respondet et Echo.
Tum me respiciens mihi sanguine proximus Acmon,
Acmon Aquinatis pastor gregis, 'Huc, puer,' inquit,
40   'huc ades, o Neore, et te his adiunge choreis
aut, spectare magis si te iuvat, aggere ab illo
prospice, dum saturae sua ducant otia caprae.'
Cui ego: 'Quin potius iuvet hoc de cespite, vestros
spectantem lusus, molli requiescere in herba.'
45   Et tum forte deus, buccas sandyce rubentes
inflans et picea frontem praecinctus acuta,
ad calamos circumsiliens, haec carmina cantu
fatidico insanus latas fundebat ad auras:
    'Dicite Io, satyrisci, et Io geminate, coloni:
50   aurea felici nascuntur saecula mundo.'
Excipiunt iuvenes, iterat nemus, assonat Echo:
'Aurea felici nascuntur saecula mundo.'
Tum sequitur deus: 'Ante tamen rex magnus Olympi
bellumque, horribilemque famem, diramque flagellis
55   armatam Alecto e tenebris et faucibus Orci
immittet terris, genus ut mortale coëcens

grove that the early Latins had consecrated to Silvanus. In the middle of it is a field encircled by dense oak trees, where the rustic gods can often be seen and heard. Here, to my amazement, I often found goat-footed satyrs and a flock of shepherds, their hands 30 linked in a circle, as they sang and joined in happy choruses. In the middle great Pan guided the exulting crowd to the music of pipes and song. While the god sang, the young men were silent. When 35 he was silent the others followed with processions and dances, as they repeated the last words sung by the chanting god. The woods reverberated with their words and Echo responded. Then my close relation Acmon, the shepherd of Aquino, looked at me and said, "Come here, young Neorus, and join in our song. Or if you prefer 40 to watch, do so from that hill, while the well-fed goats disport themselves at leisure." I replied: "I would prefer to watch your revelries from this meadow, while I lie in the soft grass." And just 45 then it happened that Pan inflated his vermilion cheeks, his forehead crowned with prickly pine, as he danced to the music of the pipes and madly sang this prophetic song to all the winds:

"Sing, then you satyrs! Shepherds, you join in!
Across the happy world the golden years begin!" 50

The youths took up the song, the grove resounded and Echo repeated: "Across the happy world the golden years begin!"

Then the god resumed: "But before that time, the great king of Olympus will loose upon the earth war and horrid famine and dread Alecto, armed with a scourge, sent forth from darkness and 55 the jaws of Orcus. Thus would he compel and punish the mortal

castiget, fraudesque hominum, fastusque superbos,
et luxus, et spes miseras, et gaudia vana,
dum tandem sese atque deos cognoscere discant.
60 Mox tantum exspectatum illud, quod carmine sacro
tot vates cecinere pii, felicibus astris
adveniet tempus, quo Mons ille arduus, ille
Mons ingens sublime caput super omnia tollat
culmina, sidereum qui vertice tangat Olympum,
65 quo neque vis ventorum adeat, non fulminis ignes.'
        'Dicite Io, satyrisci, et Io geminate, coloni:
aurea felici nascuntur saecula mundo.'
        'Hoc in Monte Dei pecudes pascentur et agni,
graminis aeterni pingues, et velleris aurei.
70 Exsilient et aquae vivae, quibus ubera caprae
grandia distendant, distendant ubera vaccae.
Non malus hic serpens, non noxia creverit herba,
non sentes, sterilisve filix, non frigida taxus,
sed bis lecta seges, sed bis gravis uva racemis,
75 corticibusque cavae sudabunt balsama pinus.
Hinc, magnis praestantem animis et fortibus ausis,
fortunata nimis pastorem haec saecula habebunt,
qui virtute regat populos et legibus aequi,
divinas qui impinguet oves, et pascua late
80 extendat, pecudesque ipsas et ovilia servet.
Hic primum diram Alecto et Cocytia monstra
Caucasea aerata religabit rupe catena.
Inde famem miseram e Latio populisque deorum
pellet in hostiles gentes et barbara regna.
85 Tum laeta Ubertas segetumque onerata maniplis
alma Ceres Italas spicis venerabitur aras,
quam circum pueri salient et rustica pubes,

race for the deceit of men, for their vaunting vanities and extrava-
gance, their sad aspirations and empty joys. Then finally they will
come to know themselves and the gods as well. Then, under auspi-   60
cious stars, the long-awaited time will come that so many pious
prophets foretold in sacred song, when that steep and massive
mountain will raise its lofty head above all the other summits and
touch starry Olympus with its peak, beyond the reach of winds or   65
lightning.

    "Sing, then you satyrs! Shepherds, you join in!
    Across the happy world the golden years begin!"

    "Upon this mountain the goats and lambs of God will graze,
fattened on eternal grass and wearing a golden fleece. Gleaming   70
water will rush in abundance and the udders of the goats and cows
will swell to fullness. Here no evil snake or noxious weed will ap-
pear, no brambles or sterile fern or frigid yew, but rather twice
gathered harvests and grapes heavy upon the vine, and from their   75
barks the hollowed pine trees will exude balm. And so, that exces-
sively favored age will hail a shepherd, conspicuous in nobility and
bold action, who will rule his people with virtue and just laws,
feeding the divine lambs and expanding their pastures, while he   80
keeps the sheep and sheepfold safe. First he will chain dire Alecto
and the monsters of Cocytus to the Caucasian cliffs with brazen
chains. Then will he repel sad hunger from Italy and the people of
God and redirect it toward his enemies, the barbarian kingdoms.
Glad abundance and nourishing Ceres, encumbered with grain,   85
will honor the altars with wheat. And the young men and rustic

ridentesque iocos incomptaque carmina dicent.
At noti Musis Damones et Alphesiboei,
90   vota patri magno laudesque et sacra canentes,
aeternis illum numeris ad sidera tollent,
heroemque, deumque, salutiferumque vocabunt.'
    'Dicite Io, satyrisci, et Io geminate, coloni:
aurea felici nascuntur saecula mundo.'
95   'Ille animum mox ad pacem et discordia regum
pectora convertet, sanctisque hortatibus iras
atque odia, et caecos regnorum et laudis amores,
horrendamque sitim caedis fusique cruoris
sedabit, pelletque feri mala semina belli.
100   Tum Pax alma ferens ramos felicis olivae,
atque Amor, et iunctis pariter Concordia dextris,
et Genius comitum, et generis Hymenaeus amator
invisent late populos, Latiique per arva
laetitiam risusque ferent. Tum iusta cupido
105   bellorum piaque arma Dei vertentur in hostes.
Iam video augustis late plena aequora velis
fervere, iam trepidare vagi septem ostia Nili,
Euphratemque Tigrimque suo se condere in amne.
Iam nec Bactra ipsum capiunt, non India tota
110   Maumethen fugientem, ipsum non Caucasus ingens,
non qui tot silvas, iuga tot comprendit Imaus.'
    'Dicite Io, satyrisci, et Io geminate, coloni:
aurea felici nascuntur saecula mundo.'
    'Quae nam, quae properant tantae per caerula puppes
115   devotae ad Tiberim magnaeque ad moenia Romae,
ceu densae ad nidos latum per inane columbae?
Agnosco gentem innocuam, numerumque beatum,
felices animas, fatis ab origine prima
dilectas, quae caelo olim divisque fruantur.

youth will dance around, laughing and telling jokes and singing
untutored songs. But then Damon and Alphesiboeus, no strangers   90
to the muses, will sing prayers and praise and sacred songs to the
great father, exalting him to heaven in eternal verse as they call
him a hero, a god and the bringer of health.

"Sing, then you satyrs! Shepherds, you join in!
Across the happy world the golden years begin!"

"Next he will bend the rage and the discordant hearts of kings   95
toward peace: with his sacred injunctions he will calm their anger
and hatred, their blind desire of conquest and praise, their horrid
thirst for slaughter and split blood, as he banishes the evil seeds of
cruel war. Then nurturing Peace, bearing branches of the fertile   100
olive, will join hands with Love and Concord, with the Genius of
friendship and Hymenaeus, lover of progeny, as they travel to all
the people, filling the Italian fields with happiness and laughter.
And so the just desire of war and pious arms will be turned   105
against the enemies of God: already I behold the great sea roiled
by august sails, as the seven mouths of the meandering Nile
tremble and the Tigris and Euphrates hide themselves among their
banks. No longer can Bactria, nor all of India, contain the fleeing   110
Mohammed, nor the vast Caucasus, nor the Himalayas with their
many mountains and woods.

"Sing, then you satyrs! Shepherds, you join in!
Across the happy world the golden years begin!"

"What, O what are these many sacred ships that hasten over
the blue waters, devoted to the Tiber and the walls of great Rome,   115
like multitudinous doves hastening to their nests through the
broad expanse of air? I recognize the spotless race and their
blessed numbers, happy souls who were chosen by fate from the
very beginning and who one day will enjoy the favors of heaven

120 En iam sanctam urbem, iam septem in collibus aras
     impositas, summique pedes pastoris adorant.
     Hos inter, video, et nostri longa aequora sulcant
     Arcades, Italiamque petunt fataliaque arva
     Arcades. O soli quondam cantare periti
125 pastores, quos Iustitia, e tellure recedens,
     postremos liquit, nunc rursus laeta revisit.
     O sancti, properate; vocat Deus aethere ab alto:
     vos alius iam grex aliudque exspectat ovile.
     Quin venit illa dies, cum nos quoque Maenala nostra
130 Arcadiamque omnem, qua immani a gente repulsi
     fugimus in Latium, longo post tempore tandem
     visamus dulcemque auram. O placidissime Peneu,
     o Ladon, vos o gelidi pineta Lycaei,
     quando ego per vestros meditabor carmina lucos?
135 Maenalios quando recinet mea tibia versus?
     Maenalus auritas dantesque oracula quercus
     semper habet, semper doctas ille audit avenas.
     Concipe Maenalios, mea tibia, concipe versus.'
         Talia cantabat memorans Pan magnus. At Acmon
140 'Haec referes, puer,' inquit, 'et hoc tibi munus habeto
     nunc parvum: ventura dies maiora reservat.'
     Tum mihi fiscellam dono dedit optimus Acmon,
     dicere et occasus astrorum, dicere et ortus,
     et quid quaeque ferat tellus, quae commoda Baccho,
145 quae Cereri, quidnam ventos, quid nuntiet imbres,
     quae tempestatum, caeli quae signa sereni,
     denique quae cunctis natura sit indita rebus,
     virtutem in primis et honestum quemque docere,
     ac, vitii ipse expers, aliena notare paratus.
150 Et iam tempus erat pastum deducere capras.

and the gods. And now they adore the sacred city and the seven 120
altars placed upon the seven hills and the feet of the supreme
shepherd. Among these, I see as well my fellow Arcadians who till
the vast sea as they seek Italy and their predestined fields. O shep-
herds, you who once were the only ones learned in song, you 125
whom Justice left behind when she abandoned the earth: how
happy she is now to see you once again. O holy men, come quickly,
for God calls you from the height of heaven! Another flock,
another sheepfold awaits you. For surely the day approaches when
we too, after so many years, will again see our beloved Maenalus
and all of Arcady, from which a wretched race sent us fleeing into 130
Italy, and we will breathe its pure air again. O peaceful Peneus, O
Ladon, and you pine groves of cool Lycaeus: when will I sing
songs within your groves? When will my pipe sing the songs of 135
Maenalus? Maenalus still has those oaks that listen and give ora-
cles, and still does he listen to the playing of learned reeds. Play
then, my flute, the songs of Maenalus!"

Such was the song of great Pan. But Acmon said, "Repeat these 140
words, lad, and in return take now this small gift. The coming day
brings greater things." For then great Acmon gave me this pipe to
describe the rise and fall of stars and which crops come from each
sort of land, which befit Bacchus and which Ceres, and which 145
signs foretell of wind and rain, of storms and of fair weather. And
finally he gave me the power to sing the essential nature of all
things, the power to teach virtue and honor and, being free of vice
myself, to be prepared to censure it in others.

And now it was time to lead the goats to pasture. 150

: XIII :

Incidens

Battus, amor Dryadum, defunctum pastor Iolam
flebat. Eum fontes, Alpinaque numina circum,
Sarcaque, pumiceoque sedens Benacus ab antro
maerentem lacrimis consolabantur obortis;
5   ille autem, nulla accipiens solamina, tantum
deserta sub rupe, in litoribus Benaci,
talia nequicquam surdas iactabat ad undas:
    'Immites divi, et crudeles vos quoque Parcae,
crudeles nimium Parcae. Vos ibitis amnes,
10   aëriae stabunt rupes; nusquam amplius ipse
his terris, numquam hoc caelo agnoscetur Iolas,
ut cecidit semel, in pratis ut purpureus flos,
quem tetigit vel hiems vel iniquo Sirius astro.
Currite iam fluviorum undae et producite vitam,
15   et rupes durate: tamen non alter Iolas
hos pecus in montes, non haec ad flumina ducet.'

: XIV :

Incidens
ad Ioannem Baptistam Turrianum Veronensem

Illa, colum exercens, saxo consedit aprico,
laeta tepore novo et liquefacta Sole pruina:
at iuxta nemore in magno grex pascitur omnis.

: XIII :

Fragment

Battus the shepherd, beloved of the dryads, wept at the death of
Iolas. All around him the streams and mountain sprites, the river
Sarca, and Benacus in his pumice cave, consoled the mourner,
covered in tears. But he would accept no consolation. Instead he   5
sat under a deserted rock on the shores of Benacus and vainly
called out as follows to the heedless waves:

   "You savage gods and cruel fates, too cruel: you streams will   10
continue to flow and you lofty cliffs will continue to stand firm.
But Iolas will never again be seen in these mountains or under this
sky, once he has died, like a beautiful flower blighted by winter or
by Sirius with its malign star. Run, then, you waters of the rivers,
with your unending life! And you cliffs, stand firm! But no other   15
Iolas will lead his flocks to these mountains or streams."

: XIV :

Fragment
To Giovanni Battista della Torre of Verona

Plying her distaff, she sat upon a sunny rock, delighted by the
warmth of spring and by the sun as it dissolved the frost. But
nearby, in the vast woods, the entire flock was eating.

: XV :

Hiems, ad eundem

Frigidus at silvis Aquilo si increverit, aut si
hiberni pluviis descendent nubibus imbres,
nos habeat domus, et multo lar luceat igne.
Upilio ingentem aut fagum vel scissile robur
5   sufficiat, tum vos, claro quando igne soletis,
iuniperi suaves, circum diffundere odores,
et vos Palladiae flammis imponat olivae.
Ante focum tibi parvus erit, qui ludat, Iulus,
blanditias ferat, et nondum constantia verba.
10   Ipse legam magni tecum monumenta Maronis.
O fortunatos nimium, si fata, quod aevi
nos manet, hanc una dederint producere vitam!

: XVI :

Ver, ad eundem

Iam veniet ver purpureum, iuvenisque revertens
annus aget Zephyros, et caelo desuper alto
deducet pleno genitalia semina cornu,
unde hominum genus et pecudum, vitaeque natantum,
5   et pictae volucres, et amantes rorida plantae
in venerem caeco aeterni rapiuntur amore.
Gaudete, o quicumque bonum speratis, agrestes,
quorum amor est sobolis, studiumque nepotibus arva

: XV :

Winter, to the same

But if the frigid north wind roars or if winter storms descend in rain filled clouds, then let us remain at home and may the hearth shine forth with a great fire. Let the shepherd prepare logs of the huge beech or oak, easily split. Then let him place you in the fire,   5 junipers, who are wont to spread sweet odors all around, and you too, olive trees of Athena. In front of the fire you will have young Giulio to play with, as he charms you and speaks words as yet incoherent. For my part, I will join you in reading the remains of   10 great Vergil. How lucky we should be if fate allowed us to pass what is left of this life in one another's company.

: XVI :

Spring, to the same

Now beauteous spring will come and, as the young year returns, it will bring on zephyrs and draw down from high heaven its generative seeds in an abundant horn. And then the race of men and beasts, of fish and parti-colored birds and plants that love dew, will   5 be ravished eternally with blind love of Venus. Rejoice, all you rustics who hope for good outcome, who are eager of offspring, who strive to cultivate your fields for the sake of your grandchildren

incolere, et parvas ulmis attollere vites:
10 annus io, novus annus adest, mutatur et aetas,
et meliora novo nascuntur saecula mundo.
Bella pater procul et diras Saturnus Erinnes
arcebit caro e Latio, ac sub Tartara mittet.
Tum Letum, et caecus Furor, et vesana Cupido
15 perpetuis extra terras religata catenis
persolvent poenas scelerum; at Pax alta per omnem
Italiam magno populos sub Caesare viset.
Ille autem insignis spoliis et mille trophaeis
instituet festos alta ad Capitolia ludos.
20 Stabit onusta ingens Tarpeii ad limina templi
quercus honore sacra et praenuntia temporis aurei.
Tum vescae glandes; tum, terra sponte ferente
omnia, comparibus disiunget colla iuvencis
agricola, et rudibus mirabitur hordea sulcis
25 sponte adolere sua, et nullo frumenta colono
undantem laetis segetem flavescere campis.
Noctibus in silvas et mollia prata serenis
aetherio dulcem commixtum nectare rorem
sudabit caelum, tenera qui lectus ab herba
30 mortales saturat mensa dapibusque deorum.
Salve, magne Tybri, et vos, natae Tybride nymphae,
tuque, senex pater Eridane, et qui flumine Tusco,
Benace, in nostro placidus perlaberis agro.
Tuque, Athesis, cunctique amnes salvete Latini,
35 diique omnes magnae Hesperiae, qui saecula soli
aurea Saturni primo meministis ab aevo,
cum sepes vel limes adhuc communibus agris
non foret aut ulli variarent iugera sulci,
sponte sua sed terra ferax daret omnia et ipsae
40 praeberent dulci victum de robore glandes.

and to join frail vines to mighty elms! For the new year has come! 10
It is a new age now, and happier centuries are dawning across a
new world. Father Saturn will keep wars and dire Furies far from
our beloved Italy, hurling them down into hell. Then Death and
blind Fury and maddened Lust, banished from these lands in per- 15
petual chains, will pay for their crimes. Instead deep Peace will
spread across Italy and visit its peoples ruled by great Caesar,
while he, resplendent in spoils and a thousand trophies, will insti-
tute festive games atop the Capitol. Beside the Tarpeian temple 20
will stand a huge and full oak tree, sacred with honors and pro-
phetic of a golden age. Then you will see tender acorns. Then, as
the earth spontaneously brings forth all things, the farmer will
untie the necks of joined oxen and will marvel as barley emerges
on its own out of the unworked furrows, and grain, in swaying 25
harvests, dazzles the fertile fields, without the help of any hus-
bandry. In the serene nights, the sky will cover the forests and
grassy fields with sweet dew and heavenly nectar. Gathered from
the soft grass, it feeds men to satiety with the feasts and fare of the 30
gods. Hail to you, great Tiber, and you nymphs born of the Tiber,
and you, aged father Eridanus, and Benacus, who with your Etrus-
can stream, glide gently through our fields. And hail to you, too,
Adige, and all you rivers of Italy, and all the gods of great Hespe- 35
ria, who alone remember from time immemorial the golden age of
Saturn: when no fence or boundary divided the common fields,
nor any furrow scarred the land. Rather the fertile earth gave all
things up spontaneously and the acorns of the sweet oak tree pro- 40
vided sustenance.

: XVII :

Incidens, ad eundem

Quarum pars, brumae impatiens et condita terrae,
exspectat ver egelidum flatusque Favonii,
pars, passura hiemem, laeta ab radice virescit,
emittitque comam: siculumque atque altera beta,
5   atque ari virides, et odoriferae calaminthae,
atque olus, atque rumex, et salsi gramina crithmi.
Quas inter suaves mollesque aspirat odores
nunc decus hortorum, menta: at, si vera loquuntur,
nympharum quondam pulcherrima Graiugenarum.
10   Tum iuvat et frondes apii, et sisymbria laeta,
intubaque, et toto florentes frigore sonchos
incolere, atque hortis Aquilonem arcere nocentem.

: XVIII :

Aliud

Nox venit, et pastae redeunt ad tecta capellae.
Prae caper it, cui barba iubat, cui cornua pendent
intorta, et grandes olido de corpore setae.
Pone gregem reliquum compellit arundine virgo
5   upilio, multo armantur cui baltea fuso.
At mater longaeva, igni dum brassica fervet,

⁚ XVII ⁚

Fragment, to the same

. . . whereof a part, impatient of winter and planted in the earth, awaits the warmth of spring and the Favonian winds. Another part will survive winter and gladly grow green from its root, and send forth leaves: among these the honey garlic and next the beet, 5 as well as green arum and fragrant calamint, weeds and sorrel and leaves of salty samphire. Also among these, the mint plant, now the pride of gardens, exhales its sweet and pleasant odors: but if report is true, the mint was once the most beautiful nymph of Greece. Next it is advisable to plant leaves of parsley and fertile 10 rocket, endives and sow thistle that flower even in the cold, and to keep the baneful north wind from the gardens.

⁚ XVIII ⁚

Another fragment

Night comes on and the sated goats return to the fold. The billy goat leads the way, with his shaggy beard, twisting horns that hang down, and the bristling coat of his pungent body. Behind him a maiden goatherd, her girdle covered in threads, drives the 5 rest of the flock with her crook. But while cabbage boils in the fire,

mulctra effert, gravidoque recens lac ubere mulget.
Rusticus interea pinguis collector olivae,
interea et validus prima de nocte bubulcus
advenere domum: congesta tum focus orno
ingenti aut fago vel fragmine roboris ardet.
Tolluntur laetae flammae lateque relucent.

10

: XIX :

Aliud incidens ad eundem

At nemora et liquidis manantia fontibus arva
et, placidus, myrteta inter laurosque virentes,
vicinus nitido Benacus labitur amne.
At focus, et circum pueri vernaeque canentes,
dum cena undanti coquitur silvestris aheno,
grandiaque exurunt crepitantes robora flammae.
Suspensae e summis pendent laquearibus uvae,
malaque, castaneaeque, et passo fistula ventre.
Hiberna de nocte, boum stabula alta petuntur.
Una omnes matresque, virique, omnisque iuventus
insomnem exercent noctem: pars pensa fatigat,
pars texit teneros Amerino vimine qualos,
atque anus hic aliqua interea, dum vellera carpit
et teretem tremulo propellit pollice fusum,
languentes oculos fabella fallit inani.

5

10

15

her aged mother take out her pales and draws fresh milk from the laden udders. Meanwhile at dusk the farmer, collector of fat olives, has returned home, accompanied by the strong cowherd. The 10 hearth burns with piles of wood from a great ash tree, from a beech and a bit of oak. The dancing flames rise up, spreading light abroad.

: XIX :

Another fragment, to the same

But amid groves and fields watered with clear streams, amid myrtle bowers and green laurel trees, neighboring Benacus, with its gleaming wave, glides placidly along. There is a hearth and around it the children and the servants are singing, while a rustic supper is 5 cooked in a boiling pot and crackling flames consume the large logs. Clustered grapes hang down from the ceiling, with apples and chestnuts and sausages. It is a winter's night and the cows seek the shelter of their lofty stable. Together, fathers and mothers and 10 all their children pass a sleepless night. Some of them perform their chores, while others weave soft baskets out of withe from Ameria. And as some old woman shears a fleece and draws the smooth thread with tremulous thumb, she beguiles their weary 15 eyes with an empty tale.

: XX :

Aliud

Mane domi validos pluvia ut conclusit agrestes,
caeditur iliceo distenta sagimine porca.
Laeta domus: tum, sollicita in farcimine, mater
pingue suis niveum, et dissecti frusta cerebri,
5   et niveum lac purpureo cum sanguine miscet.
Tum semen marathri atque arentis gramina thymbrae
adiicit, et coli insperso sale concava complet.

: XXI :

In natalem diem Iani Fregosii, Caesaris filii

Sacrorum si plena deo sunt pectora vatum,
     si norunt triplices fata futura deae,
fortunate infans, verus tibi grandia vates,
     grandia concordes concinuere deae.
5   Ecce tuo felix nasci novus annus ab ortu
     incipit, atque omen nomine habere tuo.
Cresce cito, magnique patris mirarier acta
     incipe, et invicti Caesaris arma sequi.
Tempus erit, tibi cum partis iam mille triumphis,
10   et fessi rebus compositis Latii,

: XX :

Another fragment

In the early morning, when rain has kept the strong farmers in-
doors, a sow, fattened with acorns, is slaughtered. The house is
merry. Then the solicitous mother makes a sausage out of the pig's
white fat, odd bits of brain and pale milk mixed with red blood. 5
To this she adds fennel seed and leaves of dry savory and fills the
bowl, sprinkled with salt.

: XXI :

On the birthday of Giano Fregoso, son of Cesare

If the hearts of sacred poets are filled with god and if the three
Fates can foretell the future, then, happy child, the truth-telling
poet and the concordant goddesses prophesy great, great things for
you. Behold, a new year begins since you were born and it finds 5
an omen in your name. Grow up quickly so that you can marvel at
the deeds of your great father and follow the standards of unvan-
quished Caesar. There will be a time when you will have earned a
thousand trophies and peace will reign throughout wearied Italy, 10

barbaricis captis opibus, ducibusque subactis,
    multa tibi circum tempora laurus eat.
Tum laeta ante tuum stabit Victoria templum,
    claudet et aerata limina ahena sera.

: XXII :

De partu Victoriae Farnesiae,
Guidi Ubaldi Feretrii Urbini ducis coniugis

Lucinae Iunonis opem Victoria supplex
    cum peteret, placido sic ait ore dea:
'Sis licet Aeneadum et Veneris de sanguine avito
    nata, puella, tamen digna favore meo es,
5   quam Charites tanto iunctae comitantur honore,
    grandia quam Parcae fata manere canunt:
quippe, ubi Iunonis flos et Saturnia quercus
    iungantur, faustis currere Isaurum aquis,
promittique tibi sobolem, qua pristina virtus
10   Italiae, et priscus restituatur honos.
Nascere, magne puer, patremque imitatus avosque,
    magna aude. Non vos Umbria magna capit.'
Et iam infans, sanctasque manus divamque secutus,
    optati in lumen aetheris exierat.
15 Ergo et quod potuit, risu agnovitque parentem,
    praesentisque dedit nuntia signa deae.

when Barbarian treasures have been won and generals defeated
and abundant laurels will adorn your brow. Then rejoicing Victory
will stand before your temple and shut its brazen doors with a bolt
of bronze.

: XXII :

On the birth of a son to Vittoria Farnese, wife of Guidobaldo da Montefeltro, Duke of Urbino

When Victoria, as a suppliant, sought the help of Juno Lucina, the
goddess gently replied: "Though you are born of the ancestral
blood of Venus and the sons of Aeneas, still you are worthy of my
aid. Their arms linked, the Graces escort you with much honor,   5
while the Fates prophesy a great destiny. For where the flower of
Juno has been joined to the Saturnian oak, the waters of the Isau-
ros run auspiciously, and a son will be born to you who will restore
to Italy its former virtue and honor. Come forth, great child, and   10
in imitation of your father and your forefathers, dare to do great
things. Great Umbria is not big enough for you." And already, in
obedience to the doctor's sacred hands and to the goddess, the boy
emerged into the light of the hoped-for air. Not yet able to speak,   15
he acknowledged his mother with a smile and gave proof that the
goddess was present among them.

: XXIII :

Tumulus Francisci Mariae Molsae
Mutinensis

Quod Molsae fuerat mortale, hac conditur urna,
    exstruxere suis quam Aonides manibus.
Coetibus at superum fruitur nitidissimus almis
    itque comes magno spiritus Hippolyto,
5   quem Medica de gente satum pulcherrima Virtus
    extulit et caeli templa tenere dedit,
quemque unum ante omnes coluit, dum fata sinebant,
    atque oculis vates praetulit ipse suis.

: XXIV :

Ad Ioannem Lipomanum
ex Veronensi praetura decedentem

Hadriacum, Lipomane, Athesis dum curret in aequor,
dum meritis reddetur honos et gratia, semper
praetori tibi debebit Verona patrique
linquenti monumenta annos mansura per omnes.
5   Illa tibi semper divinos solvet honores,
et condet tua perpetuis annalibus acta.
I, spes o Venetum, et quem iam moderamina parva
non capiunt, i, te maioribus insere sceptris,
et lacrimas et vota, quibus comitamur euntem,
10   accipe, discessusque tui dona ultima porta.

⁝ XXIII ⁝

The tomb of Francesco Maria Molza
of Modena

The mortal part of Molza lies buried in this urn, which the
Aonian Muses made with their own hands. But the great man
himself now, in full splendor, enjoys the nurturing friendship of
the Gods. His spirit accompanies the great Ippolito, a scion of the   5
Medici, whom beautiful Virtue exalted and admitted into the
temples of heaven. While he lived, the poet loved Ippolito more
than all other people, more even than his own eyes.

⁝ XXIV ⁝

To Giovanni Lippomano
On stepping down as podestà of Verona

Lippomano: as long as the Adige flows into the Adriatic, as long as
honor and thanks are paid to merit, Verona will always be in-
debted to you, its podestà and father, who left behind monuments
that will last forever. Verona will always pay you divine tribute and   5
ever remember your deeds in its annals. Go then, hope of the Ve-
netians, for whom a modest rule will not suffice; go seek greater
scepters. And accept these tears and vows that we bestow upon
you as you go, and take them with you, the final gifts on your de-   10
parture.

: XXV :

In mortem Ioannis Baptistae Montani
medici Veronensis

Dum medica, Montane, doces ope vincere fata
    et Lachesi invita vivere posse diu,
Lethaeo indignans pressit te Parca sopore,
    et secuit vitae grandia fila tuae.
5 Sic, animas et tu, Asclepi, dum subtrahis Orco,
    te quoque saevorum perdidit ira deum.

: XXVI :

Ad Ioannem Matthaeum Gibertum
episcopum Veronensem

Melsineae rupes subiectaque litora, Tusci
    quae suprema sonans alluit unda lacus,
annuite, agrestem dum, votum pauperis, aram
    e vivo Thyrsis cespite tollit humo.
5 Nunc herba struit, atque hederis et floribus ornat,
    et, Giberte, tibi rustica sacra facit;
ast olim auratam niveus tibi taurus ad aram
    cornibus auratis victima magna cadet.

: XXV :

On the death of Giovanni Battista da Monte, a Veronese doctor

While you were teaching us, da Monte, how to vanquish fate through the art of medicine, and how to live long, against the will of Lachesis, she vengefully oppressed you with Lethean sleep and cut the long threads of your life. Even so, Asclepius, did you res- 5
cue souls from Orcus, only to be destroyed by the anger of the raging gods.

: XXVI :

To Gian Matteo Giberti, bishop of Verona

Cliffs of Malcesine and shores beneath that are washed by the far-sounding waters of the Etrurian lake: accept this rustic altar — the vow of a poor man — which Thyrsis has raised up upon the ground out of fresh grass. Now he strews it with grass and adorns it with 5
ivy and flowers, a rustic tribute to you, Giberti. But one day a greater offering, a snow-white bull with gilded horns, will fall before your golden altar.

: XXVII :

Ad eundem

Naiades hoc, Giberte, tibi Benacides antrum
 et qui muscoso fons cadit e lapide
sacravere. Tibi sit cura et fontis et antri,
 et quandoque deus ad tua sacra veni.
5 Et sacer est, et habet spirantes suaviter auras
 hortus, et est nullo gratior umbra loco,
et nusquam est longaeva mage et felicior arbos,
 pulcher Adoni, tua, pulcher Apollo, tua.
Hic canere et tenuem posse exercere Camenam
10 ille dedit, sanctus qui mihi semper erit.
Hic herbas, succosque tuos, artemque relinquo,
 Phoebe: soles Musas tu quoque amare magis.

: XXVIII :

Ad eundem

Ipsa tibi, Giberte deus, lego lychnida Leuce,
 Melsineis Leuce cognita litoribus.
Et pulchram cyanum et canentia lilia necto:
 illa colore magis, haec et odore placent.
5 Roma caput sacro decoret tibi magna galero:
 non tamen et Leuce non sua serta dabit.

⁝ XXVII ⁝

To the same

The naiads, daughters of Benacus, have consecrated this cave to you, Giberti, and this fountain that falls from the mossy cliff. Take care of the fountain and the cave, and come every so often, like a god, to the ceremonies in your honor. The garden is sacred and ⁅5⁆ graced with sweetly breathing airs, and nowhere else has pleasanter shade. Nowhere else is there a sturdier or more fruitful tree than yours, handsome Adonis, or yours, handsome Apollo. Here Giberti allowed me to sing and honor my modest muse and so he ⁅10⁆ will always be holy to me. Here, Phoebus, I relinquish your herbs, your potions and your art. For you as well love the Muses more than medicine.

⁝ XXVIII ⁝

To the same

Godly Giberti, I, Leuce, have plucked this red flower for you, I who am well known along the shores of Malcesine. And I weave lovely cornflowers for you and white lilies too, the former dear for their color, the latter for their scent. Even if great Rome should ⁅5⁆ adorn your head with the sacred cap, Leuce will not fail to give you her flowers.

: XXIX :

Ad eundem

Et laurum et citrum hanc teneram de matre revulsam
    Giberto sacram Thyrsis utramque serit.
Hanc, Venus, ast illam iuveni servabis, Apollo,
    ne noceant aestus, ne noceatve gelu.
5   Tu quoque Benaci vicino, Naïs, ab amne
    clam gelidas teneris frondibus affer aquas,
dumque feres, dic: 'Sancte, humili tibi nunc dea rivo,
    cum venies, toto serviet amne tibi.'

: XXX :

De Marsango fluviolo,
prope villam Ioannis Baptistae Rhamnusii,
in agro Patavino

Qui te populea cingit, Marsange, corona,
    dulce ut in umbrosis cornibus aura sonet,
ac ne umquam inficiat lutulenti sordida plaustri
    te rota, sub firmo dat tibi ponte viam,
5   vicinae cultor villae, Rhamnusius, horti,
    agrique, et dominus ripae utriusque rogat:
'Lenis vere flue atque, nivali providus undae,
    arida in aestivi sidera parce Canis.

⁚ XXIX ⁚

To the same

For Giberti Thyrsis plants this laurel and this tender citron plucked from its mother, both of them sacred trees. Venus will protect the citron for the young man while you, Apollo, protect the laurel from heat and cold. And you, Naiad, quietly bear cool 5 waters from the nearby streams of Benacus to these tender plants. And when you bring them, say: "Saintly man, the goddess now serves you water from a humble stream. But when you come, she will serve you from the entire river."

⁚ XXX ⁚

On the Marsango rivulet
near the villa of Giovanni Battista Ramusio
in the Paduan plain

The man who girds you, Marsango, with a crown of poplar leaves, that the breeze might sound sweetly in your shady glens; the man who grants you passage under a sturdy bridge, that no sordid wheel of muddy wagon might pollute you; that man, Ramusio, the 5 owner of the neighboring villa, with its gardens and fields, the lord of both banks, asks this of you: Flow softly in spring and protect your cool waters against the arid stars of the dog days. So shall

Sic tibi grata Nape geminabit serta quotannis,
10   et tua par magnis amnibus ibit aqua.'

: XXXI :

De eodem

Qui modo fons, Marsange, humilis, modo cornibus ingens
    per salicum rapido laberis amne nemus,
vere novo, Marsange, mihi flue lenior undis,
    uberior, sitiens cum coquit arva Canis.
5   Frigentes aestate tibi Rhamnusius umbras
    sparget, et ad gelidas ipse sedebit aquas.
Vere rosam violasque feret pictasque corollas
    pulchra tibi hinc Naïs, hinc Galatea dabit.

: XXXII :

In calce Homocentricorum

Sed iam me, rapidi diversa volumina caeli
dimensum satis, et numquam requieta secutum
sidera per varios cursus variosque recursus,
hac iuvet insudasse tenus: nunc ultima fessum
5   accipiat finemque meo det meta labori.
Vos aeterni orbes aeternique aetheris ignes,
qui tacito circum labentes tempora cursu

pleasing Nape bring you abundant flowers each year, and your   10
waters will flow like those of the great rivers.

∶ XXXI ∶

On the same

You who glide, Marsango, now in a humble stream and now abun-
dantly in a rushing spate, meandering among the willows, flow
more softly for me in early spring and more fully when the thirst-
ing dog star scorches the fields. So will Ramusio spread refreshing   5
shade over you in summer, as he sits beside your cool waters. In
spring he will bring roses and violets, while, here and there, Galatea
and fair Nais gather for you parti-colored chaplets.

∶ XXXII ∶

From the end of the Homocentrica

But now, after I have journeyed long enough through the divers
orbits of swift heaven and followed the stars, which are never still,
through their varied courses and returns, I am pleased to end my
exertions here. Now may the finish line receive the weary author   5
and bring an end to his labors. You eternal orbs and fires of the
sky, who, as you glide, draw on the seasons in your silent course

ducitis et longum per saecula volvitis aevum,
si non aeternum (neque enim fas poscere tantum),
10   at saltem durare diu et producere vitam
hoc concedite opus, videant ut vestra nepotes
saecula, et aeternis vos admirentur ab annis,
mirenturque vias, cum iam non tramite sueto
curret iter solitum Titan, sed purpureum ver
15   et iuvenem signis conversis invehet annum.
Tuque etiam, seu te, tua tanta inventa novosque
admirantem orbes, puro fulgentia caelo
templa tenent, seu, Threiciae testudinis audens
tangere ebur, plectis numeros et carmina dictas,
20   qua Via sidereo candescit Lactea caelo,
Turri, ades, inventisque tuis nostroque labori
da, sancte, augurium, atque optatis annue nostris.

: XXXIII :

Postremo capite libri primi
De contagione et contagiosis morbis

            Saepe exiguus mus
augurium tibi triste dabit, tellure sub ima
quem non ullus amor tenuit, sed in aëra apertum
erupit scrobibus, vitaeque atque immemor usus,
5   et parvos natos et dulcia tecta reliquit.
Ipsa etiam tellus, ceu non ignara futuri,

and, through the ages, spin out your long lives: though it would be
too much to ask that this work of mine be eternal, at least grant ⟶ 10
that it may live and endure for a long time, so that future genera-
tions may view your ages and admire your eternity. And let them
marvel at your orbits when the Titan sun no longer hastens
through its wonted course according to its custom, but rather
brings in the lovely spring and the new year with the constellations 15
reversed. And whether you dwell in gleaming temples beneath a
serene heaven, della Torre, as you admire your many discoveries
and new stars, or dare to pluck the ivory of a Thracian lyre, weav-
ing rhymes and chanting poetry while the Milky Way glows in the 20
starry skies, be present, holy one, and look auspiciously upon my
labors and my hopes.

: XXXIII :

From the last chapter of the first book
On Contagious Diseases

Often a tiny mouse will send you a sad portent when, no longer
happy to dwell underground, it emerges from the bushes into the
open air, heedless of life and custom, leaving behind its offspring 5
and sweet home. Even the earth itself, as though sensing things to
come, will give signs, when it trembles and inwardly sighs from its

cum tremit atque intus gravida suspirat ab alvo,
signa dabit: tremuere urbes, et vertice toto
formidavit Athos, timuitque sub aequore Nereus.

: XXXIV :

Capite septimo libri tertii de iisdem

Proderit et latos stipularum incendere campos
et nemora intacta, et sanctos exurere lucos.

: XXXV :

Dialogo de poetica

Huc ades, o Thelayra: quid, ah quid grandia farra
aestivo sub Sole teris medioque sub aestu,
nec parcis tibi, saeva? Ah, te ne immitis adurat
Sirius! Ah, teneras ne rumpat pustula palmas!
5   Demens, o Thelayra, patri concede laborem,
cui Cereris cura est: melior te cura Diones
sollicitet. Tu, dum fervet tritura sub aestu,
dum crepitat seges, et multo sonat area pulsu,
clam te operis furare et aquas effinge ferendas.

pregnant womb. Cities have trembled and Mount Athos has shiv-
ered through its entire height, while Nereus shook beneath the
waves.

: XXXIV :

From chapter seven of the third book of the same work

It will help to set fire to the broad fields of stalks, to consume the
untouched thickets and the sacred groves.

: XXXV :

From the Dialogue on Poetry

Come here, O Thelayra. Why, O why, hard woman, do you grind
abundant wheat under the blazing sun, in the midst of sum-
mer, with no regard to yourself? Let not the savage Sirius burn
you, nor let blisters hurt your delicate hands. O mad Thelayra, 5
leave this labor to your father, who keeps a care of Ceres! Bet-
ter that you should concern yourself with the care of Dione.
While the threshed grain flies here and there beneath the sum-
mer's sun, while the harvest crackles and the threshing floor re-
sounds beneath repeated blows, say that you need to get water.

10   Hic nitidus fons est, hic plurima populus umbram
      sufficit, et gelidae summittit frigora ripae.
      Vos aurae, Alpinis placidae de montibus aurae,
      haec illi portate, aut, si pater obstat eunti,
      saltem aestum lenite, gravem lenite laborem.

: XXXVI :

Libro primo De intellectione

      Natalem, Thelayra, tuum lux crastina reddet,
      crastina lux mihi sancta. Tuos, age Lucifer, ortus
      profer, et Auroram propero dux evehe curru:
      evehe, sed sero tardus cede, Hespere, caelo,
5   longa ut eat felixque dies. Lege lychnida, Leuce,
      et viridem violis intexito amaracon albis.
      Serta duo mihi necte: unum, quod postibus ipse
      appendam, Thelayra, tuis, mea maxima dona
      nota tibi; ast aliud, quod festa luce laborum
10   immunes decoret plena ad praesepia tauros.
      Tu vulgo Venerique palam formosa videnda
      comptaque, sed clam pulchra tuo, sed compta Myconi
      incedes, tacitisque deam venerabere votis,
      ut mea tu, tuus ipse ut sim: dea maxima votis
15   annuet. At tu omnem, Thelayra, abrumpe pudorem
      tum, cum exspectatum difflabit tibia cantum,
      ardentesque sono in choreas accendet amantes.
      Tum dextram laevamque manus iungamus amicas,
      invideantque omnes; neque enim te doctior usquam
20   ulla salit, non ipsa Iole, non nata Lycotae.
      Me vero quales in caelum tollere saltus

Here is a gleaming stream; here many a poplar offers shade, re- 10
freshing the cool riverbanks. And you breezes, you placid breezes
from the Alpine mountains, bring these things to her. And if her
father refuses to let her go, at least mitigate the heat and her great
labors.

∴ XXXVI ∴

From the first book On Intellection

Tomorrow, Thelayra, is your birthday. Tomorrow is sacred to me.
Lucifer, bring on the day and lead in the dawn on your swift
chariot. Lucifer, bring on the dawn: but you, Hesperus, bear it
away only belatedly as you descend from heaven, so that the day
might be happy and long. Take up the red flower, Leuce, and in- 5
terweave the blooming marjoram with white violets. Weave me
two chaplets, one of which I can place upon your door, Thelayra,
my greatest gift to you. As for the other, may it adorn the bulls,
free of labor on this holiday, in the full stable. Reveal yourself, 10
lovely and well kempt, to Venus and the crowd. But also come
beautiful and well kempt to your Mycon, and honor the goddess
with silent vows, that you should be mine and I yours. The su-
preme goddess will favor your prayers. But set aside all modesty, 15
Thelayra, when the pipe plays the awaited song, inflaming ardent
lovers with its sound, so that they unite in choruses. Then let us
join hands in friendship, and may everyone envy us: for no one
knows how to dance better than you, not even Iole or the daughter 20
of Lycota. Truly you will see me leap up to heaven and turn you in

aspicies, Thelayra! Modo et te flectere in orbem,
et modo te contra stantem mira arte movere
ante retroque pedes, spatio nec cedere ab uno!
25 Ipsa Venus caelo ridens spectabit ab alto.

: XXXVII :

Eodem libro primo De intellectione

Ollis divina super mens
astat, magna, micans: cuius radiata nitore,
quae fuerant obscura prius simulacra, repente
fiunt coram anima, claraque in luce refulgent.
5 Non aliter quam quae caeca sub nocte tenentur,
si feriat rutilum Solis iubar, omnia late
splendescunt, pulchraque petunt in luce videri.

: XXXVIII :

In calce eiusdem libri

= XLIV

circles, Thelayra, and as I stand before you with marvelous art, I
will move my feet back and forth, yet ever in place. Venus herself
will look down from the height of heaven, and she will smile.   25

∶ XXXVII ∶

From the same book On Intellection

Over them stands the divine mind, great and resplendent: illumi-
nated by its brilliance, those things that had previously been but
obscure simulacra suddenly manifest themselves before the soul
and shine forth with a divine light. Even so are objects covered in   5
darkness: if the sun's golden splendor strikes them, they all begin
to glow abroad, eager to reveal themselves in the lovely light.

∶ XXXVIII ∶

At the end of the same book

See below, C. 44.

: XXXIX :

Libro secundo De intellectione

Carpe fugam, Galatea: ferus petit aequora Cyclops;
carpe fugam, pelagoque procul speculator ab alto
te quis amat dignumque tuo se censet amore.
Humano primum rorantem sanguine barbam,
5   et foedum os, oculumque unum, quem fronte patentem
ipse gerit media, multo lavere aequore cernes;
pectere dein rastro crines, apioque virenti
assimiles laudare; silens tum consulere aequor,
et se spectatis formosum dicere ab undis;
10   te vero, Galatea, quod hunc contemnis amantem,
nec pecoris numerum nec avenae sibila curas,
crudelem et pistri natam Scyllaque vocare;
crudelesque deos, si dii tamen aethere in alto
vel mare sunt aliqui (neque enim se posse putare
15   ullos esse deos); demum tibi dira minari:
nam fore ut, ictu uno magno cum fragmine montis,
teque tuumque Acim medium disperdat in aequor.
    At tu, tuta mari magno, Cyclopis amores
despiciens, ridensque minas et inania verba,
20   in nostros, Galatea, sinus, formosa, recurre.
Ille inter pecudes et amore uratur, et Aetna.

⁝ XXXIX ⁝

From the second book On Intellection

Run away, Galatea! The savage Cyclops is heading into the sea.
Run, and from afar, in the deep waters, watch the one who is in
love with you and thinks himself worthy of your love. You will see
him first pouring abundant water over his beard, which is be-   5
dewed with human blood, and over his filthy mouth and the soli-
tary eye exposed in the middle of his forehead. Then with a rake
he combs his hair, which looks like verdant celery, and he praises
it. Finally he looks into the silent sea and, from its reflection, he
pronounces himself a good-looking man.

   Truly Galatea, because you reject this lover and care not how   10
many flocks he has or how he plays his pipe, he swears that you
are cruel, the daughter of Scylla and of a sea monster. He says the
gods are cruel, if indeed there be any gods in heaven or in the sea.
Finally, saying that he is unable to believe that the gods exist, he   15
begins to threaten you. He says he will kill you and your beloved
Acis in the middle of the sea, with a single blow from a large
rock.

   But since you are safe in the high sea, lovely Galatea, since you
reject the love of the Cyclops and laugh at his threats and empty
words, run back into my arms. And may he be consumed by love   20
and volcanic fire amid his flocks!

: XL :

Eodem libro

Telamonius Aiax
arma rapit, superosque furens in proelia poscit,
iamque hominum hos nunc insequitur, nunc percutit illos.
At tacitus maerensque, hominum consortia vitans,
5   Bellerophon solos errat male sanus in agros:
Bellerophon, quem Martis honos, quem gloria currum
per deserta fugit, nec amor comitatur equorum.

: XLI :

Dialogo de anima, *non procul ab initio*

Ne timeas, Troiane puer, quod in ardua tantum
tolleris a terra, quod rostro atque unguibus uncis
te complexa ferox volucris per inania portat.
Audistine umquam sublimis nomen Olympi?
5   Audistine Iovis tonitru, qui fulmina torquet,
qui pluit in terras, cui templa arasque dicatis
vos homines, taurosque tua mactatis in Ida,
quique etiam vestri est, si nescis, sanguinis auctor?
Ille ego sum. Non te haec volucris, sed Iuppiter est, qui,
10   haud praeda captus, cari sed amore nepotis,
in summum amplexu innocuo te portat Olympum,
astra ubi tot spectare soles, ubi pulcher obit Sol
ortusque occasusque suos, ubi candida noctes

∶ XL ∶

From the same book

Ajax, the son of Telamon, rages as he grabs his weapons and challenges the gods to a fight. Some mortals he chases, others he strikes. But silent and sad, avoiding the company of men, Bellerophon wanders madly through solitary fields, Bellerophon whom the honor of Mars and the glory of chariot victories abandons in the wilderness, and he has no love of horses.

∶ XLI ∶

From near the beginning of the Dialogue on the Soul

Fear not, Trojan youth, that you are being lifted so high above the earth, that a fearsome bird carries you through the empty air in its beak and hooked talons. Have you never heard the name of lofty Olympus? Have you not heard the thunder of Jove, who bends the lightning bolt and rains upon the earth, Jove, to whom you mortals raise temples and altars and make offerings of bulls on Mount Ida, your home, Jove who, if you do not know it, is the creator of your blood? I am he. For it is not a bird, but rather Jupiter who, struck not with desire of prey, but rather with love of his dear offspring, carries you in his tender embrace to the height of Olympus, where you are wont to see so many stars, where the beautiful sun rises and falls, where the brightly shining moon traverses the

currit Luna nitens, Auroram Lucifer anteit.
15   Hic ego te in numero superum domibusque deorum,
ver ubi perpetuum, felix ubi degitur aetas,
aeterna et semper viridis florensque iuventa,
consistam, aequalemque annis pubentibus Heben
officioque dabo comitem, qui pocula nobis
20   laeta ministretis; reliquum caelestibus una
astragalis choreisque diem exercere licebit.
Pone metum, dilecte Iovi, melioraque longe
prospiciens, caram, puer, obliviscere Troiam,
neve deum te iam et divorum regna petentem
25   ulla canum aut Idae nemorosae cura sequatur.

: XLII :

Eodem dialogo: Psyche

Huc, Amor o dilecte, ades, o dilecte Cupido:
formosum tua te Psyche formosa requirit,
et poscit te dia deum, puerumque puella.
O tibi tam similis si te peramatque cupitque,
5   nonne et amabis Amor illam, cupiesque Cupido?
Est eadem nobis patria, est caelestis origo
ab Iove, nos terris pariter, nos aethere in alto
versamur pariter, coniunctaque munera obimus.
Ipsa bonum pulchrumque modis in pectora miris
10   insinuo, tu corda feris, tu suggeris ignes,
accendisque ardore novo, genus unde animantum
concipitur, crescitque, sua et connubia iungit.

night and Lucifer precedes the dawn. I shall place you among the 15
deities, in the house of the gods, where spring is eternal and where
one lives a happy life, an eternal life that is always green and flour-
ishing with youth. I shall give you Hebe as a companion cupbearer,
equal to you in tender years, so that you can serve us delightful 20
drafts. The rest of the day you may spend, together with the gods,
in choruses and in playing games of chance. Don't be afraid, youth
beloved of Jove, and, looking forward to better things, forget dear
Troy. And now that you are already a god, now that you are ap-
proaching the realms of the gods, have no further care of hounds 25
or of Ida and its abundant woods.

∶ XLII ∶

From the same dialogue: Psyche

Come hither dear Love, dear Cupid. The beautiful Psyche seeks
you, who are as lovely as she is. A goddess and a girl, she seeks
you, a god and a boy. O if one so like you loves and desires you,
will you not, Love, love her too? Will you not desire her, Cupid? 5
We both come from the same place: we were born of Jove in
heaven. We live our lives equally on earth and in heaven and enjoy
the same powers. Whereas I use marvelous skills to insinuate the
good and the beautiful into the hearts of men, you wound hearts 10
and start fires, inflaming those hearts with a new longing, through
which the human race is conceived, matures and joins itself in
marriage.

Me miseram, quod et ipsa meis in me artibus usa,
ah nimium tenera et pulchro nimis apta moveri,
15   ut te conspexi, ut novi, pulcherrime rerum,
continuo facibusque tuis et Amoris amore
exarsi. Iuvat hoc, paribus si et tu ignibus ardes.
Tolle, puer, vittas, atque in me lumina solve:
nempe et amabis Amor pulchram, cupiesque Cupido.
20   Ipsa tibi tenuem, qua cingas tempora, vittam
intertextam auro et molli bombyce laboro,
pictus ubi Narcissus hiat, Maeander oberrat.
Hic ego te latas terras atque alta volatu
nubila tranantem fingo, et maria uda secantem,
25   cuncta tibi imperio subdentem, hominesque, ferasque,
et pictas volucres, et quae nant aequore monstra.
Diis quoque nec parcis: curru rex Iuppiter aureo
invehitur, cinctus humeros et brachia ferro;
quos inter tua Psyche etiam religata catenis
30   it maerens, sequiturque tuos captiva triumphos.

: XLIII :

Vetus epigramma in calce Sententiae
de vini temperatura

Infantem nymphae Bacchum, quo tempore ab igne
    prodiit, inventum sub cinere abluerant:
ex illo nymphis cum Baccho gratia multa est,
    seiunctus quod sit ignis et urat adhuc.

Alas, I used my arts against myself and was no proof against them. I was too apt to be moved by beauty. As soon as I saw you, 15 as soon as I knew you, most beautiful of all beings, at once I was inflamed by your fires and by the love of Love. This is a fine thing, if you burn with the same ardor. Lift then, boy, your blindfolds, and set your eyes on me. Then, Love, you will love me in my beauty. Then, Cupid, you will desire me. I am weaving a modest 20 chaplet to bind your temples, one interwoven with gold and soft silk. Pictured therein, Narcissus gapes and Meander wanders. I have also portrayed you sailing with winged course over broad lands and high clouds, plying the watery seas, and subduing all 25 things to your will: men and beasts, brightly colored birds and the monsters of the deep. You do not spare even the gods: Jupiter himself is depicted, drawn along in a golden chariot, his shoulders and arms clamped in iron. And among the gods even Psyche, in chains, can be seen lamenting, as she, a captive, follows in your 30 triumphs.

⦂ XLIII ⦂

An ancient epigram, placed at the end of
An Opinion on the Blending of Wine

When the infant Bacchus emerged from the fire, the Nymphs found him beneath the ashes and washed him off. Since that time, there has been great friendship between Bacchus and the Nymphs: apart from them he becomes fire and still burns.

: XLIV :

Baccho conciliatori

Mero madentes largo et edacibus
    curis soluti, dum tibi candidam
    lucem deorum ducimus optime,
      Bacche, seu Dionysius
5   mavis vocari, seu magis Evius,
    seu tu Lyaeus, seu Bromius magis,
    Liberve, Iacchusve, aut Semele satus,
      et magni soboles Iovis,
adsis Bassareu, laetitiae dator,
10   adsis. Furentes ast age Maenadas
    in iuga crebris Indica tympanis
    resona atque ululatibus.
Lyncas nec acres advehe, neu gere
    Thyrsos, venustum nec tege casside
15   horrente vultum, sed tenero veni
    cinctus cornua pampino,
tuisque mitis et placidus sacris
    adesto, qualem te memorant iugo,
    Bactris subactis, in medio deum
20   convivam Iove cum patre
sedisse, circum diis resonantibus
    Evoe, pharetra cum posita tuas
    laudes eburna grandiloquus lyra
    Latona cecinit satus:
25   ereptus igne ut fulmineo Iovis
    bis natus infans duceris ad deos,

: XLIV :

To Bacchus, the conciliator

Sated with wine and free from gnawing cares, we bring you the
dazzling day, O Bacchus, best of the gods, or if you prefer to be
called Dionysius or Evius, Lyaeus or Bromius, Liber or Iacchus, or   5
the son of Semele and the scion of great Jove. Come Bassareus,
giver of gladness, leading the raging Maenads and filling the In-   10
dian hills with an abundance of drums and shouts. Do not come
leading fierce lynxes, nor bearing the thyrsus, nor covering your
lovely face with a dread helmet: rather come having adorned your   15
horns with the tender vine. Come to your sacred festival as they
say you were when, having vanquished the Bactrians, you sat on a
mountain top as a god and a guest of Jove, your father, and all   20
around the gods cried out, "Euoe!": or when the eloquent Apollo,
born of Leto, set aside his quiver and sang your praises on an ivory
lyre. Seized from the thundering fire of Jove and twice born,   25
you were led, an infant, to the gods, and all the dwellers of heaven

at tibi magnis plausibus omnium ad-
risit caelicolum cohors;
namque ore pulchro talis erat color,
30   nitente qualis emicat in rosa,
et prominebat exsilientibus
sacrum corniculis caput;
Tyrrhenus ut te navita deprecans
sero, furoris, numinis et tui
35   expertus iras, squameus in mare
piscis desiliit rate.
Tu pertinacem, Penthee, concitas
matrem furentem. Quo fugis ah miser?
Te mater aprum, te Autonoë putans
40   saeva dilaniat manu.
Sensit Lycurgus vitibus impiam
ausus bipennem immittere; sensit et
cohors gigantum, trudere iam rata
alto caelicolas polo.
45 Tu Gange victo miles ab ultimis
Indis triumphos victor, io, refers,
et redeunti Susa et Achaemenes
aras constituit tibi.
Fremunt in altis orgia montibus
50   Evoe: solutae per iuga Thyades
crines in auras raucisonis replent
altum cornibus aethera.
Salve, repertor magne meri pater,
mentesque nostras concilia, et procul
55   iras, et arma, et bella age in impios
carentesque mero Scythas.

smiled upon you to great applause. For your beautiful face had a   30
complexion like a blushing rose. Then from your sacred head little
horns began to grow. Come as you appeared to that sailor of the
Tyrrhenian sea who belatedly begged you for mercy and, feeling
the anger of your rage and your divinity, leaped from his ship into   35
the sea as a scaly fish. You, Pentheus, goad your raging, driven
mother. Whither will you flee, wretch? For your mother and Au-
tonoe, thinking you a wild boar, tear you to pieces with their sav-   40
age hands. Lycurgus felt it when he dared to set his impious ax to
your vines. And the pack of giants felt it too when they decided to
attack the gods up in heaven. Having vanquished the Ganges, you   45
come as a victorious soldier, bringing triumphs from utmost India,
as Susa and the Acheamenians raise altars to you on your return.
On the mountain tops, your celebrants cry out "Euoe!" And the   50
Thyades, having loosed their hair to the breeze, fill the lofty air
with their raucous trumpets. Hail, great father, discoverer of wine:
gladden our minds and drive all quarrels and arms and wars away   55
from us and toward the impious Scythians, who lack the juice of
the grape.

: XLV :

In fugam Caroli V imperatoris

Tene igitur terrorem orbis, te, maxime Caesar,
victorem late, regnatoremque superbum,
conversa nunc fortuna, Germania vidit
praecipiti dare terga fuga sub nocte silenti?
5   Atque adeo non Turca ferox, non Persa secutus
te pepulit. Vix hostis erat, quem dicere posses
armatum contra iusto contendere bello:
tu tamen inclinato animo, trepidusque futuri,
hostilis fama adventus et nomine solo,
10 laberis, obscura tectus caligine noctis;
cui comes it frater pavitans, geminatque pudorem,
Romani imperii atque Augusti nominis heres.
Deseritur longo tellus pacata labore,
totque haustis opibus regnorum, ac sanguine fuso.
15 Scilicet hoc, Caesar, tua vasta ac dira cupido
dedecus, hanc peperit mansuram in saecula labem,
dum modus optandi nullus, dum quidquid ubique est
spe capis, atque auctis semper cupis addere rebus.
Praesidium, quo te in primis ac parta tueri
20 debueras, Italae misisti ad moenia Parmae,
urbis nec meritae tot duri incendia belli,
ut generi et natae spoliis potiare cruentis:
hoc tibi pro tali facto pia numina reddunt.

⁙ XLV ⁙

On the flight of Emperor Charles V

Can it be, great Caesar, that through a shift of fortune, Germany
has seen you, the terror of the world, the broad victor and proud
conqueror, turn tail in headlong flight amid the silence of night?
But it was not the ferocious Turk or the Persian who pursued you   5
and drove you away. It was scarcely an enemy that you could say
came armed against you in a proper battle. Rather with prostrate
soul, and fearful of the future, at the mere mention of the enemy
and the mere rumor of his approach, you slipped out, covered by   10
the deep darkness of night, accompanied by your brother who
doubled your shame, that heir to the might of Rome and the name
of Augustus! Thus did you abandon a land that you had subju-
gated with much effort and loss of blood and treasure. Thus did
your vast and baneful ambition beget this shame, this blot that
will last for centuries, while there is no limit to your grasping,   15
while you aspire to seize anything in your path and always to add
to the wealth you have already accumulated. That battalion that
you should have kept to protect you and what you had already
acquired, you sent instead against the walls of Parma, an Italian   20
city that had done nothing to deserve the conflagrations of harsh
war, just so that you could win possession of its bloodied spoils for
your son-in-law and your daughter. This is how the pious gods
reward that deed!

∶ XLVI ∶

In obitum Marci Antonii Turriani

Haec iuvenis, magnae Italiae spes magna, docebat
Turrensis, dum florenti Ticinidis urbis
Gymnasio fama summo sese aequat Olympo.
Ipse artes illi medicas formosus Apollo
5   cesserat, ipse illi numeros pulchramque iuventam,
quo foret exemplar studiorum praecipuum et spes.
Nondum illi sex lustra ierant, florentibus annis,
cum decus hoc Latio invidit Mors impia, et illum
abstulit, extrema positum Benacide ripa,
10   quam media inter saxa sonans Sarca alluit unda.
Illum Alpes vicinae, illum cava flumina flerunt,
patrius illum Athesis, nec non Graiae atque Latinae
cum vestro miserum flevistis Apolline nymphae.

∶ XLVII ∶

Ad Marcum Antonium Flaminium
gratiarum actio

Quas tibi reddemus grates, dulcissime vatum,
quod nos tam claro fueris dignatus honore,
nomen uti nostrum dignis Iove prodere chartis
velles, suavis amicitiae nostrae monimentum

: XLVI :

On the death of Marcantonio della Torre

These were the teachings of young della Torre, the great hope of
great Italy, when, in the flourishing University of Pavia, he raised
himself in fame to the heights of lofty Olympus. Handsome
Apollo himself would have yielded to him in medical skill, in po- 5
etry and in the beauty of youth, to be a great example and hope to
other students. He had not yet attained his thirtieth year when, in
the flower of his youth, impious death begrudged this honor to
Italy and stole him away to Benacus's distant shores, washed amid 10
its rocks by the waters of the sounding Sarca. Him the neighbor-
ing Alps and the hollow riverbanks bewept. Father Athesis wept
miserably for him, as did you nymphs of Greece and Italy, together
with your beloved Apollo.

: XLVII :

An offering of thanks
to Marcantonio Flaminio

How can I thank you, dearest of poets, for deigning to honor me
in writings that are worthy of Zeus? It is an outstanding tes-
tament to our dear friendship, one that no age will ever efface

5   egregium, quod nulla dehinc obliteret aetas,
       et multi invideant nobis post fata nepotes?
       Scilicet hoc tua mens semper tulit, hoc tua virtus
       inclita, non reges ut mirarere superbos,
       quos vulgus stupet insanum de divite gaza,
10   et solos laudans ducit dicitque beatos;
       sed, si quis sceleris vacuus et pectore puro
       vitam agat, atque animum studiis intendat honestis,
       hunc tu regum opibus praefers et regibus ipsis,
       Musaeoque tuo lepido impertiris honore.
15   Macte, vir eloquio princeps et carmine princeps!
       Macte animis, macte ingenioque et pectore sancto,
       non exspectatum Latiis decus addite Musis!
       Namque tuas laudes spargens vaga fama per urbes
       ad caelum te laeta vehit plaudentibus alis,
20   dum nos versicolore trahis super aethera curru.
       Vive diu, vates vatum doctissime, vivent
       innumeros veluti tua carmina lecta per annos.
       Vive iterum felix, nostri lux maxima saecli,
       cum Polo, unanimique tuo dulcique Priulo,
25   Farnesi ut possis laudes aequare canendo,
       quem colit atque suis oculis plus diligit una,
       pulcher honos pulchrae Italiae, pulcherrima Roma.

: XLVIII :

= XXVII 5–12

and that future generations will envy after I am gone. For it has   5
always been the cast of your mind, it has always been part of your
great virtue, not to marvel at those proud kings who move the
foolish and dazzled mob to wonder at such wealthy splendor,
those kings whom the mob praises, whom it believes and declares   10
alone to be happy. If, rather, a man is free of any crime, if he lives
his life with a pure soul and energetically pursues honorable stud-
ies, that man you prefer to the wealth of kings and to kings them-
selves, and you bestow upon him the charming honor of your
muse. Hail to you, prince of eloquence and song, hail to your   15
spirits, your wit and your holy heart, you unlooked-for honor,
added to the poets of Italy! For wandering fame has spread your
praise among the cities, gladly lifting you to heaven and beating its
wings in applause, as you take us to heaven in a chariot of many   20
hues. Live long, most learned of poets, just as your choice songs
will live on for many years. Be happy once again, preeminent light
of our age, together with Polo and the sweet and concordant Pri-
uli. So might your song do justice to the praises of Farnese, whom   25
the fair glory of fair Italy, Rome, fairest of all, worships and loves
more than its own eyes.

⁝ XLVIII ⁝

See C. 27.5–12.

: XLIX :

Hos catulos, genus audacum de stirpe Laconum,
  depulsos teneris nuper ab uberibus,
parvus alit servatque tibi, Giberte, Caryclus:
  signa Lycus matris, Thessala patris habet.
5   Et puer interea et catuli, tua munera, crescent:
  crescentem sobolem tu tibi, sancte, lege.

: L :

Fragmenta carminis in laudem
Matthaei Giberti, episcopi Veronensis

Haec tum forte, boni captus communis amore,
condebam, dulceis Sophyae digressus in hortos,
hortos, quos ver perpetuum, quos aura Favoni
semper alit, semper caelesti nectare pascit,
5   quum nova te, meritis ingens, virtutibus ingens,
fama refert sacra redimitum tempora mitra,
qui rem divinam nobis, qui sacra ministres,
antistes Gibberte deum. Quo nomine primum,
ridenteis inter colles Cerealiaque arva,
10   spicisque et viridi praecinctum tempora oliva
erexit Verona caput, venerataque numen
terque quaterque deos patrios in vota vocavit.
Tum pater exultante Athesis se flumine ab alveo
extulit, et longe matri gratatus ovanti est.
15   Tum quoque pumiceo senior Benacus ab antro
pacavitque lacum, iussitque abscedere ventos,

: XLIX :

These puppies, from the race of audacious Laconian hounds, were
but recently weaned from their mother and are being raised and
kept for you by young Caryclus. The one named Lycus bears the
markings of his mother, while Thessala resembles her father. In 5
time the boy and the puppies, your gift, will grow. May you ac-
cept, saintly friend, this growing offspring.

: L :

Fragments of a poem in praise of
Matteo Giberti, bishop of Verona

Such were the words I sang when, struck by love of the common
good, I happened to wander in the sweet gardens of Wisdom,
gardens graced with eternal springtime and Favonian winds, and
ever fed on celestial nectar. It was then that I heard new reports of 5
how you, a priest of the gods — O great in merits and in virtues! —
crowned with a sacred miter, would administer to us the sacra-
ments and God's laws. On first hearing your name, Verona herself,
amid her smiling hills and fields of grain, raised up her head, her 10
temples crowned with wheat and green leaves of olive. Venerating
your spirit, she repeatedly invoked the gods of her country in her
vows. Then father Adige rose up from his banks amid exultant
streams and far and wide he congratulated Verona, his delighted
mother. And from his pumice cave old man Benacus too becalmed 15
his lake and bade the winds depart, as he adorned with Paphian

et Paphia citro et viridanti litora lauro
ornavit laetosque olea Tyrrenide campos.
Quem circum centum virides per littora nymphae
20   Naiades in numerum laetas traxere choreas:
Tuscaque, Syrmioque, atque ignis iam Stella Vehilli,
et Saloë, et Baccho dilecta Lacusia, et horto
Limonis celebrata et Adonidis arbore dives,
Bardoque, Cesiaque, Grineaque Apollinis ardor,
25   et iam Mersa parens, et adhuc Trimelia virgo,
et demum Carita ipsa suo digressa recessu.
Quarum, quae linguas volucrum atque oracula Phoebi
et tripodes docta et cytharam Grinea sonoram,
'O centum Etruscho prognatae fonte sorores,'
30   infit, 'io, nymphae. . .'

    Quae modo, te sacris delecto antistite et aris,
et tenerum sacra caput exornante thyara,
Musa tibi, Gybberte, animo gratata benigno est,
solemnesque dies egit, sparsitque virenti
35   flore solum, cytharamque tibi pulsavit eburnam.
At nunc Romanas inter si forte Camenas
advena habere locum possit. . .

    Magna novos dum Roma tibi, Gybberte, triumphos
exigit, et sacro fulgentem heroa galero
40   donat ovans, plausuque sonat strepituque faventum,
assurgitque pater Tyberis, ripaeque resultant,
et Tirena fremunt vicini littora ponti,
haec inter, Latiasque inter si forte Camenas
advena habere locum possit, sine, nostra triumphi
45   pars etiam sit Musa tui, comitetur et ipsa
pone sequens, plaudatque tibi. Sine, laurea parvum
serta inter folium e ripa Benacide nectat,
et patrios animos conceptaque gaudia monstret.

lemons and green laurels the shore and fields rich in Tuscan olives. Surrounding him upon the shore were a hundred green Naiads 20 who rhythmically performed joyous dances: Tusca and Sirmio and Stella, already the flame of Vehillus, Saloe and Lacusia, whom Bacchus loved, Limonis, famous for her garden and rich in the trees of Adonis, Bardo and Cesia and Grinea, beloved of Apollo, 25 Mersa, already a mother, Trimelia, still a virgin, and finally Carita herself emerging from her hidden abode. One of them, Grinea, learned in the language of birds and the oracles of Apollo, in the sacred tripodes as well as the resounding lyre, thus began, "O hundred sisters born of the Tuscan stream, nymphs: . . ." 30

When, Giberti, you were chosen as priest of the sacred altars, and adorned your dear head with a sacred tiara, the muse benignly congratulated you and, declaring a holy day, strewed the ground 35 with blooming flowers and struck her ivory lyre. But if perchance a foreigner might have a place among the Roman Muses. . . .

While great Rome stages new triumphs in your name, Giberti, and exultantly bestows a sacred cap upon you, her gleaming hero; while she resounds with the cries and ovations of your admirers 40 and Father Tiber rises up from his echoing banks and the Tyrrhenian shores of the nearby sea tremble: if a stranger might partake of these rites and of the Latin Muses, allow my own Muse to be a part of your triumph, so that she might accompany you and, trail- 45 ing behind, applaud your acts. Permit her to add to your crown of laurels a humble leaf from the shores of Benacus, and so demonstrate the spirit of her country and the extent of her joy. Behold

Aspice: cuncta tuis cernunt in honoribus ingens
50   nescio quod firmantque novis applausibus omen.
Ipsa tibi ante alias, ad tantae nomina famae,
ridentes inter colles Cerealiaque arva,
praecinctum spicis et amica pacis oliva
erexit Verona caput, venerataque numen
55   terque quaterque deos patrios in vota vocavit.
Tum primum exultante Athesis se flumine ab alveo
extulit, et longe matri gratatus ovanti est,
ingens et toto sonuit tua nomina ponto.
Tunc quoque pumiceo senior Benacus ab antro
60   pacavitque lacum, iussitque abscedere ventos,
et Paphia citro et viridanti littora lauro
induit undantesque olea Tyrenide campos.
Quem circum virides centum per gramina nymphae
Naiades in numerum laetas duxere choreas:
65   Cesiaque, Grineaque, et amor iam Stella Vehilli,
et Saloë, et Baccho dilecta Lacusia, et horto
Limonis celebrata et Adonidis arbore dives,
et Thusca, et numeros servans lasciva Catulli
Syrmio, et exercens agrestem Melsina Musam,
70   et demum Charithea suo digressa recessu.
Quas inter, docta et numeros et pectora vatum
fatidica et volucrum pennas et Apollinis artem,
Syrmio, 'Proh Tusco prognatae fonte sorores,
haec,' ait, 'haec erat illa dies, tandem affore nobis
75   quam toties ita fata mihi monstrare canebam:
scilicet Etrusca reges a styrpe futuros,
qui vestri memores, priscaeque ab origine gentis,
demissum caelo, magnis virtutibus auctum
deligerent heroa, istis qui praeforet oris,
80   pacatasque sacra sub relligione teneret;
Harpiae, et dirae Eumenides, infernaque monstra

how the whole world perceives some great new omen in these
honors of yours and finds it in this unwonted applause. And on   50
hearing these titles of fame, Verona herself—before other cities
and amid her smiling hills and fields of grain—raised up her head,
crowned with wheat and leaves of olive, the friend of peace. And
venerating your spirit, she repeatedly invoked the gods of her   55
country in her vows. Then for the first time, the Adige rose up
from his banks amid exultant streams and rejoiced far and wide in
his delighted mother and massively intoned your name over the
surface of the sea. And from his pumice cave old man Benacus too
becalmed his lake and bade the winds depart, as he strewed Paph-   60
ian lemons and green laurels over the shore and the fields abound-
ing in the Tuscan olive. Surrounding him through the meadows
were a hundred green Naiads who rhythmically led joyous dances:
Cesia and Grinea and Stella, beloved of Vehillus, Saloe and Lacu-   65
sia, whom Bacchus loved, Limonis, famous for her garden and rich
in the trees of Adonis, and Tusca and playful Sirmio, guarding the
poems of Catullus, as well as Melsina with her rustic muse and   70
finally Charitea, emerging from her hidden abode. Among these
Sirmio, learned in verse and the truth-telling hearts of poets, in
the plumage of birds and the arts of Apollo, cried, "Ah, my sisters,
born of the Tuscan stream! Finally that day has come which, as I
so often prophesied, the Fates had shown to me: that there would   75
be kings, born of the Etruscan race, who, mindful of you and of
the earlier race of your land, would choose a hero sent down from
heaven and endowed with great virtues to rule this land and   80
keep it in peace, according to the holy faith. By whom Harpies
and fearsome Furies and the monsters of the underworld, bound

perpetuis extra has terras religata cathenis
penderent poenas scelerum; at Pax aurea secum,
et Pietas, et cana Fides, et lancibus aequis
85   inviolata alto descendens aethere Virgo,
et fecunda Ceres, et Copia cornibus aureis,
nexae animos nexaeque manus, saecla aurea nobis
afferrent. Date, Nayades, date lilia magno
heroi, sacraque caput praecingite lauro.'
90   Tum sanctosque ortus memorat, tuaque acta recenset
grandia, nascenti ut maiora WORD WORD.

Ipsa tibi tua bella novis gratata triumphis
ante omnes Verona alta assurrexit ab arce,
ridentesque inter colles Cerealiaque arva
95   virgineum erexit caput, et laeta omine tanto
tempora paciferae ramo praecinxit olivae,
et magnum plausu insonuit: magnum omnia plausu
insonuere, tuumque ferens super aethera nomen
clamor iit . . .

100   Omen, io, Gybberte, tuis ab honoribus annus
incipit, et melior nobis iam vertitur orbis.
Iam nova mutato procedere saecula mundo
incipiunt: tua iam regnant tria sydera, et ipsa
terrarum dea Luna novo Latonia cornu.
105   Aspice: nescio quid cuncti promittimus ingens,
firmamus novum magnis applausibus omen.
Aspice, iam plenis laetentur ut omnia votis.
Ipsa tibi tua bella animo gratata benigno
ante alias Verona, ad tantae nuntia famae,
110   tempora paciferae ramo praecinxit olivae,
ridentesque inter colles Cerealiaque arva,
virgineum e summa plausu caput extulit arce,
effuditque preces . . .

in perpetual chains beyond the borders of this land, would pay the
penalty for their crimes; while golden Peace and with her Piety
and white-haired Faith and the inviolate Virgin, descending from 85
heaven with her just scales, as well as fertile Ceres and Abundance
with her golden horns, would join hearts and hands and bring us
a golden age. Throw lilies, O Naiads, at this great hero and crown
his head with sacred laurel." Then she recalled your divine origin 90
and your great deeds, how, at your birth . . .

Before all others, your lovely Verona herself, congratulating you
in your unheard of triumphs, rose up from her lofty citadel and
raised her virginal head amid her smiling hills and fields of grain; 95
and delighted by such a great omen, she crowned her temples with
a branch of the peace-bringing olive and sang as she greatly re-
joiced. Everything resounded with a great ovation and a shout
went up, bearing your name into heaven.

Truly, Giberti, this year begins auspiciously with your elevation 100
and the world is better for us than before. Now a new age begins
to march across a transformed world. Now your three stars reign,
as does the Latonian moon, goddess of the earth, with her new
horns. Behold: all of us look forward to some signal of greatness 105
and, with great ovations, we confirm a new omen. Behold, as all
things rejoice in vows fulfilled. Before the others, your lovely Ve-
rona herself, benignly congratulating you at the announcement of
such great fame, crowned her temples with a branch of the peace- 110
bringing olive and, amid her smiling hills and fields of grain, raised
her virginal head from her utmost citadel, and spoke these
prayers.

Magna tibi meritos praestat dum Roma triumphos,
115   teque sacro, macte o iuvenis virtute, galero
donat ovans, plausuque sonat strepituque faventum,
assurgitque pater Tyberis, ripaeque resultant,
et Tyrena fremunt vicini littora ponti,
haec inter, Latiasque inter si forte Camenas
120   advena habere locum possit, sine, Musa triumphi
pars etiam sit nostra tui, comitetur et ipsa
pone sequens, plaudatque tibi; sine, laurea parvum
serta inter folium e ripa Benacide nectat.
Omen, io, Gybberte, tuis ab honoribus annus
125   incipit, et melior nobis iam vertitur orbis:
iam nova mutato procedere saecula mundo
incipiunt. Bona iam regnant tria sydera, et ipsa
terrarum dea Luna novo Latonia cornu.
Aspice, nescio quid cuncti ut promittimus ingens.
130   Aspice, iam plenis laetantur ut omnia votis.
Ipsa tibi tua bella animo gratata benigno
ante alias Verona alta assurrexit ab arce,
ridentesque inter colles Cerealiaque arva
virgineum erexit caput, et laeta omine tanto
135   tempora paciferae ramo praecinxit olivae,
solemnemque diem statuit, lustravit et aras,
et patrios divina deos in sacra vocavit.
Ipsae laetitia nemorosa cacumina sylvae
nutarunt, fremuere amnes, et vertice cano
140   Baldus, et aëriae resonis applausibus Alpes.
Tunc pater, Herculea redimitus cornua fronde,
ipse Athesis late fluvio exultavit amoeno,
longius atque urnam versavit, et aggere ab alto
in mare prorumpens rapidis sese intulit undis.

While great Rome offers you well-deserved triumphs, and exul-   115
tantly bestows a sacred cap upon you—hail to you, youth great in
virtue!—while she trembles with the ovations and clamor of your
admirers, and while Father Tiber rises up from his echoing banks,
and the Tyrrhenian shores of the nearby sea tremble: if a stranger
might partake of these rites and of the Latin Muses, allow my own   120
Muse to be a part of your triumph, so that she might accompany
you and, trailing behind, applaud your acts. Permit her to add to
your crown of laurels a humble leaf from the shores of Benacus.
Truly, Giberti, this year begins auspiciously with your elevation,   125
and the world is better for us than before. Now a new age begins
to march across a transformed world. Now three auspicious stars
reign, as does the Latonian moon, goddess of the earth, with her
new horns. Behold how all of us look forward to some signal of
greatness. Behold how all things rejoice in vows fulfilled. Before   130
the others, your lovely Verona herself, congratulating you with her
benign spirit, rose up from her lofty citadel and raised her virginal
head amid her smiling hills and fields of grain; and delighted by
such a great omen, she crowned her temples with a branch of the   135
peace-bringing olive and announced a holiday, as she consecrated
the altars and invoked the gods of the fatherland to the sacred
rites. The very woods have shaken their leafy heads with joy. The
rivers resounded, as did Baldus with his white head, and the lofty   140
Alps with their echoing applause. Then father Adige himself, his
horns crowned with the Herculean branch, rejoiced in his pleasant
stream, and spilled his urn further than was his wont, and from a
hill rushed forth into the sea with his rapid wave.

: LI :

Fragmenta eclogae in laudem eiusdem

Ibla colo, Leuce calathis, Cneorus ibisco
depositis, sola pueri sub rupe sedentes
apricum ad Solem in littoribus Benaci,
in numerum cantant eadem non vocibus iisdem:
5   Ibla gravi, Leuce media, Cneorus acuta
cantant; Melsineae responsant omnia sylvae.

Cne. O nisi me Thelayra meus consumeret ignis,
ecquis laetitia in tanta me laetior esset?
Nunc et hiems est verna, et nunc solemnia, et ipsi
10   plena coronati stant ad praesepia tauri.
Parce, precor, Thelayra, novo dum maxima sacra
semideo agricolae facimus, dumque omnibus aris
laetitia it, vallesque cavae, ripaeque recurvae,
Benacusque, Athesisque tibi, Gybberte, resultant.

15   Quin, matris puer ingratae, materque, facesse hinc,
ingrati mater pueri, qui tristia laetis,
semper qui lachrymas intermiscetis amaras.
Sancta placent. Sancto iuvenem dum Roma galero
donat ovans, magnisque parat decorare triumphis,
20   mons circum septemque sonant applausibus arces,
assurgitque pater Tyberis, ripaeque resultant,
et Tyrrena fremunt vicini littora ponti.

Hybla colo, Leuce calathis, Cneorus ibisco
depositis, sola pueri sub rupe canentes
25   apricum ad Solem, docuit quae maximus Alcon,
in numerum cantant eadem non vocibus iisdem:

: LI :

Fragment of an eclogue in praise of the same man

Hybla had put aside her distaff, Leuce her baskets and Cneorus
his twig of hibiscus. In the bright sunlight, these young people sat
upon a secluded rock by the shores of Benacus, and sang in meter
the same things, but with different voices. Hybla's voice was low,   5
Leuce's was in the middle range and that of Cneorus was high.
And the woods of Malcesine echoed with all their voices.

Cneorus: O if only my flame, Thelayra, were not consuming me,
   would anyone be happier than I am amid such happiness? Now
   even winter is like spring. Now is a sacred time and the very
   bulls stand crowned beside their overflowing pens. Pardon us,   10
   please, Thelayra, while we rustics pay our greatest tribute to a
   new demigod, while gladness fills all the altars, while the hollow
   vales, the curving shores, Benacus and the Adige all resound,
   Giberti, in your honor.

   But you, son of an ungrateful mother and you, mother of an   15
   ungrateful son, go hence, you who always mix sadness and bit-
   ter tears with joy. There is pleasure in sacred rites. While
   Rome, rejoicing, bestows a sacred cap upon this youth, and
   prepares great triumphs for him, the nearby mountains and the   20
   seven hills resound with his praise, and Father Tiber rises up
   from his resounding banks, and the Tyrrhenian shores of the
   nearby sea tremble.

Hybla had put aside her distaff, Leuce her baskets and Cneorus
his twig of hibiscus. In the bright sunlight, these young people
were singing upon a secluded rock, together, they sang in meter   25
the songs that great Alcon had taught them, but with different

Hybla gravi, Leuce media, Gneorus acuta
cantant; Melsineae responsant omnia sylvae.

G.   Nunc et hiems verna est, nunc et solemnia, et ipsi
30   plena coronati stant ad praesepia tauri.
      Nunc etiam hyrsutae ludunt per prata capellae,
      nunc etiam faciles saliunt per littora nymphae.

L.   Omen, io, novus ecce tuis ab honoribus annus
      incipit, en melior nobis iam vertitur orbis.
35   Iam caelum, Gybberte, tenent tua sydera et ipsa
      terrarum dea Luna novo Latonia cornu.
      Iam nova mutato nascuntur saecula mundo.

H.   Et Pietas, et cana Fides, et lancibus aequis
      inviolata alto descendit ab aethere Virgo,
40   et fecunda Ceres, et Copia cornibus aureis.

G.   Magna novum sacro heroa dum Roma galero
      donat, Io, septem responsant undique colles,
      assurgitque pater Tyberis, ripaeque resultant,
      et Tyrena fremunt vicini littora ponti.

45 L. Ipsae laetitia nutarunt vertice sylvae,
      ipse Athesis fluvio pater exultavit amoeno,
      largius atque urnam versavit, et aggere ab alto
      aurea concussit taurina cornua fronte.

H.   Tum quoque pumiceo senior Benacus ab antro
50   pacavitque lacum, fluctusque, fremitumque marinum
      sedavit, iussitque vagos abscedere ventos,
      et lauro et viridi ripas ornavit oliva.

G.   Syrmio, frondentes per ripas insere lauros:
      ille colit Musas, et vates educat, et iam
55   magna iterum docti nascetur Musa Catulli,
      magnanimum heroa tua quae cantet in acta.

voices. Hybla's voice was low, Leuce's was in the middle range and that of Cneorus was high. And the woods of Malcesine echoed with all their voices.

Cneorus: Now even winter is like spring. Now is a sacred time and the very bulls stand crowned beside their overflowing pens. 30 Now even the shaggy goats disport in the fields, while the agile nymphs dance upon the shore.

Leuce: Truly, Giberti, this year begins auspiciously with your elevation and the world is better for us than before. Now your 35 stars shine in the heavens, as does the Latonian moon, goddess of the earth, with her new horns. Now a new age is born across a transformed world.

Hybla: And Piety and white-haired Faith and the inviolate Virgin, with her just scales, will descend from heaven, as well as fertile 40 Ceres and Abundance with her golden horns.

Cneorus: While great Rome exultantly bestows a sacred cap upon the new hero, lo, the seven hills resound everywhere, Father Tiber rises up from his echoing banks, and the Tyrrhenian shores of the nearby sea tremble.

Leuce: The very woods have bowed their heads with happiness. 45 With his pleasant waves, Father Adige himself has leaped up, spilling out his urn in greater abundance and, from a lofty hill, he, bull-headed, has shaken his golden horns.

Hybla: Then too, from his pumice cave, did old man Benacus becalm his lake, pacifying his streams and their watery roar, as he 50 bade the wandering winds depart and adorned his banks with myrtle and green olive.

Cneorus: O Sirmione, put forth your laurel fronds, a great grove. For Giberti cultivates the muses and nurtures poets and now the great muse of learned Catullus will be born anew, to sing of 55 this greathearted hero on your shore.

L.   Ille etiam agrestes non dedignatur avenas:
      'Tyrsi, mihi cane, Tyrsi,' inquit, 'sit rustica quamvis
      Musa tibi, tamen immemorem non arguet, et me
60   gratum Melsineis non inficiabitur hortis.'
H.   Quid? Quod et agrestesque manus et munera curat.
      'Leuce,' inquit, 'decoret sacro me Roma galero,
      serta tamen tu, chara mihi, tu munera mittes:
      lilia tu lege cana mihi, lege lycnida, Leuce.'
65 G.   Tybri, quid ah nostrum retines? Ab origine Thusci
      nos tecum servamus adhuc nomenque genusque.
      Hinc et amat nos ille deus terraeque, marisque,
      qui caelos aperire potest et Tartara Clemens.
L.   Clementi nova sacra deo renovate quotannis,
70   agricolae. Hic diram Allecto, caecumque Furorem,
      Gorgones, Harpyiasque feras, infernaque monstra
      Caucasea aerata religabit rupe cathena.
H.   Hic te pastorem nobis, miseratus egenos,
      sanctum te, Gybberte, dedit, tibique optimus inquit:
75   'Tu nostrum gentisque novae curabis ovile,
      quem mox fata deum post me ad maiora reservant.'
G.   Oceano in magno pupis secura magistro
      contemnit pelagique minas, ventosque furentis.
L.   Rege sub exercetur apum studiosa iuventus:
80   mella premunt, finguntque favos, roremque reportant.
H.   Tutela pastoris oves per pabula laeta
      contemnuntque lupos, iam nec metuere leones.
        Quum venies, Gybberte, tuum visurus ovile,
      mella ferent quercus, decurrent flumina lacte.
85   Vellera ab arboreis pendebunt mollia ramis,
      inculti pretiosa ferent opobalsama vepres.
        Ros et nocte cadet caelesti nectare mistus,
      qui gentes saturet mensa dapibusque deorum.
        Salve, macte nova iuvenis virtute decorus.

Leuce: He does not disdain even rustic reeds. "Thyrsis," he said,
"sing to me. Though your muse is rustic, she will not accuse me
of being unheedful or say that I am unwelcome in the gardens   60
of Malcesine."

Hybla: "Why?" you ask. "Because he cares for the people and the
gifts of the countryside." "Leuce," he said, "though Rome be-
stows upon me a sacred cap, you, dear one, send me chaplets as
gifts. Leuce, gather white lilies for me and red flowers as well."

Cneorus: What, O Tiber, do you have in common with us? Even   65
now, as of old, we share with you the Etruscan name and race.
Therefore are we loved by that great god, Clement, who rules
the earth and sea and can open up heaven and hell.

Leuce: Rustics, let us each year renew our sacred vows to this god
Clement. For with a brazen chain will he bind upon the Cauca-   70
sian mountain dire Alecto, blind Fury and the Gorgons, as well
as fierce Harpies and the monsters of hell.

Hybla: Pitying us in our need, he bestowed you upon us, Giberti,
to be our holy shepherd. And the great man said to you: "You   75
will protect both the people and their sheepfold, while divine
destiny reserves you for greater things after me."

Cneorus: On the vast ocean, a ship, safely guided by its pilot, fears
neither the water's threats nor the raging winds.

Leuce: Led by the king of the bees, the hive's eager youth extract   80
honey, build honeycombs and bring back the dew.

Hybla: Guarded by their shepherd, the sheep pass through smiling
pastures, scoffing at wolves and no longer fearing lions.

When you come, Giberti, to look upon your flocks, the oak
trees will exude honey and the rivers will flow with milk.

Soft fleeces will hang from the branches of trees and prickly   85
underbrush will give forth pure balm.

Even at night dew will fall, mixed with heavenly nectar that
will nourish the nations upon the feasts and fare of the gods.

90 En crescit, completque tibi sua cornua Phoebe,
et tria ab aetherio felicia sydera mundo
irradiantque tibi, et caelum iam militat omne.
    Salve, aetas heroum, amnes, salvete, Latini,
diique omnes magnae Hesperiae, qui saecula soli
95 aurea Saturni primo meministis ab aevo,
quum sepes vel limes adhuc communibus agris
non foret, aut ulli variarent iugera sulci,
sponte sua sed terra ferax daret omnia, et ipsae
praeberent dulci victum de robore glandes.

100   Hybla colo, Leuce calathis, Cneorus ibisco
depositis, sola pueri sub rupe sedentes
apricum ad Solem in littoribus Benaci,
in numerum cantant, docuit quae maximus Alcon,
carmina concordes eadem non vocibus iisdem.

105   Hybla colo, Leuce calathis, Cneorus ibisco
depositis, pueri docuit quos maximus Alcon,
alternis forte sub rupe canentes
apricum ad Solem in littoribus Benaci,
concordes cantant eadem non vocibus iisdem.

110   Hybla colo, Leuce calathis, Cneorus ibisco
depositis, sola pueri sub rupe canentes
apricum ad Solem, docuit quos maximus Alcon,
una omnes cantant eadem non vocibus iisdem:
Hybla gravi, Leuce media, Cneorus acuta
115 cantant; Melsineae responsant omnia sylvae.
Cn. Nunc et hiems est verna, et nunc solemnia, et ipsi
plena coronati stant ad praesepia tauri.
Nunc etiam hirsutae ludunt per prata capellae,
nunc etiam laetatur ager, laetatur et annus.

Hail to you, young man, resplendent in your new rank. Be- 90
hold how Phoebe waxes and fills her horns for you, while in the
lofty heavens, three auspicious stars shine for you, and already
all of heaven is at your service.

Hail to you, age of heroes, hail, streams of Italy, and all you
gods of great Hesperia, who alone remember from time imme- 95
morial the golden age of Saturn: when no fence or boundary
divided the common fields, nor any furrow scarred the land.
Rather the fertile earth gave all things up spontaneously and the
acorns of the sweet oak tree provided sustenance.

Hybla had put aside her distaff, Leuce her baskets and Cneorus 100
his twig of hibiscus. In the bright sunlight, these young people sat
upon a secluded rock by the shores of Benacus and, all together,
rhythmically sang the songs that great Alcon had taught them, but
with different voices.

Hybla had put aside her distaff, Leuce her baskets and Cneorus 105
his twig of hibiscus. In the bright sunlight, these young people sat
upon a secluded rock by the shores of Benacus, and sang in unison
the songs that great Alcon had taught them, but their voices were
not the same.

Hybla had put aside her distaff, Leuce her baskets and Cneorus 110
his twig of hibiscus. In the bright sunlight, these young people sat
upon a secluded rock and, all together, sang the songs that great
Alcon had taught them, but with different voices. Hybla's voice
was low, Leuce's was in the middle range and that of Cneorus was
high. And the woods of Malcesine echoed with all their voices. 115

Cneorus: Now even winter is like spring. Now is a sacred time and
the very bulls stand crowned beside their overflowing pens.
Now even the shaggy goats disport in the fields, now the very
fields partake of their joy, and the streams too.

323

120 H.   Sit faustum felixque. Tuis ab honoribus annus
           incipit, omen habet: melior iam vertitur orbis,
           iam caelum Gybberte tenent tua sydera, et ipsa
           terrarum dea Luna novo Latonia cornu.

     L.   Iam nova mutato nascuntur saecula mundo,
125   et Pietas, et cana Fides, et lancibus aequis
           inviolata alto descendit ab aethere Virgo,
           et fecunda Ceres, et Copia cornibus aureis.

     C.   Roma sacro iuvenem donat dum magna galero,
           mons circum septemque sonant applausibus arces,
130   assurgitque pater Tyberis, ripaeque resultant,
           et Tyrena fremunt vicini littora ponti.

     H.   Ipsae laetitia nutarunt vertice sylvae,
           populiferque Athesis fluvio exultavit amoeno,
           largius atque urnam versavit, et aggere ab alto
135   aurea concussit taurino cornua vultu.

     L.   Tum quoque pumiceo senior Benacus ab antro
           pacavitque lacum, fluctus, fremitumque marinum
           sedavit, iussitque vagos abscedere ventos,
           et myrto et viridi ripas ornavit oliva.

140 G.   Syrmio proceras, magnum nemus, insere lauros:
           ille colit Musas, et vates educat, et iam
           mille habet: atque aliquis crescit tibi forte Catullus,
           magnanimum heroa tua qui cantet in acta

     H.   Ille etiam agrestes non dedignatur avenas.
145   Ille tibi caelo tandem demissus ab alto,
           'Tyrsi, canas licet usque, et agas laeta otia,' dixit,
           'En agrum, en tibi do, quod numquam duxeris, hortos.'

     L.   Ex illo nobis deus est. Illi annua sacra
           montibus his faciemus: erunt et rustica grata.
150   Hybla, deo tua texta para, quae munera mittas.
           Lilia tu lege, cana, mihi, lege lycnida, Leuce.

Hybla: May it pass happily and auspiciously. This year begins with 120
your elevation and it brings auspices. Now the world is changing
for the better, now your stars shine in the heavens, Giberti, as
does the Latonian moon, goddess of the earth, with her new horns.

Leuce: Now a new age is born across a transformed world, and 125
Piety and white-haired Faith and the inviolate Virgin, with her
just scales, will descend from heaven, as well as fertile Ceres
and Abundance with her golden horns.

Cneorus: While great Rome bestows a sacred cap upon this youth,
the nearby mountains and the seven hills resound with his
praise, Father Tiber rises up from his echoing banks and the 130
Tyrrhenian shores of the nearby sea tremble.

Hybla: The very woods have bowed their heads with happiness.
With its pleasant waves the Adige, rich in poplars, has leaped
up, spilling out his urn in greater abundance and, from a lofty
hill, he, bull-headed, has shaken his golden horns. 135

Leuce: Then too, from his pumice cave, did old man Benacus be-
calm his lake, pacifying his streams and their watery roar, as he
bade the wandering winds depart and adorned his banks with
myrtle and green olive.

Cneorus: O Sirmione, put forth your tall laurels, a great grove. For 140
Giberti cultivates the muses and has already raised up a thou-
sand poets. Perhaps another Catullus is emerging, to sing of
this greathearted hero on your shore.

Hybla: Giberti does not disdain even rustic reeds. At last, sent 145
down from on high for you, Thyrsis, he said, "You can keep
singing and enjoy happy leisure: here do I give you fields and
gardens beyond your expectations!"

Leuce: From that time forth he is a god to us: in these mountains
we will perform yearly rites in his honor. Even our rustic tribute
will please him. Hybla, prepare your weavings to send as a gift 150
to the god. Leuce, gather white lilies for me and red flowers as
well.

C.   Tybri, quid ah nostrum retines? Ab origine tecum
nos Thusci servamus adhuc nomenque genusque.
Hinc et amat nos ille deus, cui temperat orbis,
155   qui caelos aperire potest et Tartara Clemens.

H.   Clementi nova sacra deo renovate quotannis,
agricolae. Hic diram Alecto, caecumque Furorem,
Gorgones, Harpyasque feras, infernaque monstra
Caucasea aerata religabit rupe cathena.

160 L.   Hic te pastorem nobis, miseratus egenos,
hic patrem, Gybberte, dedit, tibique optimus inquit:
'Et genus interea, et nostrum servabis ovile,
dum te fata deum mox ad maiora reservant.'

C.   Oceano in magno pupis secura magistro
165   contemnit pelagique minas, ventosque furenteis.

H.   Rege sub exercetur apum studiosa iuventus:
mella premunt, finguntque favos, roremque reportant.

L.   Tutela pastoris oves per gramina laetae
despiciuntque lupos, iam nec metuere leones.

170 C.   Quum venies, Gybberte, tuum visurus ovile,
mella ferent quercus, decurrent flumina lacte.

H.   Vellera ab arboreis pendebunt mollia ramis,
puraque dumosi sudabunt balsama vepres.

L.   Ros et nocte cadet caelesti nectare mistus,
175   qui gentes saturet mensa dapibusque deorum.
     Salve, magna aetas, et vos salvete, beati
heroes. Salvete, amnes, fontesque Latini,
diique omnes magnae Hesperiae, qui saecula soli
aurea Saturni primo meministis ab aevo,
180   quum sepes vel limes adhuc communibus agris
non foret, aut ulli variarent iugera sulci,
sponte sua sed terra ferax daret omnia, et ipsae
praeberent dulci victum de robore glandes.

Cneorus: What, O Tiber, do you have in common with us? Even now, as of old, we share with you the Etruscan name and race. Therefore are we loved by that great god, Clement, who rules 155 the world and can open up heaven and hell.

Hybla: Rustics, let us each year renew our sacred vows to this god Clement. For with a brazen chain will he bind upon the Caucasian mountain dire Alecto, blind Fury and the Gorgons, as well as fierce Harpies and the monsters of hell.

Leuce: Pitying us in our need, he bestowed you upon us, Giberti, 160 to be our shepherd and our father. And the great man said to you: "You will protect both the people and their sheepfold, while divine destiny reserves you for greater things."

Cneorus: On the vast ocean, a ship, safely guided by its pilot, fears 165 neither the water's threats nor the raging winds.

Hybla: Led by the king of the bees, the hive's eager youth extract honey, build honeycombs and bring back the dew.

Leuce: Guarded by their shepherd, the sheep lie happily in the grass, scoffing at wolves and no longer fearing lions.

Cneorus: When you come, Giberti, to look upon your flocks, the 170 oak trees will exude honey and the rivers will flow with milk.

Hybla: Soft fleeces will hang from the branches of trees and prickly underbrush will give forth pure balm.

Leuce: Even at night dew will fall, mixed with heavenly nectar that 175 will nourish the nations upon the feasts and fare of the gods.

Hail to you, great age, and hail, you blessed heroes! Hail to you, rivers and springs of Latium, and all you gods of great Hesperia, who alone remember from time immemorial the golden age of Saturn: when no fence or boundary divided the 180 common fields, nor any furrow scarred the land. Rather the fertile earth gave all things up spontaneously and the acorns of the sweet oak tree provided sustenance.

Salve cura deum iuvenis, cui militat aether:
185   en crescit, completque tibi sua cornua Phoebe.

     Ibla colo, Leuce calathis, Gneorus ibisco
     depositis, sola pueri sub rupe sedentes
     apricum ad Solem in littoribus Benaci,
     in numerum cantant eadem non vocibus iisdem:
190   Ibla gravi, Leuce media, Gneorus acuta
     cantant; Melsineae responsant omnia sylvae.

C.   O nisi me Thelayra meus consumeret ignis,
     ecquis laetitia in tanta me laetior esset?
     Nunc et ver placidum est, et nunc solemnia, et ipsi
195   plena coronati stant ad praesepia tauri.

L.   Quemque suus tenet ignis. Adesto, candide Ayla,
     laetitiae, nunc luce sacra duc gaudia mecum.
     Postridie curabis oves, aut, si magis horti
     detineat te cura, virens tondebis anethum.

200 H.   Quin, matris puer ingratae, materque, facesse hinc,
     ingrati mater pueri, qui tristia laetis,
     semper qui lachrymas intermiscetis amaras.
     Sancta placent: agitur iuveni lux optima sancto.

G.   Dum decorat, Gybberte, sacro te Roma galero,
205   mons circum septemque sonant applausibus arces,
     assurgitque pater Tyberis, ripaeque resultant,
     et Tyrena fremunt vicini littora ponti.

L.   Ipsae laetitia nutarunt vertice sylvae,
     populiferque Athesis fluvio exultavit amoeno,
210   largius atque urnam versavit, et aggere ab alto
     aurea concussit taurino cornua vultu.

H.   Tum quoque pumiceo senior Benacus ab antro
     pacavitque lacum, fluctus, fremitumque marinum
     sedavit, iussitque vagos abscedere ventos,
215   et myrto et viridi ripas ornavit oliva.

Hail to thee young man, beloved of the gods, whom heaven
serves. Behold how Phoebe waxes and fills her horns for you.   185

Hybla had put aside her distaff, Leuce her baskets and Cneorus
his twig of hibiscus. In the bright sunlight, these young people sat
upon a secluded rock by the shores of Benacus, and sang in meter
the same things, but with different voices. Hybla's voice was low,   190
Leuce's was in the middle range and that of Cneorus was high.
And the woods of Malcesine echoed with all their voices.

Cneorus: O if only my flame, Thelayra, were not consuming me,
  would anyone be happier than I am amid such happiness? Now
  is mild spring, now is a sacred time and the very bulls stand   195
  crowned beside their overflowing pens.
Leuce: Each man after his passion. Come, handsome Aylas, and
  on this sacred day, partake with me of the common joy. Tomor-
  row you will care for your flocks, or, if the garden concerns you
  more, you will clip the green dill.
Hybla: But you, son of an ungrateful mother and you, mother of   200
  an ungrateful son, go hence, you who always mix sadness and
  bitter tears with joy. There is pleasure in sacred rites. And this
  is a great day for our saintly youth.
Cneorus: While Rome bestows a sacred cap upon you, Giberti, the   205
  nearby mountains and the seven hills resound with his praise,
  Father Tiber rises up from his echoing banks and the Tyrrhe-
  nian shores of the nearby sea tremble.
Leuce: The very woods have bowed their heads with happiness.
  With its pleasant waves the Adige, rich in poplars, has leaped
  up, spilling out his urn in greater abundance and, from a lofty   210
  hill, he, bull-headed, has shaken his golden horns.
Hybla: Then too, from his pumice cave, did old man Benacus be-
  calm his lake, pacifying his streams and their watery roar, as he
  bade the wandering winds depart and adorned his banks with   215
  myrtle and green olive.

G.   Sit faustum felixque tuis ab honoribus omen:
nescio quid quercu volucris cantabit ab alta.
En caelum Gybberte tenent tua sydera et ipsa
terrarum dea Luna novo Latonia cornu.

220 L.   Iam nova mutato nascuntur saecula mundo,
et Pietas, et cana Fides, et lancibus aequis
inviolata alto descendit ab aethere Virgo,
et fecunda Ceres, et Copia cornibus aureis.

H.   Vos quoque Clementi, agricolae, renovate quotannis
225   sacra deo . . .

G.   Clemens hunc nobis iuvenem, miseratus egenos,
ipse dedit, dixitque: 'Meum servabis ovile
Etrusci, puer, armenti, puer inclyte, pastor,
dum te fata deum mox ad maiora reservant.'

230 H.   Pastori, Benace, tuo flue lenior undis:
tempus erit quum sancta pedum vestigia lambes.
Tunc tibi et Amphrysus concedat, Apolline quamvis
labatur pecoris nivei pastore superbus.

H.   Syrmio proceras, magnum nemus, insere lauros:
235   ille colit vates, et Musas educat, et iam
mille habet, atque aliquis crescit tibi forte Catullus,
magnanimum heroa tua qui cantet in acta.

G.   Ille etiam agrestes non dedignatur avenas:
ille tibi caelo tandem demissus ab alto,
240   Tyrsi, 'canas licet usque, et agas laeta otia,' dixit,
'en agrum, en tibi do, quod numquam duxeris, hortos.'
    Quid? Quod et agrestes flores et munera curat,
'Leuce,' inquit, 'decoret sacro me Roma galero,
serta tamen tu, chara mihi, tu munera mitte:
245   lilia tu lege cana mihi, lege lycnida, Leuce.'
    Quin tua ipse etiam parvum quod laurea nectat
serta inter folium e ripa Benacide misi.

Cneorus: May a happy and auspicious omen arise from your eleva-
tion. A bird, sitting in a lofty oak, will sing it. Behold, your
stars shine in the heavens, as does the Latonian moon itself,
goddess of the earth, with its new horns.

Leuce: Now a new age is born across a transformed world, and   220
Piety and white-haired Faith and the inviolate Virgin, with her
just scales, will descend from heaven, as well as fertile Ceres
and Abundance with her golden horns.

Hybla: Rustics, let us each year renew our sacred vows too to this
god Clement . . .   225

Cneorus: Pitying us in our need, Clement himself gave us this
young man and said: "You will preserve my pen, noble youth,
shepherd of the Tuscan flock, while divine destiny reserves you
for greater things.

Hybla: Flow softly, Benacus, for your shepherd. There will come a   230
day when you will wash the tracks of holy feet. Then even Am-
phrysus must yield to you, although as it glides, it boasts of
Apollo as the shepherd of its snowy flocks.

Leuce: O Sirmione, put forth your tall laurels, a great grove. For   235
Giberti cultivates the muses and has already raised up a thou-
sand poets. Perhaps another Catullus is emerging, to sing of
this greathearted hero on your shore.

Cneorus: Giberti does not disdain even rustic reeds. At last, sent
down from on high for you, Thyrsis, he said, "You can keep   240
singing and enjoy happy leisure: here do I give you fields and
gardens beyond your expectations!"

"Why?" you ask. "Because he cares for the flowers and the
gifts of the countryside." "Leuce," he said, "though Rome be-
stows upon me a sacred cap, you, dear one, send me chaplets as
gifts. Leuce, gather white lilies for me and red flowers as well."   245

To him I too sent a small leaf from the shores of Benacus, to
bind together his laurel chaplets. That the young man should

Quod veniat munus iuveni, nova texta paravi,
pictus ubi Narcissus hiat, Maeander oberrat.

250   Hybla, Almo, Gneorus: apum studiosa puella,
venatus Almo, pecoris Gneorus . . .
idem consueti sylvas et littora cantu
assiduo mulcere, sonumque adiungere Musis,
forte simul sola pueri sub rupe sedentes
255 apricum ad Solem in littoribus Benaci,
Hybla colo, iaculis Almo, Gneorus hybisco
depositis . . .

    Forte simul pueri Leuce, Cneorus, et Almo,
Almo arcu, Leuce calathis, Cneorus ibisco
260 depositis, sola pueri sub rupe sedentes
apricum ad Solem in littoribus Benaci,
idem consueti sylvas et littora cantu,

    Forte subalpini Leuce, Gneorus, et Almo,
Almo arcu, Leuce calathis, Cneorus hybisco
265 depositis, sola pueri sub rupe sedentes
apricum ad Solem in littoribus Benaci,
in numerum cantant eadem non vocibus iisdem,
Almo gravi, Leuce media, Gneorus acuta,
adiunguntque sonum tenuis Cneorus avenae,
270 arguti Leuce crotali, testudinis Almo.
Haec Almo, illa puer Gneorus, at ultima Leuce
cantat; Melsineae responsant omnia sylvae.

    Forte subalpini iuvenes Gneorus, et Almo,
Hyblaque, venatus Almo, Gneorus aratri,
275 Hybla horti studiosa, iidem nemora omnia cantu
assueti mulcere, in littoribus Benaci
apricum ad Solem aëria sub rupe canebant.
Hybla bidente, Almo iaculis, Cneorus aratro

332

receive these gifts, I have prepared new weavings, in which Narcissus is depicted gaping while Maeander wanders.

There were Hybla, Almo and Cneorus: the girl delighted in the 250
care of bees, Almo in hunting, Cneorus in sheep-breeding, and
they were wont to beguile the woods and the shores with their assiduous singing, joining music with words. It happened once that
the youths sat together beside a deserted rock in the bright sun- 255
shine on the shores of Benacus: Hybla had put aside her distaff,
Almo his arc, and Cneorus his twig of hibiscus . . .

It happened once that the youthful Leuce, Cneorus and Almo
(Almo having put aside his arc, Leuce her baskets and Cneorus
his twig of hibiscus) sat together beside a deserted rock in the 260
bright sunshine on the shores of Benacus. They were wont to beguile the woods and the shores with their assiduous singing.

It happened once, at the foothills of the Alps, that the youthful
Leuce, Cneorus and Almo (Almo having put aside his arc, Leuce
her baskets and Cneorus his twig of hibiscus) sat beside a deserted 265
rock in the bright sunshine on the shores of Benacus, singing in
meter the same things, but with different voices. Almo's voice was
low, Leuce's in the middle range and Cneorus's high. Cneorus
added the sound of the slender flute, Leuce that of the shrill casta- 270
net and Almo that of the lyre. These were the songs first of Almo,
then of young Cneorus and finally of Leuce. And the woods of
Malcesine echoed with them all.

It happened once that, at the foothills of the Alps, the youths
Cneorus, Almo and Hybla loved farming, hunting and gardening 275
respectively. They were accustomed to beguile all the woods with
their song. On the shores of Benacus, in the bright sunlight, they
were singing beside a lofty cliff. Hybla had set aside her hoe, Almo
his spears and Cneorus his plow as they exchanged words and

depositis, numeros partiti et verba vicissim,
280 addiderantque sonum tenuis Cneorus avenae,
Hybla cavi crotali, resonae testudinis Almo.
Haec Almo, illa puer Cneorus, at Hybla supremum
cantant: Melsineae responsant omnia sylvae.

Al. O nisi me Thelayra meus consumeret ignis,
285 ecquis laetitia in tanta me laetior esset?
Nunc et ver placidum est, nunc et solemnia, et ipsi
plena coronati stant ad praesepia tauri.
Parce, precor, Thelayra, novo dum sacra dies est
semideo, dum ridet ager, laetatur et amnis.

290 Quemque suus tenet ignis. Adesto, candida Leuce,
laetitiae: nunc luce sacra duc gaudia mecum.
Postridie lustrabis apes, aut, si magis horti
tunc habeat te cura, virens tondebis anethum.
Nunc etiam hyrsutae ludunt per prata capellae,
295 nunc etiam virides saliunt per littora nymphae.

Quin, matris puer ingratae, materque, facesse hinc,
ingrati mater pueri, qui tristia laetis,
semper qui lachrymas intermiscetis amaras.
Sancta placent. agitur iuveni lux optima sancto,
300 cui caelum egelidum, cui ridet florigerum ver,
gramine terra novo vestitur, frondibus arbor.

Forte subalpini iuvenes Cneorus, et Almo,
Hyblaque, Cneorus pastor gregis, optimus Almo
venatu, lanae studiosa et Palladis Hybla,
305 iidem, consueti sylvas et littora cantu
assiduo mulcere, alta sub rupe canebant.
Haec ego; namque licet lusus agitetur ubique
multum laetitiaeque . . .

music in alternation, each according to his part. Cneorus added   280
the sound of the slender flute, Hybla of the hollowed castanet and
Almo of the resounding lyre. Almo sang first, then Cneorus and
finally Hybla. And the woods of Malcesine echoed with them all.

Almo: O if only my flame, Thelayra, were not consuming me,
would anyone be happier than I am amid such happiness? Now   285
it is mild spring, now is a sacred time and the very bulls stand
crowned beside their overflowing pens. Pardon us, please, The-
layra, while we celebrate a sacred day for a new demigod, while
the field smiles and the stream rejoices.

Each man after his passion. Join in the happiness, lovely   290
Leuce, and on this sacred day, partake with me of the common
joy. Tomorrow you will tend to the bees or, if the garden inter-
ests you more, clip the green dill. Now even the shaggy goats
disport themselves in the fields. Now even the youthful nymphs   295
dance upon the shore.

But you, son of an ungrateful mother and you, mother of an
ungrateful son, go hence, you who always mix sadness and bit-
ter tears with joy. There is pleasure in sacred rites. And this is a
great day for our saintly youth, upon whom the clement heav-   300
ens and the flowering spring smile, as the earth decks itself in
new grass and the trees in new leaves.

It happened once that young Cneorus, Almo and Hybla stood
at the foothills of the Alps: Cneorus tended flocks, Almo was ex-
pert at hunting and Hybla delighted in wool and weaving. They   305
were wont to beguile the woods and the shores with their assidu-
ous singing, and now they sang beside a lofty cliff.

These things I said: for although great joy and playfulness are
everywhere . . .

Forte subalpini iuvenes Cneorus, et Almo,
310   Hyblaque (Cneorus pastor gregis, optimus Almo
venatu, lanae studiosa et Palladis Hybla),
Hybla colo, iaculis Almo, Gneorus hybisco
depositis, sola pueri sub rupe canebant,
flumina Benaci residentes propter amoeni,
315   addiderantque sonum gracilis Gneorus avenae,
Hybla cavi crotali, resonae testudinis Almo.
Haec Almo, illa puer Gneorus, at Hybla supremum
cantat; Melsineae responsant omnia sylvae.

Al.   O nisi me Thelayra meus consumeret ignis,
320   ecquis laetitia in tanta me laetior esset?
Nunc et festa dies, nunc et solemnia, et ipsi
plena coronati stant ad praesepia tauri.

Cn.   Quemque suus tenet ignis. Ades, formosa Lycori,
laetitiae: nunc luce sacra duc gaudia mecum.
325   Nunc etiam hyrsutae ludunt per prata capellae,
nunc etiam virides saliunt per littora nymphae.

Hy.   Quin matris puer Idaliae, materque, facesse hinc,
Idalii mater pueri, qui tristia laetis,
semper qui lachrymas intermiscetis amaras.
330   Sancta placent: agitur iuveni lux optima sancto.

Al.   Sit faustum felixque: tuo, Gybberte, refulsit
aether in adventu, et caelo felicia ab alto
nescio quid micuere novum tria sydera, et ipsa
terrarum dea Luna novo Latonia cornu.

335 *Al.*   Iam nova mutato nascuntur saecula mundo,
et Pietas, et cana Fides, et lancibus aequis
inviolata alto descendit ab aethere Virgo,
et fecunda Ceres, et Copia cornibus aureis.

It happened once, in the foothills of the Alps, that the youthful
Cneorus, Almo and Hybla were singing under a deserted rock,   310
Cneorus a shepherd of flocks, Almo an expert hunter and Hybla
skilled in wool and the arts of Athena. Now Hybla had put aside
her distaff, Almo his shafts and Cneorus his twig of hibiscus, as
they sat beside the streams of charming Benacus. Cneorus played   315
on the slender flute, Hybla on the hollowed castanet and Almo on
the resounding lyre. Almo sang first, then Cneorus and finally
Hybla, and the woods of Malcesine echoed to them all.

Almo: O if only my flame, Thelayra, were not consuming me,
would anyone be happier than I am amid such happiness? To-   320
day is a holiday, a time of solemn rites, and the very bulls stand
crowned before their overflowing pens.

Cneorus: Each man after his passion. Join in the happiness, lovely
Lycoris, and on this sacred day, partake with me of the com-
mon joy. Now even the shaggy goats disport themselves in the   325
fields. Now even the youthful nymphs dance upon the shore.

Hybla: But you, son of the Idalian mother, and you, mother of the
Idalian boy, go hence, you who always mix sadness and bitter
tears with joy. There is pleasure in sacred rites, and this is a   330
great day for our saintly youth!

Almo: May it pass happily and auspiciously. The air glowed, Gi-
berti, at your coming, and in high heaven three prosperous stars
shone in a new way, as did the moon itself, daughter of Leto
and goddess of the earth, with her new horns.

Already the world has changed and a new age is being born.   335
Piety and white-haired Faith, and the inviolate Virgin, descend-
ing from heaven with her fair scales, as well as fertile Ceres and
Abundance with her golden horns.

Gn.	Hac iuveni nova sacra die renovate quotannis,
340	agricolae. Hic diram Alecto, caecumque Furorem,
	Gorgones, Harpyasque feras, infernaque monstra
	Caucasea aerata religabit rupe cathena.
Gn.	Ipsae laetitia nutarunt vertice sylvae,
	populiferque Athesis fluvio exultavit amoeno,
345	largius atque urnam versavit, et aggere ab alto
	aurea concussit taurino cornua vultu.
H.	Tunc quoque pumiceo senior Benacus ab antro
	pacavitque lacum, fluctus, fremitumque marinum
	sedavit, iussitque vagos abscedere ventos,
350	et myrto et viridi ripas ornavit olivo.
Hyb.	Pastori, Benace, tuo flue lenibus undis:
	tempus erit quum sancta pedum vestigia lambes.
	Tunc tibi et Amphrysus concedat, Apolline quamvis
	labatur pecoris nivei pastore superbus.
355 *Al.*	Syrmio frondosas, magnum nemus, indue lauros:
	ille colit Musas, et vates educat, et iam
	mille habet: atque aliquis crescit tibi forte Catullus,
	magnanimum qui heroa tua decantet in acta.
Gn.	Ille etiam agrestes non dedignatur avenas:
360	ille tibi caelo tandem demissus ab alto,
	'Tyrsi, canas licet usque, et agas laeta otia,' dixit,
	'en agrum, en tibi do, quod numquam duxeris, hortos.'
Hy.	Quid? Quod et agrestes flores et munera curat.
	'Leuce,' inquit, 'decoret sacro me Roma galero,
365	serta tamen tu, chara, mihi tu munera mitte:
	narcissum lege, chara, mihi, lege lycnida, Leuce.'
	Cervus in Alpinis errat tibi, Delia, sylvis:
	hunc si, diva, dabis viventem in retia, sancto
	dona feram iuveni, et ramosis serta iubebo
370	cornibus ex hedera pictis pendere corymbis.

338

Cneorus: Each year, O Gods and rustics, perform these new rites
for the youth, for with a brazen chain upon the Caucasian   340
mount he will bind dire Alecto, blind Fury and the Gorgons, as
well as fierce Harpies and the monsters of hell.

    The very woods have bowed their heads with happiness.
With its pleasant waves the Adige, rich in poplars, has leaped
up, spilling out his urn in greater abundance and, from a lofty   345
hill, he, bull-headed, has shaken his golden horns.

Hybla: Then too, from his pumice cave, did old man Benacus be-
calm his lake, pacifying his streams and their watery roar, as he
bade the wandering winds depart and adorned his banks with   350
myrtle and green olive.

    Flow softly, Benacus, for your shepherd. There will come a
day when you will wash the tracks of holy feet. Then even Am-
phrysus must yield to you, although as it glides, it boasts of
Apollo as the shepherd of its snowy flocks.

Almo: O Sirmione, put forth your laurel fronds, a great grove. For   355
Giberti cultivates the muses and has already raised up a thou-
sand poets. Perhaps another Catullus is emerging, to sing of
this greathearted hero on your shore.

Cneorus: Giberti does not disdain even rustic reeds. At last, sent   360
down from on high for you, Thyrsis, he said, "You can keep
singing and enjoy happy leisure: Here do I give you fields and
gardens beyond your expectations!"

Hybla: "Why?" you ask. "Because he cares for the gifts and flowers
of the countryside." "Leuce," he said, "though Rome bestows
upon me a sacred cap, you, dear one, send me chaplets as gifts.   365
Bring me narcissus and red flowers, O Leuce."

    Delian goddess, your stag wanders through Alpine groves. If
you cause him to fall alive into my nets, will I bring gifts to the
holy youth and cause ivy wreathes to hang from the stag's   370
branching horns in colorful bouquets.

Est mihi Cretaeis aries delatus ab oris,
cuncta niger, camuris grandes sub cornibus aures
cui pendent atque ora tegunt: Pan diligit unum.
Hic iuveni aurato felix cadet hostia cornu.

375   Quod potui, mitto: Hesperidum quae ex arbore legi,
mala dabo septena uno pendentia ramo.
Mox sancto quae dona feram, nova texta paravi,
pictus ubi Narcissus hiat, Maeander oberrat.

     Oceano in magno pupis secura magistro
380   contemnit pelagique minas, ventosque furentes.

     Rege sub exercetur apum studiosa iuventus:
mella premit, fingitque favos, roremque reportat.

     Tutela pastoris oves per gramina laetae
despiciuntque lupos, nec iam metuere leones.

385   Rura deus noster tandem sua viset et urbem:
mella ferent quercus, decurrent flumina lacte.

     Vellera ab arboreis pendebunt mollia ramis,
puraque dumosi sudabunt balsama vepres.

     Ros et nocte cadet, tenera qui lectus ab herba
390   mortales saturet mensa dapibusque deorum.

: LII :

Fragmentum de theriaca

Magne Nero, nobis qui das tuta otia, Caesar,
hanc insignem audi viribus antidotum,
hanc audi, quam Theriacen voluere vocari,
quod tranquilla omnis vita per illam agitur.

I have a buck, entirely black, brought over from the Cretan shores. His large ears hang down from his curving horns all the way to his mouth. Pan loves him especially. His horns etched with gold, he will be presented to the youth as an auspicious offering.

I offer what I can. I shall send seven fruits that I picked from 375 the tree of the Hesperides and that hang from a single branch. Then I have prepared new weavings to offer as a gift to the holy man: in them Narcissus is depicted gaping while the Meander wanders.

On the vast ocean, a ship, safely guided by its pilot, fears neither the water's threats nor the raging winds. 380

Led by the king of the bees, the hive's eager youth extract honey, build honeycombs and bring back the dew.

Guarded by their shepherd, the sheep lie happily in the grass, scoffing at wolves and no longer fearing lions.

Our god finally visits his groves and town: the oak trees will 385 exude honey and the rivers will flow with milk.

Soft fleeces will hang from the branches of trees and prickly underbrush will give forth pure balm.

Even at night, dew will fall: gathered from the tender grass, it can nourish mortals upon the feasts and fare of the gods. 390

: LII :

Fragment on poisons

Great Nero, Caesar, you who grant us leisure in safety, hear of this important antidote to poison, which the ancients chose to call Theriaca, because it allows one to lead one's entire life in safety.

5   Nec tibi letalis noceant mala pocula succi,
       pocula de nigris pressa papaveribus;
    non seu praegelidam quis hauserit ore cicutam,
       seu quis hyosciamum, sive aconita bibat,
    non tibi vel medes noceat, non fervida tapsos,
10   non extillato sanguine cantharides,
    nec sitiens dipsas, nec, fraus metuenda, cerastes,
       nec quae letali vipera dente necet;
    incassum cauda consurgat scorpius unca.

: LIII :

Fragmentum carminis de theriaca

Magne Nero, qui das nobis tuta otia, Caesar,
cui debet quicquid praeclarum parturit orbis,
antidotum hanc insignem audi, quam nomine dicunt
Theriacen, tranquilla omnis quia vita per illam
5   degitur, et longos hilaris ductatur in annos.
Qua letale nihil poteris custode timere,
non si nigra malo porrecta papavera succo
hauseris, si gelidam dent Susa cicutam,
non tibi hiosciamus torpens, aconitave dira,
10   non mede, thapsusque, tibi non cantharis urens
sanguineum missura, acri non vipera dente,
nec sitiens dipsas, nec, fraus metuenda, cerastes.
In cassum e saxo cauda insidietur adunca
scorpius assurgens, magno metus Orioni;
15   in cassum squamis maculosa horrentibus aspis.
Nec mihi sit fugienda ptyas, quamquam improba caecis
ardeat insanumque micet deprehensa latebris.

Baneful drafts of lethal liquid will not harm you, nor extract of 5
black poppies. Not even if one has imbibed chilling hemlock, or
drunk nightshade or aconite, will one suffer harm. No medes, no
feverish mullein can harm you, no Spanish fly dripping with 10
blood. Neither can the dipsas snake, which induces thirst, do
harm to you, nor the fearful wiles of the horned snake, nor the
viper that kills with its lethal bite. In vain let the scorpion rise up
with its curved tail.

: LIII :

Fragment on poisons

Great Nero, Caesar, you who grant us leisure in safety, to whom
the earth owes whatever noble thing it brings forth: hear of this
great antidote which they call Theriaca, because it allows us to
pass our entire life in peace and happiness over many years. Under 5
its protection you will fear no poison, not even if you have drunk
black poppy distilled into a maleficent liquid, not even if Susa has
brought forth its chilling hemlock. You will have no need to fear
nightshade, which induces torpor, nor dire aconite, nor medes or 10
mullein or burning Spanish fly that draws out blood, nor the
sharp-toothed viper, the thirst-inducing dipsas snake or the wiles
of the horned snake. In vain let the scorpion scheme against you,
rising up from under a rock with its curved tail, the terror of great
Orion, or the spotted asp, with its bristling scales. Nor need I flee 15
from the Phtyas snake, though it flames immoderately from its
darkened lairs, and flashes wildly when captured. Indeed, I would

Quin ausim et pastum in sicco tractare chelydrum,
fessus et herbosi dormire ad flumina Nili,
20   multa ubi littorea sit foeta haemorrhois alga.
Iam neque chersidrum, nec bicipitem amphysibaenam
formidem; iam nec Calabris demessor in agris
devitem tremulum factura phalangia corpus.
Hac fidens, dum tu Lybien tua sub iuga, Caesar,
25   victor et immensi subigis regna ultima mundi,
iam malefida potes colubrum deserta vagari.

: LIV :

Aliud fragmentum

Felix, qui chara et pura cum coniuge vivit,
educitque suam sobolem, charosque nepotes,
humani generis memor, et servator honesti.
Fortunatus et ille, sibi qui caelibe vita,
5   mentem animumque colens, diis se caelestibus aequat.
Ille nequam est qui non aliis, qui nec sibi vivit.

: LV :

Initium Syphilidis
a vulgato diversum

Quae causae morbum insolitum, quae fata tulere
tempestate ista . . .

even dare to draw onto dry land the well fed water snake and, when I am tired, to lie beside the streams of the reedy Nile, where 20 dwells the Haemorrhois snake, well fed on an abundance of seaweed. No longer need I fear the trunk snake or the two-headed amphisbaena. No longer, as a reaper in the Calabrian fields, need I fear the harvestman spider, that sets one's body trembling. Confident in this cure, Caesar, when you triumphantly subject Lybia to 25 your yoke, as well as the far-flung kingdoms of the great world, you can wander among the treacherous, snake-infested deserts.

: LIV :

Another fragment

Happy the man who lives with his dear and decent wife, raising his sons and dear grandsons, respecting the human race and guarding his honor. He as well is fortunate who, living a life of celibacy, makes himself the equal of the gods by cultivating his mind and 5 his soul. That man alone is worthless who lives neither for others nor for himself.

: LV :

Beginning of the Syphilis,
different from the published version

What causes, what accidents brought forth a strange affliction at this time . . .

Bembe, deus quando medica haud contemnit Apollo,
et nova amare solent atque admiranda Camenae,
5   nunc ego, naturae et dulci accensus amore
Musarum, quae fata novum, quae semina morbum
attulerint, nostra qui tempestate per omnem
saeviit Europam, et Latium per tristia bella
Gallorum invasit, nomenque a gente recepit,
10   hinc canere et longe secretas quaerere causas
aëra per liquidum et vasti per sydera Olympi
incipiam, nec non et opis quid comperit usus,
magnaque in angustis hominum solertia rebus,
et monstrata deum auxilia, nullique parentum
15   nostrorum memorata prius nec cognita, pandam.
    Tu mihi, quae series causarum et fata ministras,
et caelo curru inveheris, perque aethera tranas,
quae tenues Solis radios elementaque misces,
quam pictae volucres, et amantes roscida plantae,
20   atque hominum, pecudumque genus, vitaeque natantum
eductricem unam vitae matremque salutant,
ipsa ades, et mecum placidas assiste per umbras,
dum tenues aurae, dum mirtea sylva canentem
invitat, resonatque cavis Benacus ab antris.

25   Principio quaeque in terris, quaeque aethere in alto
atque mari in magno natura educit in ortum,
cuncta quidem nec sorte una, nec legibus iisdem
proveniunt: sed enim quorum consurgit origo
e paucis, crebro et passim pars magna creantur;
30   rarius ast alia apparent et non nisi certis
temporibusve locisve, quibus violentior ortus
et longe sita principia; ac nonnulla, priusquam
erumpant tenebris et opaco carcere noctis,
mille trahunt annos spatiosaque saecula poscunt.

Bembo: because the god Apollo hardly disdains the arts of medicine and because the Muses are wont to love what is new and marvelous, I will now begin, inflamed with the sweet love of nature and the muses, to tell what events, what seeds brought forth a strange new disease which, in our time, has raged throughout Europe and invaded Italy in the sad wars of the French, from which race it received its name. I shall seek far off, through the liquid air and the stars of vast Olympus, the hidden causes of the disease and I will relate what benefits accrued through experience and through humanity's great resourcefulness in trying circumstance, and through the assistance provided by the gods, assistance neither recorded nor known to any of our ancestors.

You who reveal to me the consequences and causes of events, who float through heaven and through the sky in a chariot, you who commingle the elements and the tender rays of the sun, you whom the colorful birds and the dew-loving plants, the race of beasts and men and swimming flocks hail as the nurse and mother of life, assist my task and stand by me through the calm shades, while the soft breezes and the myrtle grove invite our song, and Benacus reechoes from his hollow caves.

In the first place, all of those things that Nature brings into being on earth, in high heaven or on the vast sea, do not arise from a single source or according to the same laws. But because their component elements are few in number, a large quantity of these ailments arise frequently and in many places. Other diseases, however, appear more rarely, at specific times and in specific places, and, because they emerge after long incubation, they are more virulent. Some require a thousand years and many ages before they burst forth from darkness and night's dusky prison:

35   Tanta vi coëunt genitalia semina in unum.
      Ergo et morborum quoniam non omnibus una
      nascendi est ratio, facilis pars maxima visu,
      et faciles ortus habet, et primordia praesto;
      rarius emergunt alii et post saecula longa:
40   difficiles causas et inextricabile fatum
      et sero potuere altas superare tenebras.

: LVI :

In funere Matthaei Giberti

1   Quem iustum prius et suum Camenae
      dicebant equitem prius, suumque
      dicebant comitem et suum poëtam,
      et blande prius hospitem vocabant,
5   cui lauro violas olentiores,
      et laurum violis perenniorem
      Benaci nitidis dabant ab undis,
      suo quas dederant prius Catullo,
      nunc iustum miserae, et suum Camenae
10   lugent nunc equitem, et suum misellae
      nunc lugent comitem, et suum poëtam,
      quem non amplius hospitem vocabunt,
      nec lauro violas olentiores,
      nec laurum violis perenniorem,
15   Benaci nitidis dabunt ab undis,
      suo quas dederant prius Catullo.

so great is the violence with which the generative seeds of such af- 35
flictions are joined. Therefore, since not all diseases have the same
process of generation, the great majority are easy to observe and
emerge readily and promptly. Others arise more rarely and after
many years, having had to overcome more resistant causes, intrac- 40
table destiny and deep darkness.

: LVI :

On the death of M. Giberti

The man whom the Muses once called their true knight, their
companion and their poet, whom they once dearly called their
guest, whom they gave violets more fragrant than laurel and laurel 5
more lasting than violets from the gleaming waters of Benacus,
such as they once bestowed on their dear Catullus — that man the
sad Muses now mourn, their knight, their friend and their poet, 10
whom they will no longer call their guest, nor any longer adorn
with violets more fragrant than laurel or laurel more lasting than
violets from the gleaming waters of Benacus, such as they formerly 15
gave to their dear Catullus.

⁝ LVII ⁝

1　Bacche Ceresque veni: exiguum nam lustrat agellum
　　　Simulus et nobis reddere vota parat.
　　Aurea, sancte, tibi lentis datur uva racemis
　　　nec non et flavae spicea serta deae.
5　Tuque Giberte veni et dulcis tibi ponitur uva
　　　maiori ambobus et tibi spica deis.

: LVII :

Come Bacchus and Ceres, for Simulus plows his little field and
stands ready to fulfill our wish, for the golden grape will be given
to you, holy one, from the slow-winding vine, and sheaves of
wheat await you, fair-haired goddess. And you come too, Giberti,
and sweet wine and grain will be served to you, who are greater   5
than both these gods.

Note on the Text

❧⸙❧

The Latin text of *Syphilis, or the French Disease*, in three books, fol-
lows that of the 1530 *editio princeps*. We depart from this text only
in the case of clearly unacceptable readings, and in the case of lines
1.407–8, which have been imported from the edition published in
Rome in 1531 (see below).[1]

Syphilis had a long incubation, and Fracastoro may have been
working on it as early as 1510.[2] Around 1522 Fracastoro sent a first
draft to his friend, the poet Andrea Navagero for comment; this
draft was surreptitiously copied and distributed. Soon more than
fifty copies were in existence, and, to Fracastoro's embarrassment,
one even reached Pietro Bembo, to whom he was planning to
dedicate the work.[3] This spurred Fracastoro to continue with his
revisions, and in 1525 he was able to send a second draft of the
poem (still only in two books) to Bembo, accompanied by a letter.[4]
In a reply dated November 26, 1525, Bembo thanked Fracastoro
and praised his poem; but he also attached a series of 111 suggested
corrections, now known as the *Avertimenti*.[5] These included the
advice that Fracastoro should eliminate the *aition* of Ilceus (now *S.*
2.281–423), leaving only the *aition* of Syphilus (now *S.* 3.288–379).

A new phase of revision now started, during which Fracastoro
took stock of Bembo's *Avertimenti*. He did not always take the
older poet's advice: in particular he rejected the idea of eliminating
Ilceus's story. But in order to avoid two long *aitia* in a single book,
he decided — over Bembo's protests[6] — to add a third book, trans-
ferring to it his discussion of the properties of the *guaiacum* tree
and the story of Syphilus. The rest of Book 3, including the entire
description of Columbus's journey to the New World, was created
during this phase of revision, while the loss of lines in Book 2 was

balanced out by expanding the section on decoctions and oint-
ments.[7]

After five years of reworking, the *Syphilis* was finally sent to
press in Verona in 1530.[8] A year later, a second edition was pub-
lished in Rome, which, apart from numerous new typographical
errors, exactly reproduced the *editio princeps*, with one exception.
This was the addition of two lines, 1.407–8, which are certainly
authentic, as they appeared in the 1525 draft sent to Bembo,[9] and
are generally considered as a *pentimento* or a late correction of Fra-
castoro himself.[10] In fact, Fracastoro may have kept working on his
poem even after its publication (see his letter to Paolo Ramusio,
dated January 22, 1533 [1534]: see n. 1 above).[11] Perhaps to this
phase may also belong the draft of the beginning of Book 1 pre-
served in *aut.* (published in this volume as C. 55), since in the
manuscript it appears to be inserted among materials plausibly
datable to after 1530.[12] The 1531 Paris edition (according to the
critical apparatus by Concetta Pennuto in Vons 2011) and the 1536
Basel reproduced the *editio princeps* with no significant variants.
The 1555 *Opera omnia*, assembled by Paolo Ramusio, son of Fracas-
toro's close friend Giambattista,[13] curiously appears to be based on
the 1536 Basel edition, rather than on the *editio princeps* (note their
coincidence in error against the 1530 and 1531 editions at vv. 1.98,
110, 3.19, and 127). The second edition of the *Opera omnia* in 1574
seems to have followed the 1555 (in particular it reproduces its in-
novations at 1.418, 2.179, 226, and 3.146), but it also added the two
missing lines and introduced a number of new variants (some of
which are valuable):[14] if the lines added were not drawn from the
1531 Rome edition and the valuable new variants were not exclu-
sively editorial interventions, perhaps we can hypothesize that,
even for *Syphilis*, the editor of 1574 had independent access to au-
thorial material, as it is certainly the case for *Joseph* and, at least in
part, for the *Carmina* (see below). All later editions, up to those
issued in 1718 and 1739 by Giovanni Antonio Volpi with the assis-

tance of his brother Gaetano, ultimately depend on the 1574 text; however Volpi, already in 1718, appears to have collated one of the editions earlier than 1555 as well (cf. in particular 2.217, 444, 449, and 3.118).[15]

In modern times three significant editions of *Syphilis* have been produced. The first one was published in 1935 by Heneage Wynne-Finch, who established his text by collating the 1530 *editio princeps* with the 1531 Rome, 1531 Paris, and 1536 editions, as well as the 1555 and 1574 editions of the *Opera omnia*. Wynne-Finch was able to avail himself of John F. Fulton's contemporaneous studies on the tradition of *Syphilis*, which were published in the same year (Baumgartner-Fulton, 1935).[16] In 1984 there appeared Geoffrey Eatough's edition, still useful for its commentary: his text however relies on the one established by Wynne-Finch, with almost no changes.[17] Finally in 2011 the French publisher Les Belles Lettres issued a new edition of *Syphilis*, which, in addition to its valuable discussions of the medical content, is the first one to provide an apparatus of critical notes (prepared by Concetta Pennuto): these notes record variants from the four major editions published during Fracastoro's lifetime (1530, 1531 Rome, 1531 Paris, and 1536), while the text reproduces the 1531 Rome edition (as the only one among them attesting vv. 1.407–8), except for readings deemed untenable. The present edition differs from 2011 by allowing that the 1555 and 1574 editions, although published after Fracastoro's death, may well preserve otherwise unattested authorial variants; it also discounts 1531 Rome on the grounds that there is no evidence that, despite the addition of the two missing lines, it was prepared under Fracastoro's supervision (see n. 10 above).

The Latin text of *Joseph* given here follows the 1555 *editio princeps* except in cases of clearly untenable readings. According to Pellegrini (*Appunti* 1954, 102–3), Fracastoro started working on the *Joseph* before 1539, but afterward gave priority to other projects and was not able to finish it. In fact the poem covers only part of the biblical account of Joseph's life. Book 1 treats the events described in Genesis 37 and 39, Book 2 those of Genesis 40–43. A third book may have been planned to cover the rest of Joseph's story, found in Genesis 44–50.[18] The *Joseph* was first published only in the posthumous 1555 edition of the *Opera omnia*. The second edition (1574) shows a striking number of variants from the 1555 text,[19] which, as Volpi had already observed,[20] can be explained only on the hypothesis that two slightly different drafts of the poem existed and were separately used for 1555 and 1574. Furthermore, Fracastoro's autograph manuscript in Verona preserves two short sections of the *Joseph* (1.38–44 and 2.433–44), attesting what may be yet another redaction, which is closer to 1555 while sharing readings with 1574 as well (cf. Notes to the Text on *J.* 1.40). The 1574 text was then followed by all other editions up to and including Volpi's edition of 1718. However, in the 1739 edition Volpi gained access to the *Joseph* in the 1555 *editio princeps* and decided to prefer its authority in all instances, except in cases where its readings were deemed clearly inferior or untenable.

One further edition of the *Joseph* was produced in the sixteenth century, in 1578, included in an anthology of sacred hymns intended for the use of schools. It will be considered in the Notes to the Text, since it carries a few interesting emendations, although otherwise it exactly reproduces the text of 1555.[21]

The Latin text of C. 1–49, which gradually appeared in print from Fracastoro's lifetime on, follows, except in the case of untenable readings, the *editio princeps* of each poem. In the case of C. 50–55, however, the transcription from the Verona autograph (*aut.*) made by Girolamo da Prato and published in Volpi's 1739 edition turned out to be inadequate in various ways, which will be described in detail in the apparatus. We have therefore undertaken to present a new transcription from *aut.*, respecting the order in which the fragments appear in the manuscript and recording all deletions and variants in the Notes to the Text (for the conventions used in the transcription, see the Abbreviations). C. 56–57, hitherto unpublished, are newly transcribed from the manuscripts in which they are preserved.

The order of the poems in the *Carmina* adopted in the present volume, as well as their titles, follow, for the convenience of the reader, those of the 1739 edition, which has been widely cited as the vulgate text in the modern scholarly literature. C. 1–31 are poems from the original *Carminum liber*, as published in 1555, with reorderings and further additions made in later editions as described below.[22] C. 32–43 are poems published within various of Fracastoro's prose works; these were first added to the collection by Volpi in 1718. C. 44–49 are poems of various provenance, also first collected by Volpi in the 1739 edition. C. 50–55 are mostly fragmentary poems from Fracastoro's Verona autograph (*aut.*), first published, though inadequately, in the 1739 edition on the basis of Girolamo da Prato's transcription.[23] Finally, C. 56–57 are poems attributed to Fracastoro in a series of manuscripts, discovered in the course of research for this I Tatti volume, and are published here for the first time.

There is no evidence that the *Carminum liber*, first included in Paolo Ramusio's edition of 1555, fulfills some intention on Fracastoro's part to collect his occasional poetry into a coherent collection. Ramusio is unfortunately silent on the sources from which he drew the texts of the various poems and the principles he used to order them.[24] His edition contained only nineteen poems in the following order: C. 2–6, 8, 21, 9, 25, 10, 12, 14–20, 13, 7 (C. 17–18 were presented as a single poem until the 1718 edition). The items now numbered as C. 2–6, 8–10, 12, 21, and 25 are clearly finished poems, mostly longer, and they seem to be placed, more or less, in chronological order (cf. Pellegrini, *Appunti* 1954); at least C. 5 and 21 were already circulating in print before 1555.[25] C. 14–20 and 13

357

appear unfinished and fragmentary; they may have come from a group of drafts of bucolic poetry addressed to Giovanni Battista della Torre. The concluding poem, C. 7, also appears unfinished (see the Notes to the Text, p. 387, and n. 32 below) and may have been drawn from a manuscript draft as well.

The 1574 edition introduced several variants into the text of the poems already published in 1555, but above all it added seven new poems: C. 22–23 and 26–31 (C. 28 and 29 are presented as a single poem until the 1584 edition). Among these new poems at least C. 23 and 30–31 were already circulating in print.[26] It also partly rearranged the order of the collection (now C. 2–10, 12–23, 25–31). Hence C. 7 is moved to the group of generally longer and probably contemporaneous poems.[27] In the following group, C. 13–20, containing bucolic poetry to Giovanni Battista della Torre, C. 13 is moved to the beginning of the series, but otherwise nothing changes. Then the shorter poems C. 21 and 25 are moved from their former position and grouped in chronological order with the new C. 22 and 23. These four items thus form a group of polished shorter poems on the topic of birth and death (C. 21 and 22 are birth songs, while C. 23 and 25 are *epicedia*). In the 1574 edition, moreover, both C. 21 and 25 as well as C. 9, untitled in 1555, receive a title. Finally, after the group of C. 21–23 and 25, we find C. 26–29, a group of seemingly unfinished bucolic poems addressed to Giberti, followed by C. 30–31, also bucolic in tone, but addressed to Giovanni Battista Ramusio and probably contemporary with those to Giberti. The publication of poetic drafts, as well as the nature of some of the variants introduced in 1574 in preference to the text of 1555 (e.g. C. 5.33–34)[28] seem to confirm the hypothesis that their editors had access, at least in part, to previously unexploited authorial material, as they surely did for the *Joseph*.

The 1577 anthology by Toscani reproduced the *Carminum liber* as it appeared in the 1555 edition but added titles to C. 21, 9, 25, and 13, untitled in the earlier edition, and gave new, different titles to *C.* 14–17. Above all it adds the *Alcon* — a work of questionable paternity (see Notes to the Text, p. 379) — to the beginning of the entire collection, as *C.* 1. It also adds as an appendix *C.* 23 and *C.* 11: the former had already been published in a 1568 Brescia anthology, while the latter was printed as a liminal poem at the end of Fracastoro's prose treatise *De contagione*.

The third Giuntine edition of 1584 mostly reproduces the 1574 text but adds one more poem (C. 24), placing it within the group of shorter, finished poems on birth and death. It also separates *C.* 28 from 29 and gives it a title (see Notes to the Text, p. 393).

The 1591 Lyon edition is based on the text of the 1584, but it also imported *C.* 1 and *C.* 11 from Toscani's 1577 anthology. *C.* 11 is moved into the group of longer finished poems after *C.* 10, which is also dedicated to Alessandro Farnese. *C.* 13 is given a new title.

The organization of the *Carminum liber* as established in the 1591 edition is followed by all later editions, up to Volpi's, who innovates only by separating *C.* 18 from 17. Volpi however, already in 1718, added to the collection for the first time twelve poems extracted from Fracastoro's prose works. Then, in his second edition of 1739, he also included two more sets of poems, either newly published from various manuscript sources or collected from earlier separate editions. He also collated his 1718 text with the 1555 edition and introduced several of the latter's variants into his new text.[29]

In the Latin texts of *Syphilis*, *Joseph*, and *C.* 1–49, the orthography has been largely modernized. In *C.* 50–57 instead, the manuscript orthography has been exactly reproduced, with the exception of diphthongs and abbreviations, which have always been resolved to facilitate the text's intelligibility. In a very limited number of instances, words that appear deleted by mistake, misspelled terms, and other banal errors in the manuscript that might hinder the readers' comprehension have been corrected in the text; the original readings are recorded in the apparatus. Punctuation and capitalization have been modernized in all texts published in the present volume. With few exceptions, all editions collated were accessed through the internet.[30] The text provided by the *editio princeps* of each poem has been maintained except for clearly untenable readings, while always taking account of certain features recurring in Fracastoro's *usus scribendi*. These include his insistent accumulation of coordinative conjunctions (e.g., J. 1.352–56), the use of the indicative instead of the subjunctive in indirect questions (e.g., S. 1.118), some uncertainties with the declension of Greek nouns (e.g., *Gorgonĕs* taken as accusative instead of nominative plural at C. 51.71 and *passim* in the poem); or, on the metrical side, frequent employment of hiatus (e.g., S. 2.377 *Dii habitant*), *brevis in arsis* (e.g., C. 2.34 *arcana*, even with hiatus, e.g., *solem in* at C. 51.3 and *passim* in the poem), and sinizesis (e.g., J. 2.419 *eadem*, and especially of *-ii-* in forms such as *dii* or *iidem*). The Notes to the Text aim at providing as complete a picture as possible of the aspect of the manuscripts for C. 50–57 and of the variants attested by the different editions for all the other texts. However, in accordance with the norms and the scope of the I Tatti series, they include only readings that testify to a branch of the tradition (such as are attested in witnesses that appear to have used, at least in part, authorial material, i.e., 1555, 1574, any of the *edd. principes*, and the 1531 Rome edition of *Syphilis*), or plausible emendations, even if present in a later witness (such as are offered occasionally by 1577, 1578, 1591, and above all in the two editions by Volpi; no valuable emendations seem to be present in 1584). Banal errors, such as obvious typographical errors, even in the earliest witnesses, or clearly inferior readings attested in later editions have been excluded without comment.[31] Orthographic variants have also been generally excluded.[32]

Ornella Rossi

ABBREVIATIONS[33]

1525   Pietro Bembo's comments appended to a letter of 1525 on an early, lost draft of *Syphilis*, published in Pellegrini 1955, 35–61 (*Avertimenti*).

1530   *Syphilis*. Verona, 1530.

1531   *Syphilis*. Rome, 1531.

1536   *Syphilis*. Basel, 1536.

1538   *Homocentrica*. Venice, 1538 [= 1539].

1539   *Ioannis Secundi Hagiensis Basia*. Lyon, 1539.

1545   Bandello, *Canti XI*. Agen, 1545.

1546   *De contagione et contagiosis morbis*. Venice, 1546.

1553   *De temperatura vini sententia*. Camerino, 1553.

1555   *Opera omnia*. [Edited by P. Ramusio.] Venice, 1555.

1556   *Lettere di diversi autori eccellenti*. Edited by G. Ziletti. Venice, 1556.

1568   *Poemata selecta*. Edited by G. A. Taglietti (*alias* Taygetus). Brescia, 1568.

1574   *Opera omnia. Secunda editio*. Venice, 1574.

1577   *Carmina illustrium poetarum Italorum*. Edited by G. M. Toscano. Paris, 1577.

1578   *Hymnorum ecclesiasticorum . . . libri III*. Edited by A. Ellinger. Frankfurt am Main, 1578.

1584   *Opera omnia. Ex tertia editione*. Venice, 1584.

1591   *Operum pars [prior-] posterior*. Lyon, 1591.

1619   *In fugam Caroli V imperatoris*. Venice, 1619.

1718   *Poemata omnia*. Edited by G. A. and G. Volpi. Padua, 1718.

1739   *Hieronymi Fracastorii . . . Carminum editio secunda*. Edited by G. A. and G. Volpi. Padua, 1739.

1935   *Fracastor Syphilis*. Edited by H. Wynne-Finch. London, 1935.

1984   *Fracastoro's Syphilis*. Edited by G. Eatough. Liverpool, 1984.

2011   *La syphilis, ou le mal français*. Edited by C. Pennuto and J. Vons. Paris, 2011.

β	consensus of 1574, 1584, 1591, 1718.
aut.	Verona, Bibl. Capitolare, ms. CCLXXV volumes I and III (*Carmina* 50–55, in vol. 1, *Joseph* in vol. 3).[34]
Alecchi	Alecchi's transcription of C. 46, published in Giuliari, 1874.
Cruceius	*Carmina poetarum nobilium.* Edited by G. P. Ubalidni. Milan, 1563.
L'Estoile	*Journal d'Henri IV 1589–1611.* Paris, 1883.
Maffei 1731	*Verona illustrata*, parte seconda. Verona, 1731.
C.	Carmina
J.	Joseph
S.	Syphilis

CRITICAL SYMBOLS

in mg.	in the margin
~~words~~	words deleted in the ms.; a double strikethrough indicates a second deletion made independently of the first.
words	not fully decipherable, completely indecipherable, and illegible words
. . .	end of incomplete verses

Note: The Latin texts and apparatus in this volume were prepared by Dr. Ornella Rossi, Assistant Editor of the I Tatti Renaissance Library. The Notes to the Translation were composed by Dr. Justin Stover, Ornella Rossi, and James Gardner. The Bibliography was compiled by James Hankins and Ornella Rossi. We wish to thank Prof. Enrico Peruzzi (Università di Verona) for his extremely valuable advice on Fracastoro's Verona autograph. Above all, we would like to thank Dr. Ernesto Stagni (Università di Pisa) for his innumerable suggestions and for his immensely generous help, especially in deciphering Fracastoro's dauntingly difficult handwriting and in tracking down the more obscure sixteenth-century *editiones principes* of some of Fracastoro's *Carmina*.

James Hankins

NOTES

1. For the abbreviations used in the Note on the Text, see below; for full references to secondary literature, see the Bibliography. The *Syphilis* was Fracastoro's first published work on the topic of contagious diseases. It is likely that shortly after finishing the poem (see his letter to Giambattista Ramusio, dated January 22, 1533 [probably 1534, by the Venetian calendar], cited in the 1739 edition, 62–65), he also drafted the prose treatise on syphilis, first published from *aut.* in Pellegrini (1939). Later, expanding his scope, he composed the prose treatise *De contagione et contagiosis morbis* (which includes long sections on syphilis, in particular 2.11–12, and 3.10), and its corollary treatise *De sympathia et antipathia rerum*; these works were published together, under Fracastoro's supervision, by Giunti in Venice in 1546.

2. See Pellegrini (*Appunti* 1954, 95), and idem (1955, 14); Eatough (1984, 21).

3. On this episode, see the draft of Fracastoro's letter to Bembo in Pellegrini (1955, 30), and n. 4 below; on its chronology, see Bembo's letter quoted in the 1739 edition, 59 (= *Pietro Bembo, Lettere*, ed. Ernesto Travi [Bologna: Commissione per i testi di lingua, 1990], vol. 2, letter 621). In this letter, dated November 26, 1525, Bembo states that he had received Fracastoro's first draft two or three years before.

4. A draft of the letter in four fragments survives in *aut.* and was first published by Pellegrini (1955, 21–34).

5. Published in Pellegrini (1955), who established the numbering of the III *Avertimenti*; the original is in the Vatican Library, ms. Vat. Lat. 6557, ff. 307r–14r.

6. See the second letter from Bembo, dated January 5, 1526, published in the 1739 edition, 60–61 (= *Bembo Lettere*, ed. Travi, letter 634).

7. Bembo's letter (1739, 59–60; = *Bembo Lettere*, ed. Travi, letter 621) and the *Avertimenti* are of great interest as they allow us not only to read numerous fragments from Fracastoro's 1525 draft, but also to form an excellent idea of its structure, given that its quotations and comments appear

to follow strictly the order of the draft. The structure of Book 1 seems to differ very little from what we now read; interestingly, even the historical details of the book remained unchanged from the time of the original composition: cf., for example, the homage to Pope Leo the X, who died in 1521. The original structure of Book 2 was as follows: (a) proemion (cf. 2.1–75); (b) general practices for good health (cf. 2.76–164); (c) more invasive cures, i.e., bloodletting (cf. 2.165–73), *aition* of Ilceus (cf. 2.250–59 and 281–423) and mercury remedy (cf. 2.424–53), fumigations (cf. 2.260–69); (d) milder cures, i.e., decoctions and ointments (this was a shorter version of 2.174–244) and the guaiacum remedy, with description of the tree (cf. 3.26–46), *aition* of Syphilus (cf. 3.288–368), use of guaiacum (cf. 3.47–89); (e) conclusion (cf. 3.414–19).

8. A letter exchanged between Fracastoro and Bembo (1739, 61–62 = *Bembo Lettere*, ed. Travi, vol. 3, letter 1158) marks this moment: Fracastoro's letter, which accompanied a copy of the work, is dated September 25, 1530, while Bembo's reply is dated October 8 of the same year.

9. See Pellegrini (1955), *avertimento* n. 47.

10. The two lines appear handwritten in the margin of a rare vellum copy of the 1530 edition (Paris, Bibliothèque Nationale de France, Réserve, Vél. 2124), which must have been intended for some important figure; this gloss may have been made by Fracastoro himself or under his supervision. See Baumgartner-Fulton (1935, 38–39), Wynne-Finch (1935, 44–46), and Ruggiero (2001). The presence of these two lines in the 1531 Rome edition, however, does not imply direct supervision of this publication on Fracastoro's part (*contra* Fulton): on one hand in fact, the 1531 Rome edition has innumerable typographical errors, while these are quite rare in other publications that Fracastoro appears to have supervised (i.e., the *editiones principes* of the *Homocentrica*, the *De contagione*, as well as the *Syphilis*); on the other hand, the text of *Syphilis* with the two extra lines may have circulated among Fracastoro's acquaintances and reached the Roman publisher, Antonio Blado from Asolo, independently of the author's intention. For example, Pietro Bembo, addressee of the poem and Fracastoro's indispensable supporter throughout the process of composition, must surely have received a copy with the final *emendanda*. We know that Fracastoro personally sent him a copy of the *editio princeps* (cf. n. 8

above), probably a presentation copy similar to the rare vellum copy mentioned above, which were usually reserved for patrons and individuals of high status.

11. In this letter to Ramusio, Fracastoro, while asking his friend for a copy of certain medical texts, writes: "Forza è che io lo sappia, perchè io ho un poco emendata, al meglio che ho potuto, quella mia cosa *De morbo Gallico* al Signor M. Pietro Bembo; ed appresso ne ho poi scritto in prosa diffusamente; che a me pare non se ne sia ancora scritto come niente, benché diversi ne abbiano scritto" ("I need to learn about that, since I have emended a little, as best I could, that work of mine, *De morbo Gallico*, addressed to Pietro Bembo; and later on I have written about the topic more at length, since to me it seems as if nothing had been written about it, though so many have done so"). However, Fracastoro may here be only alluding to corrections on certain points of content that he wished to include in the prose works he had started composing after publishing the poem.

12. The nature of Fracastoro's autograph manuscript makes it extremely difficult to infer anything on the basis of the order in which the material appears, since on one hand it is uncertain when and how its fascicules were collected, and on the other, Fracastoro may have left blank pages between compositions and filled them at a later stage. In any case, according to Peruzzi's description of the manuscript (1996, 200), this poetic draft (found on ff. 143v–44r) is preceded by a prose treatise on contagions (probably the *De contagione*, f. 143r) and followed by some astronomical notes, the first of which carries the date June 28, 1533 (f. 144v). There is also a Latin prose text at f. 144r, immediately following the *Syphilis* draft, which appears to be a letter mentioning Ramusio, but this text has so far not been transcribed.

13. See the liminal poem by Ludovico Nogarola that appears in the opening pages of the 1555 edition, praising Paolo Ramusio for the task undertaken.

14. In particular see *S*. 1.272, 277, and 360 (where the variant introduced by 1574 corresponds to a suggestion made by Bembo in his *Avertimenti*; see Notes to the Text, p. 371). Furthermore, in addition to the two extra

lines at 1.407–8, a second superior reading attested in 1531 Rome is, interestingly, shared by 1574 against all earlier editions: cf. *S.* 1.301 and Notes to the Text, *ibid.*

15. The 1539 edition of Fracastoro's *Syphilis*, printed with Alfonso Ferri's *De ligni sancti medicina* (only the 1547 Lyon reprint could be consulted for the present edition), as well as the 1562 Antwerp edition and Toscani's 1577 anthology (see the Bibliography) will not be considered in the Notes to the Text for *Syphilis*, as they do not seem to carry any significant variants: the first imprint is based on the 1536 Basel edition, while the last two exactly reproduce the 1555 text. Also no edition of Fracastoro's works later than the sixteenth century has been collated, since, at the present stage of our knowledge, none of them seems likely to carry authoritative variants; in particular according to Baumgartner-Fulton (1935, 63), Peruzzi (2005, 37), and Pennuto (2008, lxxiii), all of the seventeenth-century editions of the *Opera omnia* (see the Bibliography) are dependent on the 1591 edition, which in turn depends mostly on the third Giuntine edition of 1584.

16. Wynne-Finch (1935, 43–46).

17. Eatough (1984, preface).

18. A third book was added after Fracastoro's death by Francesco Luisini, a doctor from Udine in the entourage of Alessandro Farnese, who also wrote a famous commentary on Horace's *Ars poetica*. See the Introduction at n. 9.

19. The nature of the 1574 variants in the *Joseph* reinforces the impression that they are authorial: note the frequent rearrangement of series of lines in Book 1, or the fact that several of the 1574 variants are of equivalent value to the 1555 readings. Interestingly, some of the 1574 variants seem aimed at eliminating expressions that may appear religiously unorthodox or at curtailing the use of pagan terminology as applied to biblical and Christian divine beings; see for example 1.490 and 2.562.

20. See his preface to the 1739 edition, v–vi.

21. As in the case of *Syphilis*, no seventeenth-century or later edition has been collated (cf. above, n. 15). A reference to *Hieronymii Fracastorii Jose-*

phus cum Flaminii, Strozae, et Zanchii aliquot hymnis (Venice: Giunti, 1584), listed by Friedrich Otto Mencke in his bibliographical appendix to the 1739 Volpi edition (vol. 1, pt. 2, 152), could not be verified.

22. Volpi's editions gave numbers only to the first thirty-one items; for the sake of convenience, in the present edition we have given the numbers 32–55 to the twenty-three poems Volpi appended to the *Carminum liber*, and the numbers 56 and 57 to the two newly discovered poems.

23. The last poem transcribed from the autograph and published by Volpi (a distichon listing the Works of Mercy: *Visito, poto, cibo, redimo, tego, colligo, condo. / Consule, castiga, solare, remitte, fer, ora*) has been excluded from the present edition, since it was certainly written long before Fracastoro's time; it appears, for example, as an anonymous quotation in Thomas Aquinas (*Summa Theologiae*, II.II.32.2.1).

24. From the editorial point of view, Paolo Ramusio appears in some cases to adopt a quite conservative line, respecting rather closely the original text: cf. in particular C. 7 (see n. 32 below and the Notes to the Text, p. 387), or the numerous problematic readings attested in his text. However, we know that Ramusio did not hesitate to introduce heavy editorial changes in some other cases: as Enrico Peruzzi (1998) has shown, at least Fracastoro's dialogues *De intellectione* and, above all, *De anima* underwent considerable changes; in particular, the closing section of *De anima* (para. 47.7–50.44, still attested in Fracastoro's Verona autograph and published in Peruzzi 1999) was completely excised owing to its religiously unorthodox content (as had been pointed out to Ramusio in an epistolary exchange with Sisto Medici). See also Pennuto (2008, lvii), who observes the existence of a series of variants, aimed at curtailing less classical features in Fracastoro's *usus scribendi*, introduced by Ramusio in 1555 in revising the 1546 *editio princeps* of the *De sympathia*: according to Pennuto these variants, unless derived from autograph notes for which we lack any evidence, could well be editorial changes.

25. C. 5 had been published in a 1539 Lyon anthology, while C. 21 appeared in the 1545 edition of Bandello's *Canti XI* (see the Abbreviations and the Bibliography).

26. C. 23 had been published in a 1568 Brescia anthology, while C. 30–31 were included in Ziletti's 1556 epistolary collection, since the latter were inserted in a letter to Giambattista Ramusio (see the Abbreviations and the Bibliography).

27. C. 7 may have been set in this position within the group because it was written at about the same time as C. 5–6 (cf. Pellegrini, *Appunti* 1954), and perhaps also because it is linked to C. 8 by its autobiographical theme.

28. At C. 5.34 the line skipped in 1555 is reintroduced in 1574 with a reading slightly inferior to what we read in the 1539 Lyon *editio princeps* of the poem: see Notes to the Text, p. 386.

29. The text of C. 9 attested in the 1583 collection of poems in honor of the Madruzzo family (see the Bibliography) exactly reproduces that of the 1574 and will not therefore be cited in the Notes to the Text. The 1550 and 1554 Lyon editions of the *De contagione* have not been collated, since, according to Pennuto (2008), they both appear to depend on the 1546 *editio princeps* of the work, with no significant variants. For the *Carmina*, as for *Syphilis* and *Joseph*, seventeenth-century or later editions have not been collated: see n. 15 above.

30. Physical copies preserved in the Biblioteca Nazionale Centrale of Florence were used for the 1545 edition of C. 21 within Bandello's *Canti XI* and the 1556 epistolary anthology by Ziletti. Physical copies preserved in the Yale Medical Library were used for the 1553 *editio princeps* of the *De vini temperatura sententia* (C. 43) and for the 1619 pamphlet edition of C. 45: these editions have been collated by Miss Claudia Rammelt, of the Yale Classics Department, to whom we express our gratitude.

31. The 1530 and 1536 editions of *Syphilis*, as well as the 1555 and 1574 editions of the *Opera omnia*, show a limited number of typographical errors. The 1531 Rome edition of *Syphilis*, however, is disfigured by a large number of errors (only some of which are emended in the volume's *corrigenda*). The 1577, 1584, and 1591 editions show several typos and clearly erroneous readings: in several cases 1591 maintains an error originating in 1584 (which confirms its dependence upon it). Volpi's 1718 and 1739 editions are both extremely accurate.

368

32. Spelling variants in proper names have occasionally been recorded. In particular, spelling variants in the name Giberti (*Gibertus* vs. *Gibbertus*, cf. *Gybbertus* in *aut.*) are unevenly distributed through the poems in 1555 and 1574; these readings may be evidence of a different tradition for particular poems: for example, C. 7, of unfinished aspect, is the only one in the entire *Carminum liber* where the editor of 1555 both prints two lacunae (at v. 41 and 90, later emended in 1574) and attests the spelling *Gibbertus*, closer to the spelling *Gybbertus* of *aut.*

33. Fuller bibliographical information is given in the Bibliography.

34. For a complete description of this ms. and further bibliography, see Peruzzi (1996, 197–206).

Notes to the Text

SYPHILIS

The following editions are considered in the notes to the *Syphilis*: 1530, 1531, 1536, 1555, β (= 1574, 1584, 1591, 1718), 1739, 1935 (1984 identically reproduces 1935, unless specified), 2011. Readings from the 1525 draft will also be cited, when present in the points discussed below.

Book I

1–31. *Cf. C. 55.1–24*

26. puro] pro puro *1531*

80–96. *Cf. C. 55.25–41*

98. accola] incola *1536, 1555, β, 1935*

110. incolit] accolit *1536, 1555, β, 1935*

161. secum silvas] secus silvas *1555*

271. protinus] perditus *1530, 1531, 1536, 1555, 1935 (yet 1984 has* protinus*), 2011, syntactically untenable*

272. genus] pecus *β, 1739, perhaps better (cf. Vergil,* Aeneid *3.221)*

277. mora] via *β, 1739, more appropriately (cf. Vergil,* Georgics *3.482)*

301. ingens] vigens *1531, β, 1739, 2011, perhaps better*

360. Tum *(1525 n. 41)*] Ut *β, 1739, 1935; the substitution of* tum *with* ut *was Bembo's suggestion*

407–8. *These lines are missing in 1530, 1536, 1555; however, they appear already in 1525 n. 47 (where Bembo suggested substituting* quo tandem *with* hic vero non*), and are found inserted after v. 406 in 1531 (cf. Note on the Text, p. 354); the reading is followed by β, 1739, 1935, 2011*

418. dira omina] dira omnia *1555, β, 1739*

454–69. *Cf. C. 46*

371

Book II

40. umbraeque] umbraque *1531*

94. luem] lucem *1531*

106. placidae] placide *1530, 1531, 1536*

118. quoscumque paludes] quascumque paludes *1531*

134. lumbis ne] lumbis'ne (= lumbisne) *1530*

163. ob servata (*1525 n. 73*)] observata *1574, 1584, 1591, 2011, syntactically untenable*

179. nymphis] lymphis *1555, β, 1739, 1935*

189. bdelamque] bdelenque *1555, 1574, 1584, 1591*

208. chamaedryn] chamaedrym *β, 1739*

217. sis (*1525 n. 85*)] sic *1574, 1584, 1591*   onusta (*1525 n. 85; spelled ho-nusta in 1530, 1531, 2011*)] honesta *1574, 1584, 1591*

226. thamnive (*"black bryony," cf. Columella, De re rustica 12.7 and Pliny the Elder,* Naturalis Historia *8.112*)] rhamnive *1555, β, 1935 ("buckthorn," cf. Pliny the Elder,* Naturalis Historia *1.1.79 and 24.124*)

279. colliquant: *unusually scanned* collīquant (*probably mistaking the verb* liquāre *for the deponent* līqui); *the verb* colliquāre *itself (for* colliquescere) *is never attested in classical Latin*

346. primo] prima *1531*

347. magnaeque] magneque *1531*

384. Callirhoae] Callirhoë *1530, 1531, 1536, 1935, 2011 (cf. C. 5.9)*

406. varie] variae *1530, 1531*

444. tulerit (*1525 n. 81*)] poscat *1574, 1584, 1591*

449. sed] quae *1574, 1584, 1591*

Book III

5. est *is added after* canenda *in 1531, 2011*

19. alioque] altoque *1536, 1555, β*

42. dissectae] dissecte *1531*

99. ignoti] ignota *1531*

118. dudum (*not separated from* insistite *by punctuation in 1530, 1531, 1536, 2011; perhaps to be understood as* = iamdudum; *cf. C. 6.125)*] namque *1574, 1584, 1591*

127. amico] amice *1536* (*manually corrected to* amico, *two copies inspected*), *1555,* β

135. Gyane] Cyane *1531*

146. ora] aura *1530, 1536:* arva *1531, 2011*

181. urbes] verbis *1531*

234. Ophyraeque] Ophyreque *1530, 1531*

302. vix] nix *1531*

332. Syphilidemque] Syphilidenque *1530, 1531, 2011* (*as if belonging to the first declension*)

JOSEPH

The following editions are considered in the notes to the *Joseph*: 1555, 1578, β (= 1574, 1584, 1591, 1718), 1739. Lines 1.38–44 and 2.433–44 are also attested in *aut.* (vol. 3, f. 35v, first published in Pellegrini, *Appunti* 1954, 113): variant readings found in *aut.* are recorded in the notes.

Book I

38. praecipue insignem] praesertim egregium β, *cf. v. 40 below*

39. *The following lines are added in* β *after v. 39, cf. vv. 45–47:*

qui, patre longaevo Rachele e coniuge cara
natus, erat patri ante alios dilectus Ioseph.

40. Quem] Hunc β   et Charites *written above* Quem, *to be inserted after it, in aut.*   egregium] insignem β: egregium *written above* ~~insig-~~ ~~nem~~ *in aut., cf. v. 38 above*   ~~Charites~~ *before* studia *in aut.*

41. ingenua] ingenii *aut.*   leges patrias rectumque docebant] mores, et avitae legis amorem β: verum [WORD *written above* ~~WORD~~] iustumque piumque *in aut.*

42–43. *Omitted in aut.*

42. Illi autem mens alta inerat] Cui mens alta inerat quaedam β

43. nescio quae, atque animus] atque animus semper β

44. *Two lines are added after v. 44, mostly illegible except for:* curabant . . . praecipue . . . quaedam . . . alta *in the first line*

45–47. *Omitted by* β, *cf. note to v. 39*

48. non parvam invidiam] invidiam daemon β

49. letale] mortale β

50–52. *Omitted by* β

62. solus] Solis *1578, perhaps correctly*

71. illa aliquis tibi forte deus demisit] forte, inquit, deus illa aliquis tibi mittit β

73. *Omitted in* β

75. Num] An β sume] pone β

78. dominumque vocant, regemque] regemque novum, dominumque β

79. ac] et β

82. natis] vultu β

86. *Omitted in* β, *which substitutes the line:* conspexit: nempe in celsa sibi sede locato

89. Ergo horum] Quorum ille β

91. subito nova somnia fratris] non celavere parenti β

92–94. *Omitted in* β, *which substitutes the line:* somnia, non offensum animum, non pectora amara

101. atque his falsis] levibusque istis β

102. deme] tolle β teque] et te *1574, 1584*

104. at] ac *1578,* β

107. *The following lines are added in* β *after v. 107:*

An tibi non Belus, non est tibi notus Anubis,
atque Ops, atque Hecate, non cetera turba deorum,
quos miserae gentes, aris templisque dicatis,

108. omnia quae directa Deo lex] ob responsa colunt, lex autem β

112. molle] molles *1574*

116. non gratae] placidaeve β

117. insomnia] in somnia *1574, 1584*

119. irae] iris β

120–23. *Omitted in* β, *which substitutes the line:* iniunguntque minas: dirae serpentibus atris

124. Ergo, dum iuvenes exercent] Eumenides instant. Atque haec per β

128–29. *Omitted in* β, *which substitutes the line:* producantque magis reditum, quae invisa gerebant

160. et vili] vilique *emended in 1718 metri causa (to avoid the unclassical quantity* pōlenta)

167. benedicta paterna] fausta omina patris β

174. rabidis ursove, lupove] rabidorum ursive, lupive β

215. pendent] dant ut β

216. ut] iam β

252. illaesum] *perhaps one should read* illaesus; *cf. Martial,* Epigrams *1.6.1–2*

292. neve perire fame miseros patieris] nec miseros patiere fames ut perdat β

293. illorum] eorum *1718*

326. styracem *our emendation (cf. the hiatus* styracem et *at vv. 2.610 and 656)]* styracemque *is given in all sixteenth-century witnesses:* styracen *1718, 1739; same at vv. 2.610 and 656 (but declining the Greek noun* styrax, -acis, *as if belonging to the first declension)*

332. cum] tum β

349. *Emended to* bis *in 1578, 1591, 1718, 1739 (cf. Genesis 37.28)]* is *1555, 1574, 1584.*

362. commissa] mandata β

438. Fetifarum] *the spelling of this name varies in 1555, 1574, 1584 (*Fetifar- *at vv. 1.438 and 510, while* Fetifer- *at vv. 1.445, 461, 465, 481, 485 and 2.126, 161,*

176, 196, 304); by contrast the name is always spelled Fetifer- *in 1578, and* Fetifar- *(more correctly) in 1591, 1718, 1739*

458. ulli ipse officio deest] ipse ulli deest officio β

463. ei *added after* rerum *in* β

490. deus] malus β

491. osor] hostis β

506. ipse] inde β

529. at] et β

531. portas] narras β

539. crimen] culpam β

540. ni crimen sit] culpa nisi est vel β

559. oti] ottus *1555:* otus *1578*

Book II

9. sitibunda] calcata β *(cf. Lucan,* Pharsalia *9.738)*

20. cui] quem β

22. teget] terget *1574, 1584*

28. abit] vadit *1555, 1578,* contra metrum *(perhaps influenced by* vade *at v. 26 above)*

37. ego *added after* si *by* β, *1739*

44. in puteo, neu dii alieni *(with the uncommon scansion* aljeni, *almost unattestated in Latin; cf. TLL s.v. 1567, 9–10)]* dii ne alieni aut prava β: dii ne alieni illum aut prava *1718 (avoiding the hiatus* alieni aut*): perhaps one should read the line as* in puteo neu dii alieni aut prava libido *(a correction or a gloss in Fracastoro's writing may have been misinterpreted by the editors of 1555 and 1574)*

63. se rursus anilem] convertit anum se β

64. vertit] rursus β

67. animum assuetum] animis cade β

68. adsum auxilio nutrix] praesto tibi sum matrix β

110. accumulat, pecudumque] accumulans, pecudum β

116. nulla timens] nil metuens β

126. suadet] adigit β

139. ego *added after second* en *in 1591, 1718 (to avoid the hiatus* Iphicle en*)*

147. irrepens] repens β

149–50. et viscera . . . pererrans / Tartareum *emended in 1591, 1718, 1739*] praecordia . . . pererrat / Tartareumque *1555 (v. 150 is ametric; perhaps authorial, mistaking* vīrus, -i *for* vĭr, -i*):* viscera . . . pererrans / Tartareum *1574, 1584 (probably omitting* et *before* viscera, *thus making v. 149 ametric)*

160. mancipii] mancipis *1555, 1578, 1739*

204. utrique] uterque *1555, 1578, contra metrum*

207. stabant] nutant β

218. ego] iam β

228. monstrant] monstrat *1718, 1739 (avoiding concordantia ad sensum with* terna propago*)*

296. at] ac β, *1739*

311. consistet] constituet β, *1739, more appropriately (but cf. TLL s.v.* consisto *472, 62ff.)*

348. septem prodire aliae] aliae septem oriri *1555, 1578, contra metrum*

375. sunt] re β, *1739*

400. exposcet ventura fami] exposcet venturae formi *1555:* poscet venturae formae *1578*

405. videt] vidit *1555, 1578, contra metrum*

432. comminuit] imminuit β, *1739*

433. w͟o͟r͟d͟ *written above* Urbs *in aut.*

434. et *omitted in aut.*

436. insignem *aut., 1555, 1578*] insignis β, *1739 (to avoid the unclassical use of* insignis *with the genitive, cf. TLL s.v. 1907, 13)*

437. thalamo] *written above* indigenae esse *in aut.*

438. externum fato] fato externum *aut.*

439. clari] c͟h͟a͟r͟i͟ *aut.*   in] ad *aut.*

445. et thalamo] *written in left mg. in aut.*   ~~thalamo~~ *after* Isacidem *in aut.*

447. dum] et *β, 1739*

448. ducuntur] dum fiunt *β, 1739*

451. ducebat] agitabat *β, 1739, more appropriately*

457. quin etiam siqua immittuntur] si qua etiam laetis sparguntur *β*

511. nos] *perhaps one of the two* nos *should be read as* vos

516. istuc] istic *1584, 1591, 1718*

525. cedendi] abeundi *β*

544. *Omitted in β, which substitutes the line:* atque unum pater e natis sibi vidit abesse

550. vidit] audivit *1555, contra metrum*   ab ipso] ipso a *emended in 1578 metri causa (maintaining* audivit*): perhaps one could also maintain* audivit *by eliminating* et

553. certe istas] has certe *β, 1739, more appropriately*

558. obses detur] detur obses *1555, 1578, contra metrum*

562. 'Iuppiter,' inquit] Summe deum rex *β, 1739*

564. est obses] obses et est *β*

610. styracem] styracen *1718, 1739; cf. note at v. 1.326*

635. huc *emended in 1718, 1739*] hunc *all earlier witnesses*

649. nostrum] nostro *β*

655. stactam *our emendation metri causa (otherwise one could eliminate the following* et*)*] stacten *all witnesses*

656. styracem] styracen *1718, 1739; cf. note at v. 1.326*

CARMINA

Since the collection of *Carmina* was progressively expanded and some of the poems were separately published (see Note on the Text, p. 356f.), the editions attesting each poem are noted individually below.

I. Alcon, sive de cura canum venaticorum

Attested in 1577, 1591, 1718, 1739. Fracastoro's authorship of the *Alcon* was first questioned by Volpi upon discovering a version of the poem, with numerous variants and a different coda, attributed to Luigi Annibale della Croce or Cruceius (1499–1577) in Giovanni Paolo Ubaldini's poetic anthology, *Carmina poetarum nobilium* (Milan, 1563), ff. 13v–16v. Volpi exactly reproduces the della Croce text in 1739, vol. 1, 175–80. Furthermore, the *Alcon* did not appear in any of the Giuntine editions (1555, 1574, and 1584) compiled by Fracastoro's personal acquaintances. Yet the poem seems to have circulated under Fracastoro's name well before 1563: see for example *Epitome Bibliothecae Conradi Gesneri* [. . .] *locupletata per Josiam Simlerum Tigurinum* (Zurich, 1555), f. 76v ("*Eiusdem* [sc. *Fracastorii*] *Alcon, carmen de cura canum venaticorum, excusum est in Italia, ni fallor*"); *L'Osservationi del Sig. Alberto Lavezuola sopra il Furioso di M. Ludovico Ariosto* (Venice, 1584), p. 40 ("our Fracastoro composed a poetic booklet on the cures for healing hunting dogs [. . .], which has recently been published"); *Onuphrii Panvinii Antiquitatum Veronensium libri VIII* (Padua, 1648), book 6, p. 50 (attested by a manuscript dated 1559). Since Volpi's 1739 edition, scholars have taken various stances on the authorship question: Mencke (1731, 81) and Simoni (1972) defend Fracastoro's paternity, while Barbarani (1897) and Pellegrini (1948, 153–54; *Appunti* 1954, 107–8) rule it out, arguing that an act of plagiarism on the part of a more obscure poet such as della Croce would have been patent and would have undoubtedly offended the eminent cardinal Antoine Perrenot de Granvelle (1571–1586), to whom it was addressed. More recently, Fischer (see Bibliography under "Latin Editions," 1983) has convincingly argued that della Croce may have sent an earlier version of his *Alcon* to the more famous Fracastoro for suggestions and that this copy was later found among Fracastoro's papers and believed to be his, a plausible assumption considering its similarity in style and content to his other poetic production.

Title. Eiusdem Cruceii ad Antonium Perenotum episcopum Attrebatum, nunc cardinalem, Alcon *Cruceius*

2. *Omitted by Cruceius, who instead adds the following lines:*

aestivi cupiens fastidia longa diei
fallere, dum latos exurit Seirius agros

4. viridi dum captat frigus] gelida consedit lentus *Cruceius*

5. *Omitted by Cruceius, who instead adds the line:* et iuvenem senior sic est affatus Icastum

9. densaque] densasque *1739, Cruceius, more appropriately*

10. pulvereum . . . campum] pulvereas . . . glebas *Cruceius*

11. frigusque, leves] glaciemque, levesque *Cruceius*

12. e *added before* silvis *in Cruceius*

13. validam pro me] pro me validam *Cruceius*

19. tecum semper mandata reserva] animo memori praecepta reconde *Cruceius*

22. nequaquam] nequicquam *Cruceius*

24. indomitus, saevarum et praeda] assiduus, multarum et pugna *Cruceius*

25. formamque genusque putaris] facias formamve genusve *Cruceius*

26. neque mores] nec mores *Cruceius*

28. Nam rabidas] Immanes *Cruceius*

29. variis] dubiis *Cruceius*

34. Si] Sin *Cruceius*

36–39. *Omitted by Cruceius, who instead adds the following lines:*

Petronios agiles, volucresque assume Sicambros.
Quod si te capiat, qui vi praecellat odora,
et reperire sciat latitantia lustra ferarum,
hoc tibi praestabunt Persesque, sagaxque Gelonus,
suetus et in tectas Metagon penetrare cavernas.

Cruceius's reading sagaxque Gelonus (cf. Grattius, Cynegeticon 157–58) *is clearly superior to the obscure and probably corrupt* Saxogelonus *attested in the Fracastoro editions (cf. Fischer 1983, 279–80).*

40. praesertim] tu primum *Cruceius* nec] sit *Cruceius*

41. sit] nec *Cruceius*

44. *A parenthetical sentence is added between* aures *and* cui *by Cruceius, as follows:*

> (nisi naris odorae
> si qua erit: hanc etenim promissae a vertice summo
> ad terram mollesque decent)

46. sint aeque pectora lata] latum sit pectus, et ipsa *Cruceius*

47. quae sic costis adiungitur] costis qua parte adnectitur *Cruceius*

49. ut] et *Cruceius* costis] coxis *Cruceius*

55. abstineant] abstineat *Cruceius* plena libido] aucta cupido *Cruceius*

57. Hinc maior soboles, atque inde] maiores: soboles sic ipsa *Cruceius*

58. ac sese] in lucem *Cruceius* protulit ortu] est edita partu *Cruceius*

59. selige] accipe *Cruceius*

60. sonoris] coruscis *Cruceius*

61. mota] nota *1577, 1591*

63. et inertia linquet] ignava relinquens *Cruceius*

64–65. *Omitted by Cruceius, who instead adds the following lines:*

> Ante autem catulis quam firma accesserit aetas,
> hi parvo cursu campos lustrare patentis
> incipiant, sensimque humilem conscendere collem.

66. molli assuescant] facili rursum *Cruceius*

68. facilem percurrere campum] praeda gaudere recepta *Cruceius*

69. incipiat] assuescant *Cruceius:* incipiat *should probably be corrected to* incipiant (*cf. vv. 66* assuescant, *71* hos, *75* illos, *77* discant, *78* feruntur)

70. Nulla] Parva *Cruceius* crescant] crescunt *Cruceius*

71. tuto densis] densis tuto *Cruceius*

72. per] ac *Cruceius*

73. nec minus aut] aut spumanti *Cruceius*

74. vel . . . vel dedignabere] nec . . . tu, nec dignabere *Cruceius*

76. ac mox ad tecta reverti] post vero ad tecta reversos *Cruceius*

77. vincla pati discant: ita] vincula ferre iube: sic *Cruceius*

80. silvis . . . altis] silvas . . . altas *Cruceius*

83. ore] aure *Cruceius*; *cf. Moshaim's translation of* Kynosophion 6: emittes itaque sanguinem ex auribus (*cf. Fischer 1983, 282*)

85. concoque] percoque *Cruceius*

87. Si] Sin *Cruceius*

88. succos] succum *Cruceius*

89. simul omnia miscens] fluitantiaque ova *Cruceius*

94. canem] illum *Cruceius*

96. incoquere] excoquere *Cruceius*   cani] cane 1577, 1591

97. Aut] At *Cruceius*

98. nec non] et una *Cruceius*

99. et chartam sume] chartamque assume *Cruceius*

101. taetrae causam superilline pestis] taetram placide superilline pestem *Cruceius*

102. Tum] Iam *Cruceius*

103. fluunt] cadunt *Cruceius*

104. iam] tu *Cruceius*

107. liquores] fluores *Cruceius*

109. lemiulum] ignitum *Cruceius*   meditem nomine dicunt] Graii dixere myliten *Cruceius*; *cf.* Kynosophion 27 (*Fischer 1983, 283*)

111. dulces acidosque . . . liquores] dulcemque acidumque . . . liquorem *Cruceius*

112. sumpta] molli *Cruceius*

114. tum] tu *Cruceius*

122. lente] lenteis (*sc.* lentes) *Cruceius*; *cf.* Kynosophion 24, lentis sestarium dimidium cum lacte decoquendum (*Fischer 1983, 284*)

123. et] ac *Cruceius*   immittere] iungere *Cruceius*

131. at] hic *Cruceius*   crepitantibus urere rutam] rutam crepitantibus ure *Cruceius*

132. pariter mulcere] catulum suffire *Cruceius*

133. *Omitted by Cruceius, who substitutes the following line:* perge, simulque acido vulnus perfunde Lyaeo

135. impetit usque adeo] usque adeo infestat *Cruceius*

136. ipse autem] ergo agedum *Cruceius*

137. et prius has] atque illas *Cruceius*

139. ut] et *Cruceius*   laboret] laborat *Cruceius*

142. perungens] perunges *Cruceius*

146. auxiliante] spectante *Cruceius*

147–49. *Omitted here but inserted instead after v. 154 in Cruceius.*

148. acrique] acidoque *Cruceius*

149 laesaeque adhibe haec] et laesae haec adhibe *Cruceius*

151. miserabile] penetrabile *Cruceius*

152. bovis] boum *Cruceius*

154. infectaque membra] et membra affecta *Cruceius*   *vv. 147–49 are inserted after v. 154 by Cruceius (cf. 147–49 above)*

155. tunc] tum *Cruceius*

161. lino colata nigranti] colo transmissa nitente *Cruceius*

162. revocari ad pristina tradunt] catulos ad prima reverti *Cruceius*

163. sensa canem, ac] obsequia, et *Cruceius*   rursum] tradunt *Cruceius*

167. atque ipsis foliis] ac foliis ipsis *Cruceius*

169. tandem usque adeo] tamen aeque illi *Cruceius*

172. et fauces nativo concolor auro] excrescit vermis similata figurae *Cruceius*   *The line* pustula, nativo fauces quae concolor albo *is added after v. 172 by Cruceius; cf.* Kynosophion *9:* fit autem species quaedam in formam vermis, nervo albo similis *(cf. Fischer 1983, 285)*

174. Omitted by Cruceius

175. Quem] Hanc *Cruceius*   potuit ferro] dextra potuit *Cruceius*   potentem] perita *Cruceius*

177–80. Omitted by Cruceius, who instead adds the following lines (one line is left blank after the fourth line):

    Cetera te pauco post tempore, nate, docebo.
    Nunc revocare canes, praedamque ad tecta referre
    admonet invectans sublustres Hesperus umbras,
    et qui iam posuit cantus Corydallus acutos.

    At tu, qui magni magno cum Caesare mundi
    consilio, Perenote, tuo moderaris habenas,
    incultos nostrae cantus ne despice Musae,
    pastorum a parvis ego quam paulo ante cicutis
    grandia venantum deduxi ad retia primus.
    Sic tua Caesaribus sint acceptissima semper
    obsequia, Eooque dies nascatur ab orbe,
    qua triplici tandem niteant tibi tempora mitra.

II. In obitum Marci Antonii Turriani Veronensis, ad Ioannem Baptistam Turrianum fratrem

Attested in 1555, 1577, β (1574, 1584, 1591, 1718), 1739.

Title. In obitum] In obitu *1555, 1577, 1574, 1584, 1591*   Turriani] Turrii *1555, 1577*   Turrianum] Turrium *1555, 1577*

19. sine] nisi *1574, 1584.*

62. quam *emended in 1577, 1718, 1739*] qua *all other witnesses*

65. Ticine *emended in 1577, 1718, 1739*] Ticinae *all other witnesses*

81. Turriensiaque ossa] atque ossa parentum β

86. attribuere] ah tribuere *β, 1739, perhaps better*

102. Sive] Seu *1555 (perhaps influenced by seu at v. 101)*

159. dumque aequora] dum flumina *β, 1739, more appropriately*

III. Ad Ioannem Baptistam Turrianum Veronensem,
in obitum Pauli et Iulii, ipsius Fracastorii filiorum
Attested in 1555, 1577, β (1574, 1584, 1591, 1718), 1739.

Title. Turrianum] Turrium 1555, 1577   In obitum Pauli et Iulii, ip-
sius Fracastorii filiorum *added in 1739*

60. arripit *(sc.* abripit, *not* adripit)] eripit 1591

65. tantis e patribus] e tam multis patribus β, 1739, *more correctly, but cf.*
C. 4.14

92. insudet] desudet β, 1739   praevertat] proscindat β, 1739, *more*
appropriately

100. ingentes post aestates] innumeras post aestates β, 1739, *more appro-*
priately

IV. Ad Danielem Rhainerium Veronae
praefectum senatorem amplissimum
Attested in 1555, 1577, β (1574, 1584, 1591, 1718), 1739.

Title. senatorem amplissimum *added in* β, 1739

1. Rhaineri 1718, 1739] Rheneri *all earlier witnesses; the same at vv.* 26 *and*
47

7. sacra] tecta β, 1739

14. tanta] tot iam β, 1739, *more correctly, but cf. Lucan,* Pharsalia 10.188 *and*
C. 3.65

V. Ad Ioannem Matthaeum Gibertum,
episcopum veronensem
Attested in 1539, 1555, 1577, β (1574, 1584, 1591, 1718), 1739.

Title. Hieronymi Fracastorii ad Gibertum episcopum Veronae Carpus
1539   Gibertum] Gibbertum 1574, 1584, 1591

1. Giberte] Gibberte 1574, 1584, 1591; *same at v.* 10

9. Charitae] Charite 1539, 1574, 1584 *(cf.* S. 2.384): Chariten
1591   nymphae] nympham 1591

12. per Benaci marmora 1539] Benaci sub gurgite *all later witnesses*

16. edam] eadem 1555, 1577

29. Nam quis 1539] Quis enim *all later witnesses*

30. Tu 1539] En *all later witnesses*

32. flumine 1539] flumina *all later witnesses*

33. dein 1539] tum *all later witnesses*   illos] illas 1555, 1577

34. o pueri, pretio] e pretio, pueri β, 1739; *the line is omitted in* 1555, 1577

36. iacent 1539] iacet *all later witnesses*

40. nave] navi 1555, *contra metrum*   tranant 1539] sulcant *all later witnesses*

56. pascetis] poscetis 1555, 1577 (*probably influenced by* poscitis *at v. 55 and* poscentibus *at v. 57*)

64. sunt 1539] sint *all later witnesses*

66. se condidit 1539] sub condidit *all later witnesses*

69. Iamque] Iam 1555, *contra metrum*

71. liquidas] placidus 1555, 1577, 1574, 1584, 1591: placidas 1718, 1739

73. an haec sacrumque amnem 1539] et hunc amnem sacrum *all later witnesses*

75. semper scopulo 1539] scopulo semper *all later witnesses*

78. extremo 1539] externo *all later witnesses*

80. nant 1539] nunc *all later witnesses*   caerula nautae 1539] litora nantes *all later witnesses*

81. venis 1539] venas *all later witnesses*

VI. Ad Margaritam Valesiam Navarrae reginam, Caesaris Fregosii nomine

Attested in 1555, 1577, β (1574, 1584, 1591, 1718), 1739.

Title. Navarrae] Navariae 1555

43. olivae] oliva 1574, 1584

47. se *added after* agglomerant *in* β, *but cf. Pontano*, Urania *4.409 and Servius on Vergil*, Aeneid *2.341*

58. fulmineove] fulmineosve *1574, 1584, 1591*

100. exoratque] admirans *β, 1739 (cf. Giacomo Bon,* De raptu Cerberi *2.129)*

125. dudum *(sc.* iamdudum, *cf.* S. *3.118*)] dure *β, 1739*

126. Euris vocatis] *perhaps one should read* Euros vocatos

151. ascitam] ascitum *1574, 1584*

180. non haec] non *1574, 1584:* te non *1591*

VII. Ad Marcum Antonium Flaminium et Galeatium Florimontium

Attested in 1555, 1577, *β* (1574, 1584, 1591, 1718), 1739. Placed at the end of the collection in 1555, 1577. The poem appears unfinished: in particular vv. 60–64, 65–84 and 85–90, at the end of the poem, appear rather loosely connected with the rest.

1. sensa] sensae *1555*

4. Giberto] Gibberto *1555, 1574, 1584, 1591; same at v. 65*

39. at] et *β, 1739*

40. sequitur secum] sequitur avens *1555, contra metrum:* sectatur avens *1577*

41. circum haec ipsum] *lacuna indicated between* licet *and* ipsum *in 1555:* non ipsius *1577: perhaps one could read* non his ipsum

42. Non] hic *1577 (cf. emendation at v. 41)*

64. praeceptam] praecepta *1584, 1591, 1718, 1739*

90. arcesque Sionis] *lacuna indicated after* stupuere *in 1555, 1577* (Desunt reliqua)

VIII. Ad Franciscum Turrianum Veronensem

Attested in 1555, 1577, *β* (1574, 1584, 1591, 1718), 1739.

Title. Turrianum] Turrium *1555, 1577*

70. Booten *emended in 1739*] Bootem *all earlier witnesses*

80. Gibertus *in all editions*

IX. In mortem Aliprandi Madrutii fratris Christophori cardinalis Tridentini

Attested in 1555, 1577, β (1574, 1584, 1591, 1718), 1739.

Title. *Untitled in 1555:* In obitum Aliprandi Madrutii ducis Tridentini 1577   fratris Christophori cardinalis Tridentini *added in 1739*

15. se tantum] tantum ipsam β, 1739, *more correctly*

X. Ad Alexandrum Farnesium cardinalem amplissimum

Attested in 1555, 1577, β (1574, 1584, 1591, 1718), 1739.

47. frangat] rumpat β, 1739, *but cf. Giacomo Bon,* De raptu Cerberi *2.168*

48. Tyndaridae *emended in 1739*] Tyndaridi *all earlier witnesses*

80. adcecinit] accinuit β, 1739, *more correctly*

98–101. *Omitted by 1591, possibly in deference to Protestant sensibilities*

104. stupidae] attonitae β, 1739

XI. Ad eundem illustrissimum et reverendissimum cardinalem Alexandrum Farnesium

Attested in 1546, 1555, 1577, β (1574, 1584, 1591, 1718), 1739. It was published in appendix to the *De contagione* in 1546, 1555, 1574, 1584; in appendix to the poems of the *Carminum liber* in 1577; and finally in the present position within the poems of the *Carminum liber* in 1591, 1718, 1739.

Title. Ad cardinalem Farnesium 1577   Alexandrum *added by* β, 1739   cui libros De contagione dedicavit *added in 1718:* cui libros De contagione et contagiosis morbis dedicavit *added in 1739*

34–40. *Omitted by 1591, possibly in deference to Protestant sensibilities.*

76. speratis] speretis β, 1739

XII. Ad Iulium III pontificem maximum

Attested in 1555, 1577, β (1574, 1584, 1591, 1718), 1739.

2–4. *Omitted by 1591, possibly in deference to Protestant sensibilities*

38. Acmon] Anthus *β, 1739; same at vv. 39, 139, and 142. See the Notes to the Translation, pp. 472–73.*

79. impinguet] pascat *β, 1739, avoiding the unclassical verb* impinguo

149. notare paratus] in dicere promptus *1555 (presumably a harsh anastrophe for* in aliena dicere promptus; *the editor perhaps misread* aliena indicere promptus, *although the verb* indicere *itself would be scarcely appropriate):* incidere promptus *1577*

XIII. Incidens

Attested in 1555, 1577, *β* (1574, 1584, 1591, 1718), 1739. Placed at the end rather than at the beginning of the series of bucolic poems addressed to Giovanni Battista della Torre (C. 13–20) in 1555, 1577.

Title. *No title, with a blank line separating the poem from the previous one, in 1555, 1574, 1584:* Aliud *1577:* Incidens *1591, 1718, 1739*

10. nusquam] numquam *emended in 1739, perhaps correctly (cf.* numquam *at v. 11)*

XIV. Incidens, Ad Ioannem Baptistam Turrianum Veronensem

Attested in 1555, 1577, *β* (1574, 1584, 1591, 1718), 1739.

Title. Fragmentum *1577*   Turrianum] Turrium *1555*

XV. Hiems, ad eundem

Attested in 1555, 1577, *β* (1574, 1584, 1591, 1718), 1739.

Title. Ad eundem *1555, 1574, 1584:* Hiems *1577, 1591*

12. hanc *emended in 1718, 1739*] hac *1555, 1574, 1584, 1591:* hoc *1577*

XVI. Ver, ad eundem

Attested in 1555, 1577, *β* (1574, 1584, 1591, 1718), 1739.

Title. Ad eundem *1555, 1574, 1584:* Ver *in 1577, 1591*

5. rorida] roscida *β, 1739*

26. laetis] laeti *1574*

30. saturat] saturet *emended in 1718, 1739, perhaps correctly*

XVII. Incidens, ad eundem

Attested in 1555, 1577, β (1574, 1584, 1591, 1718), 1739. First separated from C. 18 in 1718.

Title. Fragmentum 1577

XVIII. Aliud

Attested in 1555, 1577, β (1574, 1584, 1591, 1718), 1739. First separated from C. 17 in 1718.

Title first added in 1718

XIX. Aliud incidens ad eundem

Attested in 1555, 1577, β (1574, 1584, 1591, 1718), 1739.

Title. Aliud 1577

XX. Aliud

Attested in 1555, 1577, β (1574, 1584, 1591, 1718), 1739.

4. frusta] frustra 1555, 1577

7. et coli insperso] inspersoque coli 1555, 1577, *contra metrum (if authorial, perhaps mistaking* cōlon, -i *for* cŏlus, -i)

XXI. In natalem diem Iani Fregosii, Caesaris filii

Attested in 1545, 1555, 1577, β (1574, 1584, 1591, 1718), 1739. Placed between C. 8 and 9 in 1555, 1577.

Title. Hieronymus Fracastorius in Bandelli Parcas, ad Ianum Caesaris Fregosi filium 1545: *no title, with a blank line separating the poem from previous one, in* 1555: Genethliacon 1577

3. grandia 1545] gloria *all later witnesses*

8. arma] acta 1545 *(probably influenced by* acta *at v. 7)*

9. triumphis 1545] trophaeis *all later witnesses*

14. limina] lumina 1555, 1574, 1584, 1591

XXII. De partu Victoriae Farnesiae, Guidi Ubaldi
Feretrii, Urbini ducis, coniugis

Attested in β (1574, 1584, 1591, 1718), 1739.

8. Isaurum] Isauron *emended in 1718, 1739 metri causa (to avoid the hiatus*
Isaurum aquis)

15. et *omitted in 1739 (but cf.* ergo et *at S. 1.91 and* J. 2.480)

XXIII. Tumulus Francisci Mariae Molsae Mutinensis

Attested in 1568, 1577, β (1574, 1584, 1591, 1718), 1739. It is published in an
appendix after the poems of the *Carminum liber* in 1577. Fracastoro's pa-
ternity of this poem has been questioned: it has been ascribed to Trifone
Benci (one of Molza's closest aquaintances), by F. Baiocchi ("Sulle poesie
latine di F. M. Molza," *Annali della Scuola Normale Superiore*, 18 [1905]:
1–172, at 52–53 and 109) and even before Baiocchi, in Gaetano Bottari's
anthology (*Carmina illustrium poetarum Italorum, Tomus II* [Florence, 1719],
147). Indeed, this poem shows some striking correspondences to the
(somewhat generic) requests that Molza made of Benci when asking him
for an epitaph (cf. Molza's poem 10 in G. Gorni, M. Danzi, and S.
Longhi, *Poeti del Cinquecento*, vol. 1 [Milano: Ricciardi, 2001], 482; first
published in Girolamo Ruscelli, *I fiori delle rime de' poeti illustri* [Venice:
Giovanbattista e Melchior Sessa, 1558], 217): "Farai scrivendo a le fredde
ossa onore, / col favor, ch'a te sempre Apollo spira: / qui giace il Molza
de le Muse amico, / del mortal parlo, perchè 'l suo migliore / col gran
Medici suo or vive, e spira" ("You will honor my cold bones with your
writings, always touched by Apollo's favor: 'Molza, friend of the Muses,
rests here; yet I am only speaking of the mortal man, since the best part
of him now lives on, reunited with the Great Medici'"). However Benci's
authorship does not seem to be supported by any earlier testimony;
moreover, there are at least two different funerary poems for Molza that
circulated under Benci's name in the sixteenth and seventeenth centuries
(although neither one corresponds as closely as the present poem to
Molza's requests). These are a longer poem in Ubaldini's 1563 anthology
(f. 96v, *inc. Te Mutina, immo novem genuerunt Molsa sorores*), and a distichon

in the 1608 one by Gruytere (p. 398, *inc. Qui lepido veteres aequavit carmine Molsa*). Another hypothesis that would fit the facts is that this poem was composed by Fracastoro, the more illustrious poet, at Benci's request, just as C. 6 to Marguerite de Navarre was composed by Fracastoro in Cesare Fregoso's name.

Title. Epith. Francisci Marii Molsae *1568*: Epitaphium Molsae *1577*

Mariae *emended in 1739*] Marii *all earlier witnesses*

7. ante] aut *1574, 1584, 1591*

XXIV. Ad Ioannem Lipomanum, ex Veronensi praetura decedentem
Attested in 1584, 1591, 1718, 1739.

XXV. In mortem Ioannis Baptistae Montani medici Veronensis
Attested in 1555, 1568, 1577, β (1574, 1584, 1591, 1718), 1739. Placed between C. 9 and 10 in 1555, 1577.

Title. *No title, with a blank line separating the poem from the previous one, in 1555*: Ad Montanum Asclepium *1568*: Tumulus Montani medici *1577*

3. indignans pressit te Parca] oppressit Dea te indignata *1568*

5. et tu] nigro *1568*

XXVI. Ad Ioannem Matthaeum Gibertum, episcopum Veronensem
Attested in β (1574, 1584, 1591, 1718), 1739.

Title. Gibertum] Gibbertum *1574, 1584, 1591 (same variant spelling at v. 6)*

2. sonans alluit unda *emended in 1591*] sanans alluit nuda *1574*: sonans alluit nuda *1584*: sonans alluis unda *1718, 1739*

XXVII. Ad eundem
Attested in β (1574, 1584, 1591, 1718), 1739. Cf. also C. 48.

Title. Ad Ioannem Matthaeum Gibbertum episcopum Veronensem *1574*

1. Giberte] Gibberte *1574, 1584, 1591*

7. longaeva] aeterna *Venice, Biblioteca Nazionale Marciana, ms. Marc. Lat. XIV 165 (4254), cf. C. 48*

XXVIII. Ad eundem

Attested in β (1574, 1584, 1591, 1718), 1739. First separated from C. 29 in 1584. The separation does not seem particularly necessary, and yet it is attested also in the two sixteenth-century manuscripts: Venice, Biblioteca Nazionale Marciana, ms. Marc. Lat. XIV 165 (coll. 4254) and Parma, Biblioteca Palatina, ms. Pal. 555, for which see the headnote to C. 48.

Title. Ad Ioannem Matthaeum Gibbertum episcopum Veronensem *1574*

1. Giberte] Gibberte *1574, 1584, 1591*

XXIX. Ad eundem

Attested in β (1574, 1584, 1591, 1718), 1739. First separated from C. 28 in 1584 (see above, C. 28).

Title first added in 1584

2. Giberto] Gibberto *1574, 1584, 1591*

XXX. De Marsango fluviolo, prope villam Ioannis Baptistae Rhamnusii, in agro Patavino

Attested in 1556, β (1574, 1584, 1591, 1718), 1739.

Untitled in 1556

1. Marsange] Mersange *1556, 1574, 1584*

6. utriusque] utrisque *1556*

XXXI. De eodem

Attested in 1556, β (1574, 1584, 1591, 1718), 1739.

Untitled in 1556

1. Marsange] Mersange *1556, 1574, 1584; same at v. 3*

XXXII. In calce Homocentricorum

Attested in 1538 (or 1539 in the Venetian style: cf. Cibei, 2004), 1555, β (1574, 1584, 1591, 1718), 1739. Like the rest of the poems drawn from Fracastoro's prose works (C. 32–43) it was first published separately from the prose work to which it belongs in 1718, a practice repeated in 1739. For C. 32–43, the titles are first added in 1718 unless otherwise specified.

19. plectis] plectris *1584, 1591, 1718, 1739 (but cf. C. 6.76)*

XXXIII. Postremo capite libri primi De contagione et contagiosis morbis
Attested in 1546, 1555, β (1574, 1584, 1591, 1718), 1739. Cf. C. 32.

XXXIV. Capite septimo libri tertii de iisdem
Attested in 1546, 1555, β (1574, 1584, 1591, 1718), 1739. Cf. C. 32.

XXXV. Dialogo de poetica
Attested in 1555, β (1574, 1584, 1591, 1718), 1739. Cf. C. 32.

9. operis] operi β, *1739, perhaps better (cf. Statius,* Sylvae *4.4.29* temet furare labori, *and Vergil,* Aeneid *5.845)*

XXXVI. Libro primo De intellectione
Attested in 1555, β (1574, 1584, 1591, 1718), 1739. Cf. C. 32.

XXXVII. Eodem libro primo De intellectione
Attested in 1555, β (1574, 1584, 1591, 1718), 1739. Cf. C. 32.

XXXVIII. In calce eiusdem libri
See the introductory note to C. 44.

XXXIX. Libro secundo De intellectione
Attested in 1555, β (1574, 1584, 1591, 1718), 1739. Cf. C. 32.

2. speculator (*as future imperative; cf.* contemplator *at S. 1.296) manual correction in 1555 (three copies inspected), 1718, 1739*] speculatur *1555 (before manual correction), 1574, 1584, 1591*

XL. Eodem libro
Attested in 1555, β (1574, 1584, 1591, 1718), 1739. Cf. C. 32.

XLI. Dialogo de anima, non procul ab initio
Attested in 1555, β (1574, 1584, 1591, 1718), 1739. Cf. C. 32.

XLII. Eodem dialogo: Psyche
Attested in 1555, β (1574, 1584, 1591, 1718), 1739. Cf. C. 32.

Title. Psyche *1555, 1574, 1584, 1591*

21. intertextam *emended in 1718, 1739*] intertexam *all earlier witnesses*

XLIII. Vetus epigramma, in calce
Sententiae de vini temperatura
Attested in 1553, 1555, β (1574, 1584, 1591, 1718), 1739. Cf. C. 32. This epigram is set at the end of *De vini temperatura sententia* starting with 1555 (which is followed by all later editions), but it appears before Fracastoro's work, on the verso of the book's title page, in the 1553 *editio princeps*: this setting was in fact more appropriate, since Fracastoro refers to the poem in the opening chapter of the prose work (*quod vetus epigramma demonstrat*), then again in chapter 7 (here calling it *antiquum epigramma*). This poem is one among the numerous Latin translations of an epigram by the Greek poet Meleager (*Anthologia Palatina* 9.331; see the Notes to the Translation, p. 488), that were circulating in the Renaissance (see J. Hutton, *The Greek Anthology in Italy to the Year 1800* [Ithaca, 1935], 547). It is not certain whether Fracastoro was the translator of this particular Latin version of the "ancient" (*vetus*) epigram or he was just quoting a poem in Latin he had casually encountered and believed to be ancient. In fact, in 1579 Claude Binet published it within a collection of ancient poems (*C. Petroni Arbitri itemque aliorum quorundam veterum epigrammata hactenus non edita. Cl. Binetus conquisivit et nunc primum publicavit* [Poitiers: Bouchet, 1579]), declaring he had found it in a manuscript preserved in an unnamed Italian library. The poem thereafter was introduced into editions of ancient Latin poetry, first by Riese (*Anthologia Latina sive poesis Latinae supplementum*, 2nd ed. [Leipzig: Teubner, 1906], vol. 1, pt. 2, 334), and later by Bährens (*Poetae Latini minores* [Leipzig: Teubner, 1883], vol. 5, 406). However a version of this Latin epigram, apparently with a few variants, is attested in Vatican Library, ms. Vat. Lat. 9948, f. 175v, which

preserves other poems by Fracastoro, including C. 44; see the introductory note to this poem below.

Title. Vetus Epigramma 1553, 1555, 1574, 1584, 1591

XLIV. BACCHO CONCILIATORI

This poem was first published in a shorter form within the dialogue *Turrius sive de intellectione* (see above, C. 38): this first text included only vv. 13–36 (thus presenting an abrupt beginning) and 41–52. A longer version of it was rediscovered and published, first in Scipione Maffei's *Verona illustrata* (1731, vol. 2, 345–46) and then by Volpi in 1739. The texts published in 1731 and 1739 are not the same: Maffei publishes only vv. 1–12 and 53–56, i.e., three new initial stanzas and one new stanza at the end; Volpi instead prints the entire text with Maffei's additions, but also includes an additional stanza in the middle (vv. 37–40). According to Volpi's notes, it seems that in his manuscript the final stanza discovered by Maffei (vv. 53–56) replaced the one found in the vulgate (vv. 49–52); however, for the sake of completeness, Volpi decided to print both existing final stanzas, one after the other (vv. 49–52 and 53–56). It is uncertain whether Maffei simply omitted transcribing vv. 37–40 by mistake or the manuscripts seen by him and Volpi were different; in any case they both mention using a manuscript from Treviso, which Volpi describes as belonging to Giuseppe Bologni; Maffei also claims to have seen a second unspecified manuscript recently acquired by him. This longer version of the poem is attested in Vatican Library, ms. Vat. Lat. 9948, f. 174v (see Pellegrini, *Appunti* 1954, 110).

The title Baccho Conciliatori *was given to the poem in Maffei 1731 and 1739, and was probably drawn from the manuscript seen by Maffei and Volpi; the same title is also attested in Vatican Library, ms. Vat. Lat. 9948*

1–12. *Omitted by 1555,* β.

16. cornua] tempora 1555, β

22. Evoe *emended in 1718, 1739*] Heu ohe 1555, 1574, 1591, 1584; *same at v. 50*

27. omnium ad- *marked by 1739 as illegible text in ms.*

30. nitente] rubente 1555, β   emicat] enitet 1555, β

31. et] tum *1555, β*

37–40. *Omitted in 1555, β, Maffei 1731*

37. Penthee] Pentheu *is an emendation suggested in 1739 in a note*

42. bipennem] securim *1555, β*

43. iam] tum *1555, β*

48. constituit] constituunt *1555, β*

49–52. *Omitted in ms. seen by 1739*

53–56. *Omitted in 1555, β*

XLV. In fugam Caroli V imperatoris

This poem, composed shortly after Charles V's defeat in 1552, must have
started circulating widely, given the number of sixteenth-century manu-
scripts in which it is preserved (for example, Venice, Biblioteca Nazionale
Marciana, Marc. Lat. XII 122 [coll. 4173], Marc. Ital. IX 365 [coll. 7168];
Vatican Library, Vat. Lat. 5171, Barb. Lat. 3997; Milan, Biblioteca Ambro-
siana, I 48 inf.; Paris, Bibliothèque Nationale de France, Dupuy 736;
Vienna, Österreiches Nationalbibliothek, series nova 23774 [formerly
Phillipps 4561]). The poem is also attested in Pierre de L'Estoile's journal
(years 1610–11, published as *Mémoires-Journeaux: Journal d'Henri IV 1589–
1611* [Paris: Librairie des Bibliophiles, 1883], 384–85): here C. 45 appears
after a poem wrongly attributed to Fracastoro (*inc. iam nix in liquidas*) but
actually by Lazzaro Bonamico da Bassano. In 1739 Volpi published it
from an early seventeenth-century pamphlet edition of the poem (the
copy seen by Volpi can probably be identified with the one now preserved
in the Biblioteca Civica of Verona, carrying the manuscript note "1619.
Stampato dal Pinelli in Venet. ad inst. del Senator Dominico Molino").
Volpi also collated this text with some unspecified manuscripts, including
a letter in Italian by Jacopo Valvason (this ms. can probably be identified
with ms. Udine, Biblioteca Comunale, Joppi 102). The text given here
reproduces that of the 1619 pamphlet edition, which, at present, appears
to be its *editio princeps*.

8. inclinato animo] inconstans animi *L'Estoile*

10. laberis] diffugis *1739*

14. ac] et *L'Estoile*. *The line* spe nulla redeundi in tete armisque relicta *is added after v. 14 by 1739 following the text of the manuscript letter of Jacopo Valvason.*

18. capis] rapis *a reading from an unspecified ms. seen by 1739*

19. ac] et *L'Estoile*

22. potiare *(also in unspecified mss. seen in 1739)*] potirere *L'Estoile:* poterere *emended in 1739, more correctly*

XLVI. In obitum Marci Antonii Turriani

This poem appeared acephalously at the end of a manuscript containing lesson notes from a series of medical lectures by Marcantonio della Torre, collected in 1510 by a student of his named Girolamo Mantua. The manuscript, once owned by the Veronese collector Giovanni Saibante, is now lost, but a detailed description of it — with a complete transcription of our poem — was drafted in the eighteenth century by Ottavio Alecchi, a friend and close collaborator of Scipione Maffei. Alecchi's manuscript catalogue is now preserved in the Biblioteca Capitolare of Verona as ms. CCCVII (282) and was published by G. B. Giuliari in 1874. Maffei also saw the Saibante manuscript in question (calling it 834, *contra* Alecchi's numbering 110) and published the poem in his *Verona illustrata* (1731, 346–47). Yet Maffei omitted the last five lines that we read in Alecchi's transcription, which are almost identical to the closing lines of Fracastoro's *Syphilis*, book 1. (On a similar omission on Maffei's part, cf. C. 44.) Maffei attributed the poem to Fracastoro on stylistic grounds. The entire C. 46 in fact shows striking similarities with Fracastoro's lament on the death of Marcantonio della Torre at the end of *Syphilis* 1 (vv. 454–69); yet it also appears contextualized in the manuscript where it was drafted (cf. v. 1 *haec . . . docebat* referring back to the lecture notes). Unless this poem is a later plagiaristic re-elaboration of verses from Fracastoro's *Syphilis* (added at the end of Mantua's notes several years after della Torre's death), it may be a funerary poem (or part of it) for della Torre that Fracastoro perhaps never published and later reused in the *Syphilis*. This poem may have circulated among Fracastoro's acquaintances and may have been partly utilized or adapted by Mantua in order to close his collection of lecture notes.

2. florenti] florentis *Alecchi*

9–10. *Cf.* S. *1.460–61*

10. alluit] abluit *Alecchi, cf.* S. *1.461 (but* alluit *at* C. *26.2)*

11. cava] cana *Alecchi (contra metrum); cf.* S. *1.409*

13. *The following lines follow v. 13 in Alecchi (identical to* S. *1.465–69, except* rapidumque *instead of* placidumque *of* S. *1.468):*

> Tempestate illa Ausoniam rex Gallus opimam
> vertebat bello et Ligurem ditione premebat.
> Parte alia, Caesar ferro superabat et igni
> Euganeos, rapidumque Silim, Carnumque rebellem,
> et totum luctus Latium moerorque tenebat.

XLVII. Ad Marcum Antonium Flaminium gratiarum actio

This poem was discovered by Volpi, handwritten at the end of a 1504 edition of Platina's *Vitae summorum pontificum* in the possession of Francesco Maria Mancurti at Imola. It is uncertain whether the title given to the poem in 1739 was attested in its manuscript source or it was added by Volpi.

XLVIII. [Untitled]

This poem is identical to C. 27.5–12, and, rather oddly, was printed by Volpi as a new poem on the grounds that it had been discovered in a manuscript which presented C. 27 as divided into two parts (I vv. 1–4, II vv. 5–12). This manuscript, mentioned by Volpi as belonging to Apostolo Zeno, can be identified with Venice, Biblioteca Nazionale Marciana, Marc. Lat. XIV 165 (coll. 4254), s. XVI; on ff. 236r–40r it preserves the following series of poems by Fracastoro: 2, 3, 26, 27 (dividing vv. 1–4 and 5–12), 28, 29, 49. The same set of bucolic poems addressed to Giberti (with 26 and 27 divided into two parts, and including as well 28, 29, 49) is also attested, in the very same form, in Parma, Biblioteca Palatina, ms. Pal. 555 (s. XVI), pp. 218–19. This is the manuscript which also contains the newly discovered C. 57 (see below on C. 57).

XLIX. [Untitled]

Attested in Venice, Biblioteca Marciana, ms. Marc. Lat. XIV 165 (coll. 4254), f. 240r and Parma, Biblioteca Palatina, ms. Pal. 555, p. 219: see the introductory note to the previous poem.

L. Fragmenta carminis in laudem Matthaei Giberti

Attested in *aut.*, f. 149v (vv. 1–30), 150r (vv. 31–37 and 38–64, and in mg. vv. 92–113) and 150v (vv. 65–91), 153r (v. 114), 154r (vv. 114–44). It is not certain — although probable — that the order in which the material appears in the manuscript reflects the chronology of its composition: later drafts may well have been inserted on earlier pages purposely left blank. In any case, the present transcription respects as much as possible the order of lines in the manuscript. The materials can be analyzed as follows: vv. 1–30 is the first draft; vv. 31–37 is a short variant (cf. vv. 5–12 in first draft); vv. 38–91 is the second and longest draft; vv. 92–113 contain short variants (for vv. 92–99 and 108–13, cf. vv. 9–12 in first draft and 51–55 in second draft; for vv. 100–107, cf. vv. 49–50 in second draft and vv. 129–30 in third draft); vv. 114–44 represent a third draft. The 1739 edition instead published the fragments giving the longest draft first (vv. 38–91), then the earliest (vv. 1–30), followed by all the shorter variants (vv. 31–37 and 92–113), and finally the third and last draft (vv. 114–44). The title of this poem, as well as of the others from *aut.* (C. 50–55), was first added in the 1739 edition and is not found in the manuscript.

The names of some of the nymphs mentioned at vv. 21–28 and 65–73 are listed on the top right corner of f. 149 v, as follows:

Carda, Stella, Cesia, Lacusia
Saloë, Tuscula, Limonis
Grineia

7. ~~divina regas~~ *after initial* qui   nobis] *written above* divinam qui

11. ~~tantum~~ *after* venerataque

12. ~~numen ovans~~ *before* terque   quaterque] quater *aut.*

14. ~~matri~~ *after* et

15–18. *Written in mg. beside vv. 14 and 19–21 and inserted after v. 14 with an arrow*

15. ~~senior~~ *after* Tum

19. ~~circum~~ *after* Quem

22. ~~uda~~ *after* Lacusia et

25. *Written in mg. beside vv. 24–26*   iam] *written above* et Mersa

28. et tripodes docta] *written above* ~~et Fata et~~

   ~~-que humeris suspendere eburnam~~ *after* cytharam

29. ~~WORD WORD Sirmio~~ *before* O centum   ~~puellae~~ *after* fonte

30. ~~Naiades~~ *before* infit

31. sacris delecto antistite et aris] *written above* sacra caput exornante thyara, *evidently as a correction to it (although* sacra . . . thyara *is not deleted), since* sacra . . . thyara *is then used in the following line*

32. ~~tenerum dum~~ *after* et

33. Gybberte] *written above* ~~gratata~~

~~laetitiam dedit solemnesque dies tuis soles in honoribus egit~~ *after v. 33*

35. *The following partial lines are written in mg. beside vv. 35–37 (perhaps as a variant to part of v. 35 with a continuation):*

   propterque Athesim cantavit amoenum *[perhaps variant to* cytharamque . . . eburnam *in v. 35]*
   ~~heroas cytharamque manu pulsavit~~
   ~~WORD~~ heroumque humili laudes cantu

37. ~~advena· habere locum~~ *before* advena

56. ab alveo] *seems to be deleted, probably by mistake, since the line remains incomplete without it*

65. ~~Tuscaque~~ *before* Cesiaque   Grineaque] -que *should be omitted* metri causa

69. ~~sylvestrem~~ *after* exercens

~~et iam Garda parens et adhuc Trimelia virgo~~ *after v. 69*

71–73. *Written in mg. beside the following lines, which are canceled by a diagonal stroke after v. 70.*

> Affuit et nati placidum subvecta per amnem,
> coniugis et chari cumulavit gaudia Mantho,
> Mantho fatidica, in mediis quae longa recensens
> tempora, 'Proh Thusco prognatae Naiades amne,

74. nobis] *corrected from* vobis

76. ~~sty- gent-~~ a *[a is unnecessarily repeated] after* reges

78. Demissum] *written in left mg.* ~~caelo gratus vobis~~ *before* magnis; *but* caelo *needs to be reinstated after the addition of* demissum ~~auctum~~ *after* virtutibus

80. ~~et sacra~~ sanctus *before* sub relligione (*but* sanctus *should also have been deleted following the addition of* pacatasque sacra) Pacatasque sacra] *written in mg., probably as a correction to* et sacra sanctus *The following lines are canceled after v. 80:*

> quo funus et belli vobis . . .
> quo dira Allecto, quo saevae Gorgones et quo

83. penderent] *contra metrum (erroneously spelled as though from the verb* pendeo, *instead of* pendo)

86. ~~Tum memorat sanctosque ortus, tuaque acta recenset~~ *after v. 86*

87. ~~grandia~~ *before* nexae

91. ~~WORD triplex super affuit astrum~~ *after* ut sydera *written below* grandia, *perhaps as beginning of a new line*

92–113. *Written in mg. beside vv. 40–64*

92. tua bella] *written above* ~~Verona~~

98. ferens] feres *aut.*

100. Novus ecce *written above* Gybberte *as a variant to it*

103. et ipsa] *written below* sydera, *probably owing to space constraints*

105. ingens] *written above* ~~omen~~

106. firmamus] -que *rightly added by 1739 metri causa*

107. *The following lines are written after v. 107 (cf. vv. 108–10):*

> ~~Ipsa tibi ante alias ad tantae nuntia famae~~
> [WORD WORD *written above* ~~Ipsa~~] ~~tibi tua~~ bella ad tantae nuntia famae
>   tuis gratata triumphis
> ~~tempora paciferae ramo praecinxit olivae~~

109. ~~Verona~~ *before* ante

112. plausu] *written above* ~~nitidum~~

113. effuditque] efuditque *aut.*

116. strepituque] *written above* ~~Gybberte~~

119. *Written in mg. beside the line* ~~Romanas Gybberte inter si forte~~ Camenas (Camenas *not deleted by mistake), which is deleted after v. 118*

123. *The following lines are written in mg. beside vv. 123–26 (either as a variant to vv. 122–23 or meant to be inserted after v. 123):*

> Musa, tibi agresti quae quondam lusit avena,
> sacraque Melsineis persolvit rustica ripis,
> nunc vero, si qua ipsa queat, maioribus ausis
> ingreditur laudesque tuas et gaudia nostra.
> ~~explicat ab WORDque tibi gratatur WORD~~

124. Omen] *written above* ~~Annus~~   Gybberte] *written above* ~~novus ecce~~

126. iam nova] *written above* ~~magnaque~~

127. Bona] *written above* ~~Tria~~

129. ~~firmamusque novum magnis applausibus omen~~ *after v. 129*

138. WORD *written above* laetitia   nemorosa cacumina sylvae] *written above* ~~WORD vertice~~ sylvae

139. ~~macte~~ *before* nutarunt

LI. Fragmenta eclogae in laudem eiusdem

Attested in *aut.*, f. 151v (vv. 1–14), 152r (vv. 15–22), 169v (vv. 23–52), 170r (vv. 53–82), 170v (vv. 83–109), 171r (vv. 110–35), 171v (vv. 136–59), 172r (vv. 160–85), 173r (vv. 186–219), 173v (vv. 220–49), 174r (vv. 250–72), 174v (vv.

273–301), 175r (vv. 302–8), 175v (vv. 309–34), 176r (vv. 335–58), 176v (vv. 359–84), 177r (vv. 385–90); ff. 171r–v and 172r are written in a larger and clearer hand. As in the case of C. 50, it cannot be certain that the order of the material in the manuscript represents the order of composition. In any case the present transcription respects the order of the material in the manuscript as much as possible. It thus distinguishes: (a) the beginning of the poem with several variants (vv. 1–22, which may have been composed at a later stage on blank leaves, ff. 151v and 152r, left among drafts of C. 50); (b) the first draft (vv. 23–99), followed by a few more variants of the beginning (vv. 100–109); (c) the second draft (vv. 110–85, written in a larger hand); (d) the third draft (vv. 186–249); (e) numerous variants of the opening lines and initial section (vv. 250–72 being short variants of the opening lines, while vv. 273–301 represent a longer variant of the initial section and vv. 302–8 a variant of the opening lines); (f) the fourth and most polished draft (vv. 309–90). The 1739 edition instead published the fragments giving the last and most polished draft first (vv. 309–90); then the earliest one (vv. 1–22, though accepting into the text also many of the deleted parts); and finally a selection of the most significant variants present in the intermediate drafts, roughly following the order in which they appear in the manuscript (first, collecting the variants to various passages, and second, those relating to the very beginning of the poem).

1. Cneorus] *corrected from* Gneorus   *The following lines are canceled with a diagonal stroke before v. 1:*

Ibla g~ colo, Leuce calathis, Gneorus ibisco
depositis, cantant eadem non vocibus iisdem:
Ibla gravi, Leuce media, Gneorus acuta
cantant; Menaliae responsant omnia sylvae.
O nisi me Thelayra meus consumeret ignis,
ecquis laetitia in tanta me laetior esset?
Nunc etiam hirsutae ludunt per prata capellae,
nunc etiam faciles saliunt per littora nymphae.
Dumque omnis tellus, omnis dum cessat arator,
alta coronati stant ad praesepia tauri.

2. pueri] *written above* ~~iuvenes~~

4. omnes una eadem *written in mg.*

13. ripaeque] *the word is not clearly legible and -que is guesswork, but it is re-quired by the meter and context, as at v. 43 below*

14. *The following seven lines are canceled with diagonal strokes after v. 14:*

> *Ib.* Quemque suus tenet ignis. Adesto, candide A̲y̲la̲,
> laetitiae, nunc luce sacra duc gaudia mecum.
> ~~Postridie tua mala leges. sunt Medica curae~~ sine, frondeat arbos
> ~~heroi, Alcynoique arbor, grandesque volucres.~~
> ~~heroi semideo: sine, poma ferat~~, sunt Medica curae
> heroi, et sylvae Alcynoi, grandesque v̲olu̲c̲r̲e̲s̲.
> Postridie te cura ovium lactisque tenebit.

15. *The following lines are canceled with a diagonal stroke before v. 15, in the next folium (152r):*

> Nunc etiam hyrsutae ludunt per prata capellae,
> nunc etiam faciles saliunt per littora nymphae.
> Dumque omnis tellus, omnis [dum *written above* omnis cessat] cessat
>   arator,
> applaudunt cava saxa tibi, tibi condita sylvis
> applaudit, Gybberte, altis de rupibus Echo.
> Quin, matris puer ingratae, [mater *written above* ~~puerique~~], facesse
>   hinc,
> ~~ingrati mater pueri qui tristia laetis, sanctisque recedite ab aris~~
> ~~semper qui lachrymas~~ [inter- *written above* ~~faustis~~] ~~miscetis amaras~~.
> qui laetis lachrymas inter miscetis amaras [*in mg. beside previous line*]
> ~~et faustis lachrymas s̲ae̲v̲i̲ ambo et lachrymas intermiscetis amaras~~
> ingrati pueri, sacrisque recedite ab aris,
> dura parens et saeve puer, qui tristia laetis
> et semper lachrymas intermiscetis amaras.
>   Quin matris puer ingratae, materque facesse hinc,
> ingrati mater, [pueri *written above* mater qui] qui tristia semper
> laetis et lachrymas intermiscetis amaras.
>   Quemque suus tenet ignis. At, o, ne gaudia tanta,

saeve puer, laetis semper qui tristia misces,
ne turba. Sit pura dies, sint omnia laeta.
  Quemque suus tenet ignis. [eat *written above* ~~at haec~~] lux candida
    nobis,
candidus et novus annus eat: novus incipit annus.

23. Cneorus] *corrected from* Gneorus

24. ~~pueri docuit quos maximus Alcon~~ *after* depositis

25. ~~in littoribus Benaci~~ *after* Solem

~~Carminibus docuit pueros quae maximus Alcon~~ *after v. 25*

26. in numerum] *written above* ~~alternis eadem~~

28. *The following lines are written in mg. beside v. 28, but connected to v. 31 with
an arrow (maybe meant to be inserted before it, or as a variant to vv. 29–30):*

  Et nunc sacra dies agitur, nunc omnibus aris
  laetitia it . . .

31–32. *The following lines are written in mg. beside vv. 31–32, either to be in-
serted after them or as a variant of them:*

  Parce, precor, Thelayra, novo [dum maxima fiunt *written above* dum
    sacra; *the last two words were mistakenly not deleted*]
  sacra deo, dum ridet [*corrected from* ager] ager, dum ridet et a̤m̤n̤i̤s̤.

33. annus] annuis *aut.* sit faustum felixque *written in mg.*

35. tenent] *written above* ~~regunt~~

38. Et Pietas] *corrected from* Iam Pietas

41–42. *The following lines are written in mg. beside vv. 41–42, as a variant to
them:*

  Magna sacro iuvenem donat dum Roma galero,
  mons circum septemque sonant applausibus arces

41. heroa] *seems to be deleted after* sacro, *although it is required by the context
and the meter*

42. ovans *written above* io   omnia *written above* undique

46. populifer *written in left mg.*

49. H.] *wrongly placed at v. 50*

50. fluctusque] -que *is erroneously added, making the line ametric (cf. vv. 137, 213, 348)*

53. frondentes] *written above* proceras ripas] rapas *aut.*

54. Musas] *written above* vates vates ille educat et iam *written above* et word tollit et word *after* vates educat optimus et iam *written in mg.* et vates educat, et iam] *written in mg. below* educat optimus et iam

55. Educat *before* magna Catulli] Catuli *aut.*

55–56. *The following lines are written in mg. beside vv. 55–56, as variant to them:*

   mille habet, atque aliquis crescens tibi forte Catullus
   [Magnanimum heroa *written above* rursus Athim heroasque] tua
     cantabit in acta.

61. Leuce, inquit, cyanumque mihi lege lycnida Leuce *after v. 61*

63. mi *after* chara

64. lege cana, mihi] *written above* cyanumque mihi (cyanumque *was not deleted by mistake*)

66. tecum] *written above* Thusci

70. saeva- *after* hic

71. Gorgones] Gornes *aut. The ending* -ĕs *is erroneously used instead of* -ās (*i.e.,* Gorgonas) *for the accusative plural of the third declension Greek noun, as also at vv. 51.158, 341 and in the note at v. 224–25 (whereas* Gorgones *is used correctly as the nominative plural in the note to C. 50.80); perhaps Fracastoro is inappropriately echoing Vergil,* Aeneid *6.289:* Gorgones Harpyiaeque et forma tricorporis umbrae.

74. Tu *before* sanctum

77. pupis] *sc.* puppis, *same at vv. 164 and 379 below*

81. H.] *wrongly placed at v. 82*

82. lupos] *written above* contemnuntque iam

91. ~~mu· caelo~~ *after* sydera

103. cantant] *written above* ~~alternis~~ docuit

104. carmina concordes eadem] *written in left mg. as a correction to* ~~concordes cantant eadem~~ *before* non vocibus

The following lines are canceled with a diagonal stroke after v. 104 (vv. 100–104 and 105–9 are written in the blank space left around the deleted lines, above and below them respectively):

> Hybla colo, Leuce calathis, Cneorus ibisco
> depositis, pueri docuit quos maximus Alcon,
> ~~alternis~~ concordes ut forte alta sub rupe canentes
> apricum ad solem in littoribus Benaci
> convenere: eadem cantant~~ant~~ non vocibus iisdem.
> Hybla gravi . . .

107. ~~Conco-~~ *before* alternis; *the line remains metrically incomplete*

110. Cneorus] *corrected from* Gneorus

114. Cneorus] *corrected from* Gneorus

119. annus] *probably erroneously written instead of* amnis (*and cf. v. 289*), *probably influenced by* annus *at v. 120*

121. omen habet: melior] *written above* ~~et melior nobis~~

122. iam caelum Gybberte tenent] *written above* ~~Gybberte en caelo regnant~~

136. L.] *corrected from* H.

140. G.] *corrected from* L.

143. *Written above* ~~rursum Athim atque heroasque tua qui cantet in acta~~.

145. *Written above* ~~'Tyrsi, mihi cane, Tyrsi,' inquit, 'sit rustica quamvis~~.

146. *Written above* ~~Musa tibi, tamen et memorem me dicet, et usque~~.

147. *Written above* ~~gratum Melsineis non inficiabitur hortis'~~.

148. *Written above* ~~Quid? Quod et agrestes flores et munera curat~~.

149. *Written above* [~~Leuce~~ *written above* ~~Roma~~] ~~inquit, sacro decoret me Roma galero~~.

150. *Written above* ~~serta tamen tu, chara mihi, tu munera mitte~~'.

152. C.] *corrected from* H.

153. servamus] seravamus *aut.*

154. cui temperat orbis] *contra sensum, probably written by mistake instead of* qui temperat orbem (*cf.* Ovid, Metamorphoses 1.770)

157. ~~hic Alecto~~ *after* agricolae   Alecto] *written above* diram caecumque

161. hic] *written in left mg. as a correction to* ~~et~~, *before* patrem

162. interea] *written above* genus et   ~~posthac~~ *after* nostrum

163. dum te fata deum] *written above* ~~quem matura aetas~~   mox] *written above* ~~fata~~

165. ~~-que minas~~ *after* contemnit   -que minas] *written above* pelagi ventosque

168. aspectu *written in mg.*

169. ~~nec~~ *after* lupos

171. quercus] *written above* ferent decurrent

173. puraque] *written above* ~~lucida~~

176. magna] *written above* Salve aetas   et vos salvete, beati] *written above* ~~heroum, amnes salvete Latini~~

177. *Added above v. 178*

181. variarent] variaren *aut.*

184–85. *These verses, written in a smaller hand, are separated from v. 183 by a short horizontal line.*

189. cantant] cantantant *aut.*

198. magis horti] *written above* ~~WORD WORD~~

199. ~~cura mei est~~ *before* detineat

217. ~~omen iam dextrum est~~ . . . *after v. 217*

218. *The line* Ecce tua et caelo [fulserunt *written above* ~~consurgunt~~] sydera, et ipsa *is written in mg. next to v. 218, as a variant to it*

220. *The line* Incipit annus, io, melior, nova nascitur aetas *is written in mg. next to v. 220, probably as a variant to it*

224–25. Written in mg. beside the following four lines which were then canceled with a diagonal stroke:

> Clementi nova sacra deo renovate quotannis,
> agricolae. Hic diram Alecto, caecumque Furorem,
> Gorgones, Arpiasque feras, infernaque monstra
> [Caucasea *written above* ~~perpetua~~] aerata religabit rupe cathena.

Lines 224–25 may be an attempt at creating a variant to the deleted lines; or Fracastoro may have intended to restore part of the deleted text, completing v. 225 as sacra deo. hic diram Alecto, caecumque furorem *and reintegrating the following two deleted lines as well*

227. ~~sancte puer Thuscisque~~ . . . *after v. 227* The following lines are written in mg. beside v. 227–28, probably as a variant to the deleted half line and vv. 228–29:

> dum [iuvenem, dum te fata ad maiora reservant *written above* ~~tua te~~
>   ~~virtus fata ad maiora~~ reservant]
> sancte puer cui cuncta favent, cui militat aether
> WORD Etrusci pecoris . . .

231. erit] *written above* tempus quum

233. ~~Et copia~~ *written in mg.*

234. H.] L. *seems preferable; cf. v. 230*   proceras] *written above* ~~frondosas~~

235. Musas *written above* vates *as a variant to it (and a preferable one)*   vates *written above* Musas, *as variant to it (and a preferable one)*

237. atque Athim atque heroas *written in mg.*

250. The following lines are canceled with a diagonal stroke before v. 250:

> Hybla, [Almo *written above* ~~Theon~~], Cneorus, apum studiosa puella,
> ~~arm~~ venatus [Amo (*sc.* Almo) *written above* ~~iaculique~~], [curvi *written*
>   *above* ~~Theon~~] Cneorus aratri,
> iidem consueti [sylvas et littora *written above* ~~assiduo nemora omnia~~]
>   cantu

~~et parili mulcere sono~~ *[assiduo written above* ~~atque sono~~*]* mulcere
    *[*sonumque adiungere Musis *written above* ~~alta sub rupe sedentes~~*]*

Hybla <u>~~word~~</u> cicuta, ~~Almo~~ crotalo, Gneorus avena. *[in mg. next to*
    previous line; Almo is probably deleted by mistake, as it is necessary to
    meter and context]

forte simul sola pueri sub rupe sedentes *[written above the following line]*
apricum ad solem in littoribus Benaci

~~una omnes conco-~~ *[*~~concordes eadem~~ *written above* ~~In numerum~~*]*
    ~~cantant eadem non~~ vocibus iisdem

Hybla gravi, *[ast Almo written above* ~~Theon ast~~*]* media, Gneorus
    acuta

cantant; Melsineae responsant omnia sylvae.

260. sedentes] *corrected from* sedebant

262. *The following lines are canceled with a diagonal stroke after v. 262:*

    [<u>WORD</u> *written above* ~~assiduo~~*]* mulcere, *[*eadem non vocibus iisdem
        written above ~~sonumque adiungere docti Musis~~*]*,
    una omnes eadem cantant non vocibus iisdem:
    Almo gravi, Leuce media, Gneorus acuta

Below these lines (bottom of f. 174r), there is a sketch of the profile of an old
man.

263–72. *Written in mg. beside vv. 258–62 as a variant to them.*

The following lines are deleted before v. 263 (variant to vv. 258–61):

    Forte simul sola pueri sub rupe sedebant
    Apricum ad . . .

271. *The line* Haec pueri Gneorus et Almo, illa ultima Leuce *is written in*
the left mg. beside v. 271 (as variant to it)

273–77. *These lines appear to be crossed out by one or perhaps two extremely*
faint lines, whose nature and function are unclear. In the present transcription,
these verses are maintained in the text, except for the line after v. 276 (see below
ad loc.).

275. cava littora *written in mg.*

276. ~~alta sub rupe canebant~~ *after* mulcere   in littoribus Benaci]
written in mg.

277. *The line* apricum ad solem in littoribus Benaci *is perhaps deleted (and
in any case should have been) after v. 276; v. 277 is written in mg. next to the
deleted line, as a correction to it, and appears as following:*

~~aëria sub rupe~~.

~~aëria~~ apricum ad solem [aëria *written above* solem sub] sub rupe
     canebant.

288. ~~magna~~ *after* dum

289. ~~agricolae facimus~~ *after* semideo

299. *The following lines are canceled after v. 299:*

nunc etiam cui caelum, etiam cui floriferum ver
arridet, cui floret humus, cui parturit arbos,
dum decorat Gybberte sacro . . . [*written above the following line*]
cui nitidum [gelidum *written above* nitidum arridet] arridet caelum,
     cui floriferum ver

300. ~~suave viret~~ *before* cui

306. *The following thirteen lines are canceled with a diagonal stroke after
v. 306:*

flumina Benaci residentes propter amoeni,
Hybla colo, ~~Leu-~~ iaculis Almo, Cneorus hybisco
depositis, numeros partiti et verba vicissim,
addiderantque sonum raucae Cneorus avenae,
Minciados Almo cannae, thestudinis Hybla.
Carmina Melsineae responsant . . .
Haec Cneorus, at illa Almo canit, Hypla [*sc.* Hybla] suprema.
     [*written in mg. next to the previous two lines*]
Cneorus puer haec, Almo illa, Hybla ultima cantat. [*in mg. next to the
     previous two lines*]
addiderantque sonum gracilis Cneorus avenae,

Minciados Almo cannae testhudinis Hybla
Hybla colo, iaculis Almo, Cneorus hibisco
depositis, primi pueri, postrema puella
cantant Melsineae . . .

307–8. *The following lines are written in mg. beside v. 307–8 (perhaps as a variant and continuation of them):*

nam multum quamvis agitetur ubique *[probably meant to be inserted after* haec ego *of v. 307]*
ludorumque ioci, tamen p<u>ost</u> carmina <u>WORD</u> *[iocique should be read metri causa]*
c<u>onsedi</u> et numeros possem ut meminisse notavi.
Haec pueri Gneorus et Almo, illa Hybla canebat

Below these lines (bottom of f. 175r), there is a sketch of the face of a man with a hat.

310. ~~venatus~~ *after* Hyblaque

324. ~~postridie curabis oves: aut si magis horti~~ *after v. 324*

325. ~~Tunc~~ *before* Nunc

331–54. *A series of letters is marked in mg., corresponding to the initial line of each character's speech in this section:* a *at v. 331,* d *at v. 335,* e *at v. 339,* b *at v. 343,* c *at v. 347,* f *at v. 351. This would seem to indicate the following variant arrangement in the lines of this section: (a) vv. 331–34, (b) vv. 343–46, (c) vv. 347–50, (d) vv. 335–38, (e) vv. 339–42, (f) vv. 351–54. The didascaliae appear to have been inserted on the basis of this rearrangement, which in fact should avoid the repeated sequence of two speeches attributed to the same character (Alcon at 331 and 335, Gneorus at vv. 339 and 343, and Hybla at vv. 347 and 351).*

332. adventu] aventu *aut.*

339. Gn.] *wrongly placed at v. 337*

348. ~~iussit~~ *after* lacum

356. vates] vatat *aut.*

362. hortos] ortos *aut.*

368. sancto] *written above* ~~magno~~

372. sub] *written above* ~~cui~~

373. cui] *written above* ~~de~~

LII. Fragmentum de theriaca

Attested in *aut.* f. 190r, within a draft of a prose letter to Pietro Sonzio da Corfù (cf. Peruzzi 1996, 202).

5. *The line* Non illa custode malo sint noxia succo *is written in mg. beside v. 5, as a variant to it*

7. ~~quis~~ *after* seu   quis] *written above* ~~quisquam~~, *thus introducing the unclassical spelling* quīs

LIII. Fragmentum carminis de theriaca

Attested in *aut.* f. 191r, after draft of prose letter to an anonymous addressee (cf. Peruzzi 1996, 202). The poem was also attached in an appendix to a letter to Giovanni Battista Ramusio, dated January 22, 1533 (probably 1534, according to the Venetian calendar) and was first published in in Venice by Giordano Ziletti in1556, within an anthology of letters by famous men: the text in this letter is the same as the one given in *aut.* and printed here, except for the few variant readings noted below.

1. nobis] *written above* ~~Caesar~~   nobis *after* otia   qui das nobis] nobis qui das *1556, and cf.* C. 52.1

2. *Written in mg. between v. 1 and 3*

4. Theriacen] Theriacam 1556

6–23. *Written in mg., beginning beside the following six lines that are canceled with a diagonal stroke, after v. 5:*

> Nulla timens, non si quis nigra pavera *[sc.* papavera*]* succo
> expresso ~~ebiberit~~ gelidamve exhauserit ore cicutam;
> tutus hyoscyamum *[*haurire *written above* potare*]* aconitaque nigra
> et medem tapsumque potes. tibi cantaris urens

sanguineum missura, malo non vipera dente,
nec sitiens dipsas, nec, fraus metuenda, cerastes

6. letale . . . custode] custode . . . letale *1556*

8. hauseris *(contra metrum)*] *written above* ~~ebiberis, non~~, *but* ebiberis non
1556

11. missura] misura *aut.*

13. ~~cauda~~ *after* in cassum   e saxo cauda insidietur adunca] *written
above* consurgat Scorpius unca, *which was mistakenly not deleted*

14. *Written in mg. beside v. 13, as a continuation of its variant.*   *The fol-
lowing lines (cf. vv. 15–17) are canceled after v. 13:*

in cassum imprevisa aspis, nihil improba quamquam
in propriis ostensa pthyas furibunda latebris
officiat . . .

18. pastum in sicco] *written above* ~~WORD WORD~~

21. Iam neque] *written above* ~~Non~~ ego [ego *mistakenly not deleted*]; *the line is
ametric unless the quantity of* bicipitem *is understood as* bĭcipitem

22. agris] arvis *1556*

24–26. *Written in the space left blank below the deleted lines following v. 5 (see
the note above on v. 6–23), as space was lacking in mg. below v. 23. These lines
are omitted in 1556.*

26. malefida *written above* deserta, *which was mistakenly non de-
leted*   colubrum deserta *and* ~~regna~~ *are written above* qui ~~inhospita arva~~
(qui *should have been deleted as well*)

LIV. Aliud fragmentum
Attested in *aut.*, f. 1r, within botanic notes (cf. Peruzzi 1996, 197).

2. suam] sua *aut.*

6. non aliis, qui nec sibi vivit] *written below* ~~non aliis, qui nec sibi vi-
vens~~   nec generis, qui nec memor aequi *written in mg. as an additional
variant*

LV. Initium Syphilidis a vulgato diversum

Attested in *aut.*, f. 143v (vv. 1–35) and f. 144r (vv. 36–41). For the date of composition of this fragment and its relation to the published version of the *Syphilis*, see Note on the Text, p. 354.

1. *Cf.* S. 1.1

3. ~~haud~~ *after* quando   haud contemnit] *written above* ~~aspernatur~~   *For* Bembe, deus *cf.* S. 1.15 *and also 1525 draft n. 7*   *For* quando medica haud contemnit Apollo *cf.* S. 1.20

5–6. *The following lines are written after v. 4, but Fracastoro probably intended to delete them, since they are corrected by the following vv. 5–6 (cf. S. 1.12 and 14):*

> ~~nunc ego~~ dum vacat, et magno correptus amore
> Musarum feror . . .

5. dulci (*cf.* S. 1.12 *and 1525 draft n. 6*)] *written above* ~~mirum~~, *Bembo had suggested* miro captus novitatis amore   ~~accensus~~] *read by Volpi in 1739*

6. quae fata novum, quae semina morbum] *cf.* S. 1.1

7. attulerint nostra qui tempestate (*cf.* S. 1.3, *partly in accord with Bembo's suggestion*)] intulerint nostra qui primum aetate *1525 draft n. 1 and 6*

8. *Cf.* S. 1.4–5

9. *Cf.* S. 1.6 *and 1525 draft n. 2*

10. hinc canere *cf.* S. 1.10 *and also 1525 draft n. 4*   et longe secretas quaerere causas (*cf.* S. 1.10)] et eorum primordia quaerere prima *1525 draft n. 4*

11. *Exactly reproduces* S. 1.11 *and also 1525 draft n. 5*

12. nec non et opis quid comperit usus] *written above* ~~et veterum non ulli cognita pandam~~. *The line* nec et quae cura et opis quid comperit usus (*contra metrum*) *is written after v. 12 but should have been deleted too. Cf.* S. 1.12 *and* 7

13. *Exactly reproduces* S. 1.8

14. nullique parentum] *in mg. as correction to* ~~et data munera caeli~~; *before deletion v. 14 exactly reproduced* S. 1.9 *and cf. also 1525 draft n. 3*

15. *Written in mg. beside the following canceled lines, after v. 14 (cf.* S.
3.11–12*):*

> persequar, alteriusque canam miracula mundi,
> maiorumque prius non ulli cognita pandam.
> et nulli maiorum cognita pandam *written above* alteriusque . . . mundi
> > *in the first of the two deleted lines.*

16. ~~quae rerum causas, quae sydera noscis~~ *after* mihi   quae series
causarum et fata ministras *written in mg. in correction of the deleted part. Be-
fore deletion v. 16 exactly reproduced* S. 1.24 *and cf also* 1525 *draft n.* 9

17. ~~et caeli effectus varios~~ *before* et caelo   *Cf.* S. 1.25 *for text before
deletion*

18. -que ~~WORD WORD WORD~~ *after* quae (-que *should have been deleted
too)*   tenues] *read by* 1739

19. *Cf.* C. 16.5

20. *Cf.* C. 16.4

20–21. *The following lines are written in mg. beside vv.* 20–21, *as a variant to
them:*

> quadrupedumque, hominumque genus, pecudumque natantum
> altricem cuncti generis matremque salutant.

21. ~~tam~~ *before* eductricem

22. *Cf.* S. 1.29

23. tenues] *read by* 1739   aurae *is missing in aut. but it is restored by* 1739
following S. 1.30   Sophiae dum floridus hortus *written in mg. as vari-
ant to* dum myrtea sylva canentem. *Cf.* S. 1.30

24. invitat] *restored in* 1739 *from an almost illegible word, probably following* S.
1.14. *Cf.* S. 1.31

25–41. *These lines reproduce exactly* S. 1.80–96, *except for few variants noted
below*

25. quaeque] *written above* ~~atque~~

26. in ortum] in auras *in* S. 1.81

28. consurgit origo] primordia constant *in* S. 1.83

35. *vv. 30–34* (= S. *1.85–89*) *are repeated again (apparently with no variants) after v. 35, then deleted*

39. saecula longa] tempore longo *in* S. *1.94*

LVI. In funere Matthaei Giberti

This poem is attested, in identical form, in two sixteenth-century manuscripts, Venice, Biblioteca Nazionale Marciana, Marc. Lat. XII 122 (coll. 4173), f. 17v, and Vatican Library, Vat. Lat. 5171, f. 16v. In both manuscripts it is entitled *In funere Matthaei Giberti*. In ms. Vat. Lat. 5171 it is explicitly attributed to Fracastoro (*Hier.mi Fracast.* before the title) and it is placed within an anthology containing several other poems by Fracastoro (*C.* 12, 45, 56, 8, 11, 9, 25, 5). In ms. Marc. Lat. XII 122 it is inserted between two poems by Fracastoro (*C.* 45 and 24), the first of which is explicitly attributed to him, as well as the last one (*eiusdem*); later in the manuscript we also find *C.* 23. For further discussion on Fracastoro's authorship of this poem, see the Notes to the Translation, pp. 502–3.

Title. In funere Matthaei Giberti *Marc. Lat. XII 122*] Hier.mi Fracast. In funere Matthaei Giberti pontificis Veronensis *Vat. lat. 5171*

LVII. [Untitled]

This poem is preserved in a manuscript in Parma, Biblioteca Palatina, Pal. 555, p. 219, on which see the introductory note to *C.* 48. In the manuscript, the series of bucolic poems addressed to Giberti and closed by *C.* 57 (*C.* 26, 27 divided in two parts, 28, 29, 49, 57) is placed under the heading *Hieronymi Fracastorii, ut puto*, and it is followed by two blank pages. For further discussion of Fracastoro's authorship of this poem, see the Notes to the Translation, p. 503.

Notes to the Translation

❧❧❧

ABBREVIATIONS

C.	Carmina
DBI	*Dizionario biografico degli Italiani* (Rome, 1960–); also on line at www.treccani.it/biografie, but without page numbers.
J.	Joseph
New Pauly	*Brill's New Pauly: Encyclopedia of the Ancient World and the Classical Tradition*, ed. Hubert Cancik, Helmuth Schneider, and Manfred Landfester et al. (Leiden: Brill, 2006–11). Published in German and English, and in an online edition.
S.	Syphilis
TLL	*Thesaurus linguae latinae*. Published online by K. G. Saur (Munich), 2002–7.

SYPHILIS

Book I

Meter: Dactylic Hexameter

1. Cf. Lucretius, *De rerum natura* 2.1072.

4. This line is modeled on Vergil, *Aeneid* 4.173: *extemplo Libyae magnas it Fama per urbes*.

5. Latium, in the poetry of Fracastoro, usually refers to Italy as a whole, instead of, more properly, the region surrounding the city of Rome.

6. The so-called Italian Wars began in 1494, when Charles VIII of France invaded Italy and pressed the Angevin claim to the Kingdom of Naples. The wars lasted until 1559.

10. Cf. Vergil, *Georgics* 1.1–5.

11. Cf. Statius, *Thebaid* 1.294 and Lucretius, *De rerum natura* 2.146.

15. Ausonia, in Vergil, is the name for the Italian peninsula. Pietro Bembo (1470–1542) was a Venetian humanist and one of the leading Italian intellectuals of the first half of the sixteenth century. A distinguished poet in Latin and Italian, he undertook to purify the literary style of his contemporaries by advocating general adoption of the Tuscan dialect and of Petrarch as a literary model. In addition to writing a history of Venice in Latin (published in this I Tatti Library), he was a cardinal and served several popes as a diplomat and Latin secretary. One of these was Pope Leo X, born Giovanni di Lorenzo de' Medici, who was the second son of Lorenzo the Magnificent and served as pope from 1513 to 1521.

20. Among his other titles, Apollo was the god of medicine and healing.

22. The adjective *tenuis*, a key term in Vergil's poetics, is used to describe his "minor" productions (cf. *Georgics* 4.6–7, *Eclogues* 1.2 and 6.8). Fracastoro repeatedly uses it in the same sense to stress his Vergilian legacy: cf. S. 2.65, C. 27.9, and also S. 1.275 and C. 51.217 and 228; see also Fracastoro's draft of a letter to Bembo (Pellegrini 1955, 26 and 30): *Scripsi igitur ea de re* [i.e. *de morbo gallico*] *formula quadam et typo, ut dicunt, tenui*, "Therefore I wrote about the French disease in the humble genre and style, as they call it."

23. Urania was the muse of astronomy: she is the one invoked in this poem because, as Fracasotoro argues, astral influences were the first cause of the outbreak of syphilis.

27. Cf. Lucretius, *De rerum natura* 5.448.

30. Cf. Ovid, *Metamorphoses* 11.234.

31. Cf. Claudian, *Carmina* 24.310. Benacus is the ancient name of the Lago di Garda in northern Italy, as well as of the deity associated with the lake. The lake and the deity figure prominently in the poetry of Fracastoro, whose home in Incaffi overlooked the lake.

35. Cf. the image of the Argonauts in Catullus, *Carmina* 64.4–7. The reference is to Columbus and his crew.

49–50. Cf. Ovid, *Ars amatoria* 1.349–50.

51. This line is modeled on Statius, *Thebaid* 5.564–65: *dat sonitum tellus, / nemorumque per avia densi / dissultant nexus*.

61–64. The Sagra is a small river in Calabria, the modern Alaro. For Ausonia see the note on *S.* 1.15, while Iapygia was the ancient name for Apulia and Calabria. By the Eridanus, Fracastoro means the Po River in northern Italy.

70. Cf. Vergil, *Georgics* 1.50: *ac prius ignotum ferro quam scindimus aequor*.

71–72. The Pyrenees, the Rhine River, the Alps, and the sea are the natural boundaries of France.

72. Cf. Vergil, *Aeneid* 8.727.

73. By the bear is meant Ursa Minor, which contains Polaris, the North Star, and so is representative of the North generally.

74. Cf. Vergil, *Georgics* 3.245 and 531.

76. Edom, or Idumea, was the region to the south of Judea and the Dead Sea.

90. The phrase *genitalia semina* comes from Lucretius, *De rerum natura* 5.851 and Vergil, *Georgics* 2.324.

102. Cf. Vergil, *Aeneid* 5.543

106. The phrase *longaeva vetustas* comes from Martial, *Epigrammata* 6.3.

107. Cf. Ovid, *Tristia* 4.2.25.

108. Cf. Silius Italicus, *Punica* 4.399 and Vergil *Aeneid* 2.58.

112. Cf. Lucretius, *De rerum natura* 5.677: *sic fuerunt causarum exordia prima*.

117. Cf. Ovid, *Metamorphoses* 2.95–97.

126. Cf. Ovid, *Fasti* 2.399.

127. Cf. Tibullus, *Elegiae* 1.7.41.

133. Cf. Lucretius, *De rerum natura* 1.6–9 and Vergil, *Georgics* 1.469.

135. Cf. Vergil, *Aeneid* 3.213.

141. The Sun is in the constellation Cancer from July 21 to August 9, a period coinciding with the dog days of summer.

142. Cf. ps.-Vergil, *Dirae* 16: *pallida flavescant aestu sitientia prata*.

160. Cf. Horace, *Odes* 3.29.33–41.

162. The line-ending *impete magno* is from Lucretius, *De rerum natura* 6.153.

169. Cf. Vergil, *Georgics* 1.493.

170. Cf. Vergil, *Aeneid* 2.257.

172. The phrase *quis credere possit* is Ovidian: cf. *Ars* 1.79, *Heroides* 18.123, *Metamorphoses* 7.690 and 15.613, *Tristia* 1.2.81.

176. Cf. Statius, *Thebaid* 4.141.

179–81. Coeus, Enceladus, and Typhoeus were the offspring of Gaia, goddess of the earth in Ancient Greek mythology. They were respectively a Titan sired by Uranus, a giant sired by the blood of Uranus, and a sea monster sired by Tartarus. Ossa is a mountain in Thessaly which the giants attempted to place atop Mount Pelion in order to scale the heavens in their assault upon the gods of Olympus.

188. The phrase *Aurorae populi* is from Vergil, *Aeneid* 8.686.

189. The Black Death, or bubonic plague. The line-ending *pectore anhelo* is from Statius, *Thebaid* 9.402 and 12.244.

194–95. Canopus was a coastal town in Ancient Egypt, on the outskirts of what is now Alexandria. Its debauchery became proverbial. See, for example, Juvenal, *Satires* 6.80–84 and 15.44–46; for the phrase *mollis Canopus*, cf. Lucan, *Pharsalia* 8.543, *mollis turba Canopi*. Phrygia was a kingdom in Anatolia, in modern-day Turkey.

195. Cf. Statius, *Silvae* 3.5.79.

204–5. The fatal conjunction of the planets Mars and Saturn occurred under the constellation of Cancer, i.e., in the hottest days of summer (between June and July); see also *S.* 1.225–26.

210–11. The Siren is Parthenope, the mythic founder of Naples. The poet in question is Giovanni Gioviano Pontano (1426–1503), the preeminent Neapolitan humanist of the last quarter of the fifteenth century. Leader of the Academia Pontaniana, he is invoked here for his long astronomical poem *Urania*, in this context considered a prophetic work.

The phrase *senior vates* comes from Statius, *Thebaid* 4.443, applied there to Tiresias.

221. Cf. Vergil, *Aeneid* 2.251.

228. For the phrase *ferroque coruscans*, see Silius Italicus, *Punica* 1.434.

229. Mighty in war: *Bellipotens* is one of Statius' favorite epithets for Mars (cf., *inter alia*, *Achilleid* 1.443; *Silvae* 1.4.34 and 5.2.179; *Thebaid* 2.716, 3.292, etc.). For *Bellipotens* with *Mavors*, see the *Ilias latina* 532.

234. The epithet *falcifer* comes from Ovid, *Fasti* 1.234. According to classical mythology, the god Saturn was overthrown and pushed into exile by his son Jupiter.

236. The phrase *vestigia torsit* is Vergilian; cf. *Aeneid* 3.669 and 6.547.

254. For the line-ending *aethere ab alto*, see Vergil, *Aeneid* 7.25.

265. This half-line is Vergilian; cf. *Aeneid* 2.306 and *Georgics* 1.325 (*sata laeta boumque labores*).

273. This line is modeled on the ps.-Vergilian *Culex* 45–46: *propulit e stabulis ad pabula laeta capellas / pastor*.

275. Cf. Vergil, *Eclogues* 1.2.

283. Cf. Ovid, *Metamorphoses* 1.81.

286. See the note on *S.* 1.189.

296. In speaking of the seeds of the affliction of celestial origin, Fracastoro is looking back to Lucretius, *De rerum natura* 2.114–16 and Vergil, *Aeneid* 6.730–33.

298. For the phrase *turba natantum*, see Ausonius, *Mosella* 141 and 250.

307. This line looks back to the beginning of Vergil's description of the illnesses which afflict cattle in the *Georgics* 3.440: *Morborum quoque te causas et signa docebo*.

310. Cf. Vergil, *Eclogues* 3.61: *illi mea carmina curae*.

316. Cf. Ovid, *Epistolae ex Ponto* 3.3.81.

331. As Eatough (1984, ad loc.) rightly points out, *inguen* here may indicate the male genital organs and *locos* the female ones (for such a meaning of *locus* cf. *TLL* s.v. 1578, 44ff.).

360. In classical mythology Phyllis was the daughter of a Thracian king and married Demophon, son of Theseus; afterward, deserted by her husband, she hanged herself and was changed into an almond tree.

367. For the phrase *turgentia ora*, see Ovid, *Fasti* 3.757.

368. This line is modeled on Vergil, *Eclogues* 5.23: *atque deos atque astra vocat crudelia mater.*

369–70. Cf. Vergil, *Aeneid* 8.26–27: *terras animalia fessa per omnis / alituum pecudumque genus sopor altus habebat.*

374. People affected by syphilis could consume no food (here indicated by Ceres, the goddess of harvest and crops) or beverage (indicated by Bacchus, the god of wine). Cf. Valerius Flaccus, *Argonautica* 8.162–63: *quod nullae te, nata, dapes, non ulla iuvabant / tempora.*

377. Tempe was a valley in Thessaly praised in classical literature for its extreme beauty.

376. Cf. Lucretius, *De rerum natura* 3.1081.

382. The Cenomani were a tribe of the Gallic Aulerci who, in the fourth century BCE, migrated from the Maine to the region bordered by the rivers Oglio, Po, and Adige in the north of Italy and settled in the sites of the future cities of Verona, Brescia, and Cremona. The Oglio (Ollius) flows into Lago d'Iseo (Lacus Sebinus). For *ipse ego . . . memini*, see Ovid, *Metamorphoses* 15.160.

384. The young man in question is never identified. According to Eatough (1984, *ad* vv. 409–11), however, Fracastoro may perhaps be alluding to Giovanni Cotta, who died around the age of thirty. Cotta was a close friend of Fracastoro's, and his premature death is lamented along with that of Marcantonio della Torre (cf. *S.* 1.455–64; see also *C.* 2.45–50). But the identification is otherwise uncertain, as there is no evidence that Cotta ever suffered from syphilis. He allegedly died suddenly of a fever in 1510 (see the article of Roberto Ricciardi in *DBI* 30 [1984]). Fracastoro had another friend, however, who did suffer from syphilis in the early 1520s (though he did not die from it), the poet Marcantonio Flaminio (1497–1550). Flaminio wrote an affecting elegy on his own sickness (*De se*

aegrotante), the fifth poem in the second book of his *Carmina* (1739, vol. 2, 168).

386. Cf. Ovid, *Fasti* 5.525.

389. For *pictis splendescere in armis,* see Vergil, *Aeneid* 8.588 (*pictis conspectus in armis*) and Silius Italicus, *Punica* 8.465 (*pictis radiabat in armis*).

394. The phrase *optatos . . . hymenaeos* is taken from Catullus, *Carmina* 64.141.

402. Parenthetical *horrendum* without a complement is characteristic of Silius Italicus (cf. *Punica* 2.584, 10.122, and 11.231).

406. Cf. Vergil, *Aeneid* 6.497.

410–11. See the note on *S.* 1.392–93.

413. This line is modeled on Vergil, *Georgics* 2.538: *aureus hanc vitam in terris Saturnus agebat.*

418–20. Tartarus was a region of the underworld through which flowed the river Styx.

420. Fracastoro models the structure of this line on Vergil, *Georgics* 4.442: *ignemque horribilemque feram fluviumque liquentem.*

421. Cf. Vergil, *Aeneid* 9.247: *di patrii, quorum semper sub numine Troia est.*

422. According to Roman mythology (cf. Vergil, *Aeneid* 8.319–27), Saturn found a hiding place in Italy during his wanderings, after having been overmastered by Jupiter.

425–27. The death of the king of Naples, Ferrante I, in 1494 provided Charles VIII of France (1470–98) with the occasion to invade Italy.

428–32. This passage refers to the battle of Fornovo, which occurred 20 miles southwest of Parma on July 6, 1495. In it Charles VIII of France defended himself against an Italian attack on his retreat from Italy, with considerable carnage on both sides. The Taro is a tributary of the Po (or, in Latin, the Eridanus).

433–36. These lines refer to the battle of Agnadello (May 14, 1509), in which the Venetians were defeated by the League of Cambrai, again with great bloodshed. The battle was fought along the river Adda, another tributary of the Po.

443. The Erethenus, or Retrone, is a river that flows near Vicenza, another city that saw episodes of extreme brutality during the war against the League of Cambrai.

444. The Retrone is a tributary of the Bacchiglione, which flows by the Euganean Hills, the hills rising a few miles south of Padua where Petrarch spent his final years.

445–46. Cf. Statius, *Thebaid* 11.391: *io patria, o regum incertissima tellus.* With *o patria* here Fracastoro is addressing his hometown of Verona.

448. The Adige is the river that flows through Verona. For Benacus see the note on *S.* 131.

450. Cf. Statius, *Thebaid* 7.452.

452. Cf. Prudentius, *Psychomachia* 91.

456–63. Pallas is an epithet of Minerva, or Athena, the goddess of wisdom and the arts. Marcantonio della Torre, or dalla Torre (1481–1511/12, see *DBI* 32 [1986] s.v.) was a student of anatomy, a friend of Fracastoro, well known as a collaborator of Leonardo da Vinci. On della Torre's early death from the plague, the poet addressed a long poem (C. 2) to the young man's brother Giovanni Battista, who was also a friend of Fracastoro. The Sarca, which Fracastoro mentions frequently, is a river that flows into the Lago di Garda; Pietro Bembo composed a long hexameter poem on it, published in this I Tatti Library: Pietro Bembo, *Lyric Poetry*, tr. Mary P. Chatfield (Cambridge, MA, 2005; reprinted with corrections 2012). Verona was the birthplace of the Roman poet Catullus.

462. For the line-ending *voce vocare*, cf. Lucretius, *De rerum natura* 4. 711.

464. Cf. Statius, *Thebaid* 3.448.

465–66. The French King is Louis XII (1462–1515), who stormed northern Italy at the head of the League of Cambrai between 1508 and 1511 after having severely suppressed a rebellion in Genoa in 1507.

467–68. "Caesar" is here the Holy Roman Emperor Maximilian I (1459–1519), who also joined the League of Cambrai and came to invade the Venetian territories. For the Euganean Hills see the note on *S.* 1.444.

The Sile is a river that flows through Treviso into the lagoon of Venice. The Carni were an ancient Celtic tribe that inhabited east Tyrol, Carinthia, and Friuli: this territory had been conquered by the Venetians in 1508 but shortly after was lost to the League of Cambrai.

BOOK II

1. The opening of this book, in which Fracastoro explains the nature of, and cures for, the disease, is modeled on a very common Lucretian formula: cf., *inter alia*, *De rerum natura* 2.62–66, 6.495–97, 6.738–39.

11. Cf. Lucretius, *De rerum natura* 2.180 and 5.198.

14. In Latin mythology the Camenae were goddesses of poetry, later identified with the Muses.

15. Cf. Lucan, *Pharsalia* 8.366.

17. This line is modeled on Vergil, *Aeneid* 4.21: *sparsos fraterna caede penates*. The *Penates* were the tutelary gods of the Roman household.

26. Amphitrite, a sea goddess, was the wife of Poseidon and the daughter, by some accounts, of Oceanus.

27–30. Fracastoro describes here the outermost limits of the known world, according to ancient geographic lore. The Atlas Mountains stretch across much of northern Africa and, like the garden of the Hesperides (the daughters of the Titan Atlas), these mountains represented the westernmost point known to ancient geographers, just as the promontory of Prasum and of Rhaptum, in southeastern Africa (cf. Ptolemy, *Geography* 4.8), represented the southernmost point. For Arctos see the note on *S.* 1.73. Prasum was located in the southern hemisphere. Carmania (Kerman) was a Persian city and region located between the Persis mountain and the deserts of modern Baluchistan; along with Arabia, it represents the easternmost point known to ancient geographers.

31–36. Early modern explorers sought—and believed they had reached—the Far East, the mythical abode of the goddess Aurora (the Dawn), daughter of the Titan Hyperion. In fact, by 1522, when Fracastoro was still drafting the *Syphilis*, Magellan's fleet had just circumnavigated the world for the first time (the first account of his voyage was published in 1523). Catygara, or Cattigara, was already mentioned by Ptolemy as a seaport in South-east Asia, and is probably to be identified with modern Hanoi or possibly Canton (cf. *New Pauly* s.v.). Cyambe, or Champa, was a kingdom in what is now Cambodia and Vietnam that flourished in the Middle Ages.

38–42. Fracastoro reiterates his homage to the poet Giovanni Pontano: see on *S.* 1.210–11. Sebethus is a small river near Naples, often recalled in Pontano's poetry. Vergil lived for a time in Naples (cf. *Georgics* 4.563–66), and it was there that his ashes were buried (cf. Donatus, *Vita Vergilii* 36). At vv. 41–42 Fracastoro alludes to several of Pontano's works: *Urania, Meteorum liber,* and *De hortis Hesperidum.*

45–47. For Bembo and Pope Leo X see the note on *S.* 1.15.

50–51. Cf. Ovid, *Fasti* 5.545–46. The opposing stars are Saturn and Mars, according to the theory Fracastoro expressed in Book 1.

53–57. As Eatough points out (1984, ad loc.), the phrasing by which pope Leo X is addressed recalls Vergil's mention of Fabius Maximus Cunctator, the Roman general famous for his delaying tactics in the Second Punic War—tactics that, in the end, proved victorious (cf. *Aeneid* 6.845–46 *tu Maximus ille es, / unus qui nobis cunctando restituis rem*). Leo X, as well, sought to avoid warfare, stressing instead his activity as diplomat and patron of the arts.

58–60. These lines list the boundaries of the Ottoman Empire, against which Pope Leo X had planned a crusade that was never realized. The Euxine is the ancient Greek name for the Black Sea. In classical mythology Doris was a sea goddess, daughter of Oceanus and Thetis, and wife of Nereus; here *Aegea Doris* is a metonymy for the Aegean Sea.

61–65. Fracastoro closes his proemion to Book 2 with a *recusatio,* in which he humbly leaves a recital of Pope Leo X's deeds—a daunting task—to greater poets, like his friend Bembo (v. 62 *et tu*), while for himself he invokes only the Vergilian *tenuis Musa* (see the note on *S.* 1.22).

80. Cf. Ovid, *Metamorphoses* 9.778: *memorique animo tua iussa notavi.*

86. Zephyrus was the mild West Wind, carrier of Spring; Aquilo, the Roman equivalent of the Greek Boreas, was a cold wind blowing from the North.

92. This line is modeled on a simile in Silius Italicus describing a boar hunt; see *Punica* 10.80: *lustrat inaccessos venantum indagine saltus*.

130–31. Fracastoro is alluding to the legend that, when the Gauls invaded Rome in 390, they tried to seize the Capitol, but were repelled by the garrison that was stationed there and that had been awakened just in time by the cackling of geese sacred to Juno, whose temple stood on the hill.

137. For the aphrodisiac properties attributed to certain onions, see Pliny's *Natural History* 20.105. The phrase *bulbi salaces* comes from Martial, *Epigrammata* 3.75.3–4: *sed nihil erucae faciunt bulbique salaces / improba nec prosunt iam satureia tibi*.

139–42. Line 139 is modeled on Valerius Flaccus, *Argonautica* 1.260: *illum nec valido spumantia pocula Baccho*. The adjective *fumosus* refers to the ancient Roman practice of aging wines by exposing them to smoke: cf. e.g., Pliny, *Naturalis historia* 23.40 or Tibullus, *Elegies* 2.1.27–28. Cyrnos was the Greek name for Corsica. In ancient times, the Ager Falernus, at the border of Latium and Campania, was famous for its wines, as were Pucinum (Pizzino) in the Veneto and Rhaetia, a region that comprised eastern Switzerland and western Austria.

143–44. The Sabines were ancient inhabitants of Latium. In Greek mythology the Naiades are nymphs of freshwater streams and lakes.

160. Aonia was the region of Boeotia in ancient Greece that included Mounts Helicon and Cithaeron, both sacred to the Muses.

161–64. In antiquity poets were honored with a laurel chaplet, the plant sacred to their god Apollo. Those who had performed acts of civil or military heroism, by contrast, were awarded a wreath (called *corona civica*) made of oak leaves, sacred to Jupiter.

174–75. Corycus was a city of Cilicia which, like Pamphylia, was a region in modern southern Turkey.

179. Here nymphs indicate water in general, one of the most important elements with which they were associated in classical mythology (and cf. C. 43).

184–86. According to Eatough (1984, ad loc.), this is the sea aster, whose Greek name, *tripolion*, means thrice-changing (cf. Dioscorides, *De materia medica* 4.130).

188. The ancient region of Nabataea comprised southern Jordan, Canaan, and the northern portion of Arabia.

190. *Panacea*, or *panaces*, an herb believed to have miraculous healing properties, was variously identified by ancient botanists, often as opoponax. Colchis is the name of an ancient kingdom located on the east shores of the Black Sea.

209. The name scordion derives from *skorodon*, the Greek word for garlic.

212–22. The *citrus* is probably to be identified with the lemon tree; cf. S. Malaguzzi, *Food and Feasting in Art* (Los Angeles, 2008), 239. In Fracastoro's elaborate reference to the plant is another homage to the Neapolitan poet Giovanni Pontano (see on *S*. 1.210–11 and 2.38–42). In fact, Pontano's poem *De hortis Hesperidum* describes the lemon tree and its cultivation, which was widely practiced in the Neapolitan region (vv. 111–24), as well as on the shores of the Lago di Garda (vv. 208–15). Pontano identified the lemon's yellow fruit with the mythic, life-granting "golden apples" that were produced in the garden of the Hesperides (see on *S*. 2.27–30) and that Hercules first brought to Italy after his eleventh labor (vv. 101–10). Pontano claimed that this miraculous evergreen first arose when Venus transformed the dead body of her beloved Adonis into the tree (vv. 67–101). The figure of Adonis and the ancient cult connected to him had eastern origins, which Pontano associates with Media, the region of the Persian Empire from which, according to ancient sources, the *citrus* or lemon had been imported (cf. e.g., Vergil, *Georgics* 2.126–35). In ancient literature, however, Venus is never associated with the *citrus* tree, and Adonis was transformed into a flower, the wind anemone (cf. Ovid, *Metamorphoses* 10.735–39). Cytherea is an epithet of Venus, who was born, according to one legend, in the waters off the Ionian island of Cythera.

225–26. Mount Dikte (from which the name "dittany" is derived) and Mount Ida are on the island of Crete.

241. For Corycus, see on 2.174–75.

269. "Chironian wounds" are incurable or extremely painful (cf. *TLL* s.v. *Chironius* 410, 11–22), like the one suffered by the centaur Chiron when Hercules shot a poisoned arrow into his leg.

281–90. Fracastoro's digression, introduced here, relates the origin of the medical use of quicksilver. He was inspired by the *aition* — a story that relates a cause — on the discovery of the "bougonia" (the spontaneous generation of bees from a cow's carcass) by the beekeeper Aristaeus, in Book 4 of Vergil's *Georgics*. As Eatough points out (1984, Introduction, 22), the name Ilceus may derive from the word *ile* ("groin") or the Greek term for "sore" (*helkos*), while the Syrian origins of Ilceus and his descent into the underworld assimilate him to the figure of Adonis (see *S.* 2.212–22). In ancient literature, the name Callirrhoe, meaning "beautiful stream," is attributed to various water nymphs and springs, some of which were located in ancient Syria and its surrounding regions (cf. Pliny, *Naturalis historia* 5.73 and 86).

287. Cf. Vergil, *Georgics* 1.14.

291. Compare Turnus's prayer to Faunus in *Aeneid* 12.777–79 and Ovid, *Metamorphosis* 8.350.

293. Cf. Vergil, *Eclogues* 7.30: *ramosa . . . vivacis cornua cervi.*

300. This line is modeled on Ovid, *Tristia* 5.3.3: *festaque odoratis innectunt tempora sertis.*

313. Trivia, "goddess of crossroads," is an epithet of Hecate, often identified with Diana.

316. Cf. Vergil, *Aeneid* 6.684.

319. Latonian refers to Apollo since he, like Diana, was the child of Leto.

329. Ops was an ancient Roman goddess of fertility.

336. The line beginning *Surge age* is Vergilian (cf. *Aeneid* 3.169, 8.59, and 10.241).

344. Cf. Vergil, *Georgics* 4.552.

351–54. Cf. Vergil *Georgics* 4.348–51.

361. The *Lipare* Fracastoro refers to is better known as *Lipara*, one of the seven daughters of Atlas by Hesperis (Evening) and a sister of the three Hesperides. Her name in Greek means "Perseverance"; see Hyginus, *Astronomica* 2.3. Lipari is also the name of a volcanic island, the largest in the Aeolian Archipelago northeast of Sicily. It is mentioned in connection with the Cyclopses by Vergil at *Aeneid* 8.417. *Lipara* is also the Latin word for a poultice.

364. Cf. Vergil, *Georgics* 4.386: *omine quo firmans animum sic incipit ipsa*.

371–74. Cf. Vergil, *Georgics* 4.363–75.

377. Proserpina, or Persephone, was the wife of Hades, ruler of the underworld.

399–400. At Etna, a volcano in Sicily, the Cyclopses assisted Vulcan, the smith god of fire, in forging the lightning bolts of Jove. Here Vulcan is a metonymy for fire itself.

410. Cf. Vergil, *Aeneid* 2.719–20.

412–14. Cf. Vergil, *Georgics* 4.384–86.

414. Cf. Silius Italicus, *Punica* 2.266: *et rapto cineres ter circum corpore lustrat*.

421. This line is modeled on Martial, *Epigrammata* 12.9.3: *ergo agimus laeti tanto pro munere grates*.

427. Oricum or Orikos was a city in the north of Epirus (modern southern Albania).

451. Cf. Ovid, *Metamorphoses* 4.765: *postquam epulis functi generosi munere Bacchi*.

452–53. Chios is an island in the Aegean Sea.

Book III

3. The Pillars of Hercules are the two promontories that flank the Straits of Gibraltar. To the ancient geographers, this, the westernmost point of the Mediterranean, was also the limit of the known world.

8. For Urania see the note on *S.* 1.23.

10. For Latium, used to indicate Italy, see the note on *S.* 1.5.

13–29. As in Book 2 (see on *S.* 2.61–65), Fracastoro closes his proemion with a *recusatio*, this time claiming for himself the humble task of discussing a curative tree discovered in the New World, while he leaves to better poets the honor of singing the epic adventures of Columbus and the other early explorers. As it happens, however, Fracastoro's account, in this book, of Columbus's first voyage to America is the earliest known poetic treatment of the subject. Cf. Eatough (1984, ad loc.).

19–20. Fracastoro refers to contemporary explorations by Europeans that had reached the southern hemisphere.

30–33. Hispaniola is the second largest island of the Caribbean, comprising modern day Haiti and the Dominican Republic. Columbus named it "Hispaniola," meaning "Little Spain," but also associated it with the mythical Ophir (see the note on *S.* 3.116–21). The island is located just below the Tropic of Cancer; hence *sub sidere Cancri*, for which see Vergil, *Eclogues* 10.68.

35. Guaiacum, the hardest known wood, came to be called the *Lignum Vitae*, or Tree of Life, because of its supposed medicinal value in combating syphilis, among other maladies.

57. Cf. this line with Vergil, *Aeneid* 7.464: *furit intus aquae vis* (according to one reading of the text); the Vergilian phrase is also found in Macrobius, *Saturnalia* 5.11.23. For Vulcan as metonymy for fire, see the note on *S.* 2.399–400.

68. Lucifer and Vesper are the morning and evening stars, respectively.

69–71. The cure using the guaiacum potion should last about thirty days (see *S.* 3.89), that is, one moon cycle. In the new moon phase, the moon (i.e., the goddess Diana) stands between the Earth and the Sun and so is in its closest position to the Sun (i.e., Diana's brother, Apollo).

77. Cf. Lucretius, *De rerum natura* 4.630.

85. The phrase *vacuas . . . in auras* is Ovidian (cf., inter alia, *Metamorphoses* 6.398 and 12.469).

93–101. Nereus was a Greek maritime deity, father of the sea nymphs, the Nereids. Calpe is the ancient name of the Rock of Gibraltar.

97. The phrase *longis erroribus actae* is Ovidian (cf. *Heroides* 2.106, *Tristia* 4.10.109, *Metamorphoses* 4.657 and 15.771).

102. Fracastoro is rewriting the first line of Horace's fifteenth *Epode: Nox erat et caelo fulgebat luna sereno*.

103. For the phrase *lumina diffundens*, see ps.-Vergil, *Culex* 176.

104. The hero is Columbus.

107. Cf. Vergil, *Georgics* 4.299: *vitulus bima curvans iam cornua fronte*. Almost two months had passed since Columbus left Spain (he set sail on August 3 and reached San Salvador on October 12).

109. The phrase *non ulla apparet tellus* seems to be taken from Vergil, *Aeneid* 3.192–93: *nec iam amplius ulla / apparet tellus*, a phrase also found in Macrobius, *Saturnalia* 5.3.3 and 5.6.1; cf. also Vergil, *Aeneid* 5.8–9.

110. For the line-ending *tangere portus*, see Vergil, *Aeneid* 4.612.

111. The epithet *noctis honos* for the moon is from Martianus Capella, *De nuptiis* 9.911–14. For *caeli decus*, see Vergil, *Aeneid* 9.18 and, in reference to the moon, Horace, *Carmen saeculare* 2 and Seneca, *Phaedra* 410. For *Latonia Virgo*, see Vergil, *Aeneid* 11.557.

112. Cf. Ovid, *Tristia* 3.4a.19. Phoebe, epithet of the moon goddess Diana, is the feminine equivalent of Apollo's attribute *Phoebus* and means "bright" in ancient Greek.

114. The Nereid Cymothoe helps Aeneas at Vergil, *Aeneid* 1.144. Clotho, one of the Fates, is not usually listed among the Nereids; according to Eatough (1984, ad loc.) she may be mentioned here because "Columbus' voyage is a harbinger of fateful events."

116–21. The first land that Columbus encounters is the island of Guanahani, in the Bahamas, which he renamed San Salvador. From there he sailed on until eventually he reached the large island of Hispaniola (see the note on *S*. 3.30–33), which he identified with the mythical Ophir—a wealthy port on the Red Sea. Ophir is mentioned in the Old Testament as the city from which King Solomon received gold and other precious merchandise.

124. The Titan is Helios, the Sun.

130–32. These lines are modeled on Vergil, *Aeneid* 3.205–8. Notus or, in Latin, Auster, is the South Wind.

133–35. The name Anthylia refers to the Antilles islands, in the West Indies; the legend of a floating island among the Antilles may have originated in the sight of cloud banks; cf. Eatough (1984, ad loc.). Since most of the islands Columbus encountered were given holy names, Hagia, from the Greek for "holy," could refer to any of a number of them. Ammerie appears to be an early version of the name "America," which was variously associated, at first, with several islands; cf. Eatough (1984, ad loc.). Gyane is a deformation of the name Guaiana, initially given to the South American shoreline facing the Caribbean sea; cf. Eatough (1984, ad loc.).

136–42. The description of Columbus's landing at Hispaniola is modeled on Vergil's treatment of Aeneas's arrival in Italy in the seventh book of the *Aeneid*. Here in particular Columbus's sighting and landing at the mouth of the Yaque del Norte River (located in the modern Dominican Republic and renamed by Columbus "Rio de Oro") is modeled on Aeneas's sighting and landing at the mouth of the Tiber (cf. Vergil, *Aeneid* 7.29–36).

144–46. The invocation of the Earth, the spirit of the place (*genium loci*), the nymphs, and the rivers is modeled on Aeneas's prayer at Vergil, *Aeneid* 7.135–38. For *aurifer amnis*, see Catullus, *Carmina* 29.17 and the *Corpus Tibullianum* 3.3.29.

146–50. Cf. Vergil, *Georgics* 4.380: *Maeonii carchesia Bacchi*. For the reference to eating bread as one disembarks, cf. Vergil, *Aeneid* 7.107–15; for the initial explorations in the surroundings, cf. Vergil, *Aeneid* 7.148–51.

151–54. The episode of the killing of the Sun's sacred birds by Columbus's men (vv. 151–99) is strikingly modeled on Aeneas's adventure in the Strophades in Vergil, *Aeneid* 3.219–65 (itself a reworking of the slaughtering of the Sun's sacred cows by Odysseus's men in Homer, *Odyssey* 12.260–419). In Vergil, Aeneas's men unwittingly kill Apollo's sacred cows and, as soon as they start feasting upon them, are assailed by Harpies. One of these disgusting creatures, half bird, half woman, explains what their sin was and prophesies that, before reaching their final target, they

435

will be greatly taxed by long wanderings and terrible hunger. In Fracastoro, the Sun's sacred birds are probably to be identified with parrots, a species that was abundant in the New World and that attracted great attention when it was imported to Europe; cf. Eatough (1984, note at v. 151).

156–58. Because they struck from afar and — in the sixteenth century — were accompanied by fire and loud noise, guns recalled the thunderbolts that Vulcan forged for Jupiter. Gunpowder was believed to have been invented in the fourteenth century by Berthold Schwartz of Freiburg in Germany.

170–73. Cf. Vergil, *Aeneid* 3.245–46, and for the line-ending *talibus infit* cf. also 10.860.

174–76. Cf. Vergil, *Aeneid* 3.247–52, and, for the line-ending *cantat Apollo*, cf. also Propertius, *Elegies* 2.1.3. Hesperia was, from the perspective of ancient Greek geography, "the land of the West," hence Italy and other regions in Western Europe: here the traditional name refers to the Italian Columbus and his Spanish crew.

177–79. Cf. Vergil, *Aeneid* 3.254–55. For Ophir see the note on *S.* 3.116–21.

182. Cf. Vergil, *Aeneid* 1.597.

182–89. In the prophecy delivered by the sacred bird, the wars alluded to must be the destruction of La Navidad, the first settlement on Hispaniola, which occurred between Columbus's first and second voyages. Probably, the loss of ships refers to the sinking of the Santa Maria before Columbus returned from the first voyage. The Cyclops, i.e., a primitive one-eyed monster who feeds on human flesh — the most famous being Polyphemus in Homer's *Odyssey* (9.287–98) — is invoked in connection with reports of cannibalism among the natives. The discord to which the bird refers is the mutinous dissent among Columbus's crew. Finally, the bird prophesies the outburst of a syphilis epidemic among Columbus's men and at the same time throughout Europe; cf. Eatough (1984, ad loc.).

193–95. Cf. Vergil, *Aeneid* 3.258–60.

196–99. Cf. Vergil, *Aeneid* 3.261–62.

198. For *supplicibus . . . votis*, see Vergil, *Aeneid* 8.61.

202–3. Cf. Vergil, *Aeneid* 8.116.

204. Cf. Vergil, *Aeneid* 6.490: *videre virum fulgentiaque arma.*

220–23. The native chieftain's attire is composed of elements typical of the New World: cotton, emeralds (abundant in Colombia and, later, Brazil), and large snakes; spears made of sharpened cane were the native's only weapons; cf. Eatough (1984, ad loc.). His holding of the spear is taken from Vergil's description of the young Camilla (*Aeneid* 11.574: *iaculo palmas armavit acuto*).

224–28. Columbus's bronze helmet recalls that of Statius's Hippomedon (*Thebaid* 4.129: *capiti tremit aerea cassis*), as the golden torque on his pale neck recalls the description of Silius's Gallic warrior Crixus (*Punica* 4.154: *colla viri fulvo radiabant lactea torque*). The "Spanish sword" may refer to a rapier.

230–31. Cf. Vergil, *Aeneid* 8.717: *laetitia ludisque viae plausuque fremebant.*

232–33. These lines, which introduce an account of the local festival in which the *aition* of Syphilus is included, echo Vergil, *Aeneid* 8.102–4, in which a religious ceremony in honor of Hercules is under way when Aeneas reaches Evandrus's kingdom. Like Columbus, Aeneas is invited to participate in the ceremony and hears, from the local king, a long account of the ceremony's origin. *Ultor*, "Avenger," is an epithet that in Roman religion was attributed to Mars.

235. For Hesperian, see the note on *S.* 3.174–76.

236–38. Cf. Silius Italicus, *Punica* 6.366: *omnis turba ruit, matres puerique senesque.*

245. In Greco-Roman culture, a paean is a ritual song normally addressed to Apollo. Paeonian is an epithet of Apollo and refers to his capacity of "healer."

251. See Vergil, *Aeneid* 3.265: *di talem avertite casum.*

262. Cf. Ovid, *Metamorphoses* 2.404: *terras hominumque labores.*

264. Cf. Lucretius' *De rerum natura* 1.54–55.

265. The myth of Atlantis, the wealthy island located in Ocean beyond the Pillars of Hercules and ultimately swallowed up by the sea, was first elaborated by Plato (cf. *Timaeus* 24e–25d and *Critias* 113b–121c). The eponymous first king of Atlantis was the Titan Atlas (see the note on *S.* 2.27–30). Cf. Ovid, *Epistulae ex Ponto* 2.5.33: *si forte . . . vestras pervenit ad aures.*

268. Cf. Vergil, *Eclogues* 1.74.

278–79. Cf. Vergil, *Aeneid* 11.614–15: *quadrupedantum / pectora.*

288. The origins of the name Syphilis, and of the shepherd Syphilus, have long been debated. Fracastoro invented it (cf. *De contagione* 2.11: *nos Syphilidem in nostris lusibus appellavimus*), but it is based on an earlier word or name. Some have suggested associations with Sypilus, one of Niobe's sons slaughtered by Apollo and Diana, or with the mountain of the same name in West Anatolia where Niobe was turned to stone: Niobe in fact, like Syphilus, incurred Leto's wrath by claiming to surpass the goddess as a mother; Niobe had seven sons and seven daughters, whereas Leto only had Apollo and Diana. Other scholars have suggested *sus-philos*, "lover of swine," or *sumphilos*, "one who makes love." Most likely, the word is a corruption of the dermatological malady known as erysipelas, which shares certain symptoms with syphilis and was often mistaken for it. As for the name of the king Alcithoos (see below at v. 311), this too may be entirely invented, though the closest parallel appears to be Alcithoe, one of the daughters of Minyas (founder of Orchomenos in Boeotia). They refused to take part in a Bacchic rite and were later maddened by the god.

291–92. Cf. Vergil, *Aeneid* 3.141–42, where Aeneas's men fall prey to pestilence while they are on Crete.

294. Cf. Valerius Flaccus, *Argonautica* 1.291: *rapido . . . concitus aestu.*

298. Cf. Vergil, *Aeneid* 5.745.

299–300. For *regia . . . armenta* cf. Vergil, *Aeneid* 7.485–86.

301–2. Cf. Statius, *Achilleid* 1.315: *niveo candore iuvencam.*

302–4. In Latin *Taurus, Aries,* and *Canis* (i.e., Sirius, the Dog Star) are names of constellations as well as of animals.

310–11. Cf. Vergil, *Georgics* 4.548–49: *Haud mora: continuo matris praecepta facessit; / ad delubra venit, monstratas excitat aras.*

332. Cf. Ovid, *Metamorphoses* 14.434.

335. Ammerice, like Ammerie at v. 134 above, seems to be a variant of the name America. The origin and the reference of the term *Carthesidis* are obscure; cf. Eatough (1984, ad loc.).

345. In Graeco-Roman culture oaths pronounced in the name of the gods or elements of the underworld were irrevocable; for the river Styx, see on *S*.1.418–20.

365. This line is modeled on Ovid, *Fasti* 1.321: *calido strictos tincturus sanguine cultros*, and cf. also Vergil, *Georgics* 3.492.

403. Scythia was an ancient kingdom on the Central Asian steppe that extended from the Caucasus to northern India.

414–17. Bactria (modern Balkh in Afghanistan) in ancient times was the capital of a region in the Persian Empire. Meroe was a city in South Egypt. Ammon, in the southeast of Lybia, was famous for its sanctuary and oracle. For the river Adige, see the note on *S*. 1.448. For Lake Benacus, see the note on *S*. 1.31.

418. Cf. Vergil, *Aeneid* 10.833. Bembo was in Rome, serving in the court of Pope Leo X and later of Paul III; see the note on *S*. 1.15.

JOSEPH

Book I

Meter: Dactylic Hexameter

2. Cf. Valerius Flaccus, *Argonautica* 2.550: *longis emissa tenebris*, and also Propertius, *Carmina* 2.26.55.

6. For *nunc o nunc*, see Vergil, *Aeneid* 8.579, imitated by Silius Italicus, *Punica* 3.509 and Statius, *Thebaid* 3.360.

8–10. Abraham was the father of Isaac and the grandfather of Jacob, the father of Joseph.

10. Fracastoro took this half-line from Paulinus of Nola, *Carmina* 6.218: *dederat dominus cui nosse futura.*

11–15. The tone of these verses and especially their suggestion of the hero's triumph through travails closely resemble the opening of Vergil's *Aeneid*.

12. Cf. Vergil, *Georgics* 2.171. Pharos is an island off the harbor of Alexandria, where, at the end of the third century BCE, the famous lighthouse was built.

15. For *limen Olympi*, see Vergil, *Eclogues* 5.56.

16. The epithet *decus Italiae* is taken from Turnus's address to Camilla in Vergil's *Aeneid* 11.508: *o decus Italiae virgo*.

19. Cf. Ovid, *Heroides* 16.23.

19–20. Cf. Ovid, *Metamorphoses* 14.124: *numinis instar eris semper mihi*.

20. Alessandro Farnese (1520–89) was a cardinal, diplomat, and patron of the arts, as well as the grandson of Pope Paul III.

21. This line is modeled on Vergil, *Aeneid* 3.368: *quidve sequens tantos possim superare labores*.

22–26. Jaffa is an ancient port town now part of Tel Aviv. Samaria is a mountainous region in the northern part of what is now the West Bank. It was also a city in the south of the region, the capital of the Kingdom of Israel. Sichen (Shechem) is the traditional dwelling of Abraham and his descendants. Hebron, located 17 miles south of Jerusalem, is traditionally where the biblical Patriarchs and Matriarchs were buried. Mount Thabor, 11 miles west of the Sea of Galilee, is thought to be the site of Christ's Transfiguration.

26. Cf. Silius Italicus, *Punica* 5.394 and Martial 836.11.

27–29. Fracastoro is comfortable mixing pagan and Judeo-Christian tradition. In Greek mythology, Pluto is the ruler of the underworld, Tartarus.

37. For the line-ending *perdere posset*, see Ovid, *Metamorphoses* 13.177.

47. This line is modeled on Vergil, *Aeneid* 12.391: *iamque aderat Phoebo ante alios dilectus Iapyx*.

49–52. Fracastoro combines elements of Vergil's description of the Fury Allecto in this passage (*Aeneid* 7.323–45).

50. Cf. Vergil, *Georgics* 3.551: *Stygiis emissa tenebris*.

55–56. For *pecudes . . . lanigeras*, cf. Lucretius, *De rerum natura* 6.1237 and Vergil, *Aeneid* 3.642.

77–79. Fracastoro uses Juvencus's description of the soldiers' mockery of Christ to characterize Joseph's brothers' abuse (*Evangelia* 4.647–52).

126. Dothain, now Tell Dothan, is a town about 65 miles north of Hebron.

130. Cf. Lucretius, *De rerum natura* 5.1367.

161. The expression *virgata veste*, used in Vergil, *Aeneid* 8.659–60 and Silius Italicus, *Punica* 4.155 to describe a typical Gallic robe, here alludes to a detail in Genesis 37:4, where Jacob is said to have given Joseph a special garment (*tunicam polymitam*), out of his particular love for this son.

169. This apostrophe is modeled on Lucretius, *De rerum natura* 2.14: *o miseras hominum mentes, o pectora caeca!*

173. Cf. Vergil, *Aeneid* 9.381–82.

196. Cf. Vergil, *Aeneid* 8.66.

199. Cf. Claudian, *Panegyricus* 84: *manibusque revinctis*.

205. The Erynnes were the avenging Furies of Greek mythology.

212. A striking, even famous, instance of Fracastoro's religious syncretism.

238. Cf. Statius, *Thebaid* 12.296: *supero respexit ab axe*.

252. Cf. Vergil, *Aeneid* 4.245–46.

264. *Napeae* are the nymphs of valleys.

273. Cf. Vergil, *Aeneid* 9.731.

274. Cf. Vergil, *Aeneid* 2.559.

277–305. The angel's announcement of Joseph's future hardship and eventual triumph looks back to Vergil's description of Aeneas's troubles at the beginning of the *Aeneid*. The line-ending *multosque per annos* (282) is probably drawn directly from *Aeneid* 1.31. Other sources include Ovid: the opening exhortation *pone metum* is typically Ovidian (see, for example, *Fasti* 2.759 and *Metamorphoses* 3.634). The prophecy, a typical element of the epic genre, is here delivered by an angel and foretells not only the future course of Joseph's own life, but also the greater destiny awaiting his descendents, namely Moses and Christ.

300–305. This prophecy of Christ is infused with the language of Vergil's fourth *Eclogue*, which was often interpreted in messianic terms. For example, the exclamation *anni properate* looks to Vergil's *talia saecla . . . currite* (4.46); *vatum oracla canunt* to Vergil's *Cumaei carminis . . . aetas* (4.4); the phrase *demittatur ab alto* to *caelo demittitur alto* (4.7); *magna Dei soboles* to *cara deum suboles* (4.49); and the *scelus antiquum* to Vergil's *sceleris vestigia nostri* (4.13).

306. The line is modeled on Vergil, *Aeneid* 8.541: *haec ubi dicta dedit, solio se tollit ab alto*.

311. Cf. Ovid, *Metamorphoses* 2.487: *manus ad caelum et sidera tollit*.

324. For *traxit suspiria*, see Ovid, *Metamorphoses* 2.753.

325. Midian (or Madian) is a region mentioned several times in the Bible, possibly located somewhere along the eastern shores of the Sinai Peninsula.

336. Marmarica was a region on the shores of North Africa between Lybia and Egypt.

371. Isaac's lament for Joseph echoes Amata's plea to Turnus in the *Aeneid* (12.57–58: *spes tu nunc una, senectae/ tu requies miserae*).

373. Cf. Vergil, *Aeneid* 9.617.

416–24. The description of Joseph's arrival in Memphis, in the midst of athletic performances by the local youth, is modeled on Aeneas's arrival at the court of Latinus in Vergil, *Aeneid* 7.160–65.

416. Cf. Vergil, *Eclogues* 1.61.

417. The city of Osiris is here probably Memphis (cf. below vv. 2.429 and 629) and not Abydos, in Upper Egypt, most sacred city to the Egyptian god of the dead and of the afterlife, who was believed to have been buried there.

427. Cf. Vergil, *Aeneid* 1.717–18: *haec oculis, haec pectore toto / haeret*.

430. For the phrase *Mavortia munera*, see Statius, *Thebaid* 2.587–88: *Mavortia munera magni / Oeneos.*

435. Cf. Ovid, *Ars amatoria* 1.557: *munus habe caelum.*

460. See Paulinus of Nola, *Carmina* 28.176: *simul et nova vita sit et prudentia cana.*

469–81. The episode of the prophetic swarm of bees nestling in Potiphar's tree is absent in Genesis and is modeled on Vergil, *Aeneid* 7.59–70.

469. Camesis, or Cameses, can perhaps be identified with the Egyptian god Horus, to whom Isis gave birth on a floating island named Chemmis, located near the sanctuary of Buto in Lower Egypt: cf. Herodotus, *Histories* 2.156. Chemmis was also the name of a city in Upper Egypt (modern-day Achmim), where, again according to Herodotus (*Histories* 2.91), the Greek demigod Perseus was worshipped with a temple and annual games (Herodotus probably identified Perseus with the local god Min). The *persaea* tree (*persea* in Greek) was an Egyptian plant, of still uncertain identification, but probably close to a pear tree: Plutarch (*De Iside*, 68) mentions it as sacred to Isis; according to Diodorus Siculus (*Bibliotheca*, 1.34.7) it owed its name to the fact that it was imported into Egypt from Persia, while Pliny the Elder (*Naturalis Historia*, 15.45) prefers the hypothesis that Perseus was the first to plant it in Memphis (cf. S. S. Munguía and J. T. Ripa, *Historia de las plantas en el mundo antiguo* [Bilbao: Universidad de Deusto, 2009], 102–3).

472. Isis is the powerful Egyptian goddess married to her brother Osiris and responsible for his resurrection.

474. For *versicoloribus alis*, see Paulinus of Nola, *Carmina* 23.15.

490. In Greek mythology, Cocytus is one of the rivers in the underworld.

494. Cf. Ovid, *Metamorphoses* 1.130.

506. See Claudian, *De raptu Proserpinae* 1.92.

508. The Acidalian spring was located in Boeotia and was sacred to Venus; the goddess's epithet Acidalia derived from this spring (cf. Vergil, *Aeneid* 1.720).

509. Tisiphone is one the Furies in Greek Mythology.

528. Cf. Vergil, *Aeneid* 9.251.

533. For *vincla iugalia*, see Vergil, *Aeneid* 4.59.

536–37. For a similar sentiment, see Horace, *Odes* 3.16, Propertius, *Elegies* 2.16.47–48, or Ovid, *Ars Amatoria* 1.633–34.

541–42. Fracastoro nods here to the famous saying of the Roman elegist Tibullus, "Be bold; Venus herself favors the brave" (*Elegies* 1.2.16: *Audendum est: fortes adiuvat ipsa Venus*).

556. For *ensemque coruscum* cf. Vergil, *Aeneid* 2.553–54; followed by Prudentius, *Psychomachia* 137.

Book II

1–9. The second book's opening with the passion of Iempsar is a reimagining of the passion of Dido at the beginning of the fourth book of the *Aeneid*. Cf. particularly these lines with *Aeneid* 4.66–69: *est mollis flamma medullas / interea et tacitum vivit sub pectore vulnus. / Uritur infelix Dido totaque vagatur / urbe furens*. For the river Styx see the note on *S*. 1.418–20.

9. Cf. Lucan, *Pharsalia* 9.738: *dipsas calcata momordit*.

61. This line is modeled on the description of Dido in Vergil, *Aeneid* 4.300–301: *saevit inops animi totamque incensa per urbem / bacchatur*.

79. Orcus, in Roman mythology a god of the underworld, here stands for the underworld itself.

80. For *dictis . . . amaris*, cf. Vergil, *Aeneid* 10.368 and 10.591.

84. Cf. Vergil, *Aeneid* 5.716.

90. In Greek mythology, Hymenaeus was the god of marriage.

93. The phrase *meliora ferant dii* is taken from the *Corpus Tibullianum* 3.4.1.

96. Cf. Martianus Capella, *De nuptiis* 6.583.15: *nitidus rutilum Titan succenderat orbem*.

100. For *matrum numerosa cohors*, cf. Paulinus of Nola, *Carmina* 21.77: *procerum numerosa cohors*.

120. Cf. Ovid, *Heroides* 1.83.

125. Cf. *Corpus Tibullianum* 4.3.7.

129. For *de Stygiis emissa tenebris*, see the note on *J*. 1.50.

136. Cf. Ovid, *Metamorphoses* 3.60.

140. See the note on *J*. 1.50 and 2.129.

172. In Roman mythology, Dis, equivalent of Hades or Pluto, was the ruler of hell. In Dante and elsewhere, he is associated with Satan.

199. This line is modeled on Martial, *Epigrammata* 9.31.3: *luna quater binos non tota peregerat orbes*.

202. For Ceres, see on *S*. 1.374.

239–40. This is an adaptation of the famous proverb "To err is human" (A. Otto, *Die Sprichwörter und sprichwörtlichen Redensart der Römer* [Hildesheim, 1988], no. 821), a sentiment found expressed variously among classical and patristic Latin authors, such as Cicero (*Philippics* 12.2.5: *hominis est errare* and *Epistula ad Atticum* 13.21.5: *possum falli ut homo*), ps.-Quintilian (*Declamationes maiores* 9.12: *errare hominis est*), and Jerome (*Epistola* 57.12: *errasse humanum est*).

245. Cf. Ovid, *Metamorphoses* 15.120.

263–64. The expression *alta solstitia* indicates the summer solstice (cf. Lucan, *Pharsalia* 9.531–32) and, in general, for the meaning of the periphrasis in these two lines, cf. Genesis 41:1: *post duos annos vidit Pharao somnium*.

270. Chaldea, a part of the Kingdom of Babylon in what is now southern Iraq, was proverbially considered by the Greeks and Romans as the source of astrology and various forms of divination.

277–78. The expression *iungere arenae fatalem numerum*, may refer to the practice of geomancy (*geomantia*), a divinatory technique about which we have extremely scattered information in ancient times (cf. TLL s.v. *geomantia*). Presumably it consisted in interpreting the patterns formed on the ground by tossing handfuls of granular materials, such as sand, soil, or even leaves. This techinque developed into much more complex forms, thorugh Arabic influences, during the Middle Age, and then became extremely popular in the Renaissance.

285. The phrase *pallor in ore* is lifted from Ovid, *Metamorphoses* 8.801, where the goddess Famine is described.

289–90. *Noctemque diemque* (*noxque diesque*) is a classic epic phrase, first used by Vergil (*Aeneid* 5.766 and 8.94), and subsequently borrowed by every major Latin epic poet.

304. Cf. Ovid, *Ibis* 619.

314. This line is modeled on the famous line at the beginning of Ovid's *Metamorphoses* (1.2–3): *di coeptis (nam vos mutastis et illas) / adspirate meis.*

316. Cf. Ovid, *Metamorphoses* 5.428.

334–35. The nature of the plants *meda* and *mynians* is obscure: on the *meda* (or *medes*), which Fracastoro found in the text of Andromachus's *Theriaca* (cf. C. 52.10 and 53.10), he himself expressed doubts (see on C. 52.10): here these plants are perhaps generically mentioned as exotic and mysterious herbs.

342. The phrase *ardor edendi* is taken from Ovid's *Metamorphoses* (8.827), the same passage Fracastoro alluded to above (see the note on J. 2.285).

385. Cf. Ovid, *Heroides* 5.115: *quid harenae semina mandas?*

429. Memphis was capital of Aneb-Hetch, in antiquity the first nome of Lower Egypt.

432. The expression *equorum comminuit numerum atque hominum* probably refers to Joseph's great need for horses and couriers, owing to his extensive travels all over Egypt (cf. also Genesis 41:46: [*Joseph*] *circuivit omnes regiones Aegypti*).

433. Heliopolis, one of Egypt's oldest cities, was the capital of the thirteenth nome of Lower Egypt and stood five miles from the northern apex of the Nile Delta.

434. Cf. Vergil's description of the priest Panthus (*Aeneid* 2.319: *arcis Phoebique sacerdos*) and the king and priest Anius (*Aeneid* 3.80: *rex idem hominum Phoebique sacerdos*).

437–39. The prophecy about Joseph's future wife is modeled on the one concerning Lavinia, daughter of Latinus and future wife of the "foreigner" Aeneas, in Vergil, *Aeneid* 7.96–101. Cf. also Vergil, *Aeneid* 3.158: *venturos tollemus in astra nepotes*.

476. Cf. Vergil, Aeneid 11.330: dicta ferant et foedera firment.

478. The phrase *populos it fama per omnes* nods to Vergil's famous description of Rumor in the *Aeneid* (4.173: *magnas it Fama per urbes*). At the same time, Fracastoro is playing with the similarity between the Latin words "rumor" (*fama*) and "famine" (*fames*).

495. For Samaria, see the note on *J.* 1.22.

504–5. For *ficto . . . dissimulans*, cf. Statius, *Silvae* 5.1.159–60: *comites tamen undique ficto / spem simulant vultu*.

513. *Sufferre laborem* is a favorite Lucretian line-ending; cf. *De rerum natura* 3.999, 5.1272, and 5.1359.

518. The phrase *potest pietas si in te ulla* may have been adapted from Ovid (*Metamorphoses* 6.503 and 7.336: *si pietas ulla est*); nevertheless, it may also represent an elegant hexameter rendering of Cicero's attack on Antony (*Philippics* 2.99.49): *si ulla in te pietas esset*.

568. Cf. Vergil, *Aeneid* 3.344.

577. See the note on *J.* 1.37.

584. For *illacrimans . . . sic fatur*, cf. Vergil, *Aeneid* 9.303 and 11.29: *sic ait illacrimans*.

609. Cf. Vergil, *Eclogue* 4.30.

616. Cf. Vergil, *Aeneid* 4.6: *postera Phoebea lustrabat lampade terras / umentemque Aurora polo dimoverat umbram*.

620–22. Jacob's blessing to Benjamin is modeled on Evander's words to his departing son Pallas in Vergil, *Aeneid* 8.574–77: *si numina vestra / incolumem Pallanta mihi, si fata reservant, / si visurus eum vivo et venturus in unum: / vitam oro, patior quemvis durare laborem*.

626–28. Edom was a region south of Judea and the Dead Sea. Gerar was a Philistine town in southern Israel. The Syrbotae are mentioned by Pliny (*Naturalis historia* 6.190 and 7.31) as a people of Ethiopia.

631. This line is Vergilian; cf. *Aeneid* 1.520 and 11.248, which both read *postquam introgressi et coram data copia fandi.*

640. For *male numen amicum*, see Vergil, *Aeneid* 2.735.

668. The expression *bona luce*, modeled on Ovid, *Tristia* 1.1.97 and *Epistulae ex Ponto* 3.1.159, here renders the word *meridie* used in Genesis 43:16 and 24.

668–92. This ekphrastic passage, in which a work of art is described at some length, is inspired by *Aeneid* 1.450–58, where Aeneas visits the temple of Juno in Carthage and finds the events of the Trojan War depicted upon its walls. The present passage relates the story of Jacob as told in Genesis. At Genesis 27:41, Esau, believing that his twin Jacob has stolen his birthright, seeks to murder him. At Genesis 29 Jacob finally marries his beloved Rachel after working for fourteen years for her father, Laban (who was also Jacob's uncle).

CARMINA

1. Alcon, or On the care of hunting dogs
Meter: Dactylic Hexameter

Fracastoro's authorship of the *Alcon* is doubtful: for a discussion of the question see Notes to the Text, p. 379. In Greek mythology, both Alcon and Acastus were hunters, with Hercules, of the Calydonian Boar and are mentioned by (ps.-) Apollodorus in his *Bibliotheca* 3.10–13. Alcon also appears as a young shepherd in the Roman bucolic tradition (cf. Vergil, *Eclogues* 5.10; Calpurnius Siculus, *Eclogues* 6; and Nemesianus, *Eclogues* 2), while in Pontano's *Eclogues*, as in the present poem, he becomes an older man (cf. *Eclogues* 1.2.42: *octogenarius Alcon*; cf. also 4.39). In general this name is rather popular among Renaissance poets (cf. for example, Baldassare Castiglione's 1505 bucolic epicedion on the death of Domizio Falcone, for whom Alcon was a pseudonym). A character named Alcon, also an older man and a teacher, reappears in Fracastoro's *C. 51*. Though the *Alcon* is cast as an eclogue, it invokes a number of didactic poems on hunting, such as those attributed to Oppian in Greek and those of Grattius and Nemesianus in Latin. Furthermore the text (especially the long section on canine diseases, vv. 80–176) closely recalls Robert Moshaim's

Latin translation of the Byzantine work *Kynosophion, seu de cura canum liber* (published in Vienna by Singriener in 1535; see Fischer 1983). Its closest parallel as a didactic eclogue, however, is the fifth *Eclogue* of Calpurnius Siculus, whose subject is the care of sheep. Interestingly Calpurnius's *Eclogue* 5 was included in the 1534 Aldine anthology of texts on hunting that also provided the *editio princeps* of Nemesianus's and Grattius's poems (cf. Fischer 1983).

3. The reference to Corvinus is unclear, although there is a town that was called Corvino (later Corvino San Quirico) in the hills south of Pavia.

5. Cf. Vergil, *Aeneid* 2.544.

8. Cf. Silius Italicus, *Punica* 7.443.

9. See S. 2.92; Vergil, *Aeneid* 4.121: *saltusque indagine cingunt.*

11. The Molossians were an ancient tribe that inhabited Epirus on the Balkan Peninsula. Vergil mentions their hounds at *Georgics* 3.404–13, together with the Spartan hounds: cf. v. 30 of the present poem.

13. This line is modeled on Calpurnius Siculus, *Eclogues* 5.11: *iam pro me gnavam potes exercere iuventam.*

18. Cf. Statius, *Thebaid* 1.397: *saetigerumque suem et fulvum adventare leonem.*

20–79. This section, on the selection, breeding and training of hunting dogs, is closely modeled on Nemesianus's *Cynegetica* 103–94. Fracastoro signals his dependence in the *incipit* of this section, which recalls Nemesianus, *Cynegetica* 103: *principio tibi cura canum non segnis ab anno / incipiat primo.*

24. Cf. Ovid, *Heroides* 11.111: *rapidarum praeda ferarum.*

26–27. Fracastoro took this idea from Grattius, *Cynegeticon* 154–55: *mille canum patriae ductique ab origine mores / quoique sua.*

29. Cf. Vergil, *Aeneid* 2.751: *et rursus caput obiectare periclis.*

30–39. This passage on the breeds of dogs looks to a later passage in the *Cynegetica* 224–80, where Nemesianus discusses the Spartan hound, as well as the Molossian, Briton, Pannonian, Spanish (or perhaps Georgian, depending on the interpretation of *Hiberus*), Libyan, and Tuscan hounds. Grattius includes the Celtic, Gelonian, Persian, Chinese, Hyrcanian, Briton, Molossian, Sycambrian, and other hounds (*Cynegeticon* 154ff.). Pannonia was an ancient Roman Province in the north of the Balkan Peninsula. Hyrcania was a region south-east of the Caspian Sea. Seria refers to the land inhabited by the *Seres*, i.e., China. The Paeonians occupied the territory in what is now Macedonia, while the Sicambri were a Germanic tribe in what is now the Netherlands. The reference to the Saxogeloni is unclear (the name *Saxogelonus* is unattested, and probably corrupt), but the Geloni were a tribe that occupied a region of Scythia some three hundred miles east of the Black Sea (cf. Grattius, *Cynegeticon* 157–58: *arma negant contra martemque odere Geloni, / sed natura sagax, Perses in utroque paratus*, and see Notes to the Text, p. 380).

30. Cf. Nemesianus, *Cynegetica* 107: *seu Lacedaemonio natam seu rure Molosso*, 224; cf. also Vergil, *Eclogues* 3.404 (see note on v. 11 above).

34–35. Cf. Vergil, *Georgics* 3.539–40.

36. Cf. Grattius, *Cynegeticon* 202: *volucresque Sycambros*.

37. Cf. Vergil, *Georgics* 2.471.

46–50. For the description of the perfect hound, compare Nemesianus, *Cynegetica* 108–13, and Grattius, *Cynegeticon* 269–78.

52. Cf. Nemesianus, *Cynegetica* 114: *huic parilem submitte marem*.

53. Cf. Lucretius, *De rerum natura* 1.163: *genus omne ferarum*.

81. See the note on *S.* 1.307.

83. Moshaim's translation of the *Kynosophion* prescribes letting blood from the dog's mouth rather than its ears (cf. Notes to the Text, p. 382).

88. Lyaeus, meaning "one who releases from care," is an epithet of the wine god Dionysus/ Bacchus, and here is a metonymy for wine itself.

109. The parenthetical *nomine dicunt* line-ending is Vergilian (cf. *Aeneid* 7.607). The nature of the stone here called *Lemiulum* or *Medis* remains unclear (cf. Notes to the Text, p. 382).

148. For Mount Ida see on *S.* 2.225; for Lyaeus see above, v. 88.

150. Cf. Vergil, *Aeneid* 2.215.

171. Both Grattius (*Cynegeticon* 386–87) and Pliny the Elder (*Naturalis historia* 29.100) mention a worm on the tongue as a possible cause of rabies in dogs; cf. also Notes to the Text, p. 383.

179. The name Coridallus is probably a diminutive of the typical bucolic name Corydon (cf. e.g., Theocritus, *Idylls* 4, and Vergil, *Eclogues* 2 and 7), deriving from the Greek noun *Korydallos*, meaning "small lark."

180. Cf. Vergil, *Aeneid* 9.373.

2. ON THE DEATH OF MARCANTONIO DELLA TORRE
Meter: Elegiac Distichs

This poem invokes a long classical tradition of *epicedia* (funerary poems), as well as Roman elegiac verse, especially Catullus 65. It was probably written in 1511 or 1512 (see Pellegrini, *Appunti* 1954, 91–93). Marcantonio della Torre (1481–1511) was a medical doctor who taught at Padua and Pavia and studied anatomy together with Leonardo da Vinci. Della Torre's brother Battus, or Giovanni Battista, was also a student of medicine and died in 1534. He appears in several of Fracastoro's poems and was one of the main influences on the author's prose work on astronomy, the *Homocentrica*.

1–6. The opening of the poem recalls that of a consolatory letter by Cicero to his friend T. Fadius (*Epistulae familiares* 5.18).

3. Cf. Catullus, *Carmina* 68.55–56: *neque assiduo tabescere lumina fletu / cessarent*; and Ovid, *Metamorphoses* 4.674: *tepido manabant lumina fletu*.

4. Cf. *Corpus Tibullianum* 3.2.6: *frangit fortia corda dolor*.

5. The rare word *amaror* at line end is Lucretian (*De rerum natura* 4.224 and 6.930).

6. Cf. Catullus *Carmina* 65.12.

7. For the Camenae, see on *S.* 1.14.

10. For the wind Notus see on *S.* 3.131.

17–24. Lampetia was one of the daughters of the sun god, Helios, and one of the sisters of Phaeton, who commandeered the chariot of the sun, but lost control and threatened to incinerate the Earth until he was killed by one of Zeus's thunderbolts. According to Ovid's account (*Metamorpho-*

ses 2.1–366), in which he mentions Lampetia, the body of Phaeton landed on the banks of the river Eridanus, where he was endlessly lamented by his sisters, until they were changed into trees and their tears became drops of amber. For Eridanus see on *S.* 1.64.

29. This line imitates Statius, *Thebaid* 9.53: *quando alius misero ac melior mihi frater ademptus.*

32. Fracastoro took the evocative phrase *columen domus* from the nurse's lament for Britannicus in the play *Octavia* falsely ascribed to Seneca (168: *columen augustae domus*).

39–42. Fracastoro refers to the so-called Italian Wars fought in Italy, primarily by France and the Holy Roman Empire, between 1494 and 1559.

40. The sentiment and wording of the half-line *nec feret ulla dies* are lifted directly from one of Ovid's elegies, *Amores* 3.6.18.

44. I.e., syphilis.

45. Giovanni Cotta (1480–1510) was a neo-Latin poet, born near Verona and connected to the circle of local literary figures there as well as to the Accademia Pontaniana in Naples. He served under the condottiere Bartolomeo d'Alviano, with whom he allegedly had an extremely close relationship. The premature death of Giovanni Cotta recalls that of Marcantonio della Torre and is perhaps alluded to in the *Syphilis* (see on *S.* 1.382–412).

57. Cf. Vergil, *Aeneid* 6.782: *animos aequabit Olympo.*

61. Cf. ps.-Vergil, *Catalepton* 9.41: *nam quid ego immensi memorem studia ista laboris.*

63–66. For Orcus, see on *J.* 2.79. Among Apollo's several attributes, he was the god of medicine and healing (cf. the note on *S.* 1.20). The Ticino and the Brenta (whose Latin name was *Medoacus*) are rivers in northern Italy. For the Euganean Hills see the note on *S.* 1.444.

67. Cf. *C.* 3.20.

74. In ancient literature, Calliope (or Calliopea) was the muse of epic poetry, and later also of elegy. By "Etruscan" Fracastoro means the Tuscan dialect of Italian.

76. The Hyperboreans were a mythical people believed to inhabit the regions "beyond the North wind," i.e., the northernmost edge of the world.

77–82. For Benacus see the note on *S.* 1.31; for the river Sarca, the note on *S.* 1.456–63; for Adige, the note on *S.* 1.448. Marcantonio della Torre died at Riva del Garda, but his body was later transferred to his native city of Verona, where he received a solemn burial (cf. Pellegrini, *Appunti* 1954, 91–92). One could easily travel from Rovereto to Verona by sailing down the river Adige.

79. Cf. Vergil, *Aeneid* 6.161.

81–82. Cf. Catullus 68.98–100: *nec prope cognatos compositum cineris / sed Troia obscena Troia infelice sepultum / detinet extremo terra aliena solo.*

83. For the Naiads see on *S.* 2.143–44.

91. As Pellegrini has rightly interpreted (*Carmina* 1954, *ad loc.*), Nacus refers to the town of Nago, at the foot of Monte Brione (here named *Brianus*), located beside Riva del Garda, where Marcantonio died.

92. Cf. Vergil, *Eclogues* 2.3: *tantum inter densas umbrosa cacumina fagos.*

98–102. Fracastoro refers to the Thracian poet Orpheus, who ceaselessly lamented his dead wife Eurydice. Rhodope was a mountain range in Ancient Thrace, in what is now Bulgaria and northern Greece. The Strymon (Struma) is a river that flows through the ancient lands of Thrace.

113. In classical mythology, Diana, the goddess of the Moon, and her brother, Apollo, were the children of Leto, who in turn was the daughter of the Titans Coeus and Phoebe.

121. Cf. Silius Italicus, *Punica* 13.883–85.

131. This Christianizing use of *semideus* is already attested in the Christian poetry of late antiquity: cf. Paulinus of Nola, *Carmina* 6.2.52.

143. Girolamo della Torre (1444–1506), father of Giovanni Battista and Marcantonio, was an illustrious doctor. He worked mostly at the University of Padua, where Fracastoro was one of his students.

157. This half-line is modeled on Silius Italicus, *Punica* 10.572: *i, decus Ausoniae.* For Ausonia, see on *S.* 1.15.

160. Fracastoro concludes his poem with a well-known Vergilian tag; cf. *Aeneid* 7.99 and 272: *nomen in astra ferant.*

3. On the death of Paolo and Giulio,
Fracastoro's sons

Meter: Dactylic Hexameter

For Battus, Giovanni Battista della Torre, see the introductory note to C. 2. According to Pellegrini (*Appunti* 1954, 94–95), this poem was probably written between 1515 and 1517.

1. Cf. Manilius, *Astronomica* 4.12: *solvite, mortales, animos curasque levate.*

4. Cf. Ausonius, *Parentalia* 14.1: *o mihi funus acerbum.*

5. Cf. Lucretius, *De rerum natura* 6.850: *terribili . . . caligine texit.*

11. For *teneris . . . ab annis,* cf. Ovid, *Epistulae ex Ponto* 2.3.73: *teneris mihi semper ab annis.*

16. Cf. C. 4.31, 7.89, and 50.35.

17. Cf. C. 7.34.

20. Cf. C. 2.67.

21. This line was evidently one of Fracastoro's favorites; he supplies versions of it in C. 4.32, 7.20, 10.83–84, 11.1, and 50.2.

22. Favonius, also called Zephyrus (cf. v. 13 above and note on S. 2.86), was the personification of the West Wind, carrier of Spring. See C. 4.33 and 17.2 (*flatusque Favonii*).

23. See C. 4.34.

24. This line is modeled on Catullus *Carmina* 68.119: *nam nec tam carum confecto aetate parenti.*

25. Cf. Vergil, *Aeneid* 6.884: *purpureos spargam flores.*

26. Thracian here alludes, as in the previous poem (see the note on C. 2.98–102), to the mythical poet Orpheus.

27. Fracastoro elegantly nods to Vergil's description of Orpheus's grief in the *Georgics*, where the poet compares the mourner to a nightingale mourning her lost hatchlings under the shade of a poplar tree (4.511–12:

qualis populea maerens philomela sub umbra / amissos queritur fetus); cf. also *Aeneid* 10.190–91: *populeas inter frondes umbramque sororum / dum canit et maestum musa solatur amorem.*

28. For the river Adige see the note on *S.* 1.448.

30. For *fortunate senex*, cf. Vergil, *Eclogues* 1.45 and 51. For the expression *ore referri*, cf. Vergil, *Aeneid* 4.328–29.

31–46. This cosmogony is essentially Platonic, as mediated through the Latin Platonists Boethius and Macrobius. Much of the vocabulary is drawn from Ovid's creation story, *Metamorphoses* 1.5–88.

49. Lachesis and her sisters Clotho and Atropos were the three *Moirai* (also called *Parcae* or Fates): Clotho spun the thread of one's life, while Lachesis (meaning "the lot-casting") measured its length and Atropos (meaning "the unavertable") finally cut the thread.

52. For Orcus, see the note on *J.* 2.79.

68. Cf. Vergil, *Aeneid* 6.882: *heu miserande puer*, addressed to Marcellus, who was the nephew and presumptive heir of Augustus, and who died prematurely in 23 BCE.

73–74. Fracastoro adopts this simile from Vergil's description of the death of the youth Euryalus (*Aeneid* 9.435: *purpureus veluti cum flos succisus aratro*).

81. In ancient mythology, the Elysian Fields were a beautiful region of the underworld where the souls of noble and heroic mortals went after death.

82. Cf. *Corpus Tibullianum* 3.7.10: *puro testantur sidera caelo.*

97–99. For the river Eridanus see the note on *S.* 1.64; Hister is the ancient name of the Danube. The Taygetus is a mountain in the Peloponnese in southern Greece, while the Sypilus is a mountain in the Manisa Province of Turkey, near the Aegean Sea (and see the note on *S.* 3.288). Cymbotus is a mountain of uncertain location, mentioned in Pliny, *Naturalis Historia* 2.205, together with the Sypilus, as suffering the effects of geological change.

4. To Daniele Rainieri, prefect of Verona

Meter: Dactylic Hexameter

According to Pellegrini (*Appunti* 1954, 93–94), this poem was written in 1517, after Verona, which had been under the dominion of the Holy Roman Emperor Maximilian I from 1508 to 1517, was reintegrated into the Venetian Republic, but before 1518, when the Venetians removed many key buildings in the interests of urban planning. Daniele Rainieri, prefect of Verona at the time, was a doctor and a poet. The poem is a plea to him, from one doctor to another, to petition the Venetians to spare the Collegio dei Medici, which, Pellegrini believes, was located in or near the Ospedale della Tomba.

1. Cf. Vergil, *Aeneid* 8.470, and here below, v. 48.

5. Bromius, meaning "noisy," is an epithet of the wine god Bacchus.

14. The phrase *tempus edax* is Ovidian (cf. *Epistulae ex Ponto* 4.10.7 and *Metamorphoses* 15.234).

18–20. Cf. C. 2.63–64.

29–30. The *cothurnus* was the high, thick-soled shoe worn by tragic actors in antiquity. Here it is a metonymy for tragic poetry, which evidently was Rainieri's specialty. For Aonia see on *S.* 2.160.

31–34. This section is a *cento* of lines from C. 3 vv. 16 and 21–23.

33. For the Favonian wind see on C. 3.22.

35. Cf. Statius, *Thebaid* 4.1.17 and Ausonius, *Mosella* 381.

37. Cf. the line-ending at Vergil, *Aeneid* 7.430. For the river Adige see on *S.* 1.448.

39. Cf. Vergil, *Aeneid* 2.788: *magna deum genetrix.*

40. Cf. Vergil, *Aeneid* 3.476.

41. Cf. Claudian, *Carmina maiora* 26.468: *et vivida Martis imago.*

44. Albis is the Latin name of the Elbe, one of the major rivers of Central Europe. It flowed through the heart of the Holy Roman Empire, from which Verona had recently been freed.

48. Cf. above, v. 1.

54–55. Much of the vocabulary in these and the following lines is drawn from Vergil's famous fourth *Eclogue*. With the advent of a new golden age, the Fates (*Parcae*, see on C. 3.49) will spin golden threads; on the myth of the golden age, see on C. 5.18.

5. To Giovanni Matteo Giberti, bishop of Verona
Meter: Dactylic Hexameter
This poem, which Pellegrini (*Appunti* 1954, 99) dates to 1534–35, is dedicated to Gian Matteo Giberti (1495–1543) who, in addition to being the bishop of Verona, was among the most learned Italian scholar-prelates of the first half of the sixteenth century and a leading reformer of the pre-Tridentine Catholic Church; his successful reforms of the clergy in Verona were held up as a model of church reform by St. Carlo Borromeo later in the century. In a diplomatic capacity, he served popes Leo X, Clement VII, and Paul III. The poem is presented together with a gift of lemons and carp. A good part of it is dedicated to an etiological narrative on the origin of this species of fish ("Salmo Carpio"), that only lives in the Lago di Garda. Saturn's transforming greedy Etruscan sailors into gold-eating carp appears to be modeled on the myth of the Tyrrhenian sailors who kidnapped the young Dionysus and were turned into dolphins by him (cf. Ovid, *Metamorphoses* 3.582–691 and cf. also C. 44.33–36). The legend of the gold-eating carp of the Lago di Garda was already present in Pierio Valeriano's epyllion, precisely titled *Carpio* and published in 1509; on other attestations of this legend cf. P. Pellegrini, ". . . *Donec Avogaro dicas nomine de meo salutem*: Umanisti veronesi e benacensi nei carmi di Pierio Valeriano," in F. Bruzzo and F. Fanizza (eds.), *Giulio Cesare Scaligero e Nicolò d'Arco: la cultura umanistica nelle terre del Sommolago tra XV e XVI secolo* (Riva del Garda, 1999), 197–208 (in particular 204–6). Yet its connection to the myth of Saturn seems to be first attested in our poem, and Fracastoro appears to attribute its paternity to Giovanni Battista della Torre (see v. 16). The story is then further expanded in the fourth book of the mythological poem *Benacus* (published in 1546) by Giorgio Iodoco Bergano (i.e., from Berghen), canon of S. Zeno in Verona (on the scattered information about whose life, see G. Petrella, *L'officina del geografo: la "Descrittione di tutta Italia" di Leandro Alberti*

e gli studi geografico-antiquari tra Quattro e Cinquecento [Milano: Vita e Pensiero, 2004], 112–13): cf. p. 54r of the 1546 edition: *Hic mihi fas te sit sectari culte Fragastor. / Quaeque laconismo nuper doctaque Thalia / scripsisti, longo liceat depromere cantu.*

2. Malcesine is a small town on the Lago di Garda. Giberti had a house in the hills that overlooked it, and Fracastoro used the house on occasion.

3. Cf. Vergil, *Eclogues* 6.11: *te nemus omne canet.*

4–9. As in the *Syphilis*, Fracastoro follows the re-elaboration of the ancient myth of the golden apples, devised by Giovanni Pontano in his *De hortis Hesperidum* (see the note on S. 2.212–22). Here, however, the golden fruits, identified with lemons, are imported to Italy, not by Hercules (cf. Pontano, *De hortis Hesperidum* 101–10), but by Perseus. According to ancient mythology, after Perseus defeated the Gorgon, he came to the end of the world and the kingdom of Atlas. Perseus was weary and hungry, and when Atlas refused him lodgings and food, for fear that he would steal the golden apples, Perseus turned the Medusa on the Titan and transformed him into the Atlas Mountains. For Benacus see the note on S. 1.31; the nymph Charita is a personification of the village of Garda, on the south-east shore of the homonymous lake (cf. the note on C. 50.26).

11. Fracastoro defines the sailors inhabiting the Lago di Garda as "Etruscans," in reference to the ancient Etruscan colonization of the region of the Po Valley.

16. For Giovanni Battista della Torre, see the introductory note to C. 2. Salò is a town on the southwest shore of the Lago di Garda (see on C. 50.22).

17. The identity of Aegon is unclear, but the name is common in the bucolic tradition (cf. Theocritus, *Idylls* 4; Vergil, *Eclogues* 3.1; Calpurnius Siculus, *Eclogues* 6.83). The Dryades are nymphs of the trees.

18–19. Saturn, often identified with the Greek Chronos, was married to the goddess of fertility (Opis/Rhea), and his reign was thought to coincide with the golden age. Fearing that he would be overthrown by one of his sons, Saturn devoured all of them at birth, except for Jupiter, who was saved by Opis and secretely hidden on the island of Crete. As Jupiter grew up, he joined battle with his father, defeated him, and pushed him into exile. According to Roman mythology (cf. Vergil, *Aeneid* 8.319–27), Saturn, after many wanderings, found a hiding place in Italy. The phrase *patriis . . . ab oris* is Vergilian (cf. *Aeneid* 10.198 and 11.281).

6. To Marguerite Valois, queen of Navarre
Meter: Dactylic Hexameter

This poem was composed by Fracastoro on behalf of the Genoese condottiere Cesare Fregoso (ca. 1500–1541). Son of Giano II di Campo-fregoso, doge of Genoa, he lived in the region of Verona — where Fracastoro presumably met him — from 1529 to 1536 and built a majestic palace beside the Lago di Garda. He abandoned the Venetian cause in favor of the French, to whom, in the present poem, we find him offering his services. He died near Pavia, having been assassinated by agents of Charles V, on July 3, 1541, together with Antoine de Rincon, the French ambassador to the Ottoman court. This was one of the events leading up to the so-called Italian War (1542–46), in which Charles V and Henry VIII of England fought against the French king Francis I and the Ottoman sultan Suleiman I the Magnificent. The addressee of the present poem, Marguerite of Navarre (1492–1549), was the sister of Francis I and the author of the famous *Heptameron*, a collection of stories modeled upon Bocaccio's *Decameron*. She was also the author of a religious poem, *Miroir de l'âme pécheresse*, that was condemned as heretical by the Sorbonne. The poem is presented as accompanying the gift of an image of Minerva, who is compared to Marguerite: Minerva, the Roman equivalent of the virgin Athena, was a warrior as well as the goddess of wisdom and cleverness, hence protectress of justice, of arts and crafts and, in particular, of such feminine activities as weaving and spinning. According to Pellegrini (*Appunti* 1954, 97–98), the poem was probably composed around 1538, although an earlier dating around 1533 is quite possible (cf. R. Cooper, *Litterae in tempore belli: études sur les relations littéraires italo-françaises pendant les guerres d'Italie* [Genève: Librairie Droz, 1997], 182–85).

1–4. For the Cenomani see the note on *S.* 1.382–85. Castel Goffredo is a town in the province of Mantua, which Cesare Fregoso chose as his main residence after he married, in 1529, Costanza Rangoni, sister of Luigi

Gonzaga. The Rhone is a river that flows through south-eastern France, while the Arre flows through Provence. The phrase *Itala tellus* comes from Ovid, *Fasti* 4.64, and later its use as line-ending became a fixture in Silius Italicus (e.g., *Punica* 8.352).

8. Gorgons were female monsters, with snakes in place of hair, who could turn any living being to stone with their gaze. The most famous of them was Medusa, slain by Perseus, cf. C. 5.4–9. The head of a Gorgon decorated Minerva's shield. For Minerva's epithet Pallas, see the note on S. 1.456–63.

16. Bellona was a Roman deity of war, often associated with the warrior goddess Minerva.

19–20. Polycleitus and Myron were famous Greek sculptors of the fifth century BCE.

21. This line rewrites Ovid, *Metamorphoses* 8.430: *illi laetitiae est cum munere muneris auctor.*

23. Pieria, a region of ancient Macedon, famous for its spring, was considered sacred to the Muses.

29–30. Both Minerva and Mars (the Roman equivalent of the Greek Ares) were gods of war and were born of Jupiter; *Gradivus*, of obscure meaning, is a Latin epithet of Mars. Here Minerva's brother, Mars, is compared to Marguerite's brother, Francis I king of France.

34–36. The most famous literary depiction of an allegorical battle is Prudentius's *Psychomachia*. Cf. also Vergil, *Aeneid* 2.368–69: *crudelis ubique / luctus, ubique pavor et plurima mortis imago.*

37. The aegis, which served as a shield, belonged to Minerva and to her father, Jupiter.

43. The half-line *ramis insignis olivae* is modeled on Vergil, *Aeneid* 6.808. The olive tree, sacred to Minerva, was a symbol of peace.

45. Cf. Ovid, *Heroides* 16.333: *ibis Dardanias ingens regina per urbes*, and Statius, *Thebaid* 2.362: *geminas ibis regina per urbes.*

47–49. Tritonian: i.e., of the goddess Athena, since in some legends she was raised near Lake Tritonis, a fresh water lake in northern Africa.

52–59. Francis I's propaganda insisted on giving an athletic, vigorous image of him: his accession was famously celebrated by the young king parading through the streets of Paris in magnificent armor and participating in a horse tournament. At a later period he was often identified with Hercules (here presented as killing the Cretan bull). These lines in particular may also contain an allusion to the king's victory against Swiss troops in the battle of Marignano (1515), later sometimes symbolized by the image of the Swiss bull defeated by the French salamander.

55. This line is modeled on Vergil, *Aeneid* 8.588: *chlamyde et pictis conspectus in armis*.

59. Cf. ps.-Seneca, *Octavia* 818–19: *claras / / diruit urbes*.

68–72. See on vv. 34–36 above. Among these figures, *Spes* is also found in Prudentius.

76. The Castalian spring, near the Greek town of Delphi, was sacred to Apollo and to the Muses (who, as daughters of Zeus, were also the sisters of Minerva/ Marguerite). This spring was thought, like the Pierian spring of v. 23 above, to confer poetic inspiration on all who drank from it.

92. *Pudor* is also a character in Prudentius (cf. on v. 34–36 above). Cf. also Horace's *Carmen saeculare*, 57–60: *iam Fides et Pax et Honos Pudorque / priscus et neglecta redire Virtus / audet adparetque beata pleno / Copia cornu*.

95. The Sequani were an ancient Celtic tribe in northeastern Gaul: here they are synonymous with the French.

99–101. This passage is modeled on Claudian, *Panegyricus* 7.96–98: *o nimium dilecte deo, cui fundit ab antris / Aeolus armatas hiemes, cui militat aether / et coniurati veniunt ad classica venti*. These verses of Claudian were singled out for express praise by Augustine (*De civitate Dei* 5.26).

102–6. These lines probably allude to the loss of Upper Navarre (south of the Pyrenees) to the kingdom of Castile in 1513, a loss which, despite failed attempts to reconquer it (in 1516 and 1521), left the royal house of d'Albret with only the smaller territory of Lower Navarre, north of the Pyrenees.

111. The reference of the name Meniascus is unclear, but it may refer to a river Menlascus in the north of Spain (cf. Pomponius Mela, *Geography* 3.15), probably to be identified with the modern Oria in the Basque territory, which in Marguerite's day coincided with the kingdom of Upper Navarre, lost by the royal house d'Albret.

112–13. These lines are modeled on Ovid, *Ars amatoria* 1.217–18: *spectabunt laeti iuvenes mixtaeque puellae / diffundetque animos omnibus ista dies.* Fracastoro may have gotten the idea for the chorus of youths also from Horace's *Carmen saeculare*, a hymn written for Augustus's *Ludi saeculares* in 17 BCE: cf. 5–8: *Sibyllini monuere versus / virgines lectas puerosque castos / dis, quibus septem placuere colles, dicere carmen.*

115. For Aonia see on S. 2.160.

116. Another reminisence of Horace's *Carmen saeculare* 46–48: *di . . . date remque prolemque / et decus omne.*

118–19. For the Fates see on C. 3.49.

125. The "harsh goddess" is Fortune.

126. Eurus is the easterly wind.

135. For Tartarus see the note on S. 1.418–20.

141–43. The Sequani, Remi, Cadurci, Aulerci, Hedui (Aedui), and Lingones were all ancient Celtic tribes in Gaul; cf. above, v. 95.

148–50. Iturissa, Andelus, and Bituris were all cities, of uncertain identification, mentioned by Ptolemy (*Geography* 2.6.67) as situated in the territory of the Vascones, corresponding to the kingdom of Navarre, which Marguerite ruled together with her husband, Henry d'Albret.

155. Cf. Silius Italicus, *Punica* 17.49 and Statius, *Achillleid* 1.445.

156. Mount Carmel is a mountain in northern Israel, overlooking the Mediterannean. Jaffa is a port city that is now part of Tel Aviv.

161. Cf. Statius, *Silvae* 2.2.24: *gaudet gemino sub numine portus.*

167. Mygdonia and Lycia were ancient regions in Anatolia (in the northwest and in the south, respectively): eastern archers were renowned, but in classical times the Parthians (i.e., Persian) were proverbially the most

skilled. This passage may also allude to Turkish archers, who were famous.

169–70. Ancient Hyrcania lay on the southern coast of the Caspian Sea. Bactria was part of what is now Afghanistan.

173–74. Cf. Ovid, *Metamorphoses* 4.639–41.

176. Anne de Montmorency (1493–1567) was marshal of France and constable of France, and a friend of Marguerite de Navarre. In 1536 he was chosen to lead the French troops beyond the Alps into Italy.

185. See on *S.* 1.229.

191. Cf. Vergil, *Aeneid* 1.335: *haud equidem tali me dignor honore.*

7. To Marcantonio Flaminio and Galeazzo Florimonte

Meter: Dactylic Hexameter

This poem, heavily influenced by Platonic idealism, is addressed to Marcantonio Flaminio (1497/98–1550), a Neo-Latin poet and scholar from the Veneto, and to Galeazzo Florimonte (1478–1567), bishop first of Aquino and then of Sessa Aurunca. The latter is remembered mainly as the inspiration for Giovanni della Casa's book on etiquette, *Il Galateo*. The poem was probably written between September 1535 and February 1536, when the bishop, Matteo Giberti (about whom see introductory note to *C.* 5), invited to Verona the Dutch theologian Jan van Kampen (1491–1538) to give a series of lectures on theological matters, above all on the Ancient Testament (cf. P. Salvetto, *Tullio Crispoldi nella crisi religiosa del Cinquecento: le difficili pratiche del viver cristiano* [Brescia: Morcelliana, 2009], 81–143). Fracastoro's praise of Giberti's initiative and of his theological and philosophical studies stands in contrast to his humbler claims for his own main fields of inquiry, medicine and astronomy; from a Platonic perspective, these studies, bound to the ephemeral and material world, were doomed to failure in their quest for ultimate truth. The poem, though probably unfinished (cf. Notes to the Text, p. 387), concludes with an encomion to Giberti: by singing his praises, Fracastoro claims to have finally found a worthy field of endeavor.

1. The fateful poets mentioned here are the major prophets of the Bible, on whom Jan van Kampen lectured in Verona.

9. Proteus was a Greek sea god who, by changing his shape at will, escaped anyone who tried to bind and question him.

11. *Simulacra rerum* is a key term in Lucretius (e.g., *De rerum natura* 4.30).

34. Cf. C. 3.17.

61. Bardolena (Bardolino) is a town near Verona, on the eastern side of Lago di Garda (Benacus).

64–65. Fracastoro wishes to be able to dedicate himself to theological studies as well, inquiring subjects such as the biblical prophets and the Old and New Testament.

68. Maeonian verse is the hexameter used by Homer, who was allegedly born in Maeonia, a region on the eastern coast of modern Turkey.

74. Cf. Statius, *Silvae* 3.1.166: *macte animis*. Cf. C. 47.16.

75. Cf. Silius Italicus, *Punica* 5.107, and Vergil, *Aeneid* 7.781.

78. Cf. Vergil, *Aeneid* 7.285: *pacemque reportant*.

81. Cf. Prudentius, *Psychomachia* 689: *te maxima virtus*.

83. Cf. Vergil, *Aeneid* 8.364.

85–90. The concluding lines of the poem are obscure, but the poet mentioned here and called "father" and "interpreter" (v. 88) is surely Jan Van Kampen.

87–90. David was considered the composer of the Psalms. Sion is a mountain near Jerusalem, the city of Solomon.

89. Cf. C. 3.16.

8. To Francesco della Torre of Verona
Meter: Dactylic Hexameter

This poem, which Pellegrini (*Appunti* 1954, 95–96) dates before 1534, is addressed to the son of Giulio della Torre and the nephew of Giovanni Battista della Torre (see introductory note to C. 2). But it closes, once

again, with an encomion for the bishop Gian Matteo Giberti (see intro-
ductory note to C. 5). It appears to be inspired by Horace's *Ode* 1.17, in
which the poet invites Tindaris to his Sabine farm. Pellegrini (*Appunti*
1954, 115–16) publishes an Italian translation of Horace's *Ode*, attributed
to Fracastoro.

2. On the Penates, see *S.* 2.17.

4. Fracastoro owned a villa at Incaffi, a small town in the hills between
Verona and the Lago di Garda: this villa always remained the poet's fa-
vorite place. He went there in search of solitude and in order to cultivate
his studies. The woods surrounding the villa were also the setting for his
three philosophical dialogues.

12. Cf. Ovid, *Fasti* 4.549: *noctis erat medium placidique silentia somni.*

14. Cf. Vergil, *Eclogues* 7.50: *adsidua postes fuligine nigri.*

15. Typhoeus was a fearsome monster of Greek mythology. Fracastoro's
point is that his guest will not find here the sort of expensive statuary
that he might find in a more opulent house.

28. Eos, the Greek equivalent of the Latin Aurora, was the goddess of
dawn. Here the name is used to indicate the East.

31. For Benacus see the note on *S.* 1.31.

33. Cf. Claudian, *Carmina minora* 25.107.

34. Cf. Ovid, *Remedia amoris* 183: *parte sonant alia silvae mugitibus altae.*

36–39. Cf. C. 18.2–5.

40–41. The children mentioned here are most probably Fracastoro's
grandchildren, the sons of his daughter Isabella (cf. Pellegrini, *Appunti*
1954, 96). The *rustica numina* come from Ovid (*Fasti* 6.323 and *Metamor-
phoses* 1.192) and were subsequently adopted by Claudian, *Carmina minora*
25.18 (the same poem alluded to above, at v. 33).

46. Fracastoro adapts this line from Ovid, *Fasti* 1.155–56: *et tepidum volu-
cres concentibus aera mulcent / ludit et in pratis luxuriatque pecus. Ludere* is a
verb typically used for describing birds: see, for example, Mantuano's
Parthenice 1.437–38: *gyroque volucres / aereo ludunt.* In English poetry, one

can compare Lovelace's *To Althea from Prison*, "The birds that wanton in the air."

51. The god Pan, or Faunus, was half man and half goat and lived on Mount Lycaeum (in the northeast of the Peloponnese). In classical literature that mountain was typically represented as cold and covered in pine trees.

63. Sirius, the Dog Star, who brings on the dog days at the end of July.

64. This line is modeled on Vergil, *Aeneid* 3.215: *Stygiis sese extulit undis*.

65. Cf. Vergil, *Aeneid* 6.850: *surgentia sidera dicent*.

70. These are three constellations. Cepheus was named for a mythological king of Ethiopia. Boötes, according to one tradition was a plowman who drove his herds in the constellation of Ursa Major or Great Bear. Ursa Major is another name for the constellation Arcton, identified with the beautiful nymph Callisto, beloved of Zeus, who was transformed into a bear by the jealous Hera, but raised to the stars by Zeus.

74–76. Andrea Navagero (1487–1529) was a Neo-Latin poet and editor of classical texts to whom Fracastoro dedicated his dialogue on poetry, *Naugerius sive De poetica* (composed during the 1540s). Battus is Giovanni Battista della Torre (see the note on C. 2). Cf. Vergil, *Eclogues* 2.24–25.

76. Cf. Vergil, *Aeneid* 1.171.

79. See Ovid, *Heroides* 7.149: *sensi mala murmura vulgi*.

81. The identification of the name *Bubulo* is unclear: according to Pellegrini's translation (*Vita di Girolamo Fracastoro* 1952, *ad loc.*), it indicates the town of Bovolone, south of Verona. Yet in this passage we would expect a reference to the nearby town of Povegliano Veronese, not Bovolone: see the note on v. 83.

83. The river Tartaro rises in the hills to the southeast of the Lago di Garda by the town of Povegliano Veronese, where Giberti had a villa. It is from here that the poet Francesco Berni, also a protégé of Giberti, composed the *capitolo* addressed to Fracastoro of his *Rime Burlesche* (published posthumously in 1537).

86. Cf. Vergil, *Aeneid* 10.899: *hausit caelum mentemque recepit.*

90. Cf. Vergil, *Eclogue* 4.15: *deum vitam accipiet.*

9. On the death of Eriprando Madruzzo

Meter: Dactylic Hexameter

Eriprando Madruzzo was an Italian condottiere who fought in the service of Emperor Charles V against the Turks in Hungary. He commanded imperial troops at the Battle of Ceresole (1544), was responsible for the security of the Council of Trent, and died fighting the Protestants at Ulm in 1547, on which occasion this poem was written.

2. For the title "Caesar," here indicating the Holy Roman Emperor Charles V, see the note on *S.* 1.467–68.

7. The phrase *vivida virtus* is Vergilian: cf. *Aeneid* 5.754 and 11.386.

9. Cf. Ovid, *Fasti* 3.729: *totoque Oriente subacto.*

16. Cf. Ovid, *Ars amatoria* 3.229 *pars maxima rerum.*

10. To Cardinal Alessandro Farnese

Meter: Dactylic Hexameter

One of the most eminent men of the sixteenth century, Alessandro Farnese, *il Gran Cardinale* (1520–89), was the grandson of Pope Paul III (who was also christened Alessandro Farnese). In addition to being a patron of poets, artists and architects, he was a papal legate who tried to negotiate between Charles V and Francis I and also led some papal troops against the Schmalkaldic league in 1546, the same year in which (according to Pellegrini, *Appunti* 1954, 103–4) the present poem may have been composed. On Farnese see Claire Robertson, *"Il gran cardinale": Alessandro Farnese, Patron of the Arts* (New Haven, 1992).

4. Cf. Ovid, *Metamorphoses* 10.681–82: *cui turis honorem / ferret.*

11–12. The Araxes (Aras) is a river that flows through Turkey and Armenia. For the Euganean Hills see the note on *S.* 1.444.

15–16. Cf. Vergil, *Georgics* 3.187: *depulsus ab ubere matris.*

20–21. See Vergil, *Aeneid* 11.430–31: *nec parva sequetur / gloria.*

34. Cf. Vergil, *Aeneid* 6.7–8: *densa ferarum / tecta*.

39–40. The dog's name Tybero derives from the Roman river Tevere (*Tiberis*), while Athiso derives from the river Adige (*Athesis*), on which see on *S.* 1.448.

46. The paranthetical *tantus amor* is Vergilian: cf. *Georgics* 2.301 (*tantus amor terrae*) and cf. also 3.112 and 4.205. For *cupidine praedae*, see Ovid *Metamorphoses* 3.225.

48–49. Calais, one of the sons of Boreas, the North Wind, sailed with the Argonauts, as did Pollux and his twin brother, Castor, the sons of Tyndareus, king of Sparta.

51. Emonian horse, i.e., originating in Thessaly, a region of northern Greece famous for its horses.

53. The Hamadryades, like the Dryades (see the note on *C.* 5.17), are tree nymphs; *insuetus* probably refers to their being unacquainted with love, like their leader, the virgin goddess Diana.

58–59. According to a version of the myth, Dione was Venus's mother and therefore the grandmother of Aeneas and the ancestor of his lineage, the Roman people. The Farnese family claimed descent from Aeneas, as we see in the Sala dei Fasti of the Palazzo Farnese in Rome, where Ranuccio Farnese il Vecchio is portrayed as Aeneas in Francesco Salviati's fresco (begun in 1552 and finished by Taddeo Zuccari in 1563). Cf. also v. 95 below. The most famous instance of the epithet *Aeneadum genetrix*, in reference to Venus, is the opening of Lucretius's *De rerum natura*: *Aeneadum genetrix, hominum divomque voluptas / alma Venus*.

62. By "the republic of the wide world" Fracastoro probably means the *respublica Christiana*, the Church, conceived of as a spiritual commonwealth ruling all mankind.

65–68. For Incaffi see the note on *C.* 8.4. For Benacus, see on *S.* 1.31. Catullus, the Roman poet (see on *S.* 1.456–63), was born in Verona and had a villa in Sirmione, on a peninsula in the Lago di Garda. Both places were visible from Fracastoro's home.

79. For Pallas, epithet of the goddess Minerva, protectress of the arts, see on *S.* 1.456–63.

82. For Aonia see on *S.* 2.160.

84–85. Urania, Calliope and Clio are three of the nine Muses: Urania was the Muse of astronomy (cf. the note on *S.* 1.23), Calliope of epic poetry (cf. the note on *C.* 2.74), and Clio of history.

92. The Pennine Alps rise in the western part of the Alpine range, while Noricum was an ancient Celtic kingdom in what is now Austria and part of Slovenia: they represent the western and eastern limits of the Alps, repeatedly crossed by Alessandro Farnese on his diplomatic trips.

95. For *matre dea comitante* see above on v. 58–59.

100. For the title "Caesar," here indicating the Holy Roman Emperor Charles V, see on *S.* 1.467–68.

105. Ottavio Farnese (1524–86) was sent with his brother Alessandro against the Schmalkaldic league in 1546.

106. Cf. Ovid, *Metamorphoses* 13.296: *duri fugientem munera belli.*

108. For Castor and Pollux, sons of Tyndareus, see above on vv. 48–49.

110–11. The people of Italy descend both from Aeneas (see above on v. 58) and from Mars, who fathered the twins Romulus and Remus, founders of Rome. Cf. Vergil, *Aeneid* 10.752: *haut expers . . . virtutis avitae.*

112. The line beginning *Bella cient* is Vergilian: cf. *Aeneid* 1.541.

115–121. Fracastoro dreams that the Italians, eagerly following Alessandro Farnese's arms, will cross the Alps to invade Germany and so finally revive the glory of the ancient Romans. The Oenus, or Aenus (Inn) is a river that flows through Austria, as does the Danube, whose ancient name was the Ister. The Hercynian Forest was a dense and mysterious woodland that, in ancient times, stretched eastward from the Rhine, covering much of the territory inhabited by the Germans (see for example Caesar's description of this forest in *De bello Gallico*, 6.24–28). Cf. Vergil, *Aeneid* 11.877: *percussae pectora matres.*

123. For *maiora . . . concipe*, see Ovid, *Metamorphoses* 15.5–6: *animo maiora capaci / concipit.*

II. To the same illustrious cardinal

Meter: Dactylic Hexameter

For Alessandro Farnese, see the introduction to the previous poem. This poem was first published in 1546 in an appendix to the *De contagione et contagiosis morbis*, on which Fracastoro's enduring fame as a doctor chiefly resides. This poem is inspired by Vergil's *Fourth Eclogue*, often interpreted by Christians as a prophecy of the Messiah.

1. Cf. C. 3.21

2. For *Italiae decus*, see the note on J. 1.16.

4–8. For the reference to Alessandro Farnese's indefatigable diplomatic and military activity, see the introductory note to C. 10 and in particular vv. 87–124.

5. This line is modeled on Lucan, *Pharsalia* 10.472: *orator regis pacisque sequester.*

12. Cf. Vergil, *Eclogues* 10.39: *et nigrae violae.*

17. Cf. Juvenal, *Satires* 8.27: *alto de sanguine.*

18. For *super aethera tollunt*, see Paulinus of Nola, *Carmina* 18.117.

22–29. For the claim of the Farnese family to descend from Aeneas, see the note on C. 10.58. The phrase *O nimium dilecta Deo* is taken from Claudian, *Panegyricus* 7.96, the same passage Fracastoro drew on in C. 6.99–101. The Ara Maxima (a monumental altar dedicated to Hercules in the Forum Boarium) was one of the earliest monuments of ancient Rome: here Fracastoro plays on the name of the monument, making it overlap with the greatest altar of Christianity, the Basilica of St. Peter.

30–32. Pope Paul III (1468–1549) was the grandfather and namesake of Alessandro Farnese. This passage is modeled on Vergil, *Aeneid* 6.845–46: *quo fessum rapitis, Fabii? tu Maximus ille es, / unus qui nobis cunctando restitues rem.* For Fabius Cunctator, see the note on S. 2.53–57, where the same line is alluded to.

31. The phrase *heroum laudes* comes from Vergil, *Eclogues* 4.26.

31–35. The Pope's tiara is decorated with three crowns that symbolize his rule over the three realms of heaven, earth, and hell. The Pope also holds

St. Peter's keys, which have the power to open and close the gates of heaven and hell through the powers of excommunication and sanctification. His putative possession of these powers was at the core of the Protestant attack on the papacy. Cf. Vergil, *Eclogues* 4.51 and *Georgics* 4.222: *terrasque tractusque maris caelumque profundum.*

36. The Bark of Peter, which holds the apostles and the faithful, ultimately derives from Mark 4:35–41; there the apostles are in a boat on the Sea of Galilee when they see Christ walking on the water. The phrase *turbante procella* comes from Statius, *Thebaid* 7.536.

41. Cf. C. 7.74.

43. Cf. Vergil, *Aeneid* 12.168, said of Aeneas's son, Ascanius: *magnae spes altera Romae.*

44. Cf. Vergil, *Aeneid* 11.312.

56. Cf. Vergil, *Eclogues* 4.15–17.

59–63. Cf. Vergil, *Eclogues* 4.52–54: *Aspice, venturo laetantur ut omnia saeclo. / O mihi tum longae maneat pars ultima vitae / spiritus et quantum sat erit tua dicere facta.*

70–71. Cf. Statius, *Silvae* 4.1.17: *salve, magne parens mundi.*

72–76. Cf. Vergil, *Eclogues* 4.39–41.

12. To Pope Julius III

Meter: Dactylic Hexameter

Julius III, born Giovanni Maria Ciocchi del Monte, was pope from 1550 to 1555. Though Fracastoro depicts him as an energetic actor and though he had some diplomatic successes prior to becoming pontiff, his reign became a by-word for indolence, even license. He is mainly remembered today as the inspiration for the Villa Giulia in Rome and as the patron of the architect Vignola, the painters Vasari and Michelangelo, and the composer Palestrina. The form of the present poem, with its recurring refrain, shares features of the bucolic tradition. The most evident models are Vergil, *Eclogues* 8; Theocritus, *Idylls* 1 and 2; and Bion, *Bucolics* 1. The poem was most probably written in 1550, upon del Monte's election as pope (Pellegrini, *Appunti* 1954, 104–5).

2–4. See the note on C. 11.31–35.

3. In Greco-Roman mythology, Dis was the name of the underworld and of its ruler.

9–12. For Pan see the note on C. 8.51; for the Parcae see the note on C. 3.49.

14–17. As punishment for killing the Cyclops — according to one version of the legend — Apollo was condemned by Zeus to a year of menial labor, herding the oxen of Admetus, king of Thessaly, beside the river Amphrysus. The young and beautiful shepherd Adonis, born of the incestuous relations between Myrrha and her father, Cinyras, became Venus's lover; on his death and metamorphosis see the note on S. 2.212–22.

22–25. Fracastoro imagines the episode described in this poem, along with its prophecy, as having taken place many years earlier. He sets this bucolic scene in the fields of Sessa Aurunca, a town in Campania: see below on vv. 38–40. The Liri is a river that flows nearby, through Abruzzi and Campania.

24. The hendiadys *umbras et frigora* comes from Vergil, *Eclogues* 2.8.

25. Cf. Ovid, *Metamorphoses* 2.509: *ad canam descendit in aequora Tethyn*.

26–29. Sylvanus was a Roman god of woods and fields, originally identified with Pan. The Satyrs (or Silenoi) were minor deities, mostly dwelling in the woods. Half man and half goat, these snub-nosed figures were known for their insatiable sexual appetites.

32. Cf. Vergil, *Aeneid* 2.797.

37. According to Ovid's account (*Metamorphoses* 3.356–510), Echo was a nymph who perished through her unrequited love for Narcissus and left only her voice behind.

38–40. The identification of the character named Acmon is problematic, all the more so because in the 1574 edition he is instead named Anthus throughout the poem (see Notes to the Text, p. 389). In classical mythology both Acmon and Anthus are minor characters who happen to share the fate of being turned into birds (see *New Pauly s.v.*). However, certain details given in Fracastoro's poem about the character of Acmon/Anthus make it likely that he is to be identified with Galeazzo Florimonte (cf. E.

Carrara, *La poesia pastorale* [Milano: F. Vallardi, 1909], 398): in this case, the name Anthus, from the Greek noun *anthos* meaning "flower," would readily bring to mind his last name; the associations of the name Acmon (corresponding to the Greek noun *akmôn* meaning "anvil" or "thunderbolt") would be more obscure. It is not impossible, however, that Fracastoro intended to connect Acmon to the Greek word *akmê*, meaning "summit," which might recall *monte* in the name Florimonte, or possibly even his first name Galeazzo, associated with the Latin term *galea*, "helmet" or "crest." Florimonte (on whom also see the introductory note to C. 7) was originally from Sessa Aurunca (cf. v. 22). Between 1542 and 1552, he was bishop of the town of Aquino (cf. v. 39). He was closely connected to Pope Julius III, who, upon his election, promptly called him to Rome. It is not clear why Florimonte is said to be *proximus sanguine*, i.e., a relative, of Fracastoro. Fracastoro gives himself the name of Neorus, which, in the spelling Cneorus/Gneorus, is also attached to one of the young characters in C. 51. Neorus is also the name that Fracastoro gives to himself in a poem in Italian, where he pays homage to Tuscan poetry (cf. 1739 edition, vol. 1, 193 and 195).

49. Fracastoro models this line on the opening line of the second book of Ovid's *Ars amatoria: Dicite "io Paean!" et "io" bis dicite "Paean!"*

55. Alecto was one of the Furies. For Orcus see on J. 2.79.

62–63. Here and in the rest of the eclogue, Fracastoro plays on the similarity between the Latin word *Mons*, "mountain," and the last name "del Monte" of Pope Julius III.

70–71. Cf. Vergil, *Eclogues* 4.21–22: *distenta capellae / ubera* (also in the context of the golden age) and 9.31: *distendant ubera vaccae*.

76. The phrase *fortibus ausis* is Vergilian: cf. *Aeneid* 9.281.

81–82. For Cocytus see the note on J. 1.490. On the hope of pushing the "infernal" Ottoman Empire back to Caucasus, i.e., beyond the easternmost limits of the civilized world, cf. below vv. 110, as well as C. 6.169–70, 11.64–65, and 51 *passim*. In Greek mythology, the Titan Prometheus was chained to a cliff in this mountain range as punishment for stealing fire from the gods and giving it to mortals.

89. Damon and Alphesiboeus are the two shepherds who compete in a singing contest in Vergil's *Eclogue* 8.

99. This line is modeled on Lucan, *Pharsalia* 3.150: *ocius avertat diri mala semina belli.*

102. Hymenaeus was the Greco-Roman deity of marriage.

106–11. Fracastoro dreams of a western crusade led by Pope Julius III against the Ottoman Empire. For Bactria see on C. 6.169–70. Imaus was the ancient name for Himalaya.

122–25. Arcadia was a mountainous region in the central Peloponnese that, in classical literature, was depicted as remote, idyllic, and inhabited by peaceful shepherds. Sacred to the god Pan, it became a typical setting for bucolic poetry and was often considered the birthplace of the genre. According to Roman mythology, a community of Arcadians, led by King Evandrus, moved to Italy, settling on the Palatine Hill and later becoming Aeneas's allies in the war against Turnus (in particular see Vergil, *Aeneid* 8). Here a group of Arcadians is imagined returning to Rome, one delegation among many that paid homage to the new pope. Cf. Vergil, *Aeneid* 5.82: *non licuit finis Italos fataliaque arva.*

129–34. Maenalus and Lycaeum (see also the note on C. 8.51) are mountains in Arcadia. Maenalus is repeatedly evoked in Damon's song in Vergil's *Eclogue* 8.17–63. The Peneus and Ladon are rivers in Thessaly and Arcadia, respectively. According to Servius's commentary at Vergil, *Aeneid* 8.51, Evander was forced to flee his country either after having murdered one of his parents or because of a popular uprising.

144. Cf. Vergil, *Georgics* 4.129.

13. FRAGMENT

Meter: Dactylic Hexameter

For Giovanni Battista della Torre (Battus), see the introductory note to C. 2. According to Pellegrini (*Appunti* 1954, 106), Iolas, whose death is here lamented by Battus, is probably to be identified with Marcantonio della Torre (see introductory note to C. 2): hence the poem would have been written some time around 1511 or 1512. It invokes the tradition of commemorative pastorals like those of Bion, Moschus and Vergil (in particular *Eclogues* 5 and 10).

3. For Benacus see the note on *S.* 1.31; for Sarca, on *S.* 1.456–63. Cf. Statius, *Thebaid* 10.574: *pumiceo pastor rapturus ab antro.*

7. Cf. Ovid, *Ars amatoria* 1.531 and *Remedia amoris* 597: *surdas clamabat ad undas.*

13. Sirius, sc. the Dog Star.

14. FRAGMENT, TO GIOVANNI BATTISTA DELLA TORRE
Meter: Dactylic Hexameter
The context of the fragment is unclear. For Giovanni Battista della Torre see the introductory note to C. 2.

15. WINTER, TO THE SAME
Meter: Dactylic Hexameter
This fragment, together with the previous one and the next five, appears to belong to a larger depiction of rustic life and to a series of drafts, perhaps intended to form one poem (or more) of a bucolic nature that Fracastoro was planning to dedicate to his friend Giovanni Battista della Torre (see introductory note on C. 2): cf. Note on the Text, p. 451. Together the fragments convey a realism and an imagistic specificity that are rare in the completed poems of Fracastoro, though they can be found in C. 8, also dedicated to della Torre. According to Pellegrini (*Appunti* 1954, 106), the child Giulio named here may be one of Fracastoro's sons, who died prematurely. If that identification is correct, the poem would have been written before his death, around 1515–16 (cf. the introductory note to C. 3). In general, according to Pellegrini (*Appunti* 1954, 105–6, following Barbarani's opinion) this series of poetic drafts collected as C. 13–20 belongs to the years 1510–20.

1. The poem's opening is modeled on Vergil, *Georgics* 2.405: *frigidus et silvis aquilo decussit honorem,* a line itself taken from the earlier Latin poet Varro Atacinus (fr. 6 Blänsdorf). Aquilo is the North Wind (see note on *S.* 2.86).

2. Cf. Vergil, *Eclogues* 6.38: *cadant summotis nubibus imbres,* and Ovid, *Metamorphoses* 11.516: *ecce cadunt largi resolutis nubibus imbres.*

10. In a tribute to his foremost poetic model, Fracastoro imagines himself and his guest reading Vergil during the long winter nights. For the phrasing, cf. Martial, *Epigrams* 11.48.1: *Silius haec magni celebrat monumenta Maronis.*

11. Cf. Vergil, *Georgics* 2.458–59: *o fortunatos nimium . . . agricolas.*

16. Spring, to the same
Meter: Dactylic Hexameter

See the introductory note to C. 15. The general tone of the opening lines recalls the invocation to Venus in the first book of Lucretius's *De rerum natura.* References to the untying of oxen and to crops growing spontaneously invoke traditional accounts of the golden age in Latin poetry, most famously in Vergil's *Eclogue* 4.

1. The phrase *Ver purpureum* comes from Vergil, *Eclogues* 9.40.

2. For Zephyr, see the note on S. 2.86.

3. Cf. Vergil, *Georgics* 2.324: *vere tument terrae et genitalia semina poscunt,* and also Lucretius, *De rerum natura* 5.851–52.

4–5. Cf. C. 42.25–26.

6. Cf. Ovid, *Fasti* 2.762: *caeco raptus amore.*

10. In many places in the sixteenth century, for example in Florence, the New Year was celebrated on the Feast of the Annunciation, March 25.

12–13. For the god Saturn's settling in Italy and bringing on a golden age, see the note on S. 1.422 and C. 5.18–19.

16–17. Cf. Lucan, *Pharsalia* 1.249–50: *pax alta per omnes / et tranquilla quies populos;* the phrase *pax alta* is a fixture in Seneca's tragedies (cf. *Agamemnon* 263, *Hercules Furens* 929, *Thyestes* 576, *Troades* 324–26). The identification of the ruler indicated here by the title "Caesar" (generally a title of the Holy Roman Emperors, cf. S. 1.467–68) is unclear (cf. Pellegrini, *Carmina* 1954, 19).

19. For *alta ad Capitolia,* cf. Silius Italicus, *Punica* 5.654 and 12.640.

20. The Tarpeian Temple is the Temple of Jupiter on the Capitoline Hill in Rome. The epithet "Tarpeian" comes from the nearby Tarpeian Rock, a place of execution in the ancient republic. The oak tree was sacred to Jupiter.

22–26. This passage recalls Vergil, *Eclogues* 4.28–30.

31–40. Cf. C. 11.70–76.

31. Cf. Vergil, *Aeneid* 8.72–3.

31–35. For the river Eridanus, see the note on S. 1.64; for Benacus see the one on S. 1.31: its waters are called Etruscan in reference to the Etruscan colonization of the region (see on C. 5.11); for the river Adige see the note on S. 1.448; for Hesperia see the one on S. 3.174–76.

17. Fragment, to the Same

Meter: Dactylic Hexameter
   See introductory note to C. 15.

2. For the Favonian wind see the note on C. 3.22. The phrase *ver egelidum* comes from Columella, *De re rustica* 10.282 and also recalls Catullus 46.1: *Iam ver egelidos refert tepores.*

4–6. This catalog of plants recalls the pseudo-Vergilian *Moretum* 71–72: *hic holus, hic late fundentes bracchia betae / fecundusque rumex malvaeque inulaeque virebant.*

8. Minthe was a beautiful nymph whom Hades tried to seduce, before his wife, Persephone, transformed her into a pungent herb (cf. Ovid, *Metamorphoses* 10.728–31).

10. Cf. Ovid, *Fasti* 4.869: *grata sisymbria.*

12. Aquilo is the North Wind (see note on S. 2.86).

18. Another fragment

Meter: Dactylic Hexameter
   See introductory note to C. 15.

2–5. Cf. C. 8.36–39.

19. ANOTHER FRAGMENT, TO THE SAME

Meter: Dactylic Hexameter

See introductory note to C. 15.

1. This line is modeled on ps.-Vergil, *Culex* 78: *novis manantia fontibus antra.*

3. For Benacus see the note on *S.* 1.31.

11. Cf. Vergil, *Aeneid* 9.166–67: *noctem custodia ducit / insomnem.*

12. The withe from Ameria (modern Amelia, in Umbria) was famous in Roman times (cf. Vergil, *Georgics* 1.264).

14. Cf. Ovid, *Metamorphoses* 6.22: *levi teretem versabat pollice fusum.*

20. ANOTHER FRAGMENT

Meter: Dactylic Hexameter

See introductory note to C. 15.

21. ON THE BIRTHDAY OF GIANO FREGOSO

Meter: Elegiac Distichs

Giano Fregoso was born in 1531, the son of Cesare Fregoso (see C. 6). After the assassination of the latter in 1541, he went with his mother to live in France, where he grew up in the small town of Agen, in Aquitaine in southwestern France. Eventually he became bishop of the town and for many years faithfully served the kings of France (and especially his protector Catherine de Medici) while indefatigably opposing the Protestant cause. He died in 1586. Since the present poem celebrates Giano's day of birth, it would seem to have been written in 1531 or, at the latest, in 1532 (cf. Pellegrini, *Appunti* 1954, 97).

2. *Triplices deae* is Ovidian: cf. *Metamorphoses* 2.654. The three goddesses are the Fates (for whom see the note on *C.* 3.49).

6. The name Giano derives from the Latin Janus, for the god of beginnings, gates, doors, etc. From this god derives the name of the first month of the year, January, and Giano himself was born on January 15.

8. Assuming the poem was written around 1530, "Caesar" most probably refers here to the boy's father, Cesare Fregoso, not the Holy Roman Em-

peror Charles V, his father's enemy in the War of the League of Cognac
(1526–30).

13–14. In ancient Rome, the gates of the temple of Janus were by custom
opened during wars and closed in times of peace.

22. ON THE BIRTH OF A SON TO VITTORIA FARNESE
Meter: Elegiac Distichs
   This poem celebrates the birth of Francesco Maria II della Rovere in
1549, one year after the marriage of his mother, Vittoria Farnese (1521–
1602), to Guidobaldo II della Rovere (1514–74). Francesco died in 1631.

1–4. In ancient Roman mythology, Lucina was the tutelary goddess of
women in labor; later Lucina became an epithet of Juno. Juno, passed
over in the judgment of Paris, was traditionally hostile to Venus, her son
Aeneas and his descendants, the Romans; for the Farnese family's claim
of descending from Aeneas, see the note on C. 10.58.

7–8. The lily, present on the coat of arms of the Farnese family, was the
flower sacred to Juno. The oak tree in Italian is *rovere*; hence, an oak ap-
pears on the della Rovere coat of arms. The oak was sacred to Jupiter, the
son of Saturn. The Isaurus was the ancient name of the Foglia River,
which flows into the Adriatic at Pesaro in Umbria, where Guidobaldo
della Rovere and his wife Vittoria lived.

11–16. The three concluding couplets of this poem are rich in allusions to
Vergil's prophetic *Eclogue* 4.

23. THE TOMB OF FRANCESCO MARIA MOLZA OF MODENA
Meter: Elegiac Distichs
   Francesco Maria Molza (1489–1544) was a poet in Latin and Italian.
He was also the teacher of Ippolito de Medici (1511–35), the short-lived
cardinal and archbishop. Fracastoro's authorship of this poem has been
questioned: see Notes to the Text, pp. 391–92.

2. For Aonia see the note on S. 2.160.

8. For the common proverbial expression, "More even than his own
eyes," cf. Catullus 3.5, 14.1, 82 passim, 105.2, as well as Fracastoro's C.
48.26 and J. 2.32, and in general TLL s.v. *oculus* 451.25–41.

24. To Giovanni Lippomano

Meter: Dactylic Hexameter

Giovanni Lippomano (1515–73?) served the Venetian state as chamberlain (*camerlengo*) in several of its eastern outposts, especially Cefalonia, in the Ionian Sea. According to Pellegrini (*Appunti* 1954, 104), this poem can be dated to 1549.

1. For the river Adige see the note on *S.* 1.448.

2. Cf. Horace, *De arte poetica* 69: *stet honos et gratia vivax.*

7. Cf. Vergil, *Aeneid* 2.281: *spes o fidissima Teucrum.*

25. On the death of Giovanni Battista da Monte

Meter: Elegiac Distichs

Giovanni Battista da Monte, or Montano (1489–1551), taught medicine in Verona and, like Fracastoro, studied the transmission of infectious diseases.

1. Fracastoro delicately alludes to Ovid's tragic account of the birth of Asclepius, the son of Apollo and the god of medicine, by adapting the first line from *Metamorphoses*, 2.617–18: *seraque ope vincere fata / nititur et medicas exercet inaniter artes.*

2. For Lachesis see the note on *C.* 3.49.

3. Lethe, one of the five rivers of Hades, induced forgetfulness of one's earlier life. The name comes from the Greek word for forgetfulness.

5. Asclepius was killed by Zeus at the bidding of Hades, who was angry that through his arts so many souls had been rescued from death. For Orcus see the note on *J.* 2.79.

26. To Gian Matteo Giberti

Meter: Elegiac Distichs

For Giberti, see the introduction to *C.* 5. According to Pellegrini (*Appunti* 1954, 103), this poem, like the following three, was written in 1533–34, while Fracastoro enjoyed Giberti's patronage and used his villa at Malcesine.

1. For Malcesine see the note on C. 5.2; for the reference to the Etruscan colonization of the region around the Lago di Garda, cf. C. 5.11.

4. The shepherd Thyrsis was a stock character in bucolic verse, appearing in Theocritus's *Idyll* 1 as well as in Vergil's *Eclogue* 7 and in Calpurnius Siculus's *Eclogues* 2 and 7. In addition to this poem, Thyrsis reappears in Fracastoro's equally bucolic C. 29 and 51.

27. To the same

Meter: Elegiac Distichs
  See introductory note to C. 26.

1. For Benacus see the note on S. 1.31.

2. Fracastoro models this line on Catullus, *Carmina* 68.58: *rivus muscoso prosilit e lapide.*

7–8. The tree of Apollo is the laurel; the tree of Adonis is not the myrrh (though it is traditionally associated with him), but rather the lemon tree: cf. the note on S. 2.212–22.

11–12. Apollo was the god of poetry as well as of medicine; for the epithet Phoebus see the note on S. 3.112.

28. To the same

Meter: Elegiac Distichs
  See introductory note to C. 26.

1–2. In classical mythology, Leuce was a beautiful nymph associated with the white poplar tree, mentioned by Fracastoro as typical of his region (see e.g., C. 50.133 and *passim*). In the bucolic tradition, Leuce appears first in Calpurnius Siculus, *Eclogues* 1.13; she also appears in C. 36 and 51. For Malcesine see on C. 5.2.

29. To the same

Meter: Elegiac Distichs
  See the introductory note to C. 26.

2. For Thyrsis see the note on C. 26.4.

3. For the laurel, sacred to Apollo, and the lemon, sacred to Venus or to her lover Adonis, see the note on *C*. 27.7–8 and also *S*. 2.212–22.

5. For Benacus see the note on *S*. 1.31.

30. ON THE MARSANGO RIVULET
Meter: Elegiac Distichs

Giovanni Battista Ramusio (1485–1557) lived in or near Padua and achieved fame as a classical scholar and geographer. In addition to editing Quintilian and Livy for the Aldine press, he was the author of *Delle navigationi et viaggi* (published between 1550 and 1606), which is considered a major account of the Western voyages of discovery and one which provided material for the writings of Richard Hakluyt and others. This poem and the following one were inserted in a letter to Ramusio, dated May 18 (probably 1550; cf. Pellegrini, *Appunti* 1954, 104); see Notes to the Text, p. 393. Here Fracastoro responded to his friend's request for an epigram to engrave on a bridge that Ramusio wished to build over a rivulet, flowing through his property in Marsango, a township in the Paduan province.

1. Cf. Horace, *Odes* 1.7.23: *tempora populea fertur vinxisse corona*.

9. The name Nape seems to be connected to the *Napeae*, nymphs of woods and valleys.

31. ON THE SAME
Meter: Elegiac Distichs

See the introductory note to the previous poem.

8. Nais is a nymph of fresh waters, while Galatea is a sea nymph and a traditional character in bucolic poetry (see *C*. 39).

32. FROM THE END OF THE *HOMOCENTRICA*
Meter: Dactylic Hexameter

The *Homocentricorum libri, sive de stellis*, published together with the *De causis criticorum dierum libellus* (first published in 1538, or more correctly in 1539: cf. Cibei, 2004), was Fracastoro's main contribution to astronomy and astrology. In writing it, he made use of the extensive knowledge and research of his good friend Giovanni Battista della Torre (see introductory note to C. 2), and it is to this same man, who had recently died (1534), that Fracastoro dedicates this final homage.

3. This line is modeled on Vergil, *Aeneid* 5.583: *inde alios ineunt cursus aliosque recursus.*

5. Cf. Vergil, *Aeneid* 2.619: *finemque impone labori.*

14. Cf. C. 16.1. For the Titan Helios see the note on S. 3.124.

18. In antiquity, Thrace was a region to the north of Greece, roughly equivalent to modern-day Bulgaria. It was the birthplace of the mythical poet Orpheus, to whom Fracastoro alludes.

22. Cf. Vergil, *Aeneid* 3.89: *da, pater, augurium, atque animis inlabere nostris;* and Ovid, *Ibis* 85: *adnuite optatis omnes ex ordine nostris.*

33. From the first book *On Contagious Diseases*
Meter: Dactylic Hexameter

On *De contagione et contagiosis morbis* (1546), see the introductory note on C. 11. The work discusses earthquakes, among other possible causes and harbingers of epidemics.

1. This poetic fragment begins as a quotation and reelaboration of Vergil, *Georgics* 1.181–82: *saepe exiguus mus / sub terris posuitque domos atque horrea fecit* (a passage in which Vergil gives advice on how to prevent mice or grass from appearing in holes and thus ruining a farmer's front yard).

6. Cf. Vergil, *Aeneid* 4.508: *haut ignara futuri.*

9. Mount Athos, a steep mountain in the Macedonian region of modern Greece, now contains some twenty Orthodox Christian monasteries. For the sea god Nereus see the note on S. 3.93–101.

34. From the third book of the same work
Meter: Dactylic Hexameter

On *De contagione et contagiosis morbis* (1546), see the introductory note on C. 11. This poem is inserted in a passage discussing the necessity of abandoning contaminated areas and even burning them in order to sterilize the environment.

1–2. This poetic fragment, like the previous one, appears to be a reelaboration of Vergil, here *Georgics* 1.84: *saepe etiam sterilis incendere profuit agros, / atque levem stipulam crepitantibus urere flammis* (a passage in which Vergil explains how to fertilize a field by burning it).

35. FROM THE *DIALOGUE ON POETRY*
Meter: Dactylic Hexameter

This poem comes from the dialogue *Naugerius, sive de poetica*, named for Fracastoro's friend Andrea Navagero (see the note on C. 8.74). This is the first in a series of three dialogues that were mostly composed in the last decade of Fracastoro's life and left unpublished at his death (see Peruzzi 1999, 12–14 and 77–81). The three dialogues are imagined as taking place during three consecutive days in the woods of Monte Baldo. The present poem, set about halfway through the *Naugerius*, serves as an interlude in the discussion and is presented (like all the other poetic interludes in Fracastoro's dialogues: i.e., C. 36, 38–39, and 41–42) as a performance by a young boy, who, at Navagero's bidding, is in charge of amusing the company with songs (cf. *Naugerius* 3.13). Here the bucolic love song reverberates in the rural setting of the dialogues and recalls Navagero's enraptured reading of Vergil's *Eclogues* at the onset of the discussion (*Naugerius* 2.10–12). This poem was translated into English and discussed by the Scottish poet John Black (1777?–1825) in *The Falls of Clyde, or the Fairies: A Scotish Dramatic Pastoral in Five Acts* (Edinburgh: William Creech, 1806), 89–90.

1. The name Thelayra may be connected to the root of the Greek verbs *thelgô*, "to charm," or *thelô*, "to wish or desire." The character appears again in C. 36 and also in Andrea Navagero's *Lusus Pastoralis* XIX, titled *Acon*.

4–5. Sirius is the Dog Star, bringer of warm weather. This couplet is modeled on Tibullus, *Elegies* 2.3.9–10: *nec quererer, quod sol graciles exureret artus, / laederet aut teneras pustula rupta manus.*

6. Ceres was the goddess of harvest, while Dione was an ancient goddess of the earth and of fertility, who, according to one version of the myth, was the mother of Aphrodite, goddess of love.

7. Cf. Vergil, *Georgics* 1.190: *cum magno veniet tritura calore.*

36. From the first book *On Intellection*

Meter: Dactylic Hexameter

This poem is included in the prose dialogue *Turrius, sive de intellectione*. On Fracastoro's dialogues see the introductory note to C. 35; on Giovanni Battista della Torre see the introductory note to C. 2. Like C. 35, this poem is a bucolic love song that suits the rural setting of the dialogues and works as an interlude in the discussion.

1. For Thelayra see the note on C. 35.1.

2–4. For Lucifer and Hesperus/Vesper see the note on S. 3.68.

5. For Leuce see the note on C. 28.1–2.

10. Cf. Vergil, *Georgics* 3.495: *et dulcis animas plena ad praesepia reddunt*.

12. Mycon, a shepherd, is mentioned in passing in Theocritus's *Idyll* 5 and in Vergil's *Eclogues* 3 and 7.

20. Iole, the beloved of Hercules, is the subject of Ovid's *Heroides* 9. Lycotas figures in *Eclogues* 6 and 7 of Calpurnius Siculus.

37. From the same book

Meter: Dactylic Hexameter

In the *De intellectione* this fragment, suffused with Neoplatonic language and imagery, is given as an example of the fanciful way in which a poet, as opposed to a philosopher, would describe the human process of cognition.

4. Cf. Vergil, *Aeneid* 1.588: *claraque in luce refulsit*.

38. At the end of the same book

Meter: Dactylic Hexameter

C. 38 concluded the first book of the dialogue *Turrius*. A more complete version of it (adding three stanzas at the beginning, one in the middle, and substituting the last stanza with a new one) was rediscovered in the eighteenth century and added to the 1739 edition of Fracastoro's poetry: see Notes to the Text, p. 396. In the present volume we give the text of the poem only once, in its most complete form, as it appeared in the 1739 edition: see C. 44.

39. FROM THE SECOND BOOK *ON INTELLECTION*

Meter: Dactylic Hexameter

This poem, included in the prose dialogue *Turrius, sive De intellectione*, invokes the same myth of the Cyclops Polyphemus and his misbegotten love for the nymph Galatea as appears in Theocritus's *Idyll* 11: the topic of this interlude (a brute's capacity to love) seems to anticipate the following discussion on the intellect of animals.

1. The phrase *carpe fugam* comes from Silius Italicus, *Punica* 10.62. Cf. also 14.221: *quique per Aetneaos Acis petit aequora fines*, which obliquely references the story of Galatea. For Galatea see the note on *C.* 31.8; for the Cyclops see the one on *S.* 3.182–89.

2. Cf. Ovid, *Tristia* 3.9.11: *quem procul ut vidit tumulo speculator ab alto*.

12. Scylla, together with Charybdis, was a sea monster who guarded the Straits of Messina (though other locations have been suggested).

16. Cf. Vergil, *Aeneid* 9.569 and 10.698, both reading *saxo atque ingenti fragmine montis.*

17. As we read in Ovid, *Metamorphoses* 13, Galatea's love for the handsome shepherd Acis ignited the jealousy of Polyphemus, who killed the young man by hurling a boulder at him. Yet Poseidon saved Acis from utter extinction by transforming him into the Acis River in Sicily.

40. FROM THE SAME BOOK

Meter: Dactylic Hexameter

This poetic fragment is inserted within a discussion of the various manifestations of madness. The only hero of the Trojan War to commit suicide, Ajax takes his own life after Odysseus tricks him out of the arms of the dead Achilles. But before this, in Sophocles's play of the same name, Ajax goes on a rampage. According to another myth, Bellerophon, on slaying the mythical beast Chimera, flies up to Olympus on Pegasus, his winged horse, but he is thrown by the horse and falls to earth, where, crippled and blind, he shuns humanity as he wanders through the plains of Aleion.

2. Cf. Vergil, *Aeneid* 10.661: *illum autem Aeneas absentem in proelia poscit.*

41. From the *Dialogue on the Soul*

Meter: Dactylic Hexameter

This poem is placed at the opening chapter of Fracastoro's third and final prose dialogue, *Fracastorius, sive de anima*; on Fracastoro's dialogues see the introductory note to C. 35. In it, Zeus addresses the beautiful Trojan youth Ganymede, whom Zeus, after transforming himself into an eagle, has just abducted from Mount Ida in Phrygia. He is carrying the youth off to Olympus where, together with the maiden Hebe, he will be a cupbearer to the gods. The ascent of the mortal Ganymede to heaven has often been seen as a metaphor of the soul's aspirations to immortality: see Plato, *Phaedrus* 255c, and *Laws* 1.636d (cf. Peruzzi 1999, ad loc.).

8–11. Zeus was the father of Dardanus, the eponymous founder of the Dardanian, i.e., Trojan, dynasty. In the ancient myth of Ganymede, Zeus kidnapped the boy because he had fallen in love with him; the Christian Fracastoro, however, shuns the traditional version and presents Jupiter as moved only by paternal sentiment. Cf. Ovid, 13.142–43: *nostri quoque sanguinis auctor / Iuppiter est.*

14. For Lucifer see on *S.* 3.68.

16. Among Christian authors, *ver perpetuum* is often used to describe Paradise; see, for example, Prudentius, *Cathemerinon* 3.103: *ver ubi perpetuum redolet.* The phrase, however, is first attested in Ovid, *Metamorphoses* 5.391.

42. From the same dialogue: Psyche

Meter: Dactylic Hexameter

In this poetic interlude, set about halfway through the dialogue, Psyche, like Ganymede in the previous poem, is a traditional metaphor for the human soul (*psyche* being the Greek word for "soul"). In an untranslatable way, this poem puns upon the two names of the Roman god whom she loves, *Amor* and *Cupido*, and the related verbs *amare* and *cupire*, which mean "to love" and "to desire," respectively. Fracastoro's representation of Cupid and Psyche owes much to the tale in Apuleius's *Golden Ass*, Books 4–5.

11–12. As elsewhere in Fracastoro's *Carmina*, the language recalls the invocation to Venus, the mother of Cupid, in the first book of Lucretius's *De rerum natura*.

15. For *pulcherrime rerum*, see Ovid, *Ars amatoria* 1.213 and *Heroides* 4.125.

18. In art and literature, Cupid is often depicted as blindfolded.

22. Narcissus, a handsome youth of Boeotia, spreads his arms to embrace his own reflection in a pond. Meander is a deity who guarded the Meander River that flowed through Caria, in what is now Turkey.

25–26. Cf. C. 16.4–5.

43. An ancient epigram, from *Blending Wine*
Meter: Elegiac Distichs

This poem accompanied Fracastoro's short essay on blending wines with water (*De vini temperaturae sententia*, published in 1553, but composed in 1534) and elegantly summarized its tenor. It is a translation, possibly by Fracastoro himself (see the Notes to the Text, p. 395), of the following epigram (9.331) in the *Greek Anthology*, attributed to Meleager of Gadara (1st century BCE):

> Αἱ Νύμφαι τὸν Βάκχον, ὅτ᾽ ἐκ πυρὸς ἥλαθ᾽ ὁ κοῦρος,
> νίψαν ὑπὲρ τέφρης ἄρτι κυλιόμενον.
> Τοὔνεκα σὺν Νύμφαις Βρόμιος φίλος· ἢν δέ νιν εἴργῃς
> μίσγεσθαι, δέξῃ πῦρ ἔτι καιόμενον.

The poem invokes one version of the Dionysus myth, in which he was born to Semele after Zeus struck her with a lightning bolt. Dionysus was then nurtured by the rain nymphs of Nysa, whom Zeus, in gratitude, transformed into the constellation Hyades. In antiquity, and down to the Renaissance, pure wine, without any added water, was considered to be unhealthy as well as a sign of intemperance; hence the "great friendship" between the rain nymphs and Bacchus.

44. To Bacchus, the conciliator
Meter: Lyric stanza composed of three alcaic hendecasyllables, followed by a glyconic

The Ode *Baccho conciliatori* concluded the first book of the prose dialogue *Turrius, sive de intellectione*. The text of C. 44 is a longer version of the poem first included with Fracastoro's poetry in 1739: see C. 38 and Notes to the Text, p. 396. This is the only poem by Fracastoro—aside from the newly discovered C. 56, of questionable attribution—to be written in a meter other than the standard hexameters or elegiacs.

1–2. The opening paraphrases Horace, *Odes* 2.11.17–18: *dissipat Euhius* [sc. Bacchus]/*curas edacis.*

4–9. Following a convention of ancient religious hymns, the poet invokes the god by listing all of his names and epithets. Liber ("the free one") is a Latin name, while all the others have a Greek origin: Bacchus (meaning "maddened"), Euius (from the cry "Euhoe" of his followers), Lyaeus ("releaser from cares"), Bromius ("noisy"), Iacchus (related to the sound of an ecstatic cry), and Bassareus (related to the word for the fox skin worn by the god's Thracian female acolytes). Semele, the daughter of Cadmus, king of Thebes and of Harmonia, was impregranted by Zeus and gave birth to Dionysius. The phrase *laetitiae dator* comes from Vergil, *Aeneid* 1.738.

10–11. Maenads were female devotees of Dionysus who frequented mountaintops in a Bacchic frenzy. According to one legend, Dionysus made an expedition to India.

13–14. The thyrsus was a staff made from fennel and covered in ivy that the celebrants of Bacchus carried around in their festivals. Bacchus was borne in a chariot drawn by such exotic animals as tigers or lions.

16. Cf. Horace, *Odes* 3.25.20: *cingentem viridi tempora pampino.*

19. For Bactria see the note on C. 6.169–70: here it refers again to Bacchus's eastern origins and to his incursions into the East.

22. "Euoe" was the cry made by the followers of Bacchus.

24. The son of Leto is Apollo (see on S. 3.288).

25–26. According to legend, after Semele, the mother of Dionysus, was consumed by one of Zeus's lightning bolts, Zeus took the fetus and hid it in his thigh until it was brought to term. Hence Dionysus was said to have two mothers and thus to be "twice-born."

33–36. According to one legend, some pirates seized young Dionysus, hoping to sell him into slavery. But when he revealed himself in his divinity, they jumped into the water and were transformed into fish: also see introductory note to C. 5.

37–40. In The *Bacchae* of Euripides, Pentheus, the king of Thebes, bans the cult of Dionysus. In revenge, the god maddens Agave and Autonoe, the mother and the aunt of Pentheus, who tear him apart with their bare hands.

41–42. Lycurgus, king of Thrace, on hearing that Dionysus had arrived in his land, imprisoned all of the god's followers. Dionysus avenged himself by causing drought and insurrection in the land and by maddening Lycurgus, who killed his son with an ax, mistaking him for a patch of ivy sacred to the god.

43–44. Giants rose up against Zeus at the instigation of Earth, whose sons, the Titans, he had imprisoned in the underworld. They were vanquished, however, by the Olympian gods, Bacchus among them.

45–48. According to the myth, Bacchus wandered for a number of years in India, spreading his cult, before he continued on to Greece. Susa was a city of ancient Persia, in the Zagros Mountains. The Achaemenians (descended from the mythical first king Achaemenes) were the dynasty that ruled Persia from the sixth to the fourth centuries BCE.

50. The Thyades were female followers of Dionysus.

56. For Scythia see the note on S. 3.403. The wish, expressed in the last stanza, to destroy the barbaric Scythians living far to the East may contain an allusion to the Ottoman Empire.

45. ON THE FLIGHT OF EMPEROR CHARLES V
Meter: Dactylic Hexameters

This poem can be dated to 1552 (cf. Pellegrini, *Appunti* 1954, 105) and seems to have circulated as a pamphlet soon after its completion (see Notes to the Text, p. 397). It refers to the events following the Schmalkaldic War (1546–47), which ended at the Battle of Mühlberg, with Charles V's defeat of the Protestant forces. He then decreed the so-called Augsburg Interim (1548), which made certain allowances to the Protestants. In 1552, however, the Protestant princes, in alliance with Henri II of France, rose up against Charles, who retreated to the Netherlands.

11. Charles V's brother and adjutant was Ferdinand I (1503–64), who ruled over the eastern half of the Hapsburg domains and became, after Charles's abdication in 1556, the Holy Roman Emperor.

22. Margaret of Parma, duchess of Parma, was a natural daughter of Charles V. After her first husband, Alessandro de' Medici, duke of Florence, was assassinated in 1537, she was married off to Ottavio Farnese, duke of Parma, in 1542.

46. On the death of Marcantonio della Torre
Meter: Dactylic Hexameter

For Marcantonio della Torre, see the introductory note to C. 2. According to Pellegrini (*Appunti* 1954, 93), this poem, like C. 2, was composed shortly after Marcantonio's death in 1511. On the vexed questions regarding the tradition and authorship of this poem, which resembles Fracastoro's lament on Marcantonio della Torre's death in the closing lines of S. 1 (454–69), see Notes to the Text, p. 398.

2. Marcantonio della Torre taught anatomy at the University of Pavia, by which the river Ticino flows.

3. Cf. Vergil, *Aeneid* 6.782: *animos aequabit Olympo.*

4. Apollo was the god of medicine, as well as of poetry.

9–10. For Benacus, see the note on S. 1.31; for the river Sarca see the note on S. 1.456–63. Cf. S. 1.460–61.

11. As already noted by Volpi, this line recurs at S. 1.409.

12. For the river Adige see on S. 1.448.

47. An Offering of thanks to Marcantonio Flaminio
Meter: Dactylic Hexameter

For Marcantonio Flaminio see the introductory note to C. 7. According to Pellegrini (*Appunti* 1954, 107), this poem was probably written around 1546, probably in response to Flaminio's poem to Fracastoro (1739, 1:vol 1, p. 184).

2. This line imitates Ovid, *Metamorphoses* 8.569: *quosque alios parili fuerat dignatus honore.*

4. Cf. Vergil, *Aeneid* 5.538 and 572: *monimentum et pignus amoris.*

5. Cf. Ovid, *Metamorphoses* 2.418: *quod nulla ceciderat aetas.*

12. Cf. Horace, *Epistles* 1.2.36: *intendes animum studiis et rebus honestis.*

16. Cf. C. 7.74.

18. This line closely imitates Ovid, *Metamorphoses* 8.267: *sparserat Argolicas nomen vaga fama per urbes.*

24. Both the English cardinal Reginald Pole (1500–1558) and the Venetian Alvise Priuli (1471–1560) were bound to Marcantonio Flaminio by friendship and common intellectual interests. Flaminio and Priuli belonged to the Circle of the Spirituals, created in Viterbo by Reginald Pole, which adopted a rather critical stance toward the Catholic Church.

25. Farnese is presumably Alessandro Farnese (1520–89), the cardinal, rather than his grandfather and namesake, Pope Paul III. Flaminio, like Pole, was strongly connected to the two Farnese.

26. On the proverbial expression "more than his own eyes," see the note on C. 23.8.

27. For *pulcherrima Roma,* see Vergil, *Georgics* 2.534.

48.

This poem, found by Volpi in a manuscript that belonged to Apostolo Zeno and hence was added to the appendix of newly discovered poems in the 1739 edition, coincides with C. 27.5–12 (see Notes to the Text, p. 399). The text and translation are not, therefore, repeated here.

49.

Meter: Elegiac Distichs

For Giberti, see the introductory note to C. 5. This poem bears some obvious similarities to C. 10, in which Fracastoro's son sends two puppies to Alessandro Farnese. Since one of those dogs is mentioned as being sired by Lycus — assuming it is the same dog as the one who bears that name in the present poem — it would follow that this poem was written before C. 10 (ca. 1546). In that case, however, it would be peculiar for Lycus to remain in Fracastoro's household long enough to sire the next generation.

3. The reference of the name Caryclus is obscure.

50. Fragments of a poem in praise of Giberti
Meter: Dactylic Hexameter

Like the following composition, this poem was dedicated to Gian Matteo Giberti (see the introductory note to C. 5) in the expectation of his being created cardinal. Because that promotion never came to pass, this poem, like the following one, was left incomplete, and part of its material was later reused for C. 11 and 12. The fact that C. 50 and 51 have many lines in common supports the idea that they were composed at the same time. Indeed, their drafts appear intermingled in the pages of the manuscript (see Notes to the Text at C. 50 and 51). Both of the poems (and in particular C. 51) also present many similarities with the series of bucolic fragments addressed to Giberti that were published in the *Carminum liber* as C. 26–29 and that seem to have been composed around the same time as C. 50–51. Both C. 50 and 51 in fact were written during the pontificate of Clement VII (1523–34), and more probably toward the end of it, while Fracastoro was enjoying the use of Giberti's villa at Malcesine (ca. 1533–34): cf. Pellegrini (*Appunti* 1954, 100).

1–30. Earliest draft of the poem that appears in the manuscript.

2. Cf. C. 3.21.

3. For the Favonian wind see the note on C. 3.22.

13–18. For the river Adige see the note on *S*. 1.448. For Benacus see the note on *S*. 1.31. For the association of the *citrus*, or lemon, with Venus, see the note on *S*. 2.212–22. Paphos is a town on Cyprus, an island that was sacred to Venus because, in some versions of her myth, she was born there. Cf. Vergil, *Aeneid* 5.539: *viridanti . . . lauro.*

15. Cf. C. 13.3.

20–26. In Greco-Roman mythology Naiads were aquatic nymphs associated with streams, fountains, and brooks. The names listed in this passage are tutelary deities of various towns on the Lago di Garda: many of them are mentioned and further described in Iodoco Bergano's poem *Benacus* (published 1546); for his appreciative response to Fracastoro's *aition* poem about the carp of the Lago di Garda, see introductory note on C. 5.

21. Tusca corresponds to the village of Toscolano. Sirmio is the town of Sirmione, where Catullus had his villa (cf. his poem 31). Stella refers to a cliff of that name near the small peninsula of Punta San Vigilio: Bergano (*Benacus*, book 5, ff. 79v–80r) narrates the story of the nymph Stella who was turned to stone as she tried to escape the satyr Viggilius.

22. Saloe corresponds to Salò, and Lacusia to Lazise. Lacusia was said to be the beloved of Bacchus, probably because this region is rich in wine production.

23. Limonis corresponds to the village of Limone, famous for its lemon trees, here called the trees of Adonis (see on *S.* 2.212–22). In book 3 of Bergano's *Benacus*, we find a long description of the story of Limonis and his twin brother, Gryneus (corresponding to the village of Gargnano; see the note at v. 24 below). In this version, both children were males, born of the union of the lake god Benacus and the nymph Phyllis. According to Bergano, when Limonis grew up, he dedicated himself to tending a beautiful orchard of lemon trees, while Gryneus became a fisherman.

24. Bardo is the nymph corresponding to the village of Bardolino. Cesia can be identified with the village of Cisano. Grinea corresponds to Gargnano, a village famous for carp fishing: cf. for example Bembo's *Sarca* vv. 271–76 (published in this I Tatti Library); for its connection to Limonis, see the note above at v. 23. Grinea is said to have been loved by Apollo and to have had prophetic powers (see vv. 27–28 below), possibly on account of the similarity between her name and the town of Grynium in Asia Minor (modern west Turkey), which was home to a sanctuary and an oracle of the god (cf. Vergil, *Aeneid* 4.345).

25. Trimelia may correspond to the village of Trimosine, or better to Trimelone, a small island along the coast south of Malcesine. The iden-

tity of Mersa is unclear, but if the text is read as Melsa (cf. v. 69), it can be seen as a variant of Malcesine (see also Pighi 1966, 17 n. 2). It is unclear why Trimelia is said to be a virgin, or Mersa a mother.

26. Carita corresponds to the village of Garda, surrounded by the slopes of Mount Baldo.

29. On the reference to the Etruscan colonization of the region around the Lago di Garda, see on C. 5.11.

31–37. Variant to vv. 5–12.

35. Cf. C. 3.16.

38–91. Second draft appearing in the manuscript.

39. Sacred cap (sacro . . . galero), i.e., that of a cardinal.

64. This line is modeled on Ovid, *Metamorphoses* 8.746: *dryades festas duxere choreas*.

68. This couplet discreetly alludes to Propertius's famous mention of the *scripta lascivi Catulli* (*Elegies* 2.34.87), imitated by Ovid, *Tristia* 2.427.

69. Melsina corresponds to the village of Malcesine (cf. Mersa above at v. 25) where Giberti had a villa that Fracastoro was occasionally permitted to use and in which he could devote himself to "rustic" poetry.

70. Charitea, which at v. 26 was spelled Carita, corresponds to the village of Garda.

76. The "Etruscan kings" to which Fracastoro refers are the Florentine Medici family, from which Pope Clement VII (Giulio de' Medici) was descended.

81. For Harpies see the note on S. 3.151–54; for the Eumenides, also called Erynnes or Furies, see the note on J. 1.205.

85. The Virgin is Lady Justice.

92–99. Variant of vv. 9–12; cf. also 51–55 in second draft and 131–37 in third draft.

96. Cf. Vergil, *Aeneid* 8.116: *paciferaeque . . . olivae*.

100–113. Variant of vv. 49–55 in second draft and 129–40 in third draft; for vv. 109–13, cf. also 9–12 and 92–99.

103–4. These lines refer to Giberti's coat of arms: a crescent moon surmounted by three stars (cf. the letter by Da Prato to Volpi in Fracastoro 1739, appendix on autograph, p. 7). For Leto, mother of Diana, the goddess of the moon, see on S. 3.288.

115–44. Third draft appearing in the manuscript.

140. For Mount Baldo see above on v. 26.

141. In classical iconography and texts, river gods often appeared as bull-headed men. The white poplar tree, very common in Italy, was sacred to Hercules (cf. e.g., Seneca, *Hercules furens* 912, or Vergil, *Aeneid* 8.276).

51. FRAGMENT OF AN ECLOGUE IN PRAISE OF GIBERTI
Meter: Dactylic Hexameter

Like the previous composition, this poem is dedicated to Gian Matteo Giberti in the expectation of his being created cardinal. That promotion, however, never came to pass: see the introductory note on C. 50. Unlike the previous work, whose form is that of a panegyric, the present poem is conceived as an eclogue in which a trio of young men and women engage in a singing contest, as is often the case in pastoral poetry (cf., for example, Vergil's *Eclogue* 5).

1–22. Fragments of the beginning of the poem, perhaps composed at a later stage and written over a set of pages that were left blank in the manuscript.

1. Hybla is the name of several towns in Sicily, home of Theocritus and the setting for several of his Idylls. Cneorus (also spelled Gneorus *passim*) seems to be a variant of Neorus, for whom see the note on C. 12.38–40 For Leuce see the note on C. 28.1–2. The twig of hibiscus is used by the shepherd as a goad: cf. Vergil, *Eclogues* 2.30.

3. For Benacus see the note on S. 1.31.

6. For Malcesine see the note on C. 5.2 and 50.69. Cf. Vergil, *Eclogues* 10.8: *respondent omnia silvae.*

7. For the name Thelayra see the note on C. 35.1, where, as in C. 36, it is attributed to a female character in a bucolic setting.

14. For the river Adige see the note on S. 1.448.

15–17. The mother and son alluded to here are Venus and Cupid. Cf. Ovid, *Fasti* 6.463: *miscentur tristia laetis*.

18–22. For these lines, alluding to Giberti's expected nomination as cardinal, cf. C. 50. 114–18.

23–99. First draft of the poem in the manuscript.

25. Alcon is the older hunter who gives instructions on dog breeding to the youth Acastus in C. 1 (v. 5 *senior*); see introductory note to C. 1.

35–36. For the reference to Giberti's coat of arms, see the note on C. 50.103–4.

39. The virgin alluded to here is the personification of Justice; cf. C. 50.85.

46–48. For the ancient representation of river gods as bull-headed men, see the note on C. 50.141.

49–52. Fracastoro deftly alludes to a passage in Vergil describing Benacus, *Georgics* 2.159–60: *te, Lari maxime, teque, / fluctibus et fremitu adsurgens Benace marino?*

53–60. For Sirmione see the note on C. 10.65–68. These lines allude to Giberti's patronage of poets. It is also likely that they were written in thanks to Giberti for permission to use his villa at Malcesine. They echo Vergil's first *Eclogue*, in which the shepherd Tityrus obtained his parcel of land through the intervention of a godlike figure (i.e., Augustus). For Thyrsis, see the note on C. 26.4.

65–68. For the allusion to Pope Clement VII and the Etruscan origins that he shared with the inhabitants of the Lago di Garda, see the note on C. 50.76. Cf. Vergil, *Aeneid* 10.149: *memorat nomenque genusque.*

70–72. For the Caucasus Mountains and the allusion to the myth of Prometheus, see the note on C. 12.82; for Alecto see the one on C. 12.55; for the Gorgons see the one on C. 6.8; for the Harpies see the one on S. 3.151–54.

78. Cf. Vergil, *Aeneid* 10.37: *ventosque furentis*.

79. In speaking of the "king of the bees," Fracastoro follows Vergil's *Georgics* 4 in attributing the masculine gender to the queen bee.

90–91. For the reference to Giberti's coat of arms, see the note on C. 50.103–4; for the moon's epithet Phoebe see the one on S. 3.112.

94–99. For Hesperia see the note on S. 3.174–76. Lines 94–99 are identical to those in the closing of C. 16.35–40, and cf. also the closing of C. 11.72–75. For the myth of Saturn, hiding in Italy and establishing a golden age, see the notes on S. 1.422 and C. 5.18–19. The millenarian tone of these lines echoes Vergil's *Eclogue* 4.

100–9. Variants of the beginning of the poem: cf. vv. 1–6 and 23–28.

133. Cf. Ovid, *Amores* 2.17.32: *populiferque Padus*.

140. For *proceras . . . laurus*, cf. Catullus, *Carmina* 64.289.

186–249. Third draft of the poem.

196. The reference of the name Aylas is obscure; however a character named Asylas appears several times in Boccaccio's pastoral poetry (cf. *Bucolicum carmen* 4.119, 6.126, 14.225–27).

232–33. For Amphrysos and the myth of Apollo tending the herds of Admetos, see the note on C. 12.14–17.

248–49. For the Meander and its connection to Narcissus, see the note on C. 42.22.

250–308. These lines contain short drafts of the initial sections of the poem. They elaborate a variant that was later incorporated into the final draft of the poem (cf. vv. 309–90).

250. Almo is the name of a small affluent of the Tiber, now called Acquataccio, and also the name of a character in a late-antique short bucolic poem contained in the *Anthologia Latina* (393) that certainly served as a model for the initial lines of Fracastoro's C. 51 (cf. Notes to the Text at v. 250 for the presence of a character named Theon as well):

> *Almo Theon Thyrsis orti sub colle Pelori*
> *semine disparili: Laurente, Lacone, Sabina.*
> *Vite Sabina, Lacon sulco, sue cognita Laurens.*
> *Thyrsis oves, vitulos Theon egerat, Almo capellas,*
> 5 *Almo puer pubesque Theon et Thyrsis ephebus;*
> *Canna Almo, Thyrsis stipula, Theon ore melodus.*

Nais amat Thyrsin, Glauce Almona, Nisa Theonem;
Nisa rosas, Glauce violas dat, lilia Nais.

304. The arts of Athena refer to Hybla's weaving skills: see the introductory note to C. 6. For the epithet Pallas, see on *S.* 1.456–63.

306. Cf. Vergil, *Eclogues* 1.56: *alta sub rupe canet.*

309–90. Fourth and most polished draft of the poem.

327. In Greek mythology, there are two Mount Idas, one in Crete, sacred to Zeus, the other in the Troad, sacred to Venus, who, together with her son, Cupid, is alluded to here.

367–70. Diana, the goddess of hunting, was born, like her brother, Apollo, on the Aegean island of Delos. Cf. Vergil, *Eclogues* 7.29–30: *saetosi caput hoc apri tibi, Delia, parvos / et ramosa Micon vivacis cornua cervi.*

372. Cf. Vergil, *Georgics* 3.55 *camuris hirtae sub cornibus aures.*

375–76. For the Hesperides and their golden apples, see the note on *S.* 2.212–22.

52. Fragment on poisons
Meter: Elegiac Distichs

This fragment and the next one (C. 53) are free translations of the opening lines of the *Theriaca*, a Greek poem on antidotes to poisons, especially snake bites, by Andromachus the Elder (*floruit* 60 CE), court physician to the emperor Nero. The word *theriaca* (from which the modern English word "treacle" remotely derives) was a honeyed medication to combat snake bite. The original Greek poem, which in its entirety runs to 174 lines, is transmitted via two passages of the eminent Greek physician Galen (ca. 130–ca. 200 CE): *De antidotis* 1.6, and *De theriaca ad Pisonem* 6–7. It seems probable that Andromachus was familiar with the extant poem of the same name by the Alexandrian poet Nicander of Colophon, who lived in the second century BCE.

The Greek text of the opening of Andromachus's poem (vv. 1–28, also including the lines translated in the longer version of C. 53) is given here for the convenience of the reader:

Κλῦθι πολυθρονίου βριαρὸν σθένος ἀντιδότοιο,
    Καῖσαρ, ἀδειμάντου δῶτορ ἐλευθερίης.

Κλῦθι Νέρων, ἱλαρήν μιν ἐπικλείουσι, Γαλήνην,
    Εὔδιον, ἢ κυανῶν οὐκ ὄθεται λιμένων.
5   Οὐδ᾽ εἴ τις μήκωνος ἀπεχθέα δράγματα θλίψας,
    χανδὸν ὑπὲρ στυγνῆς χεῖλος ἔχοι κύλικος.
    Οὐδ᾽ εἰ κωνείου πλήσοι γένυν, οὐκ ἀκονίτου,
    μέμψατο δ᾽ οὐ ψυχροῦ χυλὸν ὑοσκυάμου.
    Οὐ θερμὴν θάψον τε καὶ ὠκύμορον πόμα Μήδης,
10   οὐδὲ μὲν αἱμηρῶν ἕλκεα κανθαρίδων.
    Οὐ ζοφερῆς ἔχιός τε καὶ ἀλγεινοῖο κεράστου
    τύμματα, καὶ ξηρῆς διψάδος οὐκ ἀλέγοι.
    Σκορπίος οὐκ ἐπὶ τήνδε κορύσσεται, οὐδὲ μὲν αὐτὴ
    ἀσπὶς, ἀδηρίτων ἰὸν ἔχουσα γόων.
15 Οὐ μὲν ἀπεχθόμενος καὶ δρύας ἀντιάσειε,
    καὶ κατὰ φωλειὸν θερμὸς ἔνερθε μένοι.
    Οὐκ ἀλέγοι δρύϊνα ἂν ἀναίμακτον δ᾽ ἔχει ἰὸν
    αἱμόρρους, τοιῷ δαμναμένη πόματι.
    Οὐ μὲν ἀπεχθήεντα φαλάγγια σίνεται οὕτως
20   ἀνέρα, φρικαλέον δ᾽ ἄχθος ἔθηκε πόνων,
    οὐχ ὕδρος, οὐκ ἐπὶ χέρσον, ὅθ᾽ ὕδατα καρκίνος αἴθει
    βοσκόμενος, θερμῆς ἤρξατο πρῶτον ἄλης,
    χέρσυδρος, θανάτῳ πεπαλαγμένα χείλεα σύρων,
    ἀντόμενος, γλυκεροῦ τέρμα φέροι βιότου.
25 Τῇ πίσυνος λειμῶσι θέρους ἐπιτέρπεο Καῖσαρ,
    καὶ Λιβυκὴν στείχων οὐκ ἀλέγοις ψάμαθον.
    Οὐδὲ μὲν ἀμφίσβαινα φέρει μόρον, οὐδέ τις ἤδη
    φρύνος ἐνὶ ξηροῖς βοσκόμενος πεδίοις.

9. In a letter to Ramusio (see introductory note to C. 53), Fracastoro admits that he is uncertain of the meaning of the word "Medes."

53. FRAGMENT ON POISONS

Meter: Hexameters

This poem, like its predecessor (see the introductory note to C. 52) is a translation of the opening lines (1–28) of the *Theriaca* of Andromachus. It is somewhat closer to the original in substance than C. 52, but not in meter, for this version is composed in hexameters, while the original, like the previous translation, was composed in elegiac distichs. Fracastoro included this version in a letter, dated January 22, 1533, that he wrote to Giovanni Battista Ramusio (see Notes to the Text, p. 414), in response to his friend's request to compose a verse translation of the entire *Theriaca*. For the original Greek text see the introductory note to C. 52.

8. Susa was the capital of ancient Persia. It is not mentioned in Andromachus's original, but it is mentioned as the source for the best hemlock by Theophrastus, *Historia plantarum* 9.15.8.

14. According to one version of the myths concerning these two constellations, the hunter Orion boasted to Artemis that he would kill every animal on earth,   whereupon she dispatched a scorpion, who killed him.

20. The following reference occurs in Isidore of Seville, *Etymologiarum libri* 12.4.15: *Haemorrhois aspis nuncupatus quod sanguinem sudet qui ab eo morsus fuerit, ita ut dissolutis venis, quidquid vitae est, per sanguinem evocet. Graece enim sanguis* αἷμα *dicitur.* (The snake Haemorrhois is so called because whomever it has bitten loses so much blood that, the veins having been opened, the life departs with the blood. For in Greek the word for blood is αἷμα [*haema*]).

21. The amphisibaena was a mythical lizard with two heads, one at either end.

54. Another fragment
Meter: Elegiac Distichs
   Similar in tone and spirit to Claudian's *Carmina minora* 20 (beginning *Felix, qui propriis aevum transegit in arvis*) which concerns an aged farmer from the region around Verona.

4. Cf. Horace, *Epistulae* 1.1.88: *melius nil caelibe vita.*

55. Beginning of the *Syphilis*, another version
Meter: Dactylic Hexameter
   On this slightly different opening of the *Syphilis* and its relation to the published version, see the Note on the Text, p. 354.

19–20. Cf. C. 16.4–5.

56. On the death of M. Giberti

Meter: Phalaecean Hendecasyllables

This poem is attested in two sixteenth-century manuscripts, both of which attribute it to Fracastoro and give it the same title, "On the death of Matteo Giberti." Regarding Giberti, who died 1546, see the introductory note to C. 5. See also the Notes to the Text, p. 418.

In this poem, Fracastoro was inspired by the Roman poet Catullus (84–54 BCE), not only in terms of its meter, which was much favored by Catullus, but also in its tone, with its elaborate repetitions. Certainly Catullus (see the note on C. 10.65–68) was an important model for Fracastoro and, as a native of Verona, Catullus was an especially apt model for an encomium of the late bishop of Verona: Fracastoro mentions Catullus in his praise of Giberti's patronage of poets at C. 50 and 51. Catullus is invoked again when Fracastoro laments the death of another citizen of Verona, Marcantonio della Torre, at S. 1.456–63.

However, if the present poem is indeed by Fracastoro, it is one of only two (the other being C. 44) that he wrote in a meter other than hexameters or elegiac distichs. Also, the poem's syntactical structure, with its long, uninterrupted sentence and extremely marked parallelism, finds no exact analogy in Fracastoro's poetic corpus (although parallelism and anaphora are features that he appreciates: e.g., in the account of the young man's death at S. 1.392–94 and 409–11).

Above all, it is the identity of the addressee that raises doubts. The use in the present poem of the term "knight" may seem odd as a description of Bishop Giberti: the term *eques* is nowhere else attested in Fracastoro's poetic works, while Giberti is rather styled *heros* by Fracastoro at C. 28.5, 50 *passim*, and 51 *passim*. Moreover, there is no mention of the religious activity that was central to Giberti's life, and the title of *poeta* applied to the famous scholar-bishop (at vv. 3 and 11) seems off the mark: Giberti was never a poet himself, merely a patron of poets. His celebrated patronage of literature, however, is consonant with the expressions *hospes* (in the sense of "host") of the Muses (vv. 4 and 12), and "companion" (*comes*) of the Muses (vv. 2–3 and 10–11; cf. also C. 2.101–3 *Illi . . . semper Musa comes*, said of the mythical poet Orpheus).

In any case, no other text exists within Fracastoro's oeuvre on Giberti's death: the two poems on the subject in Italian attributed to him in ms. Vat. Lat. 9948 almost certainly are not authentic (see Pellegrini, *Appunti* 1954, 103 and 114–15). Some scholars have seen this absence as evidence of a cooling in the relationship between the two men, but Pellegrini's arguments against this view are convincing (ibid., 99–103).

7. For Benacus see on *S.* 1.31.

57.

Meter: Elegiac Distichs

This poem is attested and attributed to Fracastoro in a sixteenth-century manuscript; see the Notes to the Text, p. 418. Its explicit address to Giberti (v. 5) and its pastoral content evidently assimilate it to the series of *C.* 26–29 and to *C.* 50–51, thus making the attribution quite plausible. If the attribution is correct, this poem as well was probably written in the years 1533–34, while Fracastoro was enjoying Giberti's hospitality at his villa in Malcesine (see introductory note to *C.* 26).

2. Simulus, or Simylus, is the farmer who serves as the protagonist of the *Moretum*, one of the poems in the *Appendix Vergiliana*, often thought to contain Vergil's juvenilia.

3. Cf. a line from another poem in the *Appendix*, *Copa* 21: *et lentis uva racemis*.

6. Giberti is frequently compared with the gods by Fracastoro; cf., in particular, *C.* 8.89–90 and 27.4.

Bibliography

꧁꧂

LATIN EDITIONS AND VERNACULAR TRANSLATIONS
OF FRACASTORO'S POETICAL WORKS*

Syphilis sive morbus gallicus. Verona: [Stefano dei Nicolini da Sabbio], 1530.

Syphilis sive morbus gallicus. Paris: Louis Blaubloom, 1531.

Syphilis sive morbus gallicus. Rome: Antonio Blado, 1531.

Syphilis sive morbus gallicus. Basel: [Johann Bebel], 1536.

Hieronymi Fracastorii Homocentrica. Eiusdem De causis criticorum dierum per ea quae in nobis sunt. Venice: Girolamo Scoto, 1538 [i.e., 1539]. Includes C. 32.

Alfonsi Ferri Neapolitani . . . ligni sancti multiplici medicina et vini exhibitione libri IV, quibus nunc primum additus est Hieronymi Fracastorii Syphilis sive Morbus Gallicus. Paris: Jean Foucher, 1539. With numerous reprints. Based on the 1536 edition.

Ioannis Secundi Hagiensis Basia et alia quaedam. Lyon: Sébastien Gryphe, 1539. Includes C. 5 (pp. 57–60).

Matteo Bandello, *Canti XI.* Agen: Antonio Robiglio, 1545. Includes C. 21 (f. 202v).

De sympathia et antipathia rerum liber unus. De contagione et contagiosis morbis et curatione libri III. Venice: Giunti, 1546. Includes C. 11 and 33–34.

Liber unus de sympathia et antipathia rerum. De contagione et contagiosis morbis et curatione libri III. Lyon: Guillaume Gazeau, 1550.

---

* For a complete list of the vernacular translations of the *Syphilis* before 1935, see Baumgartner–Fulton 1935. For a list of dubious editions of Fracastoro's *Opera omnia* known only through catalogs (cited by Otto Mencke in 1739, vol. 2 pt. 2, 148–52), cf. Pennuto (2008, xxxvi–xxxvii). Note also that the two editions of Fracastoro's *Opera omnia* given in WorldCat as printed in Lyons, 1550 (OCLC 27893081) and Venice, 1553 (OCLC 27307296) are both ghosts, originating in the microfilm corpus, *French Books before 1601*, published by the Center for Research Libraries.

Hieronimi Fracastorii Veronensis De temperatura vini sententia. Consalvi Barredae Hispani sententiam perpendens libellus. Camerino: Antonio Gioioso, 1553. Includes C. 43.

Hieronymi Fracastorii Veronensis Liber unus de sympathia et antipathia rerum. Item De contagione et contagiosis morbis et eorum curatione libri III. Lyon: Jean de Tournes and Guillaume Gazeau, 1554.

Opera omnia, in unum proxime post illius mortem collecta . . . . Accesserunt Andreae Naugerii patricii Veneti orationes duae carminaque nonnulla. [Edited by Paolo Ramusio.] Venice: Giunti, 1555.

Lettere di diversi autori eccellenti. Venice: Giordano Ziletti, 1556. Includes two letters containing C. 53 (pp. 742–43), and C. 30 and 31 (p. 774).

Syphilidis sive morbi gallici libri III. Ioseph libri II. Item Carminum liber I. Antwerp: Widow of Martin Nuyts, 1562. Based on the 1555 edition.

Carmina poetarum nobilium. Edited by Giovanni Paolo Ubaldini. Milan: Antonio Antoniano, 1563. Includes (ff. 13v–16v) the Alcon (= C. 1), attributed to Luigi Annibale della Croce or Cruceius.

Poemata ex quam plurimis autorum probatissimorum scriptis. Edited by Giovanni Antonio Taglietti (alias Taygetus). Brescia: Tommaso Bozola, 1568. Includes C. 25 and 23 (p. 49).

Opera omnia in unum proxime post illius mortem collecta. Secunda editio. Venice: Giunti, 1574.

Carmina illustrium poetarum Italorum. Edited by Giovanni Matteo Toscano. 2 vols. Paris: Egidio Gorbino, 1576–77. Includes the *Syphilis* and *Carmina* in vol. 2, based on the 1555 edition, with the addition of Alcon (= C. 1) and, in an appendix, of C. 11 and 23.

Hymnorum ecclesiasticorum ab Andrea Ellingero . . . emendatorum libri III. Accessere Ioseph libri II, autore Hieronymo Fracastorio . . . . Omnia nunc primum ita edita, ut studiosae iuventuti in scholis utiliter proponi possint, de sententia Henrici Petrei Herdesiani, rectoris Scholae Francofurti. Frankfurt am Main: Franz Bassée, 1578. Based on the 1555 edition.

Johann Engerd, *Madruciados libri tres: panegyrin heroicam . . . Madruciorum . . . familiae complectentes.* Ingolstadt: Wolfgang Eder, 1583. Includes C. 9 (p. 86). Based on the 1574 edition.

Opera omnia. . . . . Ex tertia editione. Venice: Giunti 1584. Based on the 1574 edition.

Opera omnia in unum proxime post illius mortem collecta. . . . In two volumes: *Operum Pars Prior, philosophica et medica continens* and *Pars Posterior:* . . . *continens . . . poemata item varia hac ultima editione et aucta et emendata.* Lyon: François Le Febure, 1591. Reprinted in 1601. Based on the 1584 edition.

Delitiae CC. Italorum poetarum, huius superiorisque aevi illustrium. Edited by Jan Gruytere. Frankfurt am Main: Jona Rosen, 1608. Contains *Syphilis* and *Carminum Liber,* based on the 1577 edition.

Hierakosóphion. Rei accipitrariae scriptores nunc primum editi. Accessit Kynosó-phion. Liber de cura canum, ex bibliotheca regia Medicea. Edited by Nicolas Rigault. Paris: Jérôme Drouart, 1612. Contains the Alcon (= C. 1, on pp. 113–20).

In fugam Caroli V imperatoris. [Edited by Domenico Molino.] [Venice: Pinelli, 1619.] Pamphlet edition of C. 45.

Operum pars [prior-] posterior. Geneva: Samuel Crespin, 1621. In two vol-umes. Based on the 1591 edition.

Operum pars [prior-] posterior. Geneva: Pierre and Jacques Chouët, 1622. Some copies listed as printed in Montpellier: Pierre and Jacques Chouët, 1622. In two volumes. Dependent on the 1591 edition.

Operum pars [prior-] posterior: . . . Poemata item varia hac ultima editione et aucta et emendata. Geneva: Jacob Stoër, 1637. In two volumes. Depen-dent on the 1591 edition.

Philippe Labbé, ed. *Heroicae poeseos deliciae ad unius Virgilii imitationem ex summis poetis . . . Fracastorio . . . selegit.* Paris: G. Meturas, 1646. Con-tains Book 3 of the *Syphilis* and C. 5, 6, 10, 12, 11.

Operum pars [prior-] posterior. Geneva: Samuel Chouët, 1671. In two vol-umes. Dependent on the 1591 edition.

Opera omnia poetica, nunc iterum in lucem data. Naples: Giacomo Raillard, 1683. Contains the *Syphilis, Alcon* (= C. 1), *Joseph,* and a selection from the *Carmina.*

Anthologia seu selecta quaedam poemata Italorum qui latine scripserunt. Edited by Thomas Power. London: R. Green and F. Hicks, 1684. Contains the *Syphilis* (pp. 40–77) and C. 2 (pp. 209–12).

Gratii Falisci Cynegeticon . . . Accedunt Hieronymi Fracastorii Alcon, carmen pastoritium. London: Charles Harper, 1699. Contains C. 1. *Poemata omnia, nunc multo quam antea emendatiora.* Edited by Giovanni Antonio and Gaetano Volpi. Padua: Giuseppe Comino, 1718.

Carmina illustrium poetarum Italorum. Edition attributed to Giovanni Gaetano Bottari. 11 vols. Florence: Giovanni Gaetano Tartini and Santi Franchi, 1719–26. Vol. 5 contains *Syphilis, Joseph,* and the *Carminum Liber.*

Syphilis sive morbus gallicus. Edited by Charles Peters. London: Jonas Bowyer, 1720. Based on the Verona edition of 1530.

Aphrodisiacus sive de lue venerea. Edited by Luigi Luisini. Corrected edition by Hermannus Boerhaave. Leiden: Langerak and Verbeek, 1728. Contains the *Syphilis.*

Scipione Maffei. *Verona illustrata.* 4 vols. Verona: Jacopo Vallarsi and Pierantonio Berno, 1731–32. Vol. 2 (1731). Contains C. 44 and 46 (pp. 345–47).

La sifilide, poema di Girolamo Fracastoro. Translated by Sebastiano degli Antoni. Bologna: Tommaso Colli, 1738. With Latin and Italian *en face.*

Carminum editio secunda, mirum in modum locupletior, ornatior, et in duos tomos distributa. Edited by Giovanni Antonio and Gaetano Volpi. Padua: Giuseppe Comino, 1739.

Hieronymi Fracastorii et Marci Antonii Flaminii carmina. Verona: Pierantonio Berno, 1740. Contains the *Syphilis, Joseph,* and *Carmina.*

Poemata omnia, nunc multo quam antea emendatiora. Accesserunt reliquiae carminum ad usum Seminarium Veronensis. Verona: Agostino Carattoni, 1740.

Selecta poemata Italorum qui latine scripserunt. Cura cuiusdam anonymi anno 1684 congesta, item in lucem data, una cum aliorum operibus, accurante Alexandro Pope. Volumen I. London: J and P. Knapton, 1740. Contains the *Syphilis* on pp. 53–101.

Hieronymi Fracastorii et Marci Antonii Flaminii carmina. Verona: Pierantonio Berno, 1747. Contains the *Syphilis, Joseph,* and *Carmina.*

Syphilis ou Le mal vénérien, poème latin de Jerôme Fracastor avec la traduction en françois, et des notes. [Translation ascribed to Philippe Macquer and Jacques Lacombe in the catalog of the Bibliothèque National de

France.] Paris: Jacque-François Quillau, 1753. With the Latin text *en face*.

Di Girolamo Fracastoro Veronese l'Alcone, o sia del governo de' cani da caccia. Traslatato in rima con alcune osservazioni necessarie alla materia. Translated by Salvatore Spiriti. Naples: [n.p.], 1756. With the Latin text.

Hieronymi Fracastorii et Marci Antonii Flaminii carmina. Venice: Remondini, 1759. Contains the *Syphilis, Joseph,* and *Carmina.*

Della sifilide ovvero De morbo gallico . . . libri III. Volgarizzati da Vincenzo Benini colognese. A cui, oltre il testo latino, si aggiungono alcune annotazioni. Bologna: Lelio della Volpe, 1765.

Hieronymi Fracastorii et Marci Antonii Flaminii carmina. Bassano: Remondini, 1782. Contains the *Syphilis, Joseph,* and *Carmina.*

Syphilis, ou Le mal vénérien. Paris: Lucet, 1796. Latin and French.

Poésies de M. Aurelius Olympius Némésien, suivies d'une Idylle de J. Fracastor sur les chiens de chasse. Translated by Souquet de Latour Paris: Chapelet, 1799. The Alcon (= C. 1) with facing French translation.

Poemata selecta Italorum qui seculo decimo sexto latine scripserunt. Oxford: Slatter and Munday; London: Longman, Hurst, Res and Orme, 1808. Contains the *Syphilis* and C. 2, 7–12.

Lemaire, Nicolas Eloi, ed. *Poetae Latini minores.* Paris: [Firmin Didot], 1824–26. 8 vols. Contains the Alcon (= C. 1) in 1:171–76.

Syphilis libri tres. Vita eius eodemque res gestae. Edited by Enrico Ratti. Milan: F. Rusconi, 1825.

Budik, P. A. *Leben und Wirken der vorzüglichsten lateinischen Dichter des XV–XVIII Jahrhunderts.* 3 vols. Vienna: J. B. Wallishausser, 1828, 2:184–213, "Aus den lateinischen Gedichten des H. Fracastoro," contains Syphilis 1.382–412 and C. 9, 16, 22, 23, in Latin and German.

La sifilide. Poema di Girolamo Fracastoro. Tradotto da Giovanni Luigi Zaccarelli. Parma: Bodoni, 1829. With the Latin text and Zaccarelli's Italian translation.

Syphilis sive morbus gallicus. Carmen ad optimarum editionum fidem edidit, notis et prolegomenis ad historiam morbi gallici facientibus instruxit Ludovicus Choulant. Leipzig: Leopold Voss, 1830.

La Sifilide, poema di Girolamo Fracastoro, recato in altrettanti versi italiani, con note. Edited and translated by Filippo Scolari. Venice: Tipografia all'Ancora, 1842. Latin and Italian verse, *en face*.

La syphilis: poème en vers latins de Jerôme Fracastor, traduit en vers français, précédé d'une étude historique et scientifique sur Fracastor, et accompagné de notes par Prosper Yvaren. Paris: J.-B. Baillière, 1847. French translation with Latin *en face*.

La syphilis, poema latino de Gerónimo Fracastor. Madrid: José M. Ducazcal, 1863. Latin text with facing Castilian translation and notes by Luis Maria Ramirez y de las Casas-Deza.

La Syphilis (1530). Le mal français (extrait du livre De contagionibus, 1546). Translation and commentary by Alfred Fournier. Paris: Adrien Delahaye, 1869. With Latin text.

Syphilis sive morbus gallicus. Leipzig: O.Wigand, 1881. Latin text with a German translation by Theodorus Lenz.

L'Estoile, Pierre de. *Mémoires-Journeaux: Journal d'Henri IV 1589–1611.* Paris: Librairie des Bibliophiles, 1883. Includes C. 45 (pp. 384–85).

Giuliari, G. B. "Sopra alquanti codici della Libreria Saibante in Verona che esularono dall'Italia." *Archivio Veneto* 7 (1874): 143–87. Includes Alecchi's transcription of C. 46 (p. 180).

Syphilis, or, The French Disease: A Poem in Latin Hexameters. London: The Sloane Society, 1884. English and Latin *en face*.

Prose e poesie latine di scrittori italiani: Dante, Petrarca, Pontano, Poliziano, Sannazaro, Bembo, Vida, Flaminio, Fracastoro, Vitrioli, Leone XIII, Pascoli. Edited by Ugo Enrico Paoli. Florence: Le Monnier, 1927. Contains excerpts from the *Syphilis* (1.421–53 and 3.93–129).

Fracastor Syphilis, or, The French Disease, a Poem in Latin Hexameters by Girolamo Fracastoro. With a translation, notes, and appendix by Heneage Wynne-Finch and an introduction by James Johnston Abraham. London: W. Heinemann Medical Books, 1935. Text based on the *editio princeps*, Verona 1530, Paris 1531, Rome 1531, Basel 1536, and the *Opera omnia* editions of 1555 and 1574.

Carmina. Edited by Francesco Pellegrini. Verona: Edizioni di Vita Veronese, 1954. Latin text of selected *Carmina* (C. 2, 4, 13, 7, 16, 27, 39, 41,

42, 44) based on the Volpi edition of 1739, with Italian translation, introduction, and notes.

Sifilide, ossia Del mal francese libri III. Traduzione, introduzione e note di Fabrizio Winspeare, col testo latino del poema separatamente impresso. Florence: Olschki, 1955.

Syphilidis sive de morbo gallico. Edited by Francesco Pellegrini with introduction, translation, and notes. Verona: Edizioni di Vita Veronese, 1956.

Pighi, Giovanni Battista. *Benacensia.* Verona: Stamperia Valdonega, 1966. Text of C. 5, with Italian translation and notes.

Alcone, ossia Del modo di allevare i cani da caccia. Edited by Pino Simoni. Verona, 1972. Latin text with an Italian translation by Gian Paolo Marchi.

Fischer, Klaus-Dietrich. "Alcon, sive de cura canum venaticorum: kritische Textausgabe und Bemerkungen zur Urheberschaft." *Humanistica Lovaniensia* 32 (1983): 266–88.

Fracastoro's Syphilis. Introduction, text, translations and notes, with a computer-generated word Index. Edited and translated by Geoffrey Eatough. Liverpool: F. Cairns, 1984. Generally follows the text of the Wynne-Finch edition (1935).

De vini temperatura sententia. Edited by Luciano Bonuzzi with an Italian translation by Alvise del Negro. Verona: Consorzio tutela Valpolicella e Recioto della Valpolicella, 1986. Includes C. 43; the text is an astatic reprint of an earlier edition.

Alcone. With an Italian translation and notes by Enzo De Matté. Milano: Edizioni di Vanni Scheiwiller, 1987. Reprinted. Treviso: Ateneo di Treviso, 2002.

Lehrgedicht über die Syphilis. Edited and translated by Georg Wöhrle. Bamberg: S. Wendel, 1988. With Latin text *en face*. Second enlarged edition. Wiesbaden: Harrasowitz, 1993.

L'anima. Edited with an Italian translation and notes by Enrico Peruzzi. Firenze: Le Lettere, 1999. Includes C. 41–42. Based on the 1555 *editio princeps* and on *aut*.

Navagero: Della poetica. Edited with an Italian translation and notes by Enrico Peruzzi. Firenze: Alinea, 2005. Includes C. 35. Based on the 1555 *editio princeps*.

Turrius oder über das Erkennen/Turrius sive de intellectione. Edited with a German translation and notes by Michaela Boenke. Munich: Fink, 2006. Includes C. 36–40. Based on the 1555 *editio princeps*.

De sympathia et antipathia rerum liber I. Edited with an Italian translation and commentary by Concetta Pennuto. Roma: Edizioni di storia e letteratura, 2008. Includes C. 11. Based on the 1546 *editio princeps*.

Syphilis sive morbus gallicus. French translation by Christine Dussin. Paris: Classiques Garnier, 2010.

La syphilis, ou Le mal français. Syphilis sive morbus gallicus. Edited, translated, introduced, and annotated by Jacqueline Vons and others. Paris: Les Belles Lettres, 2011. Text, established by Concetta Pennuto, based on the edition of Rome 1531.

SECONDARY LITERATURE

Barbarani, Emilio. *Girolamo Fragastoro e le sue opere*. Verona: G. Zannoni, 1897.

Baumgartner, Leona, and John F. Fulton. *A Bibliography of the Poem* Syphilis, sive Morbus Gallicus, *by Girolamo Fracastoro of Verona*. New Haven: Yale University Press, 1935.

Biow, Douglas. Doctors, *Ambassadors, Secretaries: Humanism* and *Professions in Renaissance Italy*. Chicago: The University of Chicago Press, 2002. See especially chap. 2.

Cairns, Francis. "Fracastoro's Syphilis, the Argonautic Tradition, and the Aetiology of Syphilis." *Humanistica Lovaniensia* 43 (1994): 246–61.

———. "The Numeri of Niccolò d'Arco and the Veronese Circle of Francastoro." *Studi Umanistici Piceni* 15 (1995): 19–29.

Campbell, Mary B. "Carnal Knowledge: Fracastoro's Syphilis and the Discovery of the New World." *Literature Criticism from 1400 to 1800*, 144 (2008): 267–79.

Cibei, Gabriella. "Osservazioni sulla tradizione degli Homocentrica di Girolamo Fracastoro." *Quaderni per la storia dell'Università di Padova* 37 (2004): 31–82.

Cristofolini, Paolo. "La medicina eroica e il fisicare presente: la Sifilide di Fracastoro nella prospettiva Vichiana." *Bollettino del Centro di Studi Vichiani* 35 (2005): 123–29.

Della Corte, Francesco. "Il Colombo di Girolamo Fracastoro." *Columbeis* 1 (1986): 139–55.

Eatough, Geoffrey. "Fracastoro's Beautiful Idea." In *Poets and Teachers: Latin Didactic Poetry and the Didactic Authority of the Latin Poet from the Renaissance to the Present. Proceedings of the Fifth Annual Symposium of the Cambridge Society for Neo-Latin Studies, Clare College, Cambridge, 9–11 September, 1996*, pp. 105–124. Edited by Yasmin Haskell and Philip Hardie. Bari: Levante, 1999.

Filippetti, Andrea. "La *Syphilis* di Girolamo Fracastoro: Analisi del proemio." *Belfagor* 64 (2009): 327–38.

Frank, Richard. "Fracastoro: Poetry vs. Prose." *International Journal of the Classical Tradition* 9 (2003): 524–34.

Gigliotti, Gilbert L. "The Alexandrian Fracastoro: Form and Meaning in the Myth of Syphilus." *Renaissance and Reformation/Renaissannce et Réforme* 26.4, n.s. 14 (1990): 261–69.

Girolamo Fracastoro fra medicina, filosofia e scienze della natura: Atti del Convegno internazionale di studi in occasione del 450° anniversario della morte, Verona-Padova, 9–11 ottobre 2003. Edited by Alessandro Pastore and Enrico Peruzzi. Firenze: Leo S. Olschki, 2006.

Goddard, Charlotte. "Lucretius and Lucretian Science in the Works of Fracastoro." *Res Publica Litterarum* 16 (1993): 185–92.

Haskell, Yasmin. "Between Fact and Fiction: The Renaissance Didactic Poetry of Fracastoro, Palingenio and Valvasone." In *Poets and Teachers* (as above), pp. 77–103.

Hofmann, Heinz. "La *Syphilis* di Fracastoro: immaginazione ed erudizione." *Studi Umanistici Piceni* 6 (1986): 175–81.

—— . "Aspetti narrativi ed unità epica della *Sifilide* di Gerolamo Fracastoro." *Studi Umanistici Piceni* 7 (1987): 169–74.

Kempkens, Klaus. *Joseph und Aeneas; Untersuchungen zum Joseph des Girolamo Fracastoro, einem Bibelepos Italiens aus dem 16. Jahrhundert*. Inaugural dissertation. Bonn, 1972.

Mencke, Friedrich Otto. *De vita, moribus, scriptis, meritisque in omne literarum genus prorsus singularibus Hieronymi Fracastorii . . . commentatio.* Leipzig: Breitkopf, 1731.

Nutton, Vivian. "The Reception of Fracastoro's Theory of Contagion: The Seed that Fell among Thorns?" *Osiris,* 2nd ser., 6 (1990): 196–234.

Pantin, Isabelle. "Poetic Fiction and Natural Philosophy in Humanist Italy: Fracastoro's Use of Myth in *Syphilis.*" *Fiction and the Frontiers of Knowledge in Europe, 1500–1800,* edited by Richard Scholar and Alexis Tadié, 17–30. Burlington: Ashgate, 2010.

Pearce, Spencer. "Fracastoro on Syphilis: Science and Poetry in Theory and Practice." *Literature Criticism from 1400 to 1800,* 144 (2008): 279–89. Previously published in *Science and Literature in Italian Culture: From Dante to Calvino,* edited by Pierpaolo Antonello and Simon A. Gilson, 115–35. Oxford: European Humanities Research Centre, 2004.

Pellegrini, Francesco, ed. and tr. *Trattato inedito in prosa di Gerolamo Fracastoro sulla sifilide. Codice CCLXXV–I, Biblioteca Capitolare di Verona.* With a preface by Luigi Messedaglia. Verona: La Tipografica Veronese, 1939.

———. *Fracastoro.* Trieste: Zigiotti, 1948.

———, ed. and tr. *Vita di Girolamo Fracastoro, con la versione di alcuni suoi canti.* Verona: Stamperia Valdonega, 1952. With an Italian translation of C. 5, 8, 10, 3, 19.

———. "Appunti per una disposizione cronologica dei componimenti poetici del Fracastoro, con l'aggiunta di alcune poesie in volgare a lui attribuite." *Studi Storici Veronesi* 5 (1954): 89–123.

———, ed. *Scritti inediti di Girolamo Fracastoro, con introduzione, commenti e note.* Verona: Edizioni Valdonega, 1955.

Peruzzi, Enrico. "Manoscritti Fracastoriani nella Biblioteca Capitolare di Verona." *Physis* 18.3–4 (1976): 342–48.

———. "Verona, Biblioteca Capitolare." In the *Catalogo di manoscritti filosofici nelle biblioteche italiane,* 8:135–247. Firenze: Leo S. Olschki, 1996.

———. "Fracastoro, Girolamo." In *Dizionario biografico degli Italiani,* 49:543b–548a. Rome, 1997.

——. "Le censure di Sisto Medici O. P. ai dialoghi De Intellectione e De Anima di Girolamo Fracastoro." *Per Alberto Piazzi. Scritti offerti nel 50° di sacerdozio*, edited by Carlo Albarello and Giuseppe Zivelonghi, 299–328. Verona: Biblioteca Capitolare di Verona, 1998.

Roccasalva, Alessandro. *Girolamo Fracastoro: astronomo, medico e poeta nella cultura del Cinquecento italiano*. Genoa: Nova scripta, 2008.

Ruggiero, Raffaele. "La *Syphilis* di Girolamo Fracastoro e le *Stanze per la giostra*." *Schede Umanistiche* 9 (2001): 73–97.

Scaliger, Julius Caesar. *Poetices libri septem*. Lyons: Crespin, 1561. Contains a series of critical notes on points of style in the *Syphilis* (pp. 315–17, published with English translation in Eatough 1984: 215–23).

Ziolkowski, John E. "Epic Conventions in Fracastoro's Poem *Syphilis*." In *The Classical Continuum in Italian Thought and Letters*, edited by Anne Reynolds, 57–73. (Altro Polo: A Volume of Italian Studies.) Sydney: Frederick May Foundation for Italian Studies, University of Sydney, 1984.

Index

ॐᏚᎥ᯾

Names in notes are indexed by the page on which they occur. Note numbers refer to the line numbers of the various poetical works included in the Notes to the Translation or parts thereof. Thus, "420n49–50" indicates a note found on page 420 referring to lines 49–50 of the relevant work, in this case Book I of the *Syphilis*. Introductory notes to individual poems in the *Carmina* are indexed by page number plus the poem number followed by "n." Thus, "486 40n" refers to the introductory note to poem 40 on page 486.

Naples, 419n6, 422n210–11,
    428n38–42, 452n45
Narcissus, 295, 341, 488n22
Nature, 3, 347
Navagero, Andrea, x, xi, xii, 229,
    466n74–76, 484 35n
Navarre, 461n102–6, 462n148–50
Nemesianus, 448 1n; On Hunting,
    449n20–79, 449n30–39,
    450n30, 450n46–50, 450n52
Neoplatonism, 463 7n, 485 37n
Neorus, 249, 473n38–40
Neptune/Poseidon, 427n26,
    486n17
Nereids, 65, 67, 433n93–101,
    434n114
Nereus, 65, 283, 428n58–60,
    433n93–101
Nero (emperor), 341, 343, 499 52n
Newton, Isaac, xviii
New World, xiv, xv, 433n13–29,
    436n151–54, 437n220–23
Nicander of Colophon, 499 52n
Night, 53, 55
Nile River, 7, 9, 35, 105, 109, 143,
    145–47, 149, 217, 233, 253, 345
Niobe, 438n288
Noricum, 239, 469n92
Nymphs, 51, 295, 429n143–44,
    429n179, 441n264, 458n17,
    468n53, 482n9, 488 43n,
    494n20–26. See also names of
    nymphs
Nysa, 488 43n

Ocean/Oceanus, 5, 9, 61, 65, 71,
    427n26, 428n58–60, 438n265

Oenus (river), 239, 469n115–21
Oglio/Ollus (river), 25, 27,
    424n382
Olympus, 13, 15, 17, 63, 107, 249,
    251, 291, 303, 347, 422n179–81,
    486 40n, 487 41n
Ophir, 67, 71, 73, 433n30–33,
    434n116–21
Opis/Rhea, 458n18–19
Oppian, 448 1n
Ops, 51, 53, 431n329
Orcus, 183, 193, 249, 273, 444n79
Oricum/Orikos, 432n427
Orion, 343, 501n14
Orpheus, 185–87, 453n98–102,
    454n26, 483n18, 502 56n
Osiris, 113, 151, 442n417, 443n472
Ossa, 13, 422n179–81
Ottoman Empire, 428n58–60,
    473n81–82, 474n106–11,
    490n56
Ovid, ix; Art of Love 1,
    420n49–50, 443n435,
    444n536–37, 462n112–13,
    467n16, 475n7, 488n15; Art of
    Love 2, 473n49; Art of Love 3,
    467n16; Cure for Love, 465n34,
    475n7; Heroines 1, 445n120;
    Heroines 2, 434n97; Heroines 4,
    488n15; Heroines 5, 446n385;
    Heroines 9, 485n20; Heroines 11,
    449n24; Heroines 16, 460n45;
    Heroines 18, 422n172; Ibis,
    446n304, 483n22; Letters from
    Ponto, 423n316, 438n265,
    448n668, 454n11, 456n14; Loves,
    452n40, 498n133; Metamorphoses

· INDEX ·

ps.-Quintilian, *Major Speeches*, 445n239–40

Rachel (wife of Jacob), 91, 165
Rainieri, Daniele, 197–201, 456 4n
Ramusio, Giovanni Battista, x, xix n4, 277–79, 482 30n, 500n9, 500–501 53n
Ramusio, Paolo, xvi, xix n4
Rangoni, Costanza, 459n1–4
Remi, 215, 462n141–43
Reuben (brother of Joseph), 99–101, 111–13, 161
Rhaetia, 429n139–42
Rhaptum, 33, 427n27–30
Rhine (river), 7, 239, 421n71–72, 469n115–21
Rhodope, 187, 453n98–102
Rhone (river), 207, 460n1–4
Rincon, Antoine de, 459 6n
Riva del Garda, 453n77–82, 453n91
Rome, x, 35, 185, 223, 237, 239–41, 243, 245, 253, 275, 301, 305, 317, 321, 325, 329, 429n130–31, 439n418, 468n58–59, 469n110–11, 470n101, 471 12n, 473n38–40, 474n122–25, 477n20, 479n13–14
Rossi, Ornella, xvii

Sabines, 429n143–44
Sagra/Alaro (river), 5, 421n61–64
Salò, x, 203, 494n22
Saloe, 309, 311, 494n22
Salviati, Francesco, 468n58–59

Samaria, 89, 103, 153, 155, 161, 440n22–26
Sannazaro, Jacopo, *On the Virgin Birth*, xvi
Sarca (river), x, 31, 185, 257, 303, 426n456–63
Satan, 445n172
Saturn (planet), 11, 13, 422n204–5, 428n50–51
Saturn/Chronos, 15, 27, 203–7, 261, 269, 323, 327, 423n234, 457 5n, 458n18–19, 476n12–13, 479n7–8, 498n94–99
Satyrs/Silenoi, 472n26–29
Saxogeloni, 450n30–39
Saxogelonian hound, 171, 450n30–39
Schmalkaldic league, 467 10n, 469n105
Schmalkaldic War, 490 45n
Schwartz, Berthold, 436n156–58
Scylla and Charybdis, 289, 486n12
Scythia/Scythians, 299, 439n403, 450n30–39, 490n56
Sebethus (river), 33, 428n38–42
Second Punic War, 428n53–57
Semele, 297, 488 43n, 489n4–9, 489n25–26
Seneca, 476n16–17; *Madness of Hercules*, 496n141; *Phaedra*, 434n111
ps.-Seneca, *Octavia*, 452n32, 461n59
Sequani, 213, 215, 461n95, 462n141–43
Seria, 450n30–39

Publication of this volume has been made possible by

The Myron and Sheila Gilmore Publication Fund at I Tatti
The Robert Lehman Endowment Fund
The Jean-François Malle Scholarly Programs and Publications Fund
The Andrew W. Mellon Scholarly Publications Fund
The Craig and Barbara Smyth Fund
for Scholarly Programs and Publications
The Lila Wallace–Reader's Digest Endowment Fund
The Malcolm Wiener Fund for Scholarly Programs and Publications